ACROSS WIDE ZAMBEZI

A DOCTOR'S LIFE IN AFRICA

BY

WARREN DURRANT

First published in Great Britain in 2013.

PublishNation, London.

www.publishnation.co.uk

For my wife

PART ONE - WEST AFRICA

1 - Beginnings

The personnel manager swept his hand over the beetling crag of West Africa on the wall, where a green swath ran across the lower part of the map, and announced: 'This is the rain forest.' He pointed to a spot on the line of a river, a name, and added, 'And this is Samreboi.'

I was forty, unmarried, and, after ten years in general practice, was looking for a change. I had long had an interest in Africa, so when I saw the advertisement in the British Medical Journal for a medical officer for a timber company in Ghana, I applied. I later discovered that I was the only applicant. So much for the spirit of adventure in the old country[1]! The year was 1968.

Here I was in the London office of the great United Africa Company, which many called the real government of West Africa.

Besides the personnel manager, the chief medical officer was present. He enlarged on the duties briefly indicated in the BMJ.

I would be sole medical officer to the company employees and families, and to the rest of the population of the town and a considerable area of the surrounding countryside. I would have a small hospital, where I would undertake some surgery: caesarean sections and hernias were mentioned.

My sole surgical experience then, consisted of the minor procedures of hospital casualty and general practice, and a handful of appendix operations, performed under supervision as a houseman. This experience, though limited, had given me that most important surgical initiation, the 'feel of the knife' - a breaking of the ice (to mix the metaphors), which confers that all-important first strengthening of the nerve.

---

[1] This is unfair. I doubt I would have left the country while my parents were still alive (they died before I was forty); and certainly not if I were married with young children. WD.

Nevertheless I asked the doctor if I should try and get some more surgical ex-perience before I left. He said it would probably put me off. In fact, no training appropriate to African practice (embracing both surgery and obstetrics for a start) was available in England.

He explained that in my Herculean task I would have the help of medical assistants - a breed special to developing countries: half nurse and mini-doctor. These men and women receive two or three years' training in diagnosis and simple treatment. Some receive further training to take X-rays or give anaesthetics, work in laboratory or pharmacy, etc. Some girls train as maternity assistants, and not only manage normal deliveries, but twins and breeches also. All in all, they are the backbone of African medical practice, and without them, the task of the thinly spread doctors and even more thinly spread specialists would be impossible.

For I was also informed the nearest hospital with specialists was a day's journey away: too far for emergencies, and with too few specialists to deal with any but the most difficult cases.

I had a good idea of all this when I applied for the job. It was because I was looking forward to this kind of challenge that I applied in the first place.

In those days, one flew to West Africa by daylight, in a VC 10. By midday we were over the Mediterranean, and as the lunar mountains of the Atlas appeared, I knew I had left the bounds of Europe for the first time in my life - the bounds of law and safety, for the perilous world beyond - a romantic notion, both true and not so true. And then we were over the Sahara.

The plane seemed to be flying through a vast furnace, whose rising fires obscured the horizon and met in the smoking zenith. Clarity prevailed only far below on the desert floor, where from time to time mountain ridges appeared, which would have made delightful walks in the friendly Lake District, but here were lost in the appalling emptiness of a planet inimical to life. Dunes showed in tight ripples like the tide-ribbed beaches of home. Even lonely roads were seen, leading to the occasional ant-heap of an oasis, like a space station on the moon. Beyond all was the sea of sand. After some hours of this hellish progress, the sun wheeled for a few minutes in the starboard windows, before drowning in the brown shadow, rising from the earth. Lights came on in the cabin. The stewardesses served drinks. The kindly human world was restored.

Landing at Accra was like going back to the beginnings of the world (in Conradian phrase) - the moist and muddy world of the dinosaurs: one almost expected to see one lumbering out of the black African night, the blackest of all nights. The first thing I noticed on stepping out of the plane was the smell - no, not a bad smell: what I can only describe as a 'boiled' smell, the smell of a laundry, as if the whole country had been boiled and reboiled from the day of the Creation, which I suppose in a way was true. A sinister smell, with a certain burnt edge to it: a disgraceful smell, where morality was unheard of - abandoned on another planet. In the days that followed, this smell would come and go as I went in and out of air-conditioned buildings, themselves feeling as sinister as the cold of a morgue, until one got used to it and no longer noticed it, and it became lost even to memory, like the romance of first impressions.

The airport building was then little more than a large shed, awash with a sea of black faces, as if the night had invaded the building and threatened to overwhelm the feeble electric lights. At the barrier, one of the black faces lighted up for me: 'Dr Durrant?' This was Mr Aggrey, the company representative, who led me to a battered car. We both sat in the back, which was the proper place for 'masters' like us, and the chauffeur drove us to a large bleak hotel.

The next two days were all strange old colonial buildings , the surf and golden sands at the beach club, a lush and varied landscape, glimpsed from the plane on the way to Takoradi down the coast. Then another chauffeur: Samson, to take me up country.

I sat in the front passenger seat, rather to Samson's surprise, the better to chat to him. The tarmac road was not very good, full of holes and puddles, through all of which Samson charged with ruthless speed, taking no care of whom he splashed with muddy water - and more surprisingly, they seemed not to resent it - nor of the agile children who dodged out of his way. For there were people everywhere, people who seemed to be made of rubber, so fluid were their movements, so utterly free of the tensions of the white man: the women in their long skirts, their elegant head-scarves, some carrying things on their heads, moving like water plants; the men in shorts and shirts, mostly ragged, prancing along; the darting children. A cloud of tobacco smoke actually preceded round a bend by half a minute an old woman with an enormous pipe. A social world full of greetings and talk and laughter, the talk delivered at the top of the voice, for in Africa, although I did not know it then, it is considered antisocial to talk quietly and therefore secretly.

We went through a mining town - Tarkwa - all hot tin roofs, ugly industrial workings and sheds, winding gear, shabby buildings of all colours, stores, awnings and colonnades, hoardings, a tranquil grove of palm trees: as seedy and lively and picturesque as only an African town can be. Then on to the open road again, which more and more gave way to earth - and the earth was the colour of gold. For this was the Guinea coast and the mine was a gold mine: the gold of the guinea pieces, the richest gold in the world.

Another mining town , Prestea, and then quite suddenly, the forest.

The rain forest was then in better condition than I fancy it is in now. Indeed, my son's school atlas seems to indicate that it has vanished from those parts altogether. Then it was still magnificent. The road turned to red laterite and became the aisle of a great cathedral. The forest giants stood two hundred feet high, with some, the emergents, towering even higher above the canopy: for the great trunks were naked until they met and joined together above like the surface of the ocean. The trunks were supported by buttress roots which rose about twenty feet and looked like the fins of a space rocket. Between, tangled the undergrowth, which it needed a panga (or cutlass as it was called in West Africa) to get through, except where well-worn paths had been made and kept open over the years by people travelling to the forest villages. To me it is the most beautiful forest in the world and still seduces my dreams.

Suddenly the road opened on a clearing. Industrial sheds, workers' houses, a few large houses set back in spacious gardens, where the managers lived. This was an outstation: there were two in operation at that time. Then the forest closed around us again for another ten miles.

4

And then we got there, the town of Samreboi. A long straggling street, barely tarmacked: a mile long, lined with the usual flimsy stores and full of people. Then larger buildings: the police station, churches, and, in a grove of trees, the hospital.

This was a single storey affair: the main wards and a number of other buildings all joined by concrete gangways, covered with roofing against the rain. I got out of the car. A tall handsome white man of about fifty emerged from an office and came towards me. This was Des Brennan, the locum. The previous incumbent had left some months before.

He shook hands with me and said: 'Dr Durrant, I presume.'

Well, there wasn't much else he could have said.

He took me into his office and gave me tea. Then he took me on a tour of the hospital.

There were a men's ward and a women's ward. There was a wide veranda, enclosed with mosquito mesh, where the children were put with their mothers. On the wards we met Miss Lemaire, a very pretty black girl, who was deputy matron. And in due course, we met Jenny, the matron herself, a redoubtable Scotswoman of middle age.

We met Mr Sackey, the chief medical assistant, a sort of regimental sergeant-major, with no nonsense about him. We moved on to the maternity unit, which contained a labour ward and two lying-in beds, where we met Emilia, the petite and dynamic midwife.

There were an operating theatre, a laboratory, pharmacy and X-ray department: all very rudimentary and staffed with cheerful, undaunted operatives. Lastly, there was a private ward for the managers. The hospital had about fifty beds in all, which is not many even for Africa. No food was provided. Patients were fed by relatives; and always at the front gate were women ('mammies', as they were called) selling food.

Des took me back to the office for a final briefing: he was due to leave next day. He waved his hand at an uncrowded bookshelf. 'There's some operating manuals there if you get stuck.' I may say he was a bluff Irishman.

He glanced at his watch. 'The bar'll be opening now. Come along. I'll introduce you to some of the boys.'

5

Des must have felt I needed the bar by then, and, by golly, he was right!

On our way to the club, we passed a group of black children with red curly hair. I had heard that the malnourishment disease, kwashiorkor, could produce this effect, but these youngsters were healthy and lively. I asked Des about them, and he said it must have been an Irish missionary or (with a glance at my dwindling locks and from my introductory remarks) 'a doctor from Liverpool'.

Next day, in an historic tableau, we shook hands before a large crowd of black faces, before his car disappeared in a cloud of dust and cheering small boys.

I never felt more alone.

2 - My First Caesar

I will never forget my first caesarean section. I was wakened by the telephone at three in the morning of my fortieth birthday. Emilia the midwife spoke.

'We've got a breech, and it's stuck, and we can't get it out, and there's another one inside.'

When I got to the labour ward, it was as she said. An African woman was lying on her back on the delivery couch, her long legs up in the stirrups. She stared fixedly at the ceiling, in all the fathomless impassivity of her race. Two other nurses stood beside her, one on each side. They and Emilia stared expectantly at me out of their black eyes, over their masks.

Hanging from the woman's loins was a small body, feet first, limp and grey, quite obviously dead.

When I applied the foetal stethoscope to the woman's belly, I could hear the faint heart-beat of a second twin.

My first thought was that picture which all medical students remember and never see in real life of locked twins, where the head of the first twin is trapped by the head of the second. If the reader lays his two fists together, opposite ways, he will get the picture.

I did not know how to deal with locked twins, so told Emilia frankly: 'I'm going to get the book out.'

In the office, I took down an old copy of Eden and Holland from the scantily stocked shelf, Des Brennan had indicated.

As far as I remember, Eden and Holland informed me (rather unnecessarily) that the first twin is usually dead. The head should be severed from the body (or vice versa presumably, depending how you look at it), and pushed back into the pelvis, to allow the passage of the second twin.

Armed with this knowledge, I returned to the labour ward, and, using some instrument I dare not try to remember, severed the neck. The body fell into a bucket, with a dull clunk.

Now I tried to push back the head. It would not budge. The initiated will guess what I discovered next. The first twin was a hydrocephalic - a big-headed monster. Moreover, my examination

7

revealed that the woman had a contracted pelvis, a common disability among the undernourished women of the Third World. She would have difficulty delivering any kind of baby, and this was her first pregnancy.

I decided to 'cut my way out of trouble', by which we in the trade mean a caesarean section. I asked Emilia to prepare for operation, while I repaired once more to the office and Eden and Holland.

The chief medical officer in London had told me that the classical operation is the easiest. This means a vertical incision through the uterus. It is true it is the easiest, but the lower segment (cross cut) operation is far superior, and any doctor worth his salt will learn it as soon as possible.

As it turned out, the classical operation was going to be more appropriate to this particular case.

I read up the details of the operation, and made my way to the theatre, feeling hollow and afraid in the sweltering African night. There was no time to send this woman anywhere else with any hope of saving the baby, or even, perhaps, herself. Besides, country doctors in Africa are not expected to transfer cases for caesarean section.

At the theatre, I found Mr Sackey had arrived. He was to help me. There remained the question of the anaesthetic. I had discussed this with Des Brennan, during our brief handover.

'What do you do about anaesthetics?'

'We do spoinals.'

'How do you do a spinal?'

'You do a lumbar puncture, and bung the stuff in.'

Which, I might say, is not the last word on spinal anaesthesia. I expect Des thought, if you've got to shove a fellow in the deep end, the less said about it the better.

Mr Sackey, who seemed to know more about spinals than me, had got a drip going, laid out the tray, and sat the woman up across the operating table. He looked expectantly at me.

I did the lumbar puncture, and ' bunged the stuff in'. Mr Sackey laid the lady flat, and wound the table head down for a few minutes. Presently, he levelled it again, and set up a screen over the patient's chest. During a spinal anaesthetic, of course, the subject remains fully conscious, but is numb from the waist down.

Then we scrubbed up, gowned, and gloved. I remember seeing Mr Sackey's packet of Tusker cigarettes lying somewhere, and mentally catching at this homely object, like a psychological straw.

The operation went easier than I expected. I removed the second twin from the open womb. It was small and inert and covered with meconium, which is the baby's faeces, passed in distress, and a sign that it had had little time to live, if it was not dead already.

I cut the cord, and handed the object to Emilia, like a muddy little frog. She took it into the next room, and went to work on it. Presently, I heard the cry of a baby.

'Is that our baby?' I asked.

'Yes,' replied Mr Sackey, impassively.

To confirm his statement, Emilia bounced back into the theatre, bearing aloft the blindly staring little creature, wrapped in a towel.

'Jesus Christ be praised!' I shouted. Obstetrics can be an emotional business in Africa.

I removed the two afterbirths. Now remained the problem of the severed head, still stuck rock-like in the depths of the womb.

I tried to remove it with my hands. No movement. I applied forceps. No go. Finally, I stabbed the head several times with a pair of scissors, and it came away.

At this point, the patient woke up (sic).

What was more surprising was that she had been asleep so far. I have already explained that a spinal anaesthetic leaves the patient awake. But with the screen before her eyes and finding nothing further expected of her, she decided to improve the occasion with a useful nap.

Lying there, with her belly and her womb laid open, covered in blood and meconium,
she grunted something in the vernacular.

I asked Mr Sackey what she said. He replied in these immortal words:

'She's asking for her breakfast.'

All I could say was, she would have to wait.

9

I got everything stitched up, and they took her back to the ward. Ten days later she galloped off into the bush, with her new baby on her back.

I remember the names of my first big cases: my first caesar, my first hernia, my first ectopic. I remember hers. It was Veronica.

I wonder what became of her. I wonder if she returned to the hospital for her next delivery. Perhaps not, after her drastic experience with her first. Perhaps she is lying in some grave in the forest, with an unborn baby inside her.

And I wonder what became of the baby I delivered. I cannot remember if it was a boy or a girl.

3 - The Mercy Flight

It was not exactly a flight. It was mostly a train journey. It began in the labour ward.

Emilia, the midwife, informed me that she 'had a baby which she did not like the look of'. I went with her to see.

The baby had just been born. African babies are not born black: then they are only slightly duskier than white babies. They gradually turn black over the first ten days of life. This one looked decidedly grey.

I examined it carefully, including the heart sounds, which were normal. I decided to wait and see.

Two days later, the baby looked worse; and now I could hear a loud heart murmur. Obviously we had a 'blue baby' on our hands, a baby with a congenital heart defect.

I asked Emilia where we could send it for heart surgery. She thought maybe the capital, Accra.

'Then we must send the baby to Accra,' I said.

Midwives the world over are independent figures as many doctors have found to their cost. African midwives are no exception.

Emilia drew herself up to her full five feet and declared: 'Never since I am in Samreboi have we sent a baby to Accra!'

'Well, we are starting now,' I retorted.

Emilia began to harden with that adamantine hardness which I was later to discover was a peculiar property of this otherwise docile race. In the discussion that followed, I referred to the chances the baby would have in the West End of London, with other such appeals to fair dealing. Eventually, Emilia gave way.

Once she had accepted the proposition, she threw herself into it with characteristic dedication. We made plans.

First of all, we obtained oxygen for the baby. The only oxygen available came, not in the handy medical size cylinder, but a massive industrial object it took two strong men to handle. This was connected to the baby, whose colour began to improve. Now for the journey.

The mother would have to go, as all African babies are breast-fed. Father would be needed, if only for muscle power. Moreover, father's consent must first be obtained. An African peasant woman is no more placed to take an independent decision than her baby itself. And Emilia would have to go to manage the business.

Where was the father? Another difficulty. It transpired he was not a company employee but a 'house-boy'. (Those were the days before we called them male domestic workers, comrades!) The company undertook to provide unlimited transport for employees only: others would be carried to the railhead, forty miles away at Prestea. After that, they were on their own.

Now the railways of Africa universally run up-country from the coast, being originally built to garner the products of the continent rather than with any concern for the convenience of the inhabitants. That meant that while up and down journeys were no problem, to travel cross-country was not so easy. In short, our little party would first have to travel down to the coast at Takoradi, then up-country again to Kumasi, then down once more to Accra: which is like travelling from Liverpool to London via Bristol and York.

We worked out that they would need sixty cedis (which in those days was about sixty US dollars).

Where did the house-boy work? Mother did not know. She lived in the 'boy's house', in the garden of their master, but it is no part of a poor African woman's duty to know her husband's business.

Somebody said he worked for Mr Simpson.

It was four-thirty in the afternoon, when I knew Mr Simpson would be relaxing from his labours at the bar of the club. There I found him and told him the sorry story.

Mr Simpson was a dour Scot. He listened throughout with a penetrating stare, which penetrated further when I finished.

'Ye mean ye want me tae find the sixty cedis?' You've got to hand it to them for penetration!

After sundry uncharitable noises, evidently intended to disabuse the neighbouring drinkers of any idea that he was going 'soft', Mr Simpson drew a cheque and got sixty cedis from the bar.

I carried them in triumph to his house.

The father was rooted out of the boy's house. He was followed by about ten other children. The story was told again.

The father appeared even more guarded than Mr Simpson had been.

'Ah, docketa!' he exclaimed, with that sceptical glint of the eye and click of the tongue which I was also to come to know so well. 'Dis pickin never fit go for Accra!'

Newcomers to the Coast , especially ladies for some reason, swear they will never resort to 'pidgin'. After a month or two, when the limitations of the Queen's English become evident, they change their minds.

The inevitable African crowd had gathered. I played unashamedly to the gallery like a past master.

'I never savvy you be docketa, my friend!'

This drew the expected laugh.

I produced my ace card.

'Mr Simpson has given sixty cedis for the train,' I announced, drawing the notes from my breast pocket.

A small boy, who had obviously never seen such a sum in his life, gasped: 'Sixty cedis!', clapped his hand to his head and went through a theatrical fainting fit. I might add they are born actors. Sir Laurence himself could not have faulted the lad - or done better.

The ambulance took the little party, plus the massive oxygen cylinder, to the railhead. They waited all night for the train to the coast. Then, as I have indicated, up to Kumasi, and a third journey down to Accra. The group attracted considerable interest throughout, which Emilia exploited as only a midwife can, commanding strong men to 'stop staring and lend a hand' with the oxygen cylinder. Finally they emerged from the station at Accra.

It was then that the mother saw traffic for the first time in her life.

Vehicles there were at Samreboi, even some very large ones, called 'loggers', for transporting the timber, but they never added up to 'traffic'.

It was too much for the poor mother. With a scream of 'Jee-sess!', she turned tail and clutching the baby, tore back into the shelter of the station.

Leaving the husband in charge of the oxygen cylinder, Emilia tore after her.

Eventually they got into the outpatient department of the great Korle Bu Hospital. It was, like any such institution, a sea of bodies. Emilia found a big bossy sister.

'Is this an emergency?' demanded the BBS.

Emilia faced up to her like a honey badger (which is well known to be the fiercest animal in Africa) to an elephant.

'Of course it is an emergency. We have come from boosh! FROM BOOSH!!!'

In short, the baby was admitted to the ward, where it lay for three days before being seen by a doctor - in fact, by the professor on his regular ward round. He just had time to demonstrate the interesting case to the usual train of registrars, house officers, and nurses, before the little thing expired.

The truth was, I had overestimated the level of the country's technology.

Which taught me one thing: the 'demands of the ideal' (in Ibsenian phrase) have no place in Africa, where 'the best can be the enemy of the good'

4 - At the Dirty End

The scope of the country doctor in Africa embraces everything from major surgery to public health. Today it was 'public health'.

Once a month we inspected one of the company villages where the workers lived. Our little group consisted of myself; Sam, the chief engineer; Amos, the personnel manager; and Mr Cudjo, the sanitary inspector. Sam and I were from the north of England. Amos and Cudjo were Ghanaians.

The village on this day's agenda was in a bad state. It had been flooded when the river rose thirty feet at the beginning of the rainy season in May. Many people had been evacuated. Fourteen of his relatives were crowded into the tiny house of James, my cook. An African's obligations to his extended family are irresistible; and the family usually extends very far. James had a shrewd suspicion that his relatives were spinning things out, no doubt reluctant to get back to the business of cleaning up their houses. A few days before, he had asked me in a pathetic tone, 'Please, sah, do you happen to know if that village is still flooded?'

We came upon a party of 'spray boys', spraying under the eaves of the houses against mosquitoes. For some obscure reason, the spray boys came under the matron, Jenny, the stout and stout-hearted Scotswoman, who was manfully (if that is the word nowadays) struggling under her self-imposed burden of stopping Africa from back-sliding. She used to publish 'spraying programmes' every quarter, entitled 'The Spring Spraying Programme', 'The Winter Spraying Programme', etc, perhaps in nostalgic memory of her native heath, regardless of a country which knew only two seasons - wet and dry, or rather, wet and very wet.

Africa is littered with the wrecks of white idealism. One of my predecessors viewed with disfavour the extensive ditches of the town, and declared, quite correctly, that in the rainy season they must breed mosquitoes. He proposed to the general manager the installation of powerful (and expensive) pumping machinery to keep the water in the ditches in perpetual motion. He should have read a little further in his Manson's Tropical Diseases, where he would have

15

discovered that, while moving water discouraged mosquitoes, it was highly favoured by the black fly, and if he had succeeded in reducing malaria (which is very doubtful), he might have replaced it with river blindness. Not unreasonably, the GM was not impressed with this scheme, but it did not end there. The doctor was a mad Irishman: the GM was a fiery Welshman. In the midst of the vast indifferent wilderness, the two pigmy figures became locked in claustrophobic conflict. The GM wanted to sack the MO: the MO tried to certify the GM. I think it ended in an unsatisfactory draw.

After a word with the spray boys, we came upon the 'latrine boys' at work. Some other idealist, an engineer this time, had installed septic tank latrines for the groups of workers' houses. The septic tank, of course, is a delicate instrument, and they did not last long in these circumstances. They were now blocked up, and the principal work of the latrine boys was to unblock them.

The foreman of the latrine boys approached us, expanded his dirty singlet, and made a little speech in the vernacular, which was evidently intended for the new MO. Amos explained. 'He's letting you know he is the chief latrine boy, doc. He says he is a very good latrine boy and is glad to meet the new doctor. Say something nice to him, doc.'

I said something suitable, and as we walked on, Amos continued. 'The latrine boys have a hard time, doc. We have to recruit them from the NTs (Northern Territories) because no one from the south will do the job. The latrine boys are figures of fun. People hold their noses when they see them, and none of the girls will marry them.'

We came to the end of the village, where the squatters began. These people, either relatives of company people or simple opportunists, had set up their own dwellings, made of old petrol cans, bits of corrugated iron, and other scraps. They lay beyond the reach of even the battered septic tanks and the exiguous water points of the regular village. I think they did everything in and out of the bush and the river. Sam, the engineer, stood and contemplated the scene with disgust.

In Africa, the pillars of society have their secret nicknames (sometimes an open secret) among the people. Sam was a tall craggy figure, and his nickname was 'Dee Goll', in which the reader may recognise the imperious general. The sound of his thunderous voice, or the force of his powerful personality, may have penetrated the flimsy walls of the shanties, because a woman presently slipped out of one of them, gathered up her naked child, and scurried back inside, with a nervous look over her shoulder at our group.

'The only answer to this lot, doc, is an atom bomb,' pronounced Sam.

We became aware of a small piping sound at our feet. Looking down, we saw a very small naked child, standing on a heap of dubious-looking material. He was looking boldly up at Sam, and chanting: *'Bruni! Bruni! Bruni!',* which means, 'white man'.

Sam gazed down from his great height at this phenomenon, with a look of distant curiosity. The phenomenon lost steam, and the piping dried up. It lowered its head, and contemplated its bare toes, which it wriggled in the dubious-looking material. After a minute's silence, Sam retorted: *'Bibini!'* (black man). The phenomenon looked up, with a grin of relief.

At some point, Mr Cudjo drew me aside, and confided to me that, in addition to the difficulties Amos had indicated to the recruitment of latrine boys (or 'sanitary workers', as I think he called them), was the fact that they were paid less than the 'national average'. I have wondered since what was Mr Cudjo's interest in the matter. I expect he was some kind of union official.

At any rate, when at the end of our first round of visits, I came to compile my monumental public health report on the state of the company's villages, I inserted an observation, based on this information of Mr Cudjo's, that recruitment might be prejudiced by the fact, as I understood it, that the sanitary workers were paid less than the 'national average'.

A few days after copies of the report were in the hands of senior management, I received a telephone call from Amos in my office.

'Doc,' he said. 'I've got your report on the company's villages on my desk. Look, doc, would you please tell me where you got your information that our sanitary workers were paid less than the "national average"?'

I hummed and hawed.

'Look, doc! You might as well tell me. I've got my spies. I can find out for myself soon enough.'

'Actually, it was Cudjo.'

'Yes, I thought the "national average" sounded like one of Cudjo's educated expressions. While he was about it, did he tell you that our sanitary workers only work half days?'

'No.'

'So you might say, in fact, that they were being paid more than the national average.'

'Yes.'

'Look, doc,' he went on. 'I've got a deputation of sanitary workers outside my office now, with a banner. It reads: "DOCKETA SAY MORE PAY FOR LATRINE BOYS".'

'But Amos!' I protested. 'That document was marked "Confidential"!'

'Doc, you should know that nothing in Samreboi is confidential for long. Don't worry. I will deal with it.'

Which was my first introduction to the politics of public health.

5 - Jenny

Jenny has been sufficiently introduced as a representative of a nation which has contributed a disproportionate number of vertebrae to the backbone of empire.

Unfortunately, she was having a tough time of it.

One afternoon, in a quiet moment, I was improving the vacant hour in my usual way, catching up on the vast field of knowledge required for my unique job. In short I was buried in Manson's Tropical Diseases.

Along the concrete gangway, came the sound of 'footprints' (in the old school joke): the sharp tack-tack, in which I recognised the purposeful steps of Jenny. The door rattled open, and she propelled into my presence four 'African male adults', as the police reports described them. Three were poorly dressed, bare-foot, and looked guilty. The fourth, I recognised as Mills, the 'lab boy', who seemed to be some kind of witness. He was decently dressed, shod, and bespectacled, and did not share the guilty look of the others. Indeed, his face bore a look of sanctity which would have done justice to the 'black saint', the Blessed Martin de Porres.

'Doctor Durrant!' thundered Jenny, inserting twice the usual number of 'r's' into my designation. 'These are three spray boys, who were detected in dereliction of duty. Dr Durrant, you must understand that, when not required for spraying, they are supposed to be engaged in other useful employment, such as cutting grass to discourage snakes and mosquitoes. At three o'clock this afternoon, which was well past their statutory lunch time, they were found in a local tavern - CONSUMING ALCOHOLIC BEVERAGES!'

I was not sure what was expected of me, either in the matter of judgement or penalty. For my first few months in Africa I felt like a man in a darkened room with other beings whose nature and customs were invisible to him. I wondered how the old district officers and magistrates had managed to deal with these creatures of another planet. In time the darkness would thin and I would find my way about - at least to a sufficiently practical extent. But I would never have the social advantages of an African doctor; and I was even to learn later that a town-bred African would never attain the knowledge of his poorer colleague, brought up in the rural areas.

It turned out that this demonstration was for my information only. Such cases were handed over for disposal to the 'secular power': the secular power being Amos, the personnel manager.

The prisoners were removed, and I settled down with Manson again.

But not for long. Again footsteps. This time, besides Jenny's tack-tack, I detected softer tones. The door rattled open again, and Mr Mills was propelled into the room, minus every trace of his former sanctity. Besides Jenny, he was followed by the elegant form of Miss Lemaire, the deputy matron.

'Doctor Durrant!' thundered Jenny, with even more 'r's' than before. 'I was misinformed. The spray boys were discovered by Miss Lemaire. Mr Mills didnae even know they were missing!'

This seemed to imply a considerable fall in the fortunes of Mr Mills, the extent of whose duties, apart from the blameless contemplation of what are known as 'ova, cysts and parasites' under his microscope, I was not sure of. At any rate, he was quickly marched off in his turn for the disposal of the secular power.

Mr Mills escaped execution, at all events, as a few afternoons later, when I was into a further chapter of Manson, he entered my office, after first sweeping the landscape with his head-lamp glasses, evidently for any signs of Jenny. He drew after him a plump young female, clutching her arm, like a prize heifer.

'I hear you want learning Twi,' he began, referring to the local language. 'I dash you my cousin, Comfort. She very good Twi teacher.'

I recognised the famous 'sleeping dictionary'. The 'dash' is an even older West African institution: a special gift or bribe.

'Comfort' is a popular local girl's name. Others are 'Blessing' and 'Promise', and it must be said, the owners try to live up to them.

I was sorry to disappoint them, but explained that I was already receiving Twi lessons from a local schoolmaster.

One day, Amos rang me up to say that a European manager had complained that he had seen Sackey sitting in the doctor's chair, seeing patients, and seemed to think the world was coming to an end.

Now Sackey was a medical assistant, which, I have already said, is a sort of mini-doctor. Sackey regularly took over from me while I was doing my ward round, in theatre, or having my meals, etc. In most African systems, the MAs see all the patients first, screening out the more serious cases for the attention of the doctor. I was surprised Amos did not know this.

I asked him the name of the complainant, but Amos would not tell me.

Well, I could work things out, just as Amos could, even if my system was no doubt not as highly developed as his. On the day in question, there had only been one European patient. The managers sat in their own waiting room, where he would have seen Sackey in the doctor's room. His name was Bill Cartwright. He had malaria, and I put him off sick.

The managers enjoyed home visits, which were performed by Jenny, as well as myself. At my request, she attended on Bill next day.

I asked her how she got on, and took the opportunity to tell her of Bill's offence.

Jenny's face fell. 'My word! I've put my foot in it!'

Jenny had entered the sick-room and placed a thermometer in Bill's mouth, as Bill's wife stood by. While Bill sat up in bed in his best pyjamas, cooking the thermometer, a self-conscious silence descended, which affected everyone in the room except Jenny, who stood with arms folded, regarding Bill with a clinical eye. Seeking to fill the gap, Joan Cartwright opened a social conversation with the words:

'And how are things at the hospital, matron?'

She got more than she bargained for.

Jenny had heard of the complaint, but did not know the identity of the complainant.

'Things at the hospital,' she thundered 'would be a braw sight better if some of the folks in Samreboi would learn tae mind their ain business!'

21

She recounted the story of the mystery European manager.
'Ah doan't know who he is, but ah shall, and when ah do, ah'll tear him apart!'

One of the main planks in Jenny's campaign of reform was the eradication of public spitting. The African peasantry shared with British footballers an immovable belief in the poisonous properties of their oral secretions, which must be removed at regular intervals, regardless of locality. Although Jenny put up notices and made the most terrifying examples, the offenders never seemed to connect these activities of the strange white woman with the matter in question.

One morning, Jenny stood outside her office, contemplating her domain, her thoughts upon the same. Her eye fell abstractedly on a small black girl in a body cloth, sitting with her back to her on the edge of the gangway. The almost physical pressure of this powerful gaze seemed to affect the girl, who turned her head and rolled the whites of her eyes at Jenny. As one blinded by the sun, she looked ahead again, but now froze like a small animal under observation. After a minute, she turned her head again, but the sun was still glaring. Once again she looked ahead, but this time, feeling that something was expected of her, filled her mouth with spit. When it was good and ripe, she hoicked it on to the ground a yard in front of her.

Until that moment, the girl had lain unregistered on Jenny's retina. Now she became only too visible. Jenny rose a foot in the air with a loud bang, or rather series of bangs, representing the names of Miss Lemaire, Mr Sackey, and sundry other persons, including even the disgraced Mr Mills (perhaps to examine the sputum under his microscope).

A European manager, who had been standing by observing this little comedy, now pulled his pipe out of his mouth and began laughing: 'Ha! Ha! Ha!', until Jenny rounded on him, and he managed to save his life by timeously converting it to 'Ah-tishoo!'

6 - The 'Ritual Murder'

Late one Sunday afternoon, they told me there was a casualty on male ward. When I got there, I found a middle-aged man on a bed behind a couple of screens. He had been hacked about with a cutlass and was in bad way. He told a strange tale.

It was an old custom in some parts of Africa that when a chief died, certain people were selected to go with him so that he should not lack servants in the next world. It was said that in former times, his actual servants were taken, who viewed their destiny not only without distaste but with positive enthusiasm; but with the decline in attitudes of laxer days, they became evasive, to say nothing of the officious interference of colonialism and so-called 'civilisation', and the authorities had to look elsewhere for candidates. Modern 'educated' Africans piously denied the persistence of the custom, but the masses did not share their simple faith, and it was said that the victims were sought among less traceable persons, such as vagrants and itinerant traders; but these people learn, and avoided areas where the chief had recently died, so the death was sometimes kept quiet until the heads were secured (for only these were buried with the chief, in some secret part of the forest, sometimes a river being temporarily dammed for the purpose), but rumour finds a way.

At any rate, when the paramount chief of the Bruja tribe died in the nearby town of Bongo, there was widespread fear in the surrounding country. The streets, which normally pulsed with life long after dark, were deserted at sundown, not only in Bongo itself, but in our town too. When a friend and I had gone out fishing that day, he, who had been in India, carried an old Afridi sword with him, though we did not think that anyone would go for Europeans, as being altogether too conspicuous. Nevertheless, a passing small boy advised us to be home before dark as the 'executioners' were in the neighbourhood: these being the officials whose duty it was to collect the heads.

The dead chief lay in state in a small room for a week, surrounded by his wives, who were locked in with him, while the executioners went in search of the twenty heads for which a chief of this particular rank qualified. A strong body of police had been sent to the town, as

23

soon as the chief's death became known about, as a precaution against old African customs.

Our patient told us that someone who had a grudge against him had attacked him, hoping to kill him and leave his headless body to be attributed to the work of the executioners.

I ordered him to theatre, where I did what I could for him, and after two hours returned him to the ward.

Within a few days the patient developed tetanus and died, mercifully, of pneumonia.

I heard some news from the Catholic priest at Bongo, a Dutchman. The missionaries, being fluent in the vernacular and spending their whole careers among the people, are closest of all Europeans to the African, and usually have a good idea of what is going on. Father Van told me they got the twenty heads, and even collected one from the police.

I witnessed a curious sequel to this tale, some months later. In the neighbouring town of Mango, they were holding the annual Yam Festival. This takes place in November, at the end of the rainy season, and no one may touch the new yams or cassavas until it is over. There is empirical method in this custom, as the unripe plants contain cyanide, and poisoning has resulted from their premature consumption.

The festival opens with the witch-doctors, looking very spooky, smeared with white clay, running through the streets with antelope tail switches to drive away evil spirits. It finishes with a grand procession of the chief and other important persons and their wives being borne on palanquins through the crowded streets.

On the great day, music (or something) was provided by the Mango town band, which comprised drums and bugles. One could take no exception to the drummers, who performed as to the manner born, but the playing of the buglers was somewhat idiosyncratic. I could only describe it as 'action playing', after the manner of the famous school of action painters. Their method consisted in marching up and down the main street behind the drummers, 'chucking sound about'.

This was an entertaining interlude before they headed the main procession, in which they were followed first by a crowd of young men, firing off the famous 'Dane guns'. These ancient muskets came, not from Denmark, but Birmingham, and in the sanctity of Victorian trade, were actually unloaded at a point down the coast, for transport up to Kumasi, at the same time as Wolseley's troops were disembarking to face the same wares up country, in the Ashanti war of 1874. But what caught my eye especially were the two gentlemen who brought up the rear, behind palanquins and all, marching abreast with sixteenth-century Portuguese helmets on their heads and cutlasses over their shoulders.

I had a shrewd suspicion who these might be, but decided to seek confirmation from the bystanders. I asked at least two men, and in each case, received the embarrassed reply: 'I don't know how to explain it in your language.'

Finally I saw Samson: not the ambulance driver, but my 'small boy'. A 'small boy' is a second house servant. I first met him when James crept up to me in his indoor bare feet, after lunch one day, to inform me that 'someone wants to see you, sah, at the front door'.

There I found a stalwart young man of about twenty, who mystified me with the statement: 'Please, sah. I am Samson. Dr Burns make me be small boy in the school holidays.'

Dr Burns was my immediate predecessor, and I certainly wondered at first what strange experiments he had been up to, involving the temporary conversion of full-grown men to small boys, before James, who had silently appeared beside me, explained what Samson meant.

I might also add that many Africans, for various reasons, mostly economic, like Neddy Seagoon, who came home after forty-two years at school, spend an indeterminate time on their education.

A few days after engaging Samson (who James assured me was indispensable), a little old man appeared at the door, who informed me that 'Dr Burns let me sleep in the Wendy house' (a structure I had already observed in the garden). So now I found myself with no less than three servants, including a gardener. Although I was well aware that for a bachelor this number was superfluous, I was beginning to learn enough about Africa to realise that such mercenary calculations were beside the point: this was the proper noblesse oblige of such a 'big man' as a doctor.

Samson, perhaps because of so many years at school, had the unworldliness of the scholar, and could be relied on to give an honest answer to a question, if only out of pure naivety. So it was on the present occasion. When I put my question as to the two mysterious officers to him, he answered simply:

'Those are the executioners. They cut the heads off when the chief dies.'

7 - Triumph, Tragedy, Victory

As I said, I can remember the names of my first main victims. The name of my first hernia was Sammy.

I had received some theoretical teaching in inguinal hernia repair from my old chief, Howell. This dear man had an unfortunate career. He slaved for years as a registrar - a system by which the government got a specialist for rather less than it would have to pay a plumber - before being appointed a consultant well into his forties. He enjoyed his post for less than ten years before being struck down in the operating theatre by a stroke. They found him a sinecure in a convalescent hospital, and it was at his fireside in this place with his good hand that he produced the collection of drawings I took with me to Ghana which in due course bore fruit in the case of the unsuspecting Sammy.

The operation went successfully: at any rate Sammy never came back for more. I found myself with a back-log of hernias, which are common on the Coast owing to the depredations of the filaria worm. (Des, who was a sick man by then, had confined himself to emergencies.) When a doctor gets a reputation for surgery in Africa, he does not lack customers, and I found myself doing one a week and becoming a fair exponent of the Bassini, which is not a concerto grosso but the standard operation for inguinal hernia, named after the eponymous professor of Padua.

My fame spread. One of the African managers gave a lift to some ladies in the back of his Land Rover, where he overheard them singing my praises. 'Did you hear how he fixed Kobina's hernia? Who would have married him with a thing like that?'

One evening I was called out of the club to deal with a dead woman: not to pronounce her 'dead on arrival': doctors are too thin on the ground in Africa for such nonsense as that, which is performed by the senior nurse on duty. This one had a special problem. She had died in childbirth, and the afterbirth was retained. Custom forbad burial with such an unclean object inside her. I found her lying in the back of a lorry, which had brought her miles across country.

27

I thought it was superfluous to transfer the body to the mortuary. I could just as well do the business where she was. Apron, gloves and a lamp were brought.

'Ah well!' I thought. 'Our work is altruistic,' echoing the words of one of my old chiefs in Liverpool after requesting the houseman to perform a manual removal of faeces.

How did our mentors describe the sensation of removing a retained afterbirth? Like shaking hands with a gorilla? I wonder how many of them did it on a patient six hours dead and iron-hard with rigor mortis, and how they would describe that. Having been there myself, I would compare it to the technique of the rock-climber, Joe Brown, who would thrust his hand into a crevice, close his fist and swing on it.

I did my best, and removed enough of the stuff to carry conviction, including the tell-tale umbilical cord. I stepped down, sweating and shaking with the effort.

I was greeted with contented faces around me. Honour was satisfied. The family were at ease in their grief.

In the words of Trousseau: 'to cure sometimes...to comfort always.'

A woman was brought in who had suffered bleeding after childbirth. (I do not remember a baby, which may have died.) She had been treated by a native 'herbalist', who had stuffed a great quantity of his/her wares into the affected parts, and we first had to remove and wash out a lot of foul material and exhibit antibiotics, etc.

After a day or two, Mr Sackey approached me with an expressionless face and announced that 'the patient's condition had changed' - an ominous formula in the mouth of an African nurse, only exceeded in menace by 'the patient is gasping'.

I went with him to the ward, and saw tetanus for the first time in my life.[1]

At that moment the visitors burst in: a noisy bubbling African crowd. I said to Sackey: 'Mr Sackey, the ward has got to be kept quiet.'

---

[1] This was, of course, before the 'ritual murder'. WD.

Mr Sackey turned on his heel and in the tones of RSM Brittan (who in his day was the biggest voice in the British Army), bellowed:

'Now, you visitors, listen to me! We have a very sick woman here. DEE WARD GOTTA BE KEP' QUIET!!!'

As might have been expected, the woman seized up at once. Her back arched in the dreadful spasms of the disease, and an invisible hand seized her throat and began to choke her.

Fortunately, the instruments were already prepared in the duty room, and I set about the first tracheostomy of my career.

I dispensed with local anaesthetic and cut down on the wind-pipe, separating the flesh with the fingers of my free hand, until I was rewarded with the in-suck of breath, followed by the explosion of air and blood that announced my entry into the trachea. I held open the cut with the unfamiliar forceps, which work outwards, and slipped in the tube. For the time being the woman was safe. Easier than I had expected.

I ordered Largactil and phenobarbitone, and gave antitetanic serum intravenously. It came in an enormous ampoule from Russia, which must have contained 50ml. I began working out how much drugs we would need out of our limted stocks. When the monthly drug order arrived at that place, in the universal ambulance, driven by Samson, it felt like the relief of Lucknow, and even casual bystanders cheered accordingly.

But all our efforts were of little avail beyond securing a comparatively comfortable death for the victim.

I performed a caesar on a little woman who had been in obstructed labour for five days. (It must have been her first or the uterus would have ruptured.) The baby was of course dead. In those days we had not developed the method for dealing with peritonitis which was so successful later - a method ridiculously simple in principle which consists in washing out the abdomen with saline. This brilliant idea had lain dormant in the dull brain of man since the dawn of surgery.

At any rate, when the little woman's stomach swelled up two days later, I knew what was the matter with her, and that she was very ill indeed.

I gave intravenous antibiotics. I discovered that she was anaemic. At that time I secured blood for transfusion by organising a whip-round among the managers, before I hit on the more economical method of bleeding the relatives.

I got a couple of pints out of the evening drinkers at the bar. The blood must have been well medicated, as the little woman fell soundly asleep half way through the second pint.

At any rate, they pulled her through. She hung between life and death for ten days, before making a good recovery.

When I first tackled the question of blood transfusion , as I implied, I first raised a list of volunteers, white and black, from among the managers, and most of my touting was done at that convenient venue, the club bar.

One of the first on the list was Horace, of the engineering department, which surprised everybody, as this was the first pint Horace had even put his name down for, still less stood in the club; though he had never been known to cause offence by refusing one. On top of which he had the cheek to call himself Lovewater.

I will not labour the point that Sam put him in charge of the swimming pool: but one day in the club he asked me what pH I preferred.

Being a bit tired at the end of day, I thought for a wild moment he was offering me a drink, until it dawned on me he was referring to the swimming pool.

I rejoiced in the catholicity of my new job, but this was a bit of a facer. However, resourcefulness is the first quality required in an African country doctor, and I decided to exercise some.

'What pH did Dr Burns prefer, Horace?' I asked, in a discursive tone.

'Dr Burns preferred a pH of 7.5, doc.' (I hope I have got that right.)

'I'm sure a pH of 7.5 is just right for this climate.'

Meantime, Mills the lab boy was going to work on the blood groups of the volunteers. When the list was complete, I announced it (probably in breach of confidentiality), more or less openly, to the interested parties round the bar.

(One thing the reader must understand: the existence of a certain blood group called universal recipients. In a word, while most people can give blood to most other people, universal recipients can give it only to members of their own exclusive circle, but they can take it from anybody.

Perhaps because our God has taught us it is more blessed to give than to receive, this particular group is not numerous.)

'Horace has a most rare and interesting blood group,' I said. 'He is AB positive, which means he is a universal recipient.'

The laugh which followed this was not as big as the next one, which was raised by the chief of the club wags, Danny Wilson.

'Horace is a most rare and interesting person!'

Horace had the cheek to join in both laughs, but perhaps he had no option.

Another caesar I performed on a hunchback: a victim of Pott's disease, Tb of the spine. This had to be a classical operation, as the lower segment operation was physically impossible on the doubled-up little body: Ten days later, she marched off, proudly bearing her prize in her arms. It was also impossible for her to carry the baby on her back.

The police brought in a man with an arrow stuck in his upper arm. He was a thief and had been shot by an 'NT', a guard from the Northern Territories, who watched the company premises, armed with a bow and arrow. One could recognise these little people by their almost Mongolian or Bushman-like features.

I knew that this arrow was barbed, like a fish-hook. I gave the man a shot of Pentothal and simply pushed it through: I could see there were no vulnerable structures in the way. There was a gush of venous blood, soon staunched with a pressure bandage.

In the inevitable crowd that gathered outside the theatre on this interesting occasion was Alassan, the little old cook of my fishing companion, Les Cady (who, incidentally, was the European manager who nearly died laughing at Jenny in the spitting crisis). Something did not add up as far as Alassan was concerned. I must say he was an

'NT', and in his part of the world thieves were usually dealt with by nailing them to a tree by the head.

Later he questioned Les on the matter. 'Massa,' he asked. 'Wha' for dee docketa go make dat boy better? Dun dee docketa nebba savvy dat boy be tiefman?'

Nigerians were the greatest exponents of 'pidgin'. A large Nigerian lady (I recognised her by her turban, instead of the headscarf of the Ghanaian women) sat down in the chair before me. 'Docketa,' she announced. 'I nebba see my flower tree munt. I tink I go catch belly.' I will simply say the subject was obstetrical.

Blackwater fever (that dangerous complication of malaria) is rarely seen nowadays. Nevertheless we had a case in a little fellow of ten. I assembled the regulation rack of test tubes, and we watched his urine samples turn from port wine to normal over the next few days, as the treatment took effect. We also transfused him and monitored his haemoglobin by the only method available to us - a finger prick and the Talquist coloured papers.

He was duly discharged, and his father asked to bring him back for review a week later. Faithfully they turned up. I looked the little fellow over, said, 'fine' and his father led him away. This was not good enough for the little chap. He doubled back, stood before me and pointedly tapped his thumb. I obediently sent him for another blood check. That lad should go far.

Towards the end of a hard day, Miss Lemaire found me and informed me: 'We have a woman with severe abdominal pains. She is overdue her period by two weeks.'

'Wearily I commented: 'An ectopic! That's all we need.'

I examined the patient and made a proof puncture: a needle thrust into the abdomen. Sure enough, the syringe filled with blood, making the diagnosis very probable. I ordered her to theatre.

At that time, I was still using spinal anaesthetics for everything major, until my neighbour, the young Dutch mission doctor at Mango, warned me of their dangers in cases of potential shock. At any rate, I got away with it in the present case.

For those interested, our anaesthetic resources, besides spinals, consisted of an EMO miniature ether machine, which broke down early on and had to be sent to England for repair. We were not to see it again for a year, most of which time it lay on the docks at Takoradi. Meantime I did the best I could with various substances per rag and bottle, and combinations of local anaesthetic and morphine.

Incidentally, the less sophisticated Africans (and some of the other kind) preferred to stay awake during their operations and had a profound suspicion of general anaesthesia. True, the doctor spun you some yarn about 'putting you to sleep', but what kind of child did they think they were talking to? Everyone knew that you could not operate on someone in his sleep. Obviously, that injection the doctor gave you was poison which killed you. Only then could he go to work on you with all those knives and things. When he had finished, he gave you some more medicine to bring you back to life again. The whole business seemed altogether very uncertain. Much better to stay awake, when you could keep an eye on things and have a nap now then when you felt safe.

And by golly, they were tough! Especially the 'NTs'. For a reason which will appear later, I went off spinal anaesthetics for caesars for a time and relied on local, adding morphine after the delivery of the baby, when its respiration would not be compromised by the latter drug. I experimented a good deal with the amounts of local, and eventually found that ten millilitres under the skin was enough for the tough little women of the north, but would not do for the more 'civilised' ladies of the south, who were almost European in their nervous sensibilities. Most of the pain of a caesar occurs, of course, as the knife enters the skin of the abdomen: then some later, as the womb is cut and the baby's head extracted. But the tough little NT women happily fell asleep after the first ten mil of local, and never woke up until the little present was put into their arms. I came to the conclusion that they could well take a caesar with no anaesthetic at all - just a quick slash and scream. But needless to say, I never carried my experiments that far!

The abdomen is a fearful place to enter for the first time. I am not counting the several caesars I had done by then, where you come on the uterus right away, and your bearings are clear. But here, after sundry gingery cuts, I came upon a mass of bowels, swimming in a sea of dark blood.

The latter was cleared fairly quickly with the sucker. And Miss Lemaire had set up the equipment for autotransfusion, which means collecting the patient's own blood to be returned into the vein. Soon Miss Lemaire was bottling blood as calmly as ladies in England bottling jam.

With the use of abdominal towels, I found the offending tube, cut it out and stitched up the gap. Mr Sackey reported favourably on the blood pressure. I had the great feeling that we were winning.

At that moment Jenny entered, like a good matron, hearing about the serious case. She was dressed in a party frock, on her way to a social evening. I called for a catheter, and Jenny donned an apron and dropped one into the steriliser. When she tried to remove it, the thing took on a life of its own, wriggling through the holes of the trays. 'Drat the thing!' cursed Jenny. 'Ye'd think it was a snake!', which provoked much laughter in the happy celebratory atmosphere that attends the triumph of life over death.

A sadder case was a woman, heavily pregnant, brought in bleeding profusely. She was in great pain. One question only was required: did the pain come and go, or did it stay all the time? The latter: which told me it was an accidental haemorrhage (nowadays called an abruptio) caused by bleeding behind the placenta, or afterbirth.

Suffice it to say that my efforts failed to save her. I stood at the door of the little theatre with blood all over me and my heart in my boots. Emilia stood sympathetically beside me.

I saw a woman sitting on the edge of the gangway, wailing bitterly.
'Who is that woman, Emilia?'
'That is the rival.'
'Who?'
'The rival. The junior wife.'

At the end of the Saturday morning clinic one day, a crabby little old woman was brought in by her crabby little old husband. She had a lump in her groin, which I recognised as a hernia. It had been there three days and could not be pushed back. This was a strangulated inguinal hernia. I suspected the lump contained gangrenous bowel, which would need a resection (which means cutting out the bad section and joining the rest up again). Otherwise, the little woman was going to die a lingering and painful death.

Once more I went to get the book out. On the famous shelf in my office lay two or three surgical books, as Des had said. I selected one of them.

Classical scholars recognise two approaches to science: the Greek approach, occupying itself with theory and leaving the grubby practical stuff to low fellows like carpenters and Romans; and the Roman approach itself, which gets down to the nitty gritty. My first selected book (which shall be nameless) belonged to the Grecian category.

After a learned dissertation on the subject of gangrenous bowel, the writer concluded with the lordly words: 'the many methods of operation are sufficiently well known as to require no further rehearsal in these pages'.

'Marvellous!' I thought (and probably shouted: soliloquy is not unknown in the jungle). "And here I am a hundred miles up in the bush!'

Fortunately, my second choice was the Roman kind (Scottish, actually, which is the same thing) - the redoubtable Professor Grey Turner. Quickly seeing that Professor Turner meant business, I took him home with me and studied him over lunch.

Of the 'many methods' known to the Grecian gentleman (if he kept them to himself) Professor Grey Turner knew only one - a good honest method, which was unfortunately the most pedantic and time-consuming, as you might expect...but that's enough cracks about the Scots! Anyway, after I returned to the theatre I removed four inches of gangrenous bowel. The operation lasted four hours - and a spinal anaesthetic lasts an hour and a half.

I realised this when the little woman started grunting. Happily, we were able to keep her comfortable with local and morphine.

We got her back to the ward in good condition, with the regulation collection of tubes, and strict instructions for NIL BY MOUTH.

Then I went home for supper. After a couple of hours at the club, I looked in on her on my way home. To my horror I found the little woman had pulled all these tubes either up or out. Moreover, her husband was bending over her, shovelling *fufu* down her throat (which is cassava mash, slightly less stiff than cement), demanding angrily, what sort of hospital was this, where they left the patients to starve?

The fact that the little old woman made a good recovery on this post-operative regime will be of interest to physiologists.

One afternoon, an old man brought in his son, a lad of about sixteen, whom I found on a stretcher. He had been ill for a week and three days ago had developed abdominal pain and become much worse. He was hiccupping and his cheeks were sunken. When I felt his abdomen, it was board-like. In England I would have diagnosed a perforated peptic ulcer.

I opened the abdomen but found no ulcer. In despair, I closed the abdomen and started antibiotics. Later that evening the lad died.

I wrote about this case to Howell, but received no reply. I expect Howell was past correspondence by then, if he was still alive: when I returned from West Africa, he was dead. At the end of my letter, as an afterthought, I mentioned typhoid.

Few British surgeons who had not worked in the Third World would have made the diagnosis. Howell had served in the Middle East in the Second World War, so might have guessed. The answer arrived in an article on the subject in the West African Medical Journal.

Well, I had got the two main clues, but had failed to connect them. The case was one of perforated typhoid ulcer, which occurs at the other end of the small bowel from where I was looking. The article described it as the commonest cause of acute abdomen in West African males. In the lad's condition his chances would have been small, even in the best circumstances.

A number of small children were brought in, very ill. I had barely time to examine them before they all died. But I had seen enough: a thick grey membrane over the back of the throat. Something I doubt a living Englishman has seen in his own country - diphtheria.

I informed the public health, and a couple of Indian doctors came up from Takoradi with a lorry load of vaccine and serum. They stayed at my house. Over sundowners and supper, we laid plans.

All the cases had come from one village - Bekwai. We had to vaccinate all the children under five in that place. The doctors would offer serum to all medical and nursing staff in contact. I excused myself as an already vaccinated Englishman.

The village headman was notified, and the vaccination programme planned for next day. News travels fast in Africa, and so did this news. Not the news about the epidemic - that was no more news than dog bites man - but the news that injections were being given out at the hospital. There is nothing your African peasant appreciates more than a good painful injection, and even if the babies are not actually born with the taste, they are quickly trained up to it.

I started my mornings at a separate clinic at the sawmill, designed to get the malingerers back to work as early as possible. The two other doctors went straight to the hospital.

When I arrived there later, I thought the revolution had broken out. Not one village, but the whole countryside, had received the news. The hospital was practically buried in a crowd that would have done for the Cup Final. The police were hard at work with truncheons: village headmen were beating one another's flocks with not so ceremonial staffs, each battling for his own .The Bekwai kids were a drop in the ocean: how many got their rights was anybody's guess. The doctors ran out of vaccine long before a fraction of the crowd was satisfied. Their only concern now was to save their skins before the police could remove their clientele. When the police had beaten a path for my car near enough for me to see the hospital, and Dr Patel on the veranda to see me, he waved his arms and shouted:

'The whole thing has been a disastrous failure!'

Two Ibo women staged a stand-up fight in the market place. Such is the implacability of the race, especially the female of the species, and especially the Ibo of the species, that the fight went on for three days, knocking off for meals and sleep, like a test match. It ended with one receiving a decisive kick in the abdomen; whereupon she skulked in her tent for another three days, evidently hoping to mend her wounds and return to the fray. If so, she was to be disappointed: she was brought to me instead (as Mr Pooter might have said).

In short she had a ruptured spleen, and died on the operating table.

An inquest was held in the club by the district magistrate, when I gave my melancholy evidence; which was received without question, or at any rate, without criticism. Nobody blames the doctor in Africa who, like the pianist at the party, is credited with doing his best. Years later, in Zimbabwe, a murderer had the effrontery to suggest from the dock that the doctor might have done better, and was promptly put in his place by the magistrate. (This was not a hanging matter, or I wouldn't be joking about it.)

The other woman, of course, appeared: as like as two peas in a pod. She had her baby on her back. I suppose they must have taken breaks to feed their infants. I forget the outcome of the case.

Finally, my saddest case at that time. At caesarean section, just after I had delivered a healthy baby girl, Mr Sackey informed me that the patient had stopped breathing. All our efforts at resuscitaion failed. There seemed no explanation. I sent a letter to the queries column of *The Practitioner*, and received a kind and elaborate reply from one of the most eminent anaesthetists in Britain - for I suspected it was an anaesthetic death. I had used a spinal but there had been no evidence of pre-existing shock.

The specialist made a number of suggestions, ending, almost as an after-thought, about a circulatory failure in the blood returning to the heart.

Nowadays, this would be the one and only diagnosis, called supine hypotensive syndrome, caused by pressure on the main vein (which is usual), uncompensated because of a rare defect in the collateral circulation. The condition was barely understood at that time. On my return from Ghana, I read in the British Medical Journal about three cases in UK that year, one of them fatal. The condition can be corrected simply by placing a sand bag under the right buttock, which displaces the uterus enough to relieve the pressure.

Now I had the miserable task of informing the husband, who was waiting outside. I simply said: 'The pickin she live. The mammy she die.'

The man burst into the theatre, where the dead body of his wife lay as on a sacrificial altar. He did not throw himself upon her. He did not weep or do anything a white man would have done. He danced. He danced round and round the table, shouting with grief. He danced outside. He danced away to his village, still shouting.

Zorba the Greek, it will be remembered, danced for grief when his little son died. Africans also dance for grief, strange as this form of expression may seem to Anglo-Saxons.

Years later, I was performing a post-mortem in Central Africa, when, through the window, I saw the family of the deceased beginning to dance, twisting round and round and crying: *'Mai-wei! Mai-wei!'*

Beyond the fence was a crowd of about a hundred people at a bus terminus. Africans are nothing if not social beings. Privacy, except in intimate physical matters, is anathema. They also have a mass telepathy, like birds. In no time, the crowd beyond the fence took up the dance in sympathy, until they were all twisting and leaping and crying, *'Mai-wei! Mai-wei!'*

A colleague, who was assisting me in the PM, rigidly Anglo-Saxon in spirit (although his mother was Polish), cast a cold eye on the scene, and remarked: 'Not a tear!'

But that was not the point: when you express your grief or sympathy by dancing, it takes a different direction from tears.

Back in Samreboi, on a happier occasion, I was attending a little boy with acute asthma, when he suddenly stopped breathing. His mother, who was standing by, ran out of the ward and began dancing round and round the small hospital, crying: *'Adjei! Adjei!'* I bent over and gave the little body the kiss of life. Immediately, he started breathing again, and, as if by a miracle, his asthma had disappeared (a fact for physiologists to ponder). Someone ran out and caught the mother, and she returned to the ward, still dancing, but now for joy.

The Lord of the Dance is black!

In those early days at Samreboi, I would sit on my balcony at the end of the day, with book and pipe and drink, where I could see the hospital, half a mile away across a hollow. Sometimes I would see the ambulance turn into the main entrance. My heart would sink, as I wondered what new unfamiliar trial was awaiting me.

The anxiety had begun in my London hotel, on the eve of my departure. I fell into a restless sleep, in which I was confronted by a line of black faces, with unfamiliar diseases, whose treatment I had little knowledge of. When I arrived at my post, I found myself confronted by a line of black faces, with unfamiliar diseases, I had little knowledge of; but my fear was masked to a large extent like a paratrooper, who goes into action as soon as he hits the ground.

Fortunately, at that time, the British Medical Association had put out a pamphlet on tropical diseases for British family doctors, who, in this age of increasing travel, were likely to meet some of them. This proved very useful to me.

Also, I resorted to low stratagems. I have never been too proud to learn from subordinates, though it is sometimes advisable to disguise the process. 'What do you make of that, Mr Sackey?' I would ask, like a professor testing a student. 'Hookworm, sah!', promptly replied Mr Sackey, who had seen a thousand cases before. 'And what have you got on the shelf for that?' 'Alcopar!'

But it was a full year before I got over the terrors of surgery. The feeling before an operation, like a soldier going over the top. The euphoria of winning, the desolation of losing, and worst of all, the agonies of guilt over a mistake - for a doctor's mistake can cost a life - a mistake all too obvious after the event. This fear hung over me, waking and sleeping, like a heavy and immovable cloud.

I had touched on this subject in a letter to Des, who was a frequent and encouraging correspondent. He was now the company's chief medical officer at Accra. He replied comfortingly that these things lost their terrors in time. He took the precaution of inviting me down to the coast for a few days, ostensibly to 'report', but really to give me a break - the only one I had in the eighteen months I was on that station. (My Dutch colleague at Mango and his wife, who was also a doctor, stood by for my emergencies while I was away, as I did for them.) On the golden sands beside the blue waters, and in the easy hospitality of the Brennan's house, I got some much-needed relaxation. But on my return, the cloud was still there.

Then one evening, after twelve months on the station, sitting on that same balcony, I realised that like the clear sky before me, the cloud had lifted. I had conquered a great field of fear, and I would dominate it for the rest of my life.

8 - All God's Children

All Africans are religious. I will not say how they are religious. After twenty-two years on the continent I can pretend to little more than a superficial knowledge of them. Of all Europeans, paradoxically I believe the ones who know the Africans best are the rural Afrikaners of South Africa, who live cheek by jowl with them in an uneasy love-hate relationship, like a quarrelsome husband and wife.

But I do not believe they are religious in our way. We Europeans are not very happy in this world, so we have invented an improved model elsewhere. This is especially true of the Protestants, who seem to view the world as a kind of outward bound school run by God. If you get through, you get the Duke of Edinburgh's award: if you don't, you get the other thing.

Moreover this pilgrim's progress, from this world to the next, is a model in time: a true production of the European, especially Protestant, spirit. Africans have little idea of time (as European managers know to their chagrin): their world-view is the model of eternity.

(Nowadays we Europeans no longer believe in other worlds, but we still do not enjoy this one as much as we might: which seems to leave us with the worst of all possible worlds.)

Africans may not believe in other worlds, but they believe in the next life. Though 'next' is hardly the operative word - rather a continuation of this life as an 'ancestor'. The ancestors live in an invisible old people's home at the end of the village (someone has described an African village as a 'community of the living and the dead'), and the ancestors take as keen an interest in the goings-on of this world as the retired *Telegraph* readers of Tunbridge Wells. So far from enjoying any kind of paradise, they seem to be a pretty ill-conditioned lot, visiting plague and other disasters on their descendants if they forget their birthdays, etc.

There is little idea of sin, at any rate, in our abstract sense: morality is humanistic or social, apart from the ancestral obligations referred to. Africans believe in a Supreme Being, the Sky God, but his functions seem largely confined to providing rain.

So far I have been talking about the traditional Africans. Between them and the fully Christianised ones there is a spectrum of mixed beliefs; but even the most regular Christians seem to view their faith in a social light and not as the lugubrious business of northern climes.

Jesus is a friend, and incidentally a white man, like the father at the mission. I was discussing this with a Swiss friend, who peremptorily summoned his cook from his kitchen duties to test the matter.

'Joseph!' commanded Ralph 'Tell me, was Jesus a *Bruni* or a *Bibini?*'

'He was a *Bruni,* massa,' answered Joseph, in a tone of surprise, even suspicion, at the obviousness of the question.

The black Christs and Madonnas, which the fathers so proudly exhibit as the handiwork of their charges at the white-run mission stations, are there for two reasons. One, it is a fun thing to do, and two, it is part of African good manners to do what people expect of you, rather like indulging the whims of children. No one is fooled (except the fathers). Everyone knows that Jesus was a *Bruni,* if not exactly an English public schoolboy.

Graham Greene loved West Africa with a bitter relish. He saw it as a symbol of his tragic vision. 'No one in this place could believe in a heaven on earth.' But this again is a thoroughly Eurocentric view. As Saki (before Greene of course) observed, to its inhabitants the jungle was paradise enow.

I tried to express these things in a poem of my own.

The body can be broken, maimed,
Infected inwardly.
We can fall upon misfortune.
Then Christ, the crucified, is our god.

Christ is the god of Africa,
'The continent of misery and heat',
The heroic continent.

It is Christ in the wards,
Among the sick, the poor;

The lonely doctor at the mission
Or the seedy little town, which kills romantic hopes.

But among the blacks,
With their undefeated grin,
Their unmindful mirth and movement,
Their stoic sufferings,
God is also Pan.

Churches in Africa are designed with a view to function rather than beauty. It is true there are some very beautiful ones, like the Anglican cathedral in Lagos, and the Catholic cathedral in Lubumbashi, Zaire; but the working parish churches more usually resemble the Anglican church at Samreboi, which looked like a garage.

When Father Adeloye, the parish priest, saw Kendal church on a calendar in my house, he thought it was a cathedral, and could hardly believe it was a parish church like his own. 'My word, doctor!' he mused. 'Those people must have a lot of money.'

At my first attendance, I slipped quietly into a chair at the back. This did not pass unnoticed. A small boy, evidently sent by the vicar, approached me and commanded: 'Come!' I followed him to the front row, where another small boy placed a cushion on a chair and commanded: 'Sit!'

I looked about me. I was the sole European. The church was packed. Two choir stalls contained rows of little black bodies in cassocks and bare feet. They were mostly Father Adeloye's children.

They chanted plain song. Ghana is high church, Father Adeloye explained to me. Nigeria, where he came from, is low church.

There were no black Christs or Madonnas, but they certainly put plenty of African rhythm into the singing. All the little black bodies swung together in a jazzy beat.

'Dow dat tekkest away dee sins-of-dee-well, have messy upon us!'

Father Adeloye descended to read the first lesson from a massive Victorian Bible mounted on a wooden lectern. He was preceded by two little altar boys bearing candles.

As he read, one of the lads in a bored sort of way tried to set fire to the lectern with his candle. Father Adeloye leaned over and fetched him a bang on the ear which nearly overturned boy and candle, spilling a fair quantity of wax: all without taking his eye off the Bible or interrupting the flow of his reading.

Then came the sermon.

As I was to learn on future Sundays, Father Adeloye's sermons were all on the same subject. He received no stipend and supported himself and his numerous family on the products of his 'chop' garden, the division allowed him from the plate and those pledges he referred to as 'church dues'. These matters, rather than the more elevated thoughts that fill the heads of the less indigent of God's servants, were on his mind as he ascended the pulpit. So his texts (and they were the more rebarbative ones: 'Woe unto ye, scribes, pharisees, hypocrites!' 'There shall be weeping and wailing and gnashing of teeth!', etc) all came round to the same end.

'So who was Our Lord (Abraham, God) talking about when he said dose words?'

Awful pause, during which even the sucking babies (breasts having been produced to keep them quiet during the sermon) rolled their little eyes towards the pulpit.

'HE WAS TALKING ABOUT DOSE PEOPLE DAT DON'T PAY DEIR CHURCH DUES!!!'

Two interpreters stood beside the pulpit. One in Twi for the benefit of the ladies, who understood little English; and one in Ibo, of which itinerant Nigerian tribe there were large numbers in the town. Father Adeloye delivered long passages before giving them their chance, and I marvelled at their memory (although the sermons were as stereotyped as I have hinted). But I reflected, this was the gift of peoples where literacy is low, and also that these were the lands of the 'griots', or wandering story-tellers, whose well-stocked heads entertained the long dark nights beside many a village fire.

When Father Adeloye came to the bit about church dues, the interpreters performed in the business-like tone of the tax inspector.

Naturally, there followed a collection. I placed a dollar note on the plate. But this was not the end. I might add that the proceedings went on in African fashion for considerably longer than the statutory English hour. Morning prayers and hymns were performed with great gusto and without the aid of anything in print. And then I discovered that Father Adeloye had another little fund-raising idea to shake out the remaining mites.

A table was placed at the head of the aisle. Two of Father Adeloye's brawny helpers sat at it with a yet larger plate and opened a heavy ledger.

One of them called out: 'All dose born on Sunday!'

Few Ghanaians or other Africans know how old they are. (One white old hand engagingly told me, they tell you how old they feel. On sprightly days they tell you they are twenty: in less happy moods they say fifty - which is very old! My informant thought this a most enviable system.) But all Ghanaians know on which day they were born: they are named after it.

As I remember, Kobina means born on Tuesday (Abina for a girl); Kwasi on Wednesday, etc. The late unlamented Kwame Nkrumah was born on Saturday.

The Sundays stepped up and deposited their coppers, which were duly noted in the ledger. It dawned on me this was a competition designed to stimulate interest in the daily teams.

As the days wore on, people began to look at the doctor, evidently wondering what day he was born on. The doctor wondered too. As no one had ever told him, he decided to settle for Friday, as the days were, so to speak, running out.

Now another problem. I had practically exhausted my pocket money on the collection. I managed to find a few coins. Father Adeloye made a contribution to the Saturdays. Thank God, Saturday won, so I was able to save my face without upstaging the priest.

The Harvest Festival fell in November, at the end of the rains, to correspond with the Yam Festival. I found the church loaded with the products of the African earth. When we came to the first hymn, from the throats of Father Adeloye's family choir I heard with amazement:

'He sends dee snow in winter,
Dee warmth to swell dee grain...
Den tank dee Lor', O tank dee Lor',
For a-a-all His lav.'

46

Presently, far out in the hot morning, I made out the steady beat of a drum. Colonial thoughts of an Ashanti rising came to my mind. Before long, looking out of the glassless window, I saw a drum, which carried itself like Humpty Dumpty on two little black legs, and beat itself with two little black arms. Behind the drum came a school crocodile, guided by a number of schoolteachers in their Sunday-best clothes.

When the procession reached the church, the drum was silenced with some difficulty by one of the teachers, and the crocodile metamorphosed into a colony of ants, which poured into the church - an hour late, but what did that matter in Africa!

At least they were in time for Father Adeloye's sermon. When he came to the bit about church dues, he hit the pulpit so hard with his fist that two sugar canes that had been leaning there fell down onto a couple of cocks which lay trussed and giving the occasional squawk between the choir stalls, killing one outright and miraculously striking the raffia cords off the legs of the other. The second cock jumped up, rejoiced at his new-found freedom with a loud crow, and dived into the nearest choir stall. Much scuffling of little black feet and cassocks, and he was out among the congregation, flapping his wings and jumping over the heads of the multitude, until he was caught, re-trussed, and flung beneath the altar again.

There was a collection, but I think Father Adeloye let us off the name game that Sunday as he had something else in store.

After the usual three hours the service came to an end. The familiar table was placed at the head of the aisle but supplied with more than the usual number of seats. Father Adeloye's helpers were augmented to a full committee by the 'biggest men' in town, all kitted out in the most resplendent tribal dresses. The everyday ledger was replaced with an even larger one. Biros were produced and tested. It became apparent that some kind of business was about to take place.

In fact, all the harvest gifts were to be auctioned off in aid of the church. There was no thought that Our Lord might appear with his whip, overturn the table and drive them out. This might be God's house, but were they not about their Father's business?

The first article to be auctioned was a simple glass of water. The chairman (for Father Adeloye had taken a well-earned rest in a side

47

seat) rose and extolled the virtues of water. Was it not the source of all life? Where would we be without water? What was more precious than water? How much am I offered for this glass of water?

This was of course a purely ceremonial sale, a matter of honour. I did not feel called upon to upstage any of the big men, so preserved a modest silence in my usual seat. The bids went up and up to ten dollars, and a big man had his big day drinking the water there and then, to the uninhibited cheers of the congregation.

And so on down to the unfortunate cocks. I did buy something myself: a fish-trap, made of woven cane. A work of art in itself which I knew would make a beautiful ornament. I got it home to England eventually and presented it to an uncle. It returned to me after his death, and thirty years from the day it was made it still stands sturdy and elegant in my sitting room, where guests think it is a space ship.

One day we were honoured by a visit from the archdeacon. The uniformity of the English Church is as remarkable as its catholicity. There is a certain brand mark about its officers which makes me wonder if they are not mass-produced at Canterbury and some painted black for Africa. For our archdeacon was Trollope's Archdeacon Grantly, painted very black indeed. (Father Adeloye, I might say, could have been Mr Harding.) There had been some slump in the fortunes of the Church (and when I say fortunes I mean what St Matthew the tax-gatherer would have meant by them). We had already had a meeting of the parochial church council, of which I was a member, at which some very strong-arm methods for raising the necessary had been proposed, including knocking on doors more in the spirit of the Gestapo than the Little Sisters of the Poor, until I reminded them that our initials were PCC, and not CPP (which had belonged to the party of the lately overthrown dictator, Kwame Nkrumah).

The archdeacon spoke in the church one week night to a large turn-out, more due to his star quality than any religious enthusiasm, and spoke in tones of an Oxfordian fruitiness, that would have surprised even his Victorian prototype, of the 'perishes that were not doing vary waal' which included, alas, the back-sliding Samreboi. Various members of the congregation made suggestions, which the archdeacon heard with apparent interest before cutting short the inevitable African prolixity with an un-Christian clap of the hand and an authoritative finger pointing to the next aspirant. I forget what resolutions were arrived at (if any), before the archdeacon closed the proceedings with a short prayer; nor do I know where he spent the night, but I am pretty sure it was in more commodious circumstances than Father Adeloye's house could provide.

Constable Yobo of the CID was pointing out the local places of worship to me during a Sunday morning walk along the main street. He was most proud of his own establishment, the Methodist church, which he told me was 'best for singing'. His words were amply corroborated there and then by the lusty strains of 'Bread of Heaven', which threatened to lift off the tin roof of the building. This impressive performance was one of the many fruits of that diligent labourer in God's vineyard, the Reverend Alec Jones, an unassuming Welshman. Alec bore a curious nickname among the Africans. They called him *'Bruni*-go-die', (*'Bruni'* of course meaning 'white man'). Alec collected old clothes through many contacts in his homeland, and distributed them among the poor of his parish. As none of his parishioners could believe that anyone could part with his clothes in life (especially in one piece), they concluded these must be the post mortem effects of Alec's friends in Britain. Hence the name.

Further down the street we passed the Catholic church, where, Constable Yobo dismissively informed me: 'Dey jest hollered in Italian.' (This was of course still in the days before they mucked about with the Tridentine Mass.)

As I have hinted, there was a spectrum of mixed worship between orthodox Christian and pure pagan. Somewhere near the latter end of the rainbow lay a place I looked into one evening with an African guide. In the middle of the room on a stand lay a large Victorian Bible, as good as Father Adeloye's, around which the people were enthusiastically dancing amid lot of drumming and singing. My guide informed me in a superior tone that 'dey tink it catch plenty power' - a scene to make a missionary cry.

The Reverend Alec organised a sort of Three Choirs Festival at his own establishment, in which the Anglicans and Catholics were invited to participate. Not with any idea of competition. Competitiveness is considered rather vulgar in Africa, and Lady Thatcher, I am afraid, would not be thought ladylike - at any rate, on account of her famous doctrine; though she might have been respected, even worshipped as a figure of power - a Great She-elephant. Needless to say, competition or not, Alec's team outshone all the rest. Even Alec, for all his innate modesty, could not suppress a grin of sinful pride which threatened to cut his head off. The Catholic priest sat expressionless. But poor Father Adeloye (who had of course a family interest in the matter) exhibited what I can only describe as a 'boiled' look of equally sinful envy.

One Sunday afternoon I was lying on my bed when I heard once again a distant drum. In those early days I was as eager as a puppy to learn everything about my new surroundings. I quickly got up and went in search of the sound in my car. Presently I came upon a body of scouts filing into the Methodist hall, and for the first time made the acquaintance of Alec. As the forms filled up with the scouts and cubs, evidently assembled for some improving purpose, Alec invited me to take a seat beside him at the desk. When all had settled down Alec stood up and began in his Welsh voice:
'This is our new doctor, Dr Durrant.' A big clap. 'Dr Durrant would like to say a few words to you.' Then he sat down and looked expectantly at me.
Now I don't know what gave Alec that idea, because he was dead wrong. If there is anything I loathe it is having to make a speech in public when I have nothing to say. It is not shyness: just the mere fatuity of trying to make bricks without straw.
I need not have worried. I was about to witness the genius of African interpreters, which I had merely glimpsed in the Anglican church. I rose awkwardly to my feet, and before I could even cough, one of Alec's officers sprang to my side.
'Good afternoon,' I began. The interpreter went into action as if I had pulled a lever in his back, and delivered a sentence which might

have flowed from the rambling pen of Marcel Proust. He paused and looked to me for more.

'It gives me great pleasure to be here this afternoon,' I went on, beginning to feel almost eloquent myself. This generated a whole paragraph.

After that it was dead easy, and was on every miserable occasion I had to make a speech in Africa thereafter. I had only to give the interpreter a verbal shove now and again and in half an hour we had produced a speech which would have done for the House of Lords.

At the pagan end of the religious spectrum lay the fertility clinic. I am not referring to anything at the hospital, which in Western terms is a pretty sophisticated undertaking, not much less than the open heart surgery I had hoped to find at Accra hospital. I am referring to the establishment run by the witch doctor.

Twice a week I visited the outstations. On my Friday trip to Wadjo I passed a stockade in which interesting things seemed to be going on to judge by the drumming and ululating which came from within. Samson, the chauffeur (for I was not yet trusted in the forest by myself), told me this was the place of the fetish priest for women 'catch belly', but I never pressed the inquiry any further.

Until the new matron came out. Jenny left after another of those Greek tragedy affairs had broken out between her and the GM. No reflection on either of them, who were both able managers; but in the hot-house conditions of a small station in Africa, if personalities were going to clash, they clashed resoundingly.

The new matron was a pretty English girl called Sally, aged about thirty; and it was some time before anyone in those sexist days believed in her existence as a matron at all, rather than the heroine of a steamy tropical film, played by Julie Christie, whom she certainly looked like. Even when, through diligent effort and a particular interest in midwifery, she increased the weekly attendance at the antenatal clinic from thirty to eighty, that wag, Danny Wilson, commented that most of them were women.

So while I was showing Sally the ropes, I thought it might be fun to drop in on the witch doctor's clinic, on our way to Wadjo.

As we entered some of his helpers ran forward and politely provided us with log seats. We looked around. At the back was an awning with a ladies' band, all the ladies shaking rattles, beating drums and singing. In the main area stood rows of other women, about fifty in all, stripped to the waist with tin bowls of water on their heads. They swayed gently to the music while little children, some barely able to walk, jived around them.

I might say that rhythm seems inherent in the African, almost from birth. Even the babies, after their jabs at the hospital, don't cry like white babies: an immediate rhythmic 'wa! wa! wa!' gets switched on in their bottoms, while they kick their mothers in protest and wee ditto down their backs; nappies, like the wheel, not being indigenous to the continent.

Actually, most of these ladies seemed pretty pregnant already, so we concluded it was an antenatal as well as a fertility clinic.

The witch doctor went into action. He sprinkled water from the basins with an antelope switch on to the ladies' tummies, running up and down the rows. When he saw Sally and me sitting side by side on our logs, he naturally inferred an interesting connection (if not an interesting condition in Sally), and sprinkled water over us in our turn.

All very interesting, and I expect Sally wrote home about it in her first newsy letter from the Coast. But at the end of the month, as the locals so charmingly put it, 'her flower' did not appear.

Well, this is a thing well known even to white gynaecologists: a change of circumstances, the attendant stresses, etc. But it did not charm Sally. 'That bloody witch doctor!' she cursed. 'What has he done to me?'

No account of African religion would be complete without a discussion of witchcraft, in which again some 'educated' Africans profess not to believe, just as 'educated' Europeans have no fear of the number thirteen or walking under ladders. But in their hearts they are not so sure.

In fact, in his heart, Amos, who had attended the London School of Economics, was pretty sure the other way. He told me of a man who had insulted another man, and two nights later a cobra entered the first man's house and tried to bite him. 'What about that, doc? You wouldn't say that was a coincidence, surely?'

Des had spoken about 'juju' on the day of my arrival: how a man had been 'crossed' on the golf course. Two enemies approached him and crossed (changed places from left to right) in front of him. Then they passed him on either side. The terrified man looked behind him and saw them repeat the process. Within the week he was dead.

Many of our medical cases were of juju. In the African philosophy nothing happens by accident, especially evil, which is the spiritual work of an enemy or an offended ancestor. In these cases Des had his 'juju cure', or rather, Dr Conron's juju cure, which he attributed to a compatriot and previous MO Samreboi. After satisfying himself that the man merely thought he was going to die because someone had put a spell on him, Des went to work with his 'alternative medicine'. He placed a beaker on the locker on each side of the bed. The first contained water, the second hydrogen peroxide, which of course look exactly alike to an African peasant and Albert Einstein. Then Des would remove ten millilitres of blood from one of the man's arms, and this he injected into the beaker of water, which lay on the same side of the bed. He held the glass up to the light, swirled the bloody streaks round a bit and said wisely: 'Ah yes, I see the spirits!' And sure enough the patient saw them too, with his eyes popping out of his head. Then Des would give the man a painful injection (theophylline was his favourite) in his buttock, which everyone knew was the best medicine possible. He would allow that ten minutes or so to chase the spirits round the man's body, while he got on with his ward round. Then he returned and removed a similar quantity of blood from the other arm and injected it into the hydrogen peroxide. The resulting explosion of red champagne carried powerful conviction. 'Dat chase him proper!' exclaimed Des, and the man would jump out of bed, full of the joys of spring.

At a party in an African manager's house we sat on the veranda, gazing at the moon. I asked Yao if the sun and the moon held the important place in African mythology which they do in ours. 'No,' he thought. 'What means more to us is the forest and the river.'

And indeed the forest and the river were full of stranger creatures than the ones nature had placed there. To begin with there were the Aboatia people, whom even the Europeans soon told you about. They were small creatures, about the size of chimps, very hairy, and lived in the trees: perforce, as when they sat on the branches their legs hung a hundred feet to the ground, with which they seized the unwary, who were never seen again. And what is more their feet pointed backwards. Their children (whose legs had evidently not fully developed) liked to play on the bridges over the rivers, and you could be sure the African drivers of the logging and any other vehicles never forgot to sound their horns and drive slowly at these places, for if you killed or even hurt an Aboatia child, the parents would come for you in the night.

One's European informants on these matters would offer explanations (as if they thought they were Professors Frazer or Malinowski) in terms of such nonsense as chimpanzees and the lianas which hung from the trees: but that is the kind of thing *Brunis* would say, wouldn't they?

But most dreaded of all was Tano, the spirit of the river (which bore his name) who had certainly placed a number of people on my mortuary slab. Amos (who was taking a bit of risk himself in doing so, when you think about it) would use the 'Tano' test (though he was never so facetious as to call it that) in extracting the truth from people he suspected of concealing it.

'You swear?'

'Yes, massa. I swear.'

'You swear by Jesus?'

'Yes, massa. I swear by Jesus.'

'You swear by Tano?'

'Ah - Massa!'

Nobody was going take Tano's name in vain.

9 - The Forest and the River

The forest formed the perpetual backdrop to all our lives, and surrounded the square mile of Samreboi like a green wall. Two roads ran out of town, one north, one south, passing through the outstations on their way to other places. The northern road ran over the river by a Bailey bridge about a mile beyond the town.

What the forest is like now I dare not think. Even at that time the Sahara was marching to the sea at the rate of ten miles a year. This was not due to the work of the timber companies - at least, at that time. Since then the local governments have driven them to cut down the forest as quickly as possible - a fast buck for now and devil take the future! At that time the chief culprits were illegal timber cutters and the growing mass of the population, who cleared the forest to make farms. Short-lived farms, alas! because the soil that supports the forest giants and all that teeming vegetation is thin and fragile, as was demonstrated dramatically when one of the big trees fell. Guess how deep the roots went! - about three feet. Their support came from the buttresses I have described and the interlocking of the canopy.

And the denuded soil was drastically washed away when the rains began and the sluggish brown rivers rose thirty feet and turned into boiling torrents.

The timber companies at that time actually preserved the forest through the system of forest reserves and incremental cutting, whereby only a part equivalent to the annual wastage was taken, so the forest was called the Perpetual Forest in a beautiful book of that name (long out of print) by a colonial forest officer - Collins, I think - a mine of information on every last treasure of the forest.

Once a week as I said I visited one of the outstations. I was driven by a chauffeur. It was well known that doctors were not mechanics, and there was little traffic on the laterite road in case of breakdown, which moreover turned to mud in the rainy season, when the car might get stuck. If that happened, the doctor of course was pressed to remain in his lordly back seat, while the chauffeur did his best or got some help from passing pedestrians, who were never too infrequent.

Sometimes we passed tiny villages where naked children dashed out of huts shouting: 'Docketa! Docketa!' or men and women waved: the women at their duties, the men sitting around with their cronies smoking or drinking palm wine. But though I travelled those roads scores of times, to the last the sudden appearance of the outstation was always a surprise to me. It was the same on the river when a lad would take us fishing in a canoe. Never did I guess which wind of the brown water through the green walls would bring us back to the Bailey bridge, where we were to alight. Such was the monotony of all that featureless beauty.

Sometimes a tree would fall across the road, necessitating a return journey either to town or outstation. Out would come a team with chain saws, and a section would be cut out of the giant trunk (whose thickness was the height of a man) and rolled aside to let us through. I had a photograph of a friend of average height standing against the cross-section of such a log, which must have been near the base for, so far from his equalling its diameter, he came no more than half way up it, like the minute hand of a clock at half past the hour.

At the clinic I would see cases that the medical assistants there had screened for me over the previous week: a hernia, a baby with malnutrition, an old person with heart failure - patients often needing admission to hospital. The ambulance would be sent for them on my return to the hospital. Urgent cases arriving at the clinic in office hours would be transferred to the hospital, after calling for the ambulance on the station telephone. But most of the urgent cases got themselves to the hospital direct. And they came either to clinic or hospital by many means: in the local headmaster's car or contractor's van, if they were lucky; by canoe down the river, or slung on a bamboo hammock, carried by a couple of strong and devoted friends; and when available the more regular service known as the 'mammy lorry', the main bus service - fleets of such vehicles run by those pillars of West African trade, the 'mammies' or market women.

And I never failed to educate the MAs at the clinic through the cases presented, which I early recognised as the most important purpose of such a visit.

After the clinic I would drop in on friends, usually for a cup of coffee; but at Wadjo I had a standing invitation to lunch. John, the mechanic, lived with his African mistress, and while she prepared the fufu (which I was learning to relish, especially with a delicious palm oil stew), he would play his only record: Beethoven's Violin Concerto. Sitting in the cane armchairs with our beers, listening to that utterly incongruous music, with the gloomy forest pressing in on all sides, we felt we were keeping some sort of flag flying.

Walter was the mechanic at the northern outstation, which was called Brudjo. He lived with his wife Maria and their two little girls. They were an Italian family. He was an exuberant little man as well as a clever mechanic. He had fitted up his car to play *'We were all in the garden playing leapfrog'* (or whatever the Italians call it), with which he announced his arrival on his visits to town.

Walter's Mediterranean logic sometimes clashed with the local culture.

'Massa, dee tractor never fit.'

'So!' retorted Walter. 'Why don't you take him to the witch doctor?'

'Ah, massa, he never savvy him proper.'

'But he savvy your mammies, your pickins, no?' Which was a kind advertisement for me.

No reply.

I had served in Trieste with the British Army, and had a fair knowledge of Italian. Walter and Maria came from the same city, so we had something to talk about and in. One day he invited me and an English couple to lunch.

Most West African lunch parties went on all afternoon: people usually served curry or palm oil stew. There was much liquor provided, in the West African fashion: they asked you what you wanted and simply placed bottle and glass (even a full bottle of whisky) beside you and left you to help yourself. Needless to say there were no problems with drunken driving, or at any rate with the police, though cars and their owners sometimes spent the night in ditches. For when I say afternoon, it was often midnight before they wound up, the main course being usually served about four o' clock.

Walter's repast started at a more civilised hour. Incidentally, when we pulled a bottle of Beaujolais out of the car, as the common British contribution to the feast, Walter would not hear of it and made us put it back. I think he was right: hospitality should be freely offered and freely accepted.

Now, I was ten miles away from the hospital. There was no telephone at Walter's house. There was one at the office and a 'boy' had been told off to sit by it in case of any messages for the doctor. As in many African stations I was on call all the time, night and day, year in year out. My only chance of being off duty was to leave the station - a long way! Even at the Yam Festival at Mango, or any other event within thirty miles, I was still within reach of the ambulance and a written message conveyed by Samson.

When I expressed concern that the 'boy' might be bored and did he have a book to read, my remark occasioned much amusement. An afternoon spent sleeping by a telephone was no hardship to the average African worker.

I soon had the laugh on Andy and Barbara, however, at least. Spaghetti was served, which my experience in Trieste had taught me was merely an *antipasto* to an Italian meal. Andy and Barbara enjoyed the genuine Italian article so much they called for second helpings. Maria's look of surprise escaped them, but not me. When the main course appeared, of which I only remember it was pretty substantial, it was my turn to laugh at my friends.

One Sunday afternoon I took my umbrella and went for a stroll as far as the river. It was early days but I was already kitted out in the standard white shirt, shorts and stockings of the manager's uniform. I rarely wore a hat, although I am a pretty bald red-head, but never took much harm from the sun. When outdoors I was mostly in a vehicle or used my eternal umbrella equally against sun or rain, and was never far from the shade of the trees. The sky was rarely blue except in the dry season, when sky and air were cleared by the Harmattan, a fresh northern wind from off the desert, which was annually looked forward to as a refresher, the way the rains are eagerly panted for in the drier regions of Africa. Otherwise at most times of the year the sky was as steamy as the planet Venus. But let no one be fooled: you can get very sunburned under even a cloudy sky in Africa.

If one ever did such an eccentric thing for a white man as to take a walk, you had continually to refuse people stopping their cars to give you lifts, but eventually I got to the river on my two pins.

There a remarkable sight met my eyes. It was interesting enough even to the locals, as a large crowd had gathered at the point where the road ended and the bridge used to begin: for now the road ended indeed in a stream of muddy water which slid past at about five miles an hour; and of the bridge there was no sign, except the upper rails, where a fallen tree lay trapped like a stranded ship. There was a number of canoes, manned by small boys, and one of these presently approached me and asked me if I wanted to cross the river. No, I didn't. So would I like a trip - there and back for one cedi?

Well, I was a reckless bachelor then: nowadays, as an old married man with wife and children to consider, I would certainly refuse. Thus age and marriage doth make cowards of us all. But I thought to myself, the lad knows his business (I expect my patients thought the same about me!) so gingerly stepped into the craft, which had been half dragged out on to the muddy bank. Some bystanders, who looked as if they were enjoying themselves, gave us a hearty shove-off.

I did not know it then, but anyone falling into an African river in spate was likely to end up on the mortuary slab.

The canoe was a hollowed-out log about fifteen feet long, and the lad managed it with a paddle. The vessel drew very little water and skimmed like an arrow over the sliding surface. Even so the current bore us downstream in a great bow, which we made up in the shallower water near the opposite bank, so managing to beach where the road took up again. Then about turn and in another great bow, which the grinning little fellow controlled so skilfully with his paddle, we arrived back where we had started from.

Innocent me! The new doctor had become an instant hero. There was a great clap and cheer. One man shook my hand and assured me heartily: 'You are very brave! I would never have done that!'

I later discovered that Walter and family had been content to remain cut off for a week until the waters went down. They were all right for supplies. The only problem was Walter's hair. Our usual barber was one of the managers, who had acquired a dab hand at the business. Now Walter was forced to resort to Maria who, he later complained, when they reappeared in town, had cut it 'in steps'.

I turned about to walk home. But this was Africa. Not only was I a hero but it would have been the height (or depth) of unfriendliness to leave the new doctor to walk away alone. Some people attached themselves to me. ('And how are you liking Samreboi, docketa?') In Africa things have a tendency to grow, and presently the group grew to a crowd and the crowd to a procession of about a hundred. Now, all together, in jolly good companee, what more natural than to sing? And being Africa the song turned to a hymn, so at the head of the column swinging my umbrella I felt like Dr Livingstone in a B-movie. This was bad enough but my way lay past the club and by then the hymn had become Onward Christian Soldiers. A number of my countrymen appeared on the veranda with beers in their fists and merry grins on their faces to witness the revivalist activities of the new doc.

Well, we are British after all!

Marriage may make cowards of us all but it can also make us brave. I recall the story of my old colleague, Johnny de Graaf Johnson (a family famous on the Coast), who was my surgical registrar in Birkenhead. He married a white girl and took her and their child back to Ghana. Johnny was appointed provincial surgeon at Tamale, in the Northern Territories. Soon they had more children. One day they were crossing a river on a chain ferry. Johnny's wife and the older children sat in the car: Johnny stood beside them, holding the youngest child, a baby. When the ferry landed, something gave way, and the car and its occupants were pitched into the water. Johnny just had time to step ashore and hand the baby to a bystander before plunging without hesitation into the swollen river. He well knew what his chances were. He and his loved ones were all drowned.

Les Cady, my fishing friend, spent most of his time in the bush, as far away from offices and officialdom as possible. He was a tall rangy man, a born colonial, who would have been as morose as a caged lion in an English suburb. He had a petite blonde Polish wife, Maria, whom he had met in India during the war.

Les and I would go to spots on the river system known to him, in his Land Rover. Sometimes we fished from the bank, when we employed perforce more than the number of ghillies usual to places like Scotland. Custom required one small boy to dig the worm, another to stick it on the hook and a third to remove the fish, if necessary. And I mean this number for each fisherman. All the great White Man had to do was cast the hook into the water and wind it in again.

The only fish those rivers seemed to contain were barbel, a primitive-looking scaleless creature with long whiskers from the days when the earth was mud. Indeed, the barbel can live a long time in the mud when the rivers dry up (which they seldom did in that part of the world) and even it was said cross country to find water. Certainly, if you left one on the bank it would wriggle its way back to the river. Europeans did not like eating them, so we gave them to the ghillies, and they were much appreciated by them and their families.

Once I tried eating one myself. Someone told me, although tasteless, they went down well cooked with lemon juice. First you have to leave them in the bath overnight to get the mud out of their systems. This I did, and heard things go bump in the night several times as the fish leapt out of the water onto the bathroom floor. Finally the penny dropped. I filled the bath high enough to satisfy the creature, and it settled down. Next day James did his best with it, but lemon or no lemon, it tasted like rubber.

There must have been other kinds of fish, even if I never caught any, as a merry item in the station's folklore featured a cruel trick played on one of the white managers - the sort of thing I think Italians call a *beffa*. Harry was the keenest fisherman on the station, equipped with every kind of tackle, which might well have secured more difficult prey than barbel. Harry was on long leave in England. Some of his droll friends made a cut-out fish from ply-wood (which was one of the station's products) - a very large fish. They hooked it on to a rod and line and photographed it, held up by one of Harry's smiling friends. They sent the photo (which was naturally less perfect than it would be nowadays) to Harry with the message: 'Look what we are taking out of the river just now!' Harry promptly cut short his leave, and caught the next plane back to Ghana, where he was naturally disappointed on arrival. Whether his wife accompanied him or not, and what she had to say on the subject in any case, was not told me; nor as a bachelor did it occur to me to inquire.

At the end of the afternoon's sport we would pay off the ghillies, as well as distribute any fish we had caught among them. But by then the ghillies, like all things in the tropics, had multiplied considerably. This did not fool Les, who had marked out the genuine ones with his eagle eye well in advance. But we inevitably ended up with a crowd swarming at the open windows of the Land Rover before we left.

I well remember one such scene, near a bridge. Les sat silent beside me while the little hands pushed through the windows, and the little bodies tussled and crushed one another around the doors. Suddenly, even to my surprise, Les sprang up in his seat with the roar of a lion. I have mentioned before the strange telepathy of a crowd of Africans. All at once the little creatures shot off and onto the bridge, like a herd of impala, where half-way across, just as suddenly, they all stopped together and turned round. Les glowered at them through the windscreen like the Lion King for some seconds, then his features relaxed into a grin. Immediately, all the little bodies leapt up and down and screamed with delight.

We also fished from a canoe when the river had settled later in the rainy season, or in the dry season itself. This simplified the employment situation, as one little boy served as boatman and ghillie. Mostly we just drifted, usually near to the banks, and it was as lovely as a dream to while away the afternoon on the still brown water in the shade of the great trees. Les told me much about the country and its people - of the chief's daughter, who was sent down from Edinburgh University for getting herself pregnant *(autres temps, autres moeurs!)*, and her father's mystified appeal to Les: 'But Mr Cady, I ask you! What is a woman for?' A question which nowadays, of course, would give rise to trouble of another sort. He told me of the day when the cook threatened Maria with a fate worse than death, when she was alone in the house, and she defended herself with the famous Afridi sword, not actually using it but pointing it at the man's chest and marching him backwards out of the house and down to the workshop of the outstation they then managed. And when they got there perhaps the would-be rapist wished Maria had done a proper job for the fate almost worse than death that he met at the hands of the workers.

Les asked me about my future intentions. My contract was for eighteen months, and I had a vague idea of going to Australia after that. We speculated about Australia, which neither of us had visited, and whether it might contain such beautiful scenes as then surrounded us. Les thought maybe in the Northern Territories. The conversation was idle in more ways than one. Though I did not know it then, Africa had entered my blood. I was not to leave it (and then only reluctantly) for the next twenty years.

I went fishing and canoeing with others besides Les, but he would only go with me. He was a loner, and I was flattered to be selected by him as a friend. Another companion of mine was Ralph, the large Swiss who had catechised his cook on the ethnic nature of Jesus. There was usually some competition among the canoe boys for our custom. One of them was Kwame. Then one day Ralph's shirt went missing from the line outside his house. It is hard to go undetected in the African countryside (whatever Sherlock Holmes may have said about the English ditto), and we were soon informed that the thief was Kwame. I imagine Kwame returned the shirt or Ralph would never have forgiven him. At any rate, this being the south of the country he was not nailed in the manner of Sisera to a tree; but Ralph, without any Anglo-Saxon nonsense about him, organised among his friends a three-month boycott of Kwame's canoe, which was not lifted till the day itself.

Les asked me if I would like to visit a local chief - that is, one of them, for there were two in our neighbourhood - the chief of the Brudja tribe at Bongo. Of course I did. So Les arranged an appointment for a Sunday afternoon. Off we went in his Land Rover. Les told me it was customary to take a present so we stopped at a store and picked up six bottles of beer: the large West African bottles, not the miserable things of politer climes.

We entered the chief's palace, announced ourselves and were conducted by an attendant to an awning at the top of a courtyard. Chairs were brought for us. In the centre of the awning stood the 'stool'. This was made of wood and shaped rather like an anvil. It was a sacred object as it contained the soul of the tribe and, of course, no one but the chief was allowed to sit on it, on pain of pretty dire penalties, I should think. The most famous stool in the country, the golden stool of Ashanti, was let down out of the sky to the feet of the divine first king of Ashanti, Osei Tutu. Our chief was the one whose death shortly after gave rise to the strange happenings related in an earlier chapter.

Presently he entered, attended by two or three more officials, the chief dressed in a kente, or toga, made up of squares of coloured silk sewn together, a magnificent garment. He took his seat on the stool, while the attendants stood behind him, except for one who stood at his side. This was the 'linguist', for the chief does not speak directly to anyone in public, only through the linguist, who likewise conveys messages to the chief. This is not a matter of interpretation: I doubt if this old man understood English; but whether or no, it was a matter of ceremony, which his Oxford-educated successor would certainly continue in his turn.

We presented our six bottles of beer, which were received with due expressions of appreciation; and by coincidence were presented ourselves with six identical bottles of beer, at which of course nobody showed any signs of embarrassment or amusement. Les, who appointed himself as my linguist, so to speak, introduced the new doctor; and the chief's linguist informed us that the chief was delighted to meet him, and said how much his services were appreciated in the land.

There was more polite conversation, which I tried to enliven in my fatuous way by expressing a wish to marry six Ghanaian ladies before I was another year in the country. Both linguists (that is, Les and the official one) fell silent at this remark, and Les informed me on the side that the occasion did not call for humour.

After about half an hour we got ourselves out, with every sign of mutual appreciation and gratitude, and no further breaches of protocol on my part.

It was nightfall before we got back to Samreboi. When we reached the bridge some sort of altercation was going on. Les made inquiries. Now the bridge, or rather the river, divided the territories of the two tribes: the Brudjas and the Wadjas (based on Mango). It turned out that a member of the Wadjas (a degenerate lot in the opinion of their neighbours) had been using the river for a purpose of nature and had narrowly escaped some dire fate at the hands of some Brudjas who had caught him in the act. The river was sacred to all right-thinking people, but especially to the Brudjas. At any rate, before we went on the parties had separated, if not peaceably, without bloodshed.

A sequel followed (I mean to our meeting with the chief) when Sally, the new matron, and I were introduced to the new chief, not by Les, but by Adam, one of the African managers, shortly after the death of the old one. Succession is hereditary, but the office is by no means despotic, and a chief can be removed by process of the elders - all males over forty. (An old Coaster was fond of recalling a famous headline in the *Times of Ghana*: 'DESTOOLED CHIEF LOSES MOTION'.)

The new chief was a very polished young man who sat with his attendants in a sort of levee while people filed past him. Sally and I shook hands with him, a greeting he cordially received. Afterwards Adam informed us that no one was supposed to touch the chief in public, but not to worry: everything the white man (or woman) did was all right.

Another curious fact is that a chief apparent must have no mark on his body. There is a touching novel by a Ghanaian writer, which ends with the death of a chief's son when the young man develops appendicitis and refuses operation, not only to protect his succession (which is obviously doubtful), but through the demands of custom.

One who was certainly no uncaged lion in the jungle was Ernie. One evening I came upon a new face in the club. New faces were an event in Samreboi: at any rate, new white faces, of whom the usual number including the ladies was about fifty. 'Ee, doan't you get fed up wi' the same old faces?' complained the old Coaster referred to above, who had spent most of his career on a larger station in

Nigeria. An occasional recurrent addition was Leo, the 'snake man', a herpetologist, who spent most of his time camping in the forest, and was always a welcome guest. Ernie, alas, was no herpetologist, nor was he likely to find any other comfortable diversions in his new surroundings except possibly the one he had been brought out for.

Something had gone wrong with the 'ERFs', as the locals called the logging vehicles, for an obvious reason, and Ernie had been sent out from England to fix them.

It had come like a summons from the Angel Gabriel, or some darker spirit. One Monday morning he had been sitting in his Manchester office, minding his own business, when he was plucked out of his cosy nest, not by any angel, but by his boss, who announced: 'Ernie, lad, ye're going ter West Africa!' and no argument about it. I doubt if Ernie had been any farther than Blackpool in his life, and certainly he kept bleating: 'Me and the wife have never been separated before!' He made no mention of children. He was no older than twenty-five, a sad little shrimp in navy blue shorts, an unmemorable shirt, and navy blue socks (not stockings), round his ankles. And he was very nervous. Even the beer, which his kindly hosts had placed in his hand, failed to reassure him.

'Will ah catch malaria?' he whined. 'Will we get attacked by natives?'

Neither of these questions actually deserved the hearty laughter they provoked. He had been sent out without antimalarial tablets ('On t' next plane, lad! So be quick about it!') - a deficiency at least I was able to repair next morning. But the others would have laughed the other side of their faces if they had forseen the answer to the second question. For two years later (after I had left), the place actually was attacked by natives. There was a strike, which in the common way of Africa, turned quickly to rioting, in which as many people were shot as at Sharpeville, but naturally received less attention in the world press. Black bites black! That's not news!

Meantime the crowd at the bar did their best to cheer him up. 'Don't be downhearted, Ernie. We have a great time here at Christmas.'

'Christmas!' squeaked Ernie. This was September. 'I expected to be 'ome at the end of the month. The wife and me -'

However, he was a resilient little fellow, and so far lost his fear of the natives that I actually spotted him receiving the revivalist procession treatment one evening on his way home from work, which he seemed to appreciate in his simple way more happily than I did.

In the event he did get home by the end of the month, and what a tale he would have to tell the wife! Or perhaps he preferred to forget that the whole thing had ever happened, like some dreadful dream.

When not fishing, or at the pool or tennis, we would spend week-end afternoons taking walks in the forest. We would select one of the footpaths referred to in the first chapter, calculate the time to sunset by our watches (which fell regularly at 6 pm), and walk for half that time before turning back, having left the car at a convenient spot on the road. Usually we would take Sally with us, who was the darling of the station. The rest of us were bachelors, I being the oldest. All the other white women on the station were married, long settled in the place and, with their husbands, had long lost interest in such expeditions.

Sally was very nervous of the forest, which brought out the protective male in all of us - all except Ralph, who seemed to think it was funny. One afternoon, near the end of our walk, we heard a loud garrumph! nearby in the bush, which was probably a colobus monkey clearing its throat. Sally gave a scream and never stopped running till she reached the car, a full five hundred yards away, while the mean-spirited Ralph nearly laughed his un-gallant head off.

And when we would reach the car, the evening chorus had begun. The whole forest came alive like a great orchestra: a vast throbbing and whistling and screaming, like the opening of *The Rite of Spring*. Weird hornbills flapped woodenly up to their nests like creatures of the Lost World. Flocks of parrots flew in like clockwork toys, shooting their long whistles.

Otherwise, in the forest, at all times, one heard sounds, but saw little. One of the loveliest afternoon sounds was the call of the emerald-spotted wood dove, which goes: *'Coo! Coo! Coo! Coo-coo-coo-coo-coooooo!'* in a dying fall. The Zulus (for the bird is heard all over Africa) say it is saying: *'My father is dead! My mother is dead! My brothers are dead! My sisters are dead! O! O! O-oooooo!'* But only in the West African forest have I heard two of the birds singing together in falling harmonic thirds like a pair of flutes.

But as I say, we saw little. Once a troop of colobus monkeys swinging through the trees in their dinner jackets. Sometimes the green ripple of the forest mamba crossing a laterite road. Returning from a friend's house in an outstation one night, I saw a buck with stripes and spots pause in my headlights before passing on into the opposite wall of the bush. An old hand at the club identified it as a bush buck. There were stories of the bush cow, a smaller type of buffalo, but I never saw one. There were stories of leopards but I never saw one either: they are nocturnal creatures and rarely seen anyway.

Every night we heard the scream of the tree bear (hyrax). It was said to scream to frighten other creatures, then drop to the forest floor before climbing another tree. One day my neighbour, Andy Astle, showed me a rhinoceros viper, his gardener had killed. It was the size of a man's arm and had two tusks on its snout, but side by side, more like a wart hog than a rhinoceros. Africans were afraid of snakes and killed them on sight. But most of all, and all over the continent, they fear the harmless chameleon.

One night, returning from the club, I found the forecourt of my house looking like a sand table model of the Battle of Waterloo. It was covered with columns of ants moving all over the place like the armies of Wellington and Napoleon and Blücher's besides. It soon became clear what they were after. All over the battlefield were nodes of concentrated combat. These were fallen grasshoppers which were being devoured by the ants. The globe lamp over my door illustrated the whole scene.

I leapt over the columns, fumbled for my key and quickly opened the door. I switched on the hall light inside. A big mistake, for now both grasshoppers and pursuing ants began to enter the house. I ran for the spray gun from the kitchen - an old-fashioned thing you had to pump - and turned it on the invading columns. It was quite futile: I might as well have hoped to turn back the Chinese army with a Tommy gun. Then the penny dropped. The cause of everything was the lights. I switched off both inside and outside lights and waited. When after about ten minutes I gingerly switched on the outside light again, the whole spectacle had vanished, leaving not a wrack behind.

10 - At Work and Play

Jenny, who had no more race-consciousness than she had self-consciousness or class-consciousness (or any other so-called 'consciousness' except a strong dose of good old Scots moral consciousness), had long since founded a small multiracial social group - the only one which existed in Samreboi, I might say - which began around the nucleus of her famous scrabble parties - a term which excited the derisive laughter of the GM, who was not her friend.

The group consisted mostly of unmarried whites and the more modernistic Africans. After Jenny left they evolved into the more exuberant Monopoly parties, certain features of which would not have been entirely to Jenny's taste - the main such feature being the chatty hour which preceded the actual Monopoly, when we discussed the scandal of the week.

Ghanaians are famous throughout West Africa for their sense of humour, and the object of this humour which delights them most is - themselves: which strikes me as a mark of high civilisation in any people. And of all the Ghanaians I knew, the master exponent of this brand of humour was the personnel manager, Amos Black.

Amos was a tall rangy man with a woolly head, full of restless energy. He had piercing eyes: the eyes of a strong will. 'He's a bright boy,' Des Brennan had said. 'I wonder he doesn't go in for politics.' 'No fear!' was Amos's comment. 'I thought Des was my friend. Does he want to get rid of me?'

Like many Ghanaians of the south, he had acquired his surname from one of those Caledonian vertebrae of the Empire already referred to, either through ancestry or appropriation.

In many African countries is found a curious pair of opposites: one tribe which has all the brains, and another tribe which has the more martial qualities - at any rate, by reputation; on the justice of which I will not comment. So in Rhodesia, there were the Shona and the Matabele; in South Africa, the Xhosas and the Zulus. In Ghana, the corresponding pair was the Fantis and the Ashantis.

Amos put it without prevarication. 'All Fantis are cowards. I am a Fanti and I am a coward, so I know what I am talking about.'

He questioned me more than once (perhaps in a professional sense) about a matter which seemed to obsess him, as to whether one could successfully feign death on the battlefield. 'I mean, doc, how could they tell?'

He never tired of recounting the story of the famous coup, which toppled Nkrumah in 1966, while he was out of the country staying with his friends in Hanoi; and how the daring deed was done by the Ashantis. 'If it had been left to the Fantis, That Man would be here yet.' The event was precipitated when the rumour got about that Nkrumah wanted to send his army (or at any rate, the disaffected section of it) to Rhodesia to fight Ian Smith - 'so he could look good at the United Nations, and get his army wiped out at the same time,' as Amos lucidly put it.

Then he would tell how Afrifa's battalion swept down from the north and fought a ding-dong match all day in the capital with Nkrumah's Russian-trained guards, while the Fanti armoured battalion stood on the touch line, waiting to see who looked like winning, before intervening at close of play to clinch the match in favour of the rebels.

And the day itself. 'Do I remember the day of the coup! You must know what the country was like at that time. Talk about a police state! If a policeman came to your house, even if you knew it was a simple traffic offence, you sent your wife to the door while you got out the back.

'When the news broke, at first no one could believe it. Some people thought it was a trick of That Man to get his enemies out dancing in the streets so he could arrest them.

'I was sitting at home when the telephone went. When I picked it up all I could hear was funny little noises. Then I thought it sounded like Anokye.' (Anokye was Amos's assistant.) 'Now, as you know, Anokye is an Ashanti, but while he may not have the brains of the Fantis, he doesn't have the courage of the Ashantis either. Finally I said, "Look, Anokye, if you've got something to tell me, you'd better come round to my house."

'Next I hear the scrape of Anokye's car on the gravel outside. I opened the door and Anokye came in with his finger to his mouth, looking over his shoulder as if the spirits were after him. He was making funny little noises in his throat which sounded like "coo! coo! coo!" Finally it dawned on me. I said: "YOU SAY THERE'S BEEN A COUP?!!! - I mean, coo! coo! coo!"'

Nkrumah was succeeded by the sober figure of General Ankrah. The general (now president) paid a visit to Samreboi, and the managers, black and white, were lined up to receive him - a ceremony which Amos did not find entirely comfortable. He told us without shame how when the general got to him, Amos decided his shoe lace was undone (Amos's, that is, not the general's) and bent down to mess about with it, at the same time, with a deft movement of his hip, propelling Anokye, who stood beside him, practically onto the general's bemedalled chest. The simple-hearted Anokye found himself, to his pride and delight, shaking hands with his president, as sole representative of his department, in place of the suddenly indisposed Amos, who needless to say, showed no promise of speedy recovery; leaving the general with no choice but to pass on down the line escorted by a pretty red-faced GM - fiery Welshman at the best of times, as I have said. But at the critical moment, as Amos had anticipated, the press cameras (which took a particular interest in the black managers - too particular for Amos's liking), the cameras flashed, and within a few days, very likely, a photograph on the front page of the *Times of Ghana* of Anokye shaking hands with President Ankrah landed on Kwame Nkrumah's breakfast table in neighbouring Guinea. Well, while That Man was still alive, you couldn't be too careful!

Then came an outbreak of a perennial trouble: that of illegal timber-taking. Through some obscure arrangement - a relic of the wise but delicate principle of indirect rule, which formed the basis of British colonial policy - the tenure of the forest lands was divided between government and chiefs. The effective power was the government, and negotiations, brisk at any rate by African standards, were pursued smoothly enough with them. But there remained the indispensable discussions with the chiefs, mainly ceremonial though these had become. And a pretty tedious time the company's representatives had of it, according to my informant who had served his time at the business, and whose account, which I imagine is more colourful than strictly accurate, will do.

No such barbarism as 'hustle' is known to any part of the African business world (except maybe in South Africa, but I am referring to the civilised parts), and certainly not in such venerable precincts as the chief's palace, where a working lunch, still more, breakfast, would provoke indigestion by its very idea. In short, a great part of the proceedings was taken up by old gentlemen walking up and down, hitching up their togas, making very long speeches. And sometimes they would invoke the name (in passing, but the 'passing' was to prove a very long excursion indeed), the sacred name of the divine first king of Ashanti - Osei Tutu.

This would bring the proceedings to a sudden stop. Documents would be taken up, a general exit made, and preparations begun, including the slaughter of a statutory number of goats, for the mandatory three days' celebrations due to the holy utterance.

Admittedly a good time would be had by all, including the company's representatives (at any rate, while the thing was still a novelty to them), and in due course all would return to the forum. As a matter of unquestioned courtesy, the old gentleman would be allowed to take up where he left off. And as often as not, the old fool would clear his throat and recommence - 'As I was saying about Osei Tutu!' - and the whole three days' business would start again.

Not surprisingly, the legal niceties referred to rather went over the heads of the populace, who could not understand why they were no longer allowed to cut their ancestral woods, and by what right anyone could call them 'illegal timber-takers'. Anokye was sent to deal with one specially rebellious village. He soon found himself in the middle of a riot and had only time to execute a three-point turn with his Land Rover in three feet of mud, with a speed and skill he had not known he possessed, and extricate himself and companions from what the *Times of Ghana* might have reported as 'an unfortunate fate'. Not that the mob would have been content with such small fry as Anokye. Their main wrath was reserved not even for the company itself, which to them was an impersonal abstraction, but for that traitor to his own kind, Amos Black.

So Anokye's vehicle was chased out of the village to a chant of 'WE WANT BLACK! WE WANT BLACK!'

As Amos concluded the tale, we commented as one: 'Of course, you're going, Amos! - by popular demand?'

'You must be joking!'

Amos had another trouble on his hands at this time - the return of a particular native called Mensah, with at least two feathers in his cap: a white wife, and an economics degree from Manchester University. He did not allow the former to 'cramp his style', as Amos put it, with the 'local talent'; and that was Amos's problem.

Mensah was presently focussing on the wife of Ebrahim, a clerk in the accounts department. Such liaisons have their problems in small places, so Mensah took Ebrahim's wife out into the bush with him in his Mini. But even that was not plain sailing, or even motoring.

'Now you must understand,' explained Amos, 'that the bush is practically like a cathedral to us.' (And he was not using the poetic imagery I employed in my first chapter.) 'There are so many ancestral spirits and goblins and things that you practically can't have a pee, and certainly not what Mensah had in mind. And Ebrahim's wife being an old-fashioned type, Mensah wasn't getting much joy.

'But it's all right in a house, and somehow Mensah managed to persuade Ebrahim's wife that a motorcar is the same as a house - even his Mini.

'Only I can imagine it's pretty difficult in a Mini, and I believe at one stage Mensah had one leg sticking out of the right window and another leg sticking out of the left window.

'So he decided to risk it at his own house. (Being a Fanti he was too big a coward to risk it at Ebrahim's house.) And I believe he actually enjoyed Ebrahim's wife on the floor of his sitting room while his own wife was asleep in the bedroom.'

Amos paused as if shocked at his own words.

'Well, even by our standards, that's pretty bad!'

'Well, before long Ebrahim, got to know about it, and I knew there could be murder. I got the two of them together in my office -

Mensah and Ebrahim, I mean. I said to Mensah,"Look, Mensah! This has got to stop. We are not living in Accra. You can't carry on like this in a small place like Samreboi." And Ebrahim said, "I'm only a poor clerk, but I've got my rights!" Den what you tink dat clown Mensah said to Ebrahim? He rounded on him and said: "You ought to be proud," he said. "You ought to be proud to get your wife laid by a graduate of Manchester University!"!!!'

I have implied that our little multiracial group was untypical, and that was true. The white members were mostly young unmarried birds of passage (I was a not-so-young unmarried bird of passage), and the Africans were adventurous individualists, like Amos, which most Africans (who are nothing if not conventional) most certainly are not. And most of the whites were as conventional as Surrey: Les Cady was about as typical as Lawrence of Arabia.

In short, most people on the station (of all classes, as well as races) kept to their own kind, as was only natural. They were happy enough to work together, and did so happily, but at home they preferred to be at home. They dined at one another's houses, and the dinner parties were racially unmixed. When not at home, the managers had the club, at which, apart from the bar, there were tennis, snooker, golf, etc, including the swimming pool. The latter was not greatly used: in that torpid climate most people were too overwhelmed even to 'cool off', which the tepid pool was not very good at anyway. In fact, the pool was chiefly used by the children of the African managers, who sprang in and out and ran about with much shouting and laughter and uncertain knowledge of swimming, in which they had certainly received no formal instruction. Most had started life where the only water they had seen was the river (in a few cases the sea), which was used for washing, drinking, fishing and other useful purposes - never for swimming, in which no useful purpose would have been recognised whatsoever, and would rightly be considered a dangerous form of 'exercise', if even the word or the concept existed in their languages. And those who started life in the cities rarely did so in leafy suburbs with private swimming pools. And another thing they never received was any kind of supervision from their parents, even from the tenderest of ages. As one African manager remarked to me, during a discussion of comparative African and European philosophy at the Monopoly/Scrabble Club one night: 'We are careless of our lives.' When Jesus enjoined us to take no thought for the morrow (or much else in the way of safety-consciousness), our black brethren took the words to heart more than most.

Which some of the whites much resented: the lack of supervision of the black children, I mean. Their own children were closely supervised by their parents, who felt uncomfortably responsible for the black children too. They felt morally bound to hang around until all the little black tadpoles were safely off the premises, when they wanted to be off to the bar, to say nothing of their suppers. And any white parent will understand their feelings.

For a boring month or two I had to take my turn as chairman of the club committee, and one morning a white manager rang me up at the hospital to complain about the dereliction of the black parents. In turn, in what I thought was my official capacity, I got in touch with Solomon, whose default had been especially castigated by the complainant. In short, Solomon's children had formed a conspicuously large proportion of the little black free-floating bodies (in more ways than one) in the pool the previous Sunday. Solomon sounded very penitent and promised to do something about it. Somehow the matter reached the ears of the GM - maybe that was what Solomon had 'done about it'. At any rate, the GM got on to me and explained the constitution of the Samreboi Club, which included no connection with the swimming pool. That was the exclusive province of the GM. (Maybe Solomon had an idea of this. I may say he was a good friend and was not trying to get me into trouble.) The GM explained this to me with all courtesy, but I could see I had got myself into a culture clash of long standing from which I was rescued by the GM as Amos had rescued me from the politics of labour problems. And I could also see that the GM had a trickier problem to deal with than Amos's.

British mothers-to-be were sent home to UK to have their children, and the children sent home for schooling even at primary school age, and came out in the school holidays. This subject first entered my life on my first day in the country at the beach club of the hotel,

75

when I was accosted by a very persistent Dutchman on the matter. 'Vot is the thing vith this International School?' he pressed me, who had not the least idea what he was talking about. 'All the teachers are English, but the English don't send their kids to it. All the kids there are Dutch and Germans and French and things like that. I send my kids there, but the English don't send their kids there, only all the teachers are English.' (I may say he had had a few.) 'So tell me, vot's the matter vith this International School? Vy don't the English send their kids to it?'

I forget how I wriggled out of that one - I suppose I told him it was my first day in the country. He seemed to think I was Her Majesty's High Commissioner. I need not have bothered. The questions were all rhetorical. He was thinking aloud, and thinking darkly.

'I tell you vot it is,' he said. 'The companies pay for the English kids to go to school in England. Now vot I vont to know is, vy don't they pay for the Dutch and German kids to go home to school?'

Well, not being in fact 'HE', I was not in a position to answer that question. But in time it made me think - or rather it became a factor in my growing thoughts about my whole position in Africa.

For as I said, as I lazed on the river with Les, the continent was laying its hold on me. I did not know it - I had some ideas of Australia as the next, and permanent, step (for I am not by nature a wanderer, as I shall shortly explain). But it was at work on me - and 'work' is the operative word: for not only was the deep charm of the continent seducing me, so much more was the work itself. On my first excited letters home (which were all about medical adventures and must have been a bit much even to him) my old partner and friend in England had commented, 'You're in your element, that's for sure.'

So somewhere in my heart I wanted to stay in Africa - and stay for good. But I was a normal man with a normal man's desires for wife and family and home. And I could see that was what even the married white folk in Samreboi did not have.

They had one foot in Africa and one foot in Europe, and God knows where their lives were. Most of their money was paid in Europe, and their children received expensive education there (at least the British did). But that was not what I called a life.

For what I am working up to is my great thesis: in Africa (and places like it) there are two types of European - sojourners and settlers.

I do not wish to run ahead of myself. The thesis referred to matured through much living and thinking (and some pain) over many years. But, as I have hinted, I felt dissatisfied with the situation of the expatriate in West Africa, which I have described. Though many of them spent their whole working lives there, they were still what I call 'sojourners'. They spent their long leave at home, they sent their children home to school, and eventually retired to what they called 'home'.

This is no denigration. Such people have done, and continue to do, good work. Moreover, it is now almost impossible to work in Africa on any other terms, and in a reduced form at that: the form of the short-term contract. The days are past when people went to Africa on the terms they go to Canada or Australia: the terms of the immigrant.

And those, vaguely, were the terms I had in mind, which in Africa were always called the terms of the settler.

The first-water settlers in Africa are the Afrikaners of South Africa. Indeed, they would not even recognise the term 'settler'. The last settlers, as far as they are concerned, were the 1820 Settlers, who were all *rooineks* (Englishmen) anyway. The Afrikaners called themselves (in their own secret language, at any rate) 'Africans', though as far they were concerned, in its English form, the word meant 'Kaffirs'.

I am jumping ahead, but before we move south, I will affirm that nobody ever accused the Afrikaners of what I sometimes called 'flirting' with Africa: as I have already hinted, they were married to the place.

Now I was far from that stage, but I can remember a significant conversation with the GM over Sunday lunchtime drinks at the club. I asked him whether they had ever thought of opening an English-speaking primary school.

There would be nothing 'racialistic' about this. The African managers would welcome it for their kids: most primary education in Ghana was in the vernacular. They would have readily recognised the advantage for their children of primary education in English.

The GM said they had thought about it, but there was not the demand, and I had to leave it at that. The reader will perceive the direction of my thoughts: I was against all this to-ing and fro-ing anti-family business.

There I will leave the subject for now: as far as it had developed in my mind.

Les Cady (who was technically a sojourner but spiritually a settler - indeed, I believe, like me, he will spend the first thousand years of eternity between the forests and plains of Africa, when the call comes), Les had a theory which I have learned to appreciate more profoundly since: for indeed, it is a profound theory, and has added its weight to my sojourner-settler thesis. As he had naturally given more thought to it than I to mine, he had defined it more closely, which I had yet to do. He called it the 'three tour theory'.

'On your first tour,' said Les, 'you drink one finger of whisky in your glass and think the Africans are angels. On your second tour you take three fingers of whisky and think they are devils. On your third tour you take two fingers and settle down to a comfortable view which hopefully is permanent.'

Further than that he did not elaborate. He was a philosopher of the slow pipe-smoking school. I may say he was not a member of the Monopoly Society, which he probably considered, perhaps rightly, as an affair for first tourers (or even tourists).

He did not believe in miscegenation, which he thought brought out the worst in both breeds; and even wondered if he had not overstretched things in marrying a Pole. He expressed these genetical opinions, including the last, in the presence of his wife, who heard them without comment; which in a Polish lady must have signified agreement as to the main proposition and wifely acquiescence in the codicil - as Jeeves might have put it; meaning, in Bertie Wooster's words: otherwise there would have been jolly old fireworks!

There were actually two clubs in the town: the Samreboi Club, which was for managers, and was fifty per cent black; and the Forest Club, for the workers, which was wholly black. Members of the first club were encouraged to patronise the Forest Club occasionally, in an officerly sort of way, to encourage the lads - who needless to say, would not have received much encouragement if they had tried it the other way about.

When we (meaning almost exclusively the bachelors) dropped into the Forest Club on a boring Sunday afternoon, or seduced by the jolly sounds of a Saturday night dance, which were rarely echoed in the Samreboi Club, we were treated like royalty. At the dances large if battered armchairs were manoeuvred for us, and beers pressed upon us by hands which could afford them abysmally less than our own. Other times we would join the crowd at the bar. On one occasion Ralph found himself beside two gentlemen from the Ivory Coast who, of course, spoke French, and a jolly conversation ensued.

Standing by was a beefy foreman - Henry, who did not wish his underlings to think him, though a Ghanaian, ignorant of the great world beyond. After listening in to the exchange for a minute or two with a very wise look indeed, he explained to the bumpkins: 'Dat's dee French language dey are spikkin'. But dem boys for Ivory Coas' is on'y spikkin' pidgin French. Mistah Philipp is spikkin' dee proper English French.'

Ralph and I attended at least one Saturday night hop at the Forest Club. As soon as we entered, the usual armchairs and beers were produced, under the direction of the same Henry, a bearded black Falstaff, who smoked a large Meerschaum pipe. Henry was a sidesman at the Anglican church, a member of the PCC as vicar's warden, and therefore well known to me. When he had made sure we were comfortable and had everything we wanted, I gazed into the throng of dancers, amongst whom I thought I recognised one of my nurses. (As a matter of fact, she was not.)

'Who is that girl, Henry?'

When the girl had been sufficiently identified, Henry laid aside his pipe, breasted the sea of dancers until he reached the girl, whom he briskly separated from her astonished partner by grabbing her by the hair, dragging her after him like a sheep in the market, and flinging her into an empty armchair beside me.

Reappropriating his pipe as a pointer, he instructed the girl: 'Dee docketa want you. You go wid him. You get a bath. You pleasure him, and when dee docketa say fack off, you go for house one time!'

So far from resenting this treatment, the girl (who had probably never heard of Germaine Greer) sat back with an expression of the utmost complacency, and look-at-me-I'm-the-doctor's-girl written all over her.

I thought I owed her a turn of the floor, at any rate. Then I resumed my seat. She calmly resumed *her* seat beside me.

Presently Henry returned. He had evidently expected more progress. He removed his pipe from his mouth. 'Doan' you want dat one, docketa?'

'Actually, Henry, I only wanted to dance with her.'

Without a word, Henry once more discarded his pipe, grabbed the girl again by her woolly head, and flung her back into the pool of dancers like an unwanted fish, her eyes nearly popping out of her head in dismay and astonishment.

Teresa was a pretty girl of seventeen. She had sickle-cell disease, for which there was then, and is now, little effective treatment. It was heart-breaking to see the young face creased and crying with the bone-breaking pains of the disease in its acute bouts, as she lay and writhed on the hospital bed.

She followed up in outpatients and was as merry then as any other African young girl. As I passed her in the waiting queue, she smiled and chanted without shame: 'I lav you!'; which was some compliment to a bald-headed old man of forty. Nor was she at all shy of the sympathetic grins which accompanied her on all sides.

With all the gallantry I could muster, I felt the least I could do was to reply: 'I love you too, Teresa!'

Bigger happy grins and approving 'eh-eh's' all round!

The sequel came the following Sunday as I left for church. There was Teresa at the front door. 'I have come!' she announced with a happy smile. As I closed the door behind me, her eye fell on the hymn book in my hand, and the smile vanished. 'O! You are going to church?'

Once again, I felt the least I could do was give her a lift back to her village.

At the London office they had touched on the European patients. Not much trouble with the men, they said cheerfully: they have their work to keep them occupied. The women are the trouble. They have nothing to do and are bored. I do not know what the ladies would have thought of that opinion, and I never asked them. At least I found that neither they nor their men folk gave me much unnecessary trouble: they were glad to have a doctor in such a place at all, and seemed to consider his time.

It is true the men were happy at their work. The money was good, but it would have held neither the others nor myself but for the challenge of the work. For in Africa, where skilled men (and women) are so thin on the ground, everyone's job undergoes a certain elevation of responsibility.

This must be obvious even to the lay reader in my own case. How many family doctors in England do caesarean sections?

And it was true for everybody else. Mechanics became engineers, bookkeepers became accountants, general managers only fell short of deities. And this went down to the grass roots also, to one's subordinates. I have already said how the maternity assistants delivered breeches (something a GP no longer does in England) and the medical assistants were mini doctors.

In short, as well as aspiring upwards, one had to delegate downwards. And sometimes one delegated things which one had done once but had come to forget. And one such sad case was Sam's, the chief engineer.

As he grew older and the climate weighed heavier on him, Sam saw fit to delegate. He delegated the entire telephone system to his most promising technician, whom we shall call Kwasi. Now I should explain that one's responsiblities expanded outwards as well as upwards. Just as I ranged between surgery and public health, besides the more usual engineering tasks of road-making and bridge-building, Sam embraced the telephone system too. But as he felt the strain he leaned more and more on Kwasi until he rather lost his touch with the technical side of telephones. (For I might say that later, in my general enthusiasm for my job, I once got a radiographer to teach me to take X-rays; but never having kept it up, for the life of me, now, I would not know where to start.)

This would not have mattered, except that Sam had a northern directness, which was sometimes felt in those southern climes as downright rudeness. At any rate, that is how Kwasi felt it.

Kwasi downed tools. He did not sulk in his tent, or even his house. Why should he? Africans, as D H Lawrence said of the Italians, are not creatures of the home like the introvert denizens of northern lands: they are the outgoing citizens of the street, the forum and the tavern.

In Kwasi's case it was the tavern; and there, although he was not Sam's true love, he sat him down.

And the telephones in Samreboi fell silent. And what is more, Sam could not get them going again.

This did not please the GM, who as a Welshman did not take kindly to silence, telephonic or otherwise. He told Sam to do something about it - quick!

Sam, in his Gaullist fashion, issued a command to Kwasi in his tavern (by special messenger, of course) to get back to work - or else! Kwasi replied (by return of messenger) that he required an apology first. Sam's reply to that may be imagined.

And this is where Amos came in. I never inquired into the full details, but I gather that it ended with Sam eating rather more humble pie than Kwasi. As I have hinted before, the paradoxical obduracy of the African can wear down what Kipling called the 'granite of the ancient north'.

West Africa in those days was run by gentlemen amateurs, white and black - or at least, competent amateurs (and in my experience, most of them were gentlemen); for I might say, even the great United Africa Company was not a charitable instititution, and would not carry duds for long. Qualifications were considered, and looked for, but what counted was not so much what you knew (still less, who you knew), but what you could do on the ground. There was no room for duffers, and there was no room for funkers.

(In passing, I might add that it was not surprising people had called the UAC the real government of West Africa: it was greater than most people knew, and in its house were many mansions; not only in British but French and Belgian Africa too. And the company had one great commandment: THOU SHALT NOT BREAK A CONTRACT. You would not actually be nailed to a tree for this offence, even in the Northern Territories, but sure as heaven or hell, you would never get a job in West Africa again - and I mean all West Africa. One awful example will serve.

Finding life a bore on his particular station, a certain Mr A N Other applied for what seemed a more sexy job, advertised in the *Times of Ghana,* with a French company on the Ivory Coast. Perhaps he was attracted by the name: *Société Heureuse du Soleil de l'Ouest Africain,* or perhaps he remembered the famous *filles de joie* he had met on short leave in Abidjan. But apply he did, not imagining for a moment that the Happy Society had the remotest connection with the dull old African Water Closets, where he felt he was wasting away his young life.

Unfortunately for Mr Other, there was a connection - the UAC, which owned both companies. His application, in his best fifth-form French, landed on his own manager's desk a month later, with no more than a polite *pour votre attention estimée* and the stamp of the *Société Heureuse* to realise Mr Other's hopes of a French connection.

Needless to add, Mr Other's next and last journey, as far as West Africa was concerned, was to London; unless he ever returned on a sentimental journey at his own expense, which I rather doubt.)

I was saying that performance carried more weight with the company than qualifications, and this was never more true than of John Reith, a small Scot, who, though his financial attainments carried him no farther than two stripes in the Pay Corps, he nevertheless managed the entire accounts of the great West African Timber Company at Samreboi.

A charming miracle happened to the Reiths late in their marriage. They had practically reached the despair of Zacharias and Elizabeth, when they were similarly blessed by the Lord, not through an angel but through a small quantity of West African beer (for they were both practically teetotal), which they consumed one jolly night at the club. And the miracle did not end there, for the angel of the bottle went on to give John the managership of the great Lagos Brewery itself: in which the company recognised not only his competence but, no doubt, his fiscal and spirituous probity. They knew he would syphon off neither the profits nor the products.

Nevertheless, when John left, the company thought it had better join the twentieth century and engage a 'real' accountant - with a CA after his name - and duly found one in London. I know nothing of accountancy, but I understand it is no more a seamless robe than modern medicine; and, as one of my old professors might have said, has been as much ruined by specialisation. I don't know what kind of accountant Mr Flappering was, but I understand he felt himself as a skin specialist might if suddenly required to take over the entire functions of Harley Street: (a simile which I might say John Reith had been sustaining up to then, as I was sustaining the reality at the hospital; but neither John nor I was handicapped by specialisation, which an old friend of mine had described as like taking a razor to chop wood).

In short, in less than three months, Mr Flappering had a nervous breakdown, and was carried out of town, kicking and screaming and clutching a whisky bottle.

I have every sympathy with Mr Flappering. I know what a dreadful thing a nervous break-down is from both objective and subjective experience (though he never actually consulted me). And I too have been a funker; but managed to pick myself up again, as I hope he did.

Ghanaians, I have said, are a droll race; but their humour can take a sharper edge than what has been called (no doubt, by an Englishman) 'that purest of the metals, the English laugh'.

For some months after his departure, the locals took to using Mr Flappering's name as an enigmatic formula of their own.

One would throw up his hands and exclaim: 'Flappering!'

'What's dat mean, man?'

'Dat means, "I give up!"'

Les Cady had a sardonic, even cruel, sense of humour. He had fairish hair, but brown eyes, and once told me it was only people with brown eyes who had the real killer instinct. He told me proudly of a genuine Italian-type *beffa* (a word unknown to either of us at that time, or he would have made a lasting mental note of it) he played on a former GM.

The managers lived in one-, or two-storey, houses; the second, which are unusual in spacious Africa, for the senior managers, who included myself. My ground floor, besides the kitchen (which was nearly as big as James's house in the garden), comprised dining and sitting rooms, divided by a sliding screen, left permanently open, giving me a living space, between my sofa at the far window and my dinner table, as long as a cricket pitch. The GM lived in a palace, surrounded by a small English park, which would not have been despised by the Duke of Westminster.

Once a year the GM gave a party to senior management and ladies at the great house. This particular GM was an upwardly mobile type, in the social as well as other senses, before the practice had received the name: especially the social sense. Though his provenance did not equal his aspirations, he did not mean to end up half way. In the meantime, his life's study, apart from what the company paid him for, was the habits of the upper classes - and Les Cady had him sized up to a tee.

Needless to say, dinner jacket was the order of the annual party: (the GM might have gone as far as white tie). The ladies left the gentlemen when the port came on, etc; and in due course all were reunited, not only in the spacious drawing room, but on the even more spacious lawn.

Late in the proceedings, when people were thinking of drifting away, Les came up with a jolly proposal, restricted to the gentlemen. 'Let's all go for a swim in our dinner clothes!'

He knew this would chime in with some weird superstition in the aspiring mind of the GM: the sort of thing that might wind up a jolly Guards officers' evening in Birdcage Walk. The GM was not a man of reckless outgoing temperament, but while the idea would never have naturally occurred to him, he was driven by his devil.

With a joyless smile on his undistinguished face, he said, in a strangled voice: 'Er, yes. What a jolly idea!' and Les went ahead enthusiastically with his plan. He seemed to whip up an amount of enthusiasm in the others which should have made the GM suspicious, but didn't; for Les disclosed rather more of his plan to the others than he did to his superior.

Drinks were laid aside and the male section (or a sufficient number of them; the more sober members remaining behind to look after the ladies, who must have wondered what was going on) piled into cars and led by Les (who, of course, assumed the privilege of driving his leader), drove uncertainly along the laterite roads to the club. Here they lined up on the long side of the pool. At the usual signal from Les - 'One, two, three, jump!' - nobody jumped except the GM.

After he had sat on the throne about three years, President Ankrah decided that the country had behaved itself well enough to deserve a little 'democracy'. Elections were held and the people chose as their new president, Dr Busia, a nice little man with an Oxford degree or a dog collar or something or all three, who inspired the sanguine people who lend money to places like Ghana with rather more confidence of getting some of it back than his erratic predecessor bar one.

The GM, who had some conversation with him when he came to Samreboi shortly after his election, predicted that he was too nice to last more than six months in African politics. I cannot remember how accurate his prediction was, which doesn't sound optimistic.

The UAC also thought it might be a good thing to encourage the nation to believe that it ruled itself, and the GM was instructed to make preparations for the forthcoming elections at Samreboi. The job was delegated to Amos.

I remember attending a meeting which comprised such local dignitaries as a troubled-looking Father Adeloye, and Mr Sackey, who might have been wearing a tribal mask for all his face gave away. Politics, as Amos had hinted, was viewed by most people in West Africa rather as rock-climbing is by people without a special enthusiasm for it.

Amos, who had at any rate a genuine theoretical interest in the subject, tried to strike a spark from the stony faces around the large committee table. For this was the election committee, designed to educate the people as to their rights. As most of those present seemed content to listen to him without comment or the suggestions he called for, Amos finally burst out: 'Good God! What's the matter with you people? This is our country we are talking about. We are its rulers now. What are you? Ghanaians or Gold Coasters?' The obstinate silence which prevailed failed to answer his question - or perhaps Amos thought it did.

(As I did not have the vote myself, I am not sure what I was doing at this meeting. So simple a creature as myself was not there to represent the company as a disinterested observer: even in a token sense I might have put my foot in it. Perhaps I was there to stand by against any cases of psepholophobia - or election fright - in which case I might have added not only a new name to the medical dictionaries but my own to a new eponymous syndrome.)

As I said, the new President Busia came to Samreboi where he made a speech. And Ralph Philipp, with his usual cheek, pinched my seat on the HOD row to which he had no right. Now I am a pretty lamb-like fellow, as my secret nick-name among the people (finally confided to me by Amos) testifies. Modesty forbids my revealing it to the reader; though it could be a back-handed compliment in a continent where the lion is more usually admired as an object for imitation. But I had half a mind to turn Ralph out, except I anticipated some insulting reference to 'British stuffiness' or something.

I was consoled and refreshed, after the usual protracted experience in the hot open air, not greatly improved by the awning provided, by Yao in a local bar. 'Have a beer, doc!' he invited. I said, 'I would like to try an *akpoteshie* for once, if I may.' This is palm gin, the local fire-water, also known as 'VC10' for the airborne experience it commonly gives you. Yao looked doubtful. I remembered the saying: 'everything the white man says is OK', or perhaps he thought 'on your head be it!' (in more ways than one). At any rate, I had my *akpoteshie*.

I was about half way through it when a policewoman entered the bar, who looked like Bessie Braddock painted black for Africa: a large pistol on her hip for use, I suppose, against subjects beyond the reach of her hambone fist, which otherwise might have served her purpose better by the look of it. Yao brightly said, 'I want you to meet this lady, doc, who is a friend of mine.' (Lucky Yao!) 'She is the chief policewoman of Ghana.'

In preparation for taking the lady's formidable hand, I passed my glass from my right hand to my left. I deduced this from subsequent events, for at the time I discovered I could feel nothing from the neck down. Thereafter I might have been watching a film. Yao and I moved forward together (it being improbable that our surroundings moved backwards) until some invisible railway-type buffers brought me to a halt a foot before the lady. The music of three voices (as Jeeves would say) speaking in English and Ghanaian was heard from the sound track which accompanied the film. The lady's hand advanced, and I observed my own do the same and take it. After a little more on the sound track, I found us returning to our former places.

Akpoteshie! I started having thoughts about what the profession calls 'recent advances in anaesthesia'.

As great an institution among the populace as the wandering griots or story tellers were the village letter-writers. No application for job or loan went except through their skilful hands. They performed on paper torn from school exercise books, and used long envelopes whose source had better be overlooked, and charged half a dollar a time. They used a Victorian copperplate hand, and expressed themselves in formulae as hallowed by tradition as those of the law itself, if rather more colourful. The finest example retailed to me was received by a manager of the Standard Bank, which began: 'Dear Master, I lie at your feet and wait for you to open your bowels of compassion.'

Amos (who lacked the true spirit of the connoisseur) treated these creations with contempt, casting them unopened into the waste paper basket and commanding the applicant to state his business: a degree of confidence (or something) I never achieved.

For one day I found such a one outside my house: a young man waiting for me to come home, with a long brown envelope in his hand.

The contents expressed a modest request to be adopted as my son and sent to Oxford University.

While I was wondering how to deal with this with kindness and firmness, we were joined by Braimah. Braimah was the little old man who had requested the lease of the Wendy house and become my gardener. And he was an 'NT'. He was wearing a solar topee as sole garment besides his usual ragged shorts, which proclaimed that he was on his way out to the tavern. This topee had been given him by the Reverend Alec, and his title to it once questioned, to Braimah's annoyance, by my jocular neighbour, Andy Astle.

This was not the sole insult Braimah had received from the same quarter. One evening I heard a great palaver at the back door, involving James and Braimah. Braimah had been taking his usual way home from the tavern past the sawmill of which Andy was manager. This was strictly illegal, as 'access to the industrial area was restricted to employees of the Company, etc'. Standing at the door of his office, in a moment and spirit of idleness, Andy had challenged Braimah.

'Mistah Assell say, "Who be you?" I say, "O, massa! You savvy me proper." Mistah Assell say, "You lie! I nebba savvy you. What you doin' here for workside?" Den what you tink Mistah Assell say? He say, "You be tiefman. You baggaroff!"' At which point I found Braimah fairly hopping up and down on his bare feet.

Now seeing me with the young man he came up, either through curiosity or to render assistance. He peered over my arm at the letter, which of course meant nothing to him. I questioned the young man.

'You want to go to college?'

'Yessah,' answered the youth.

Braimah seemed to think some interpretation was called for, or perhaps the services of a 'linguist'.

He echoed my question. 'You wanna go for college?'

The youth looked doubtfully at Braimah for a few seconds, trying to 'place' him - an exercise as important to the African as it was to Dr F R Leavis. Some connection with myself seemed probable, but Braimah's appearance did not inspire the same confidence.

At last he gave Braimah the benefit of the doubt and replied: 'Yessah.'

Now this was the first time Braimah had been called anything but 'old man' - and not in the chummy British sense either. His chest expanded: he decided to make the most of the opportunity.

At the head of the letter was the address of the electrical department. I took up the conversation from there.

'I see you work for the electrical department.'

'Yessah,' answered the youth.

Braimah intervened. 'You dey for 'lectical depar'ment?'

The youth looked at him again. 'Yessah.' Braimah's chest expanded further.

I saw my chance. 'I think you had better consult your own manager.'

'Yessah.'

'You berra go for you same manaja,' from Braimah.

'Yessah.'

At this point the conference broke up. Braimah proceeded on his way, by far the most satisfied of the participants.

I was resting on my couch one Sunday afternoon when there came a tap on the french window. Outside was a small boy in a body cloth. When I opened the window, he announced:

'Ee dey concert tonight for Mpeasam village.'

This meant that a folk play was to be put on at the village named. The boy knew of my interest in these events. I got in touch with Ralph, who was a fellow connoisseur, and at sun-down we drove out to the forest village.

When we arrived it was night, and the village looked charming in the moonlight, which blazed on the polished earth and streamed down the thatched roofs. The play was to be enacted at the headman's house, which lay within a stockade.

At the entrance we paid our fees at a desk. A group of little boys collected round us, chanting softly in small reptilian voices: 'Docketa! Docketa! Docketa! Mistah Fee-leep!' and, 'Mastah, please give me a penny.'

If we had been so foolish as to accede to this request, the small boys would have vanished and been replaced by a mass of furious protoplasm.

90

As we entered we were seen by the headman and invited to join him in his awning.

'You know me?' he asked. 'You dun my hennia.'

The play was to take place in a central space. A hut provided the dressing room and wing. The mass of the audience sat on benches, or the ground in front of us, and all around the rest of the enclosure.

As I have said, all Africans are born actors. Even a village of a hundred souls can put on a little play, based on a well-known story, and acted out ad lib with great fluency and perfect timing. There is a certain sameness about the stories, in which the villain is always a woman, as evidenced by their titles: The Bad Woman. The Wicked Aunt. (Perhaps there is a Freudian explanation.) Tonight it was The Wicked Aunt.

A small boy called Kwasi attached himself to us to interpret (as the play was in the vernacular) and explain the action.

The entertainment began with the beat of a drum, and an almost naked man with a skeleton painted on his body performed a dance.

Then the story started. There are a number of stock characters. First we saw the Wicked Aunt with the Daughter and the Orphan. The Daughter was dressed up like a Takoradi tart to indicate her special status. (All the characters are men, as in Elizabethan times.) The Aunt was built up with aggressive cassava breasts and a pumpkin rump. The Orphan was dressed in rags.

The Aunt and the Daughter are jealous of the Orphan, who stands to inherit the farm from the Uncle, a benevolent if somewhat ineffectual figure. The Orphan is watched over by the Boy, a 'Buttons' character who does good, nor looks for any reward, and gets none. He wears a schoolboy's cap with the peak turned up and THE BOY written on it.

In the first scene the Aunt and the Daughter were expressing their feelings about the Orphan. The Aunt struck her across the shoulders with a stick. The Daughter kicked her food bowl out of her hands.

'Dey doan' like her,' explained little Kwasi.

When it gets too much, the Boy intervenes and gives the Aunt a drubbing. While she lies crippled on the ground, the Doctor enters with an enormous syringe, with which he proceeds to bayonet her in the rump, to the huge delight of the audience.

91

On his way out he adds: 'And chop *nkuntumbre!'*

This is coco yam leaf, a rich source of vegetable protein, which I recommended daily to my patients, especially for the children. The reference is not lost on the audience, and I rise to take a bow.

The plot thickens when the Aunt takes the Orphan's blanket to the witch doctor to put a spell on it, observed by the Boy from behind an imaginary bush.

At bedtime all lie down to sleep, in African fashion, with their blankets over their heads against mosquitoes. All except the watchful Boy, who changes the blankets of the Daughter and the Orphan. Next morning the Orphan gets up and goes to work, while the Daughter lies motionless.

The Aunt does a dance of triumph over the body. Tension builds up in the audience. Little Kwasi explains, breathlessly: 'She tinks it's dee Offen, but it's not. It's dee Dotta.'

The Aunt pulls back the blanket, and makes Rigoletto's discovery. She shouts, *'Adjei! Adjei!'* and beats her cassava bosoms.

This brings the house down. Women literally roll in the aisles, to the peril of the babies on their backs. Some of these fall out of their cloths and roll in the aisles themselves, crying their protests at this rude awakening.

Next enter the undertakers, sporting bowler hats and drinking beer out of bottles. 'Dey are drunk,' explains Kwasi.

There is a good deal of fun with the body, which is tossed and dropped between them and into the audience, which rises enthusiastically to toss it back; the body remaining rigid the whole time.

The Wicked Aunt is ordered into a corner by the Uncle, and the Orphan reappears, now herself dressed like a Takoradi tart, on the arm of the Doctor. Virtue rewarded!

All this has been spun out, with a great deal of extemporisation and song and dance, to about two hours. The play concludes with a moral delivered by the Boy.

'If you do good, you do it to yourself. If you do bad, you do it to yourself.'

The audience crowds out, and we seek our car. Soft voices plead for a lift back to town. This time I am not so cautious and say, 'Jump in!' Immediately, the car is full of writhing bodies, mostly female, with legs and arms protruding from the windows.

Some men unceremoniously remove a sufficient number of bodies, and we drive away.

PART TWO - CENTRAL AFRICA

1 - Zambia

I stayed in Ghana for eighteen months and returned to England before Christmas, 1969 - the dead of winter. And of course, I felt as if I had come up from the boiler room. I found a comfortable residential hotel near my native Liverpool, and seeing no reason to follow the example of Captain Oates, I remained within its doors until the slightly kinder weather of March arrived, except for rapid dashes to the motorcars of friends who were kind enough to collect me.

At that time I still had ideas of going to Australia, and even took a book out of the local library on the country: until after a few months I discovered I had read exactly twenty-four pages, though faithfully renewing it several times. In the same period I had read John Gunther's thousand page *Inside Africa* for the second time, and several other books on Africa besides. I began to realise this could only mean one thing.

But a return to Ghana would not do. Samreboi was a lonely place for a bachelor. I was only human (to say nothing of being a male human) and I looked for wider horizons and feminine opportunity. I also looked for a more satisfactory training than a doctor can give himself working alone - which is a most unsatisfactory training.

So I applied for a post in the large company hospitals of the Copper Belt of Zambia, namely, the Anglo-American Company hospitals at Kitwe, of which there were two: a 300-bed hospital for the workers, and a smaller one for the management. These were covered by a full team of specialists: full, that is, for that type of complex in Africa, which means one consultant in each of the major specialties.

Zambia has been described as 'a vast, hot, ugly country which wears its human inhabitants, white and black, as an elephant wears its

94

fleas'[1]. Now it is a principle of mine that nothing in nature can be ugly, and since most of Zambia belongs to nature, I cannot join in that epithet; though I concede its monotonous landscape would not be one's first choice in decorating a chocolate box.

But philosophy apart, I have to admit the writer had a point, which is why I used the quotation to open this section.

Here was forest again, and as monotonous as the forest of West Africa, but without its enchanting loveliness: or so it seemed to me at first. Nor were the trees tall. The highest trees in Zambia stop at thirty feet: thirty feet of scrubby bush, like the woolly heads of its black natives, except for the exotic gum trees, which were introduced from Australia via South Africa. These were tall - fifty feet or more - with their tall trunks and long branches, sometimes in their blue skins, sometimes in white nakedness, sometimes with skins half shed, like moulting snakes. These trees were brought by the white man and marked his places: the city spaces, the parks, or giving shade to a white farmstead.

Otherwise the Bushveld, as it is called, was so monotonous it was said when people skidded in their cars on its endless roads in the wet season, did a turn or two and then resumed their journey, they sometimes travelled a hundred miles or more before a previous petrol station informed them they were retracing their steps: unless they ran out of petrol first.

Zambia must be the last part of the old Empire to be significantly occupied and developed by the white man. I have met men younger than myself who came up in the Forties in ox waggons, whose first homes were rondavels (thatched roundhouses). These were Afrikaners, of course; and this must represent the last trek of that indefatigable people, who penetrated as far as Angola and Kenya.

Kitwe itself seems to have been mostly built since the Second World War. It is the largest of the group of mining towns on what is known as the Copper Belt, which runs indeed like a belt across the waist of the large body of Zambia. It runs up into the southern Congo (Zaire), into the famous province then known as Katanga, where

---

[1] Peter Wildeblood: *Against the law.* WD.

there is another group of copper mines, which belonged to the old Union Minière of Belgium. Two companies divided the Zambian mines between them: Anglo-American (which was neither Anglo nor American, but South African), and Roan Antelope.

Kitwe was a pretty town, which certainly looked like no mining town in Britain. It was a typical Central African town (in fact, a city), consisting of a central grid of wide streets. The streets of all these towns seemed to follow the example of Bulawayo, where the streets were made wide enough to turn a span of oxen, which consists of eight pair of beasts. The buildings were all modern, no more than three storeys high, giving the city an intimate feel. There were at least two good hotels, large shops, banks, and other commercial buildings, cinemas, clubs, restaurants, and handsome public buildings. The traffic was light, and the pavements wide: a pleasant place to walk about; though more walking was done by Africans than Europeans. The main grid was based on a wide central square, known as Kaunda Square, after the first president, who was still in the early days of his long reign. There were many trees: blue gums, already mentioned; the flamboyants, which were a blaze of fire in season; frangipanis, with their fleshy, ivory-coloured blossoms; and the delicate jacarandas, which flowered in clouds of mauve. The flowery season for all was September and October, before the rains began in November. For we are now south of the equator: the rain in the tropics follows the sun, and the rainy season in the south fills the other half of the year from the north. Winter is July, and December is high summer. In fact, winter in Zambia was little more than a few cold nights in June and July: the rest of the year was summer. The hottest month is actually October, panting for the rains, which was called the 'suicide month'.

The best suburbs were built nearest to the city centre, in the usual Central African fashion. Large houses, almost always single storey, lay in large gardens. These houses were not called 'bungalows', a term unused in Central Africa. A double-storeyed house was exceptional and referred to as such: so in future, in this narrative, a 'house' means a single-storey house, unless otherwise designated.

British people will see a reversal of conditions in their own country, where the best suburbs are the farthest out and the city centre consequently dies at night (or did in the sixties). In Victorian times it seems to have been otherwise, to judge by the decayed magnificence of the old central suburbs of Liverpool and Manchester: and Central Africa was simply following an older tradition. The city centre consequently lived at night in its clubs, cafes, hotels, etc.

The better suburbs were very spacious: Kitwe must have been at least five miles across, though the total population was 100,000. You needed a motorcar, unless you lived within a mile of the city centre (as I did). The great arc of Second Avenue was the main artery of the suburbs, and that was about two miles long.

These good suburbs, which were originally built for the Europeans, lay all to the north-west of the city centre. To the south-east lay the mine and all its works, and beyond them the vast workers' townships, where the prevailing winds and uncontrolled effluvia of the mine blew over them, in the correct direction: a universal principle in Central African industrial towns.

These weather conditions were reversed for a month or two when the south-easter blew in the winter, but you can't have everything in life, and at least it brought coolness.

By the sixties many Africans were rising in the world and entering the posher suburbs. But some were less posh than others. These were the older suburbs, which were actually more central than the others. Junior white managers lived among the Africans here, and in my new (and reduced) status of general duties medical officer (GDMO), I was one of them.

I lived on Eleventh Avenue, within walking distance of the city centre, across the railway line (the famous 'line of rail' which linked the country with the south and ended, not at Cairo, as Rhodes originally hoped, but at the heads of the great river system of the Congo). On my right lived a white Rhodesian family, and on my left a black Zambian one, and I could not say who made the most noise, as our kith and kin in those parts are not the shrinking violets of the old country, any more than the blacker Africans. Mercifully, there is plenty of space between such houses in Africa, so I was not much disturbed. On the black side of the fence, the quaint obligations of

97

old Africa were observed, and a large extended family accommodated by the official occupant; the cooking fires of whose relatives dotted the large garden at supper time. As if inspired by this, the white family would throw a *braaivleis* (barbecue) for their friends about once a month, at which much beef and beer were consumed and noise produced around the smoking fire, while the house became a rowdy sound box with music (or something).

My white neighbours were the Millers. Jem was a bearded jovial giant, of Celtic appearance: Sylvia was a petite, spirited blonde, with something of the Dutch in her - in fact, she came from the Eastern Cape. They had splendid family rows, which they no more disdained to share with the rest of the avenue than the Africans did on my other side. I may say that the rest of the avenue was British, and silent. Otherwise, the Millers were charming and cultured people, who soon became my warm friends (which is more than can be said for the rest of the avenue, for reasons I had better not go into).

And they were liberals.

Yes, reader, such creatures existed in that part of the world. They were not the dangerous revolutionaries which South Africa can produce: Rhodesia was more British, and kinder (or politer, anyway), than that. But they gave me much sound information on the region.

Jem produced the best aperçu I have heard on his own country. 'Imagine UK ruled by the Jews. They would probably make a better job of it than the Anglo-Saxons; but the Anglo-Saxons wouldn't like it.'

Sylvia could be very spirited. One afternoon I heard her shrill tones, not in her own house, but in the street outside. A large black man in council overalls was half-way up a ladder, doing something with a chain saw to a tree, which had nothing to do with the Millers, except in the aesthetic way. Sylvia was half way up the rest of the ladder, punching the astonished man in the kidneys with her tiny fists, without appearing to disturb him much, and screaming about 'beauty' and 'conservation' and such-like. The man kept repeating the formula, 'Mistah Cummings, madam', who, I guessed was the city engineer, rather in the spirit of 'acting under orders', which I understand has lost force since Nuremberg. Failure of communication, as they say, was mutual and complete. Sylvia only left off to take another line of attack - via the telephone on Mr Cummings. I seem to remember the tree, or most of it, was spared.

One night I got a telephone call from Sylvia at 3 am. She had had a burglar. Jem was away, and she was in the house alone with the children. I slipped on a dressing gown. She had rung the police, and as I went round, they arrived. Prompt! Several of them jumped out of the Land Rover and ran about the garden with revolvers. If the cook had emerged for any reason, he wouldn't have stood a chance.

Sylvia was soon with us in her house coat. And she had some evidence for the police. She had woken up in the night and seen the man in her room. From whatever complicated motives - fear, rage, maternal - she went for him like a leopardess and tore the shirt off his back. I even think there was blood on it.

Well, they never caught the burglar, of course; but when I returned to my house I discovered my late father's watch was missing from my bedside. The man must have got into my house before Sylvia's and never disturbed me. I think the front door lock was broken.

Jem told me he was an admirer of Liverpool humour, at least ever since one famous experience. After one of their parties, he and Ted were the only ones left, slumped in armchairs at six o' clock in the morning; apart from Sylvia who had got a few hours in her bed, who then appeared in her nightdress and surveyed the usual wreckage of such feasts with bleary eyes. It was Sunday and they had given their servants the day off. There was going to be a lot of cleaning up to do, and the ladies take these things more seriously than we men do. My fellow citizen tried to cheer her up (or something).

'Give us a song!'

As I said, the mine ran hospitals for management and workers. To begin with, I was assigned to the workers' hospital.

It had a number of specialised departments, each under a consultant specialist, and the GDMOs like myself were rotated between them every six months. I was placed first in the surgical department, under a benign and highly competent surgeon, Mr Hunt, a man then in his fifties.

Mr Hunt did rather more than a general surgeon would do in England: or rather, he covered a wider field, for he also did orthopaedic surgery. I do not mean he did hip replacements, which had not then been invented; nor would he have attempted anything so ambitious if they had. But he nailed femurs and screwed ankles, etc, which a general surgeon certainly does not do in England; nor does he need to.

Mr Hunt also covered traumatic surgery - accident and emergency - which is also a specialty in Europe.

And, of course, he was a general surgeon who did such things as hernias and bowel resections. In other words, as even specialists are in Africa, he was an all-rounder, but worked within the limits of his own competence and the resources available to him.

And so it was throughout the other departments: obstetrics and gynae, internal medicine - all of which stretched to include sub-specialties such as ear, nose and throat, eyes and so on, at a basic level.

There were a specialist anaesthetist and pathologist. We did not run to psychiatry; and children came under the specialist physician and surgeon.

This is the usual thing in Africa - breadth and simplicity, rather than specialisation - at hospitals up to this size.

There was little formal training for the GDMOs (or general doctors), and the hospital was not very busy. The general public went to the large government hospital, which was a very different affair.

There was nothing wrong with this. The mine hospital was designed to serve the mine people, and this it did well, with ample resources, both professional and material. And it was a place where a general doctor could learn much if he was prepared to push the specialists. In a formal training establishment the teachers push the pupils - and chase them. But formal training was not within the remit of the mine hospital, nor did it need to be.

At night the GDMOs were on call for all departments together, and could summon the appropriate specialist, and so maintained their broader experience. All in all, although it was not geared for training, a person who wanted to learn could learn much through observation and some extended practice.

My contract here was for two years, and they were not years wasted.

At week-ends we helped out with the flying doctor service: the government doctors were too busy for that. I think it was some kind of private charity, and was run for the benefit of outlying mission hospitals, where there was no doctor. We made weekly trips in a Cessna with a volunteer pilot. Emergencies at these places were sent to the government hospital by ambulance, and sometimes by air. Of course, our services were also voluntary, and it was great fun and instructive too.

Flying in a Cessna is like flying in a Mini car - a pretty nervous experience for the first time, which one quickly got used to. And the broad expanse of Africa was an exhilarating sight from the air. We looked down onto the large houses, with the blue squares of their swimming pools: we crossed the bleaker areas of the townships, and were soon over the open country - like a map painted grey-green and yellow (for my first trip was in winter and the dry season), with a few straight-ruled lines of roads running across it.

That first trip, we came after an hour to a hill, rising like some beast from the ocean of the Bushveld, the hard earth shining through its crop of shrubby trees like the scalp of a Bushman. Then, over the hill, was the landing strip, which looked like a six-inch ruler placed on the ground. How on earth were we going to land on that?

The plane smashed down with a hard bang, and then hammered across the earth as if it had lost its wheels. A reception committee of brothers or nuns would be waiting, together with the usual crowd of children.

The different missions - Anglican, Catholic, etc, - rather merge together in my memory. At one Italian mission we would be met by Sister Ilaria, in a large American car: a delightful lady who would never make her living as a taxi driver in her own country, or anywhere else where there was other traffic, or anything except fresh air. Even Africa was not big enough for her. She had several square miles of it to move around in, not another vehicle in sight (except the plane, which give her her due, she never hit in my experience), but as soon as we were in ('we' being myself and the pilot), she backed into a tree - bang! - then lurched forward, in and out of a ditch, and finally, after using the dirt road as a rough guide to the mission, deposited us there, probably having been instructed to apply the brakes within twenty yards of a building; talking and waving her hands and her white habit about all the time, in the happiest spirit in the world: a spirit not always caught by her passengers.

At these places, first we would do a ward round - the bare wards, the rough beds, the ragged people. We would do the usual things, sometimes advise referral to the government hospital. Except for emergencies, patients would have to make their own way. Afterwards, we would see outpatients: men, women and children, the latter with their mothers. Not many, as we saw only the more difficult cases selected for the doctor. At one place I saw the rubbery faces of leprosy: at another, a woman with the scaly, burnt-looking skin of pellagra - vitamin B deficiency, seen in districts where maize was eaten, unsupplemented by other foods. To finish, there would be minor operations; nothing requiring more than local anaesthetic or a whiff of ether.

An Italian sister informed me: 'We 'ave some extractions.' I found a number of people, sitting hopefully, with badly rotten teeth. The sister handed me a syringe, a bottle of local - and a screwdriver!

This same sister had a problem, which appeared to exercise her Catholic conscience. If a woman died in labour, should she do a postmortem caesarean section? (The original caesarean, of course, by which Julius Caesar was reputedly delivered.) I advised her against it, remembering the legalities of Europe, and also uncertain of the feelings of the local people. Years later, I heard of a Catholic doctor in Rhodesia successfully performing such an operation.

The people showed their feelings in no uncertain fashion at this mission on one occasion. A party of white men were fishing in a nearby river, when they were attacked by a hippo, and one of them grievously wounded. He was brought into the hospital, but died before the plane arrived. The body was removed. But what about the ghost?

The locals were well used to dealing with their own - by means of ceremonies lasting up to a year - but a white man's ghost! That was a problem beyond them. The whole black population of the mission who could use their legs or had relatives to carry them, including the nurses, took off more or less into the bush, leaving only the terrified remainder and the white staff. The father superior (the white witch doctor) had to exorcise the place before they could get them to return.

Flying home on one occasion, we saw a large herd of elephant, surging across the plain. The pilot flew low to get a closer look. There we were, alone in the vast solitude, with this noble sight.

'People come and go in Africa,' said Graham Greene, 'as though the space and emptiness encourage drift.' This is no more true of most parts of Africa than it is of Europe, but it certainly applied to the Copperbelt - and, for that matter, Samreboi. In both places there were long stayers (Mr Hunt was one), but less of them in Zambia. On the other hand, in the latter country there were the English-speaking primary schools I had suggested in Samreboi, and therefore more family life. Otherwise it was true, people came and went.

The first new doctor to follow me was Sean, a tall handsome Rhodesian, who might have been his namesake in *When the lion feeds*. He was a first class doctor, and fate eventually recognised the fact, for he did well: but fate, or what was known locally as the 'Party', did not treat him kindly at first.

One day, as he entered the hospital, the matron (who, as fate would have it, was also Rhodesian) asked Sean to have a look at her dog, which had something wrong with its ear. Being a thorough-going sort of chap, Sean asked her to bring it out of her car and into the plaster room (not the operating theatre, as the *Times of Zambia* said, which got its information, or its approval anyway, from one sole source, which the reader may guess). The plaster room was used by the medical assistants for removing or changing plasters, and was not, or intended to be, squeaky clean. Sean took a look at the dog's ear, and saw immediately that it had ticks.

But the eyes of the Party where everywhere, even in the plaster room, and next day, a deputation from the Party bore down on the medical superintendent, or rather the luckless man who was standing in for him while he was on leave. Bob Speirs was a canny Scot, and anyway, had been too long in Zambia to ask daft questions like what was the Party's constitutional connection with the matter, as he already knew the answer was nil; and that was also as much as the answer counted for in the great 'humanistic'[1] democracy of Zambia. When Louis Quatorze said, *'L'État c'est moi'*, his imitators would include even 'KK' (Little Ken Kaunda), the humble schoolmaster of Zambia.

In case the reader does not understand, the actual charge was treating a dog in an 'African' hospital (a thing which did not officially exist, as all hospitals and everything else were supposed to be non-racial; but law was not the Party's strongest point, which it generally regarded as a damn nuisance, inherited from colonialism; except for the new 'humanist' laws, with which it dealt with difficult humans), and therefore equating Africans in some way with dogs. It is interesting to speculate what would have been the reaction if the dog had been treated in the (white?) management hospital.

In short, the local gauleiter (or district governor, as I think he was called) ordered Sean out of the country, and the matron too for good measure. And the great Anglo-American Company was shown to be a lesser thing than the great UAC of West Africa was always believed to be, for it bowed the knee. In fact, they found Sean a job at another of its hospitals in South Africa.

But Sean had the last laugh. In Kitwe he met and fell in love with a very nice Finnish nurse, and one day these lovers fled away *out* of the storm, and Zambia lost two able young servants it could ill afford to lose.

Soon after they left Zambia, Sean and Rita invited me for a holiday in Rhodesia. They took me to Victoria Falls and the Eastern Highlands - the Trossachs in the tropics. In Umtali I met up with an old friend from Liverpool, Jimmy Lennon.

He was a schoolmaster, then in his late fifties, and lived alone at Brown's Hotel. I knocked on his door while he was enjoying his afternoon nap. He called 'come in' and leapt out of bed at the same time, stark naked, as he always slept in the tropics, searching for his

---

[1] 'Humanism' was the doctrine of Kenneth Kaunda, a philospher some have compared to the microscopic Mao. WD.

shorts. 'Good afternoon, father!' he said, not recognising me at first after many years and unaware that I was in Africa. We soon made up for that.

Jimmy was a short bald man with a clipped military moustache and all the charm of the Liverpool Irish. In twenty years in Africa he had not lost his Scouse accent. (I had met him on his long leaves.) He would have taken the Queen by the elbow and got away with it. Someone once saw him in the Liverpool Philharmonic Hall following Sir Malcolm Sargent off the platform, clapping all the way - Jimmy below the platform, of course.

He came out (with some more clothes on) to meet my friends. Sean's sister was with us, a girl of about eighteen, as handsome as her brother. Jimmy took her by the elbow as we crossed the street to his favourite cafe. 'And what is your name, my dear? Tamara! That is a very lovely name, but then it is only like you, my dear!' sounding as if he meant it, which he did.

Unfortunately, he was not on holiday, and we were unable to see more of him then. The reader will see much more of him later in these pages.

Next came Andy and Liz, a Northern Irish couple. Andy was half-way to being a gynaecologist: Liz was a nurse but was not working. Andy was a balding Irish gnome (bigger than a leprechaun): Liz was a laughing little Irish pixie. They sang Irish folk songs together to professional standard and appeared on Zambian television. They organised many a 'come-all-ye' at their house and attended many others, for there were many Irish in the town. And it was wonderful to see how Catholic and Protestant sank their differences so far from home (the Crookes were Protestant but were never partisan) and even sang each other's songs. Newcomers were often astonished and even disapproving of this, especially the song swapping, even English people. 'You should see what's going on at home!' Of course, they were getting it every night on telly. Alf Garnett, it will be remembered wanted to solve the 'Irish problem' by towing the country into the middle of the 'Hattalantic Hocean and torpedoing the bladdy plice!' It would be wonderful to transplant the North at least to the healing air of Central Africa for a time and see if it produced

105

the same results on a general scale - even if Alf Garnett said 'and leave it there!'

Andy did everything with the skill of an artist. He accompanied the couple's singing on the guitar. Once he painted a mural of a Roman feast on one wall of his sitting room (wall paper is unknown in Africa) for a party. Even his handwriting was the hand of an artist and not the scrawl of a doctor. And he was a deft operator.

He more or less took over the obstetrics and gynaecology. He was not backward at coming forward. The GDMOs were allowed to do a certain amount: I did hernias, for example, as well as caesars. Now Andy had never done a hernia, which was not surprising for a gynaecologist in European practice, and asked me to show him one. It must have been half way through the first one I showed him that he practically took it over. (In my teaching method, which I had scarcely evolved, I allowed the pupil to take the knife at the second operation.) Thereafter he pinched hernias from under my nose, as they arrived at the operating theatre if I wasn't quick enough off the mark, to the great amusement of everybody but me.

But in return, he taught me much himself, and by the hands-on method too. And the most important thing he taught me was the subtotal hysterectomy, as will appear later.

And then came Harry Bowen, who was half way to becoming a surgeon. He had a round face, glasses and a fringe and looked about sixteen. He was as keen as a schoolboy about life in general and surgery in particular.

One morning, Sean and I came out of the operating theatre to help out with the last of the outpatients. Harry had been in this sweatshop, not the most popular place in the hospital, since he finished his ward round.

'Where have you chaps been?'

'In theatre.'

His face fell, like the little boy who missed out on the party.

'It's all right, Harry. It's your turn on the speedboats tomorrow.'

Harry overlapped the Crookes, and made his debut in polite Kitwe society at a folk-singing party - of the rather more serious kind than a come-all-ye.

He turned up late. Indeed, the first we knew was when an old African gentleman arrived at the house on a bicycle with a note addressed to the host requesting the writer (Harry) to be rescued from a ditch. He had given the man a dollar ('Was that enough, chaps?'), where a less trusting soul would have requested cash on delivery by the note. Harry was no fool, but that was his way.

When he had recovered from his experience and been given a beer, Harry looked around him with his owl-like gaze: if ever an owl looked bright and eager for fun, that is. Perhaps he had not been forewarned, but he took it in (or something like it) fast enough.

'Folk-singing? I love folk-singing.'

He was standing on the rug before the fire place - an Afghan rug, the expensive pride and joy of the lady of the house. He put down his pint of beer beside him on this article, perhaps with a view to conducting a chorus, which never in point of fact materialised, and began:

'Cats on the rooftops. Cats on the tiles -'

gently waving his hands like Sir Malcolm Sargent. I may say he was a keen rugby player, and that is how he learned most of his 'folk songs'.

The bearded faces drooped painfully over the guitars which, needless to say, remained silent: faces and guitars. Even when Harry kicked over his beer on the Afghan carpet. The lady of the house simply left the room and her husband followed solicitously after her.

Presently he reappeared alone, tapped Harry on the shoulder - 'A word, Harry!' - 'Certainly, Ivor,' from the ever eager Harry. Ivor led him to the door, opened it, thrust Harry outside, and closed it after him.

An hour later, when Andy went outside for a breath of fresh air, he found Harry standing in the middle of the lawn with tears and moonlight streaming down his face. When he discovered what was going on, with all the passion for justice of his race, Andy led a meek

Harry back into the house; and now it was Andy's turn to have a word with Ivor.

A very ugly scene followed, in which the lady of the house, who had recovered from her own tears, took a conspicuous part, with language which made us wonder where she had spent her impressionable years. Her performance was only stimulated by the persistence of Harry (who had shed his meekness by now) in calling her 'sunshine'.

'Don't effing call me "sunshine"!'

At this stage no one was in a mood for folk-singing, and the party broke up by general unspoken agreement - or general spoken disagreement.

I took Harry on an afternoon trip to Ndola zoo. A zoo in Africa has always struck me as rather amusing - at least it does not matter if the animals escape. On the way we saw what appeared to be a strip of metal, half bent upward, at the side of the road. We were almost upon it when I realised.

'That's a snake!'

'Christ! Look at it!' shouted Harry, with an excitement it did my jaded nerves good to hear. 'Get a photograph, Warren!'

There was no time. The snake, all six foot of it, snapped like a whip and shot off into the veld. I thought it was a black mamba and said so.

'A BLACK MAMBA!!!' shouted Harry, his eyes popping out as he strained in vain to get a view through the rear window.

It was certainly more impressive than anything we saw at the zoo, except perhaps an elderly crocodile, at which a group of black children had to be restrained by a keeper from throwing stones. Zoo or no zoo, they knew all about crocodiles: the keeper must have been told off specially to protect the unfortunate old fellow.

Then we saw the fish eagle with his white head, brown wings and trousered legs - caged in Africa, dear God! Another keeper was coming up from the dam, carrying a large barbel he had caught there. 'I'm going to give this to the fish eagle,' he grinned.

He opened the cage and flung the fish into the water trough, where it twisted about, then settled motionless. The fish eagle appeared not to notice, staring off at nowhere with its mad, unseeing eye.

Then it became restless. It moved up and down on the branch, on its claws and trousered legs, stooping and flapping its large wings, like a big hungry dog.

Then it pounced. It grabbed the fish with both claws and got itself and prey back onto the branch again. With the fish under its foot, it stared once more into space.

Then it proceeded to tear up the writhing fish with its eagle beak.

'Cor, look at that!' shouted Harry. 'The fish eagle thinks its Christmas!'

I got him away at last, feeling sick at the whole Creation for a time, while Harry babbled on beside me about the bloody eagle.

But, of course, Harry was right. Who knows what fish or fish eagles feel? How can you argue with nature?

Later I was sharing house with another man when Harry drew up at our front door at 11pm. One goes to bed early in the tropics (10 pm being usual) and rises early. Billy and I were already tucked up when we heard the crunch of Harry's car on the gravel.

I rose and opened the door for him before he reached it. He stepped out of his car. Billy stood behind me. Harry had just come from the mine club. He looked at our night attire.

'Don't tell me you chaps are in bed already! What's the matter with you? You're not old men! The night is yet young!'

I forget whether he wanted us to come out to play or whether he wanted to come in to play. What I do remember is that when he stepped out of his car, he had a full pint of beer in his hand in one of the club glasses.

I introduced Harry to the flying doctor business. I don't know whether he kept it up thereafter. His mental swings were as sudden as Toad of Toad Hall's, as I discovered on the way home.

On the return flight from the Anglican mission, where he had met the usual priest, brothers and nuns, gone round the bare wards, etc seen the wretched cases, and been given a cup of tea in the common room, he fell strangely silent. Normally, even the noise of the aeroplane would not have been enough to repress Harry for an hour together.

As we left the plane and walked to the shed of the tiny airport, it all burst out.

'Wonderful people! Wonderful people, Warren! There they are, doing the Lord's work, out in the bush, looking after those poor savages, while we're revelling in the fleshpots of Kitwe!'

He paused and looked me full in the face, his eyes round with earnestness.

'I've made up my mind, Warren. I was thinking about it all the way back. I'm going straight from now on!'

As I was not aware of any wide deviations from the strait and narrow on Harry's part in the past, I said nothing.

We walked on. He glanced at his watch. 'Christ, Warren! Six o' clock already! The club bar'll be open. Come on! We're losing valuable drinking time!'

I also took him to a games evening at the Catholic hall: roulette, pontoon, crown and anchor, etc, all in aid of church funds. We bought chips at the door. We did not have much money on us: as I remember, we restricted ourselves to dollar ones (kwacha). Harry soon lost all his money.

I was reluctant to lend him any. I had limited myself to ten dollars, and meant to keep to it.

Harry sat disconsolately on the edge of the roulette table. Then an astonishing thing happened. After the wheel had stopped and the croupier was going to work, I saw Harry's hand come out as if by itself. He was looking away at nowhere the meanwhile. The hand picked up a dollar chip and was about to slip it into Harry's pocket.

The croupier, a hardened Rhodesian type, rested his rake.

'Excuse me, sir! Would you mind replacing that chip, please?'

Harry seemed to jerk out of a trance, glanced at his hand as if he had accidentally cut himself and meekly replaced the chip without a word.

Then he saw a girl he knew - a white nurse or teacher. There were unattached white females on the Copperbelt, but they were greatly outnumbered by the male ditto. I lost sight of him.

She could have been a wholesome influence on him, but it didn't happen. I don't know if she leant him any money. At any rate, it could not have accounted for what I saw next.

When I saw him again, he had undergone a terrible change. Fangs were protruding over his lower lip. Fur was sprouting from his cuffs, and, in his two-inch nails, he was clutching fistfuls of chips - not dollar ones, but ten-dollar ones. His pockets were stuffed with more of the same. He staggered from table to table, his face flushed and his eyes glazed with booze and greed. He seemed not to hear or see me when I asked him what was going on.

But it all came to nothing. When at midnight Father Bunloaf brought the proceedings to a close with a short prayer, he had lost everything.

Harry came out actually as a locum - for about three months. Then he went back to UK as a surgical registrar. He meant to return to Kitwe the following year. I asked him if he ever took a holiday.

'What do you call this?' he answered, bending over his snooker cue in the club at 4.30 in the afternoon. Certainly, company work was the lightest a doctor could get in Africa (except private practice). Samreboi was busy enough, but that was an exception.

A year later he came out again, as ebullient as ever. One morning, we noticed the appearance of more than one little black boy in the clinic bearing the Christian name of 'Bowen'.

Of course, this is a compliment to the doctor, commonly when the doctor has delivered him - which would only be in complicated and therefore memorable cases anyway; otherwise it would have been a midwife.

But Harry came in for a good deal of ribbing on this matter. He looked superior about it.

'Nothing to do with me, chaps, what they choose to call their offspring. I expect the president comes in for a lot of the same sort of thing.'

Julie came out for a short tour at the beginning of 1971. She was a lithe, gipsy-looking girl from Australia. I called her a 'socialist missionary'. A hundred years before she might have been a Christian missionary - or she might have been a George Eliot, more likely the latter. She had enough 'moral earnestness' about her to satisfy F R Leavis.

Like the girl in the Nun's Story, she was not very happy to find herself assigned to the management hospital, which was mostly white. I don't know what she expected. The whole company service seemed to her old-fashioned: geared to curative medicine with little attempt at preventive medicine, which was mostly left to the government. 'They don't even have an under-fives clinic,' complained Julie, which was a fairly new idea then. Perhaps she had a word with somebody, because soon afterwards they instituted them in the mine clinics, which were situated in the townships. She also thought the management hospital hopelessly uneconomic, which it certainly was. They should have opened it up as a private hospital to the public, who would have welcomed it and made it pay. I don't think Julie was thinking quite in this 'capitalistic' direction, however. This was a suggestion I made, but it was never taken up.

You will see that Julie's orientation was towards public health. She was a fine clinician, but not enthusiatic about surgery or obstetrics ('hated them, in fact'). The chief medical officer, a hopeless old sexist, suggested that as an unmarried woman doctor she should concentrate on child medicine. Julie was far from being a rampant feminist: she was a very balanced person; but she reacted: 'Why the hell should I do that, Warren? I suppose he thinks I'm a frustrated old maid, or something.'

(Joe Cooper was something of a paternalist into the bargain. Every Friday we had lunch at the management hospital, where Joe held a mortality meeting on all the deaths of the week. I supposed this served a purpose. Among other things, he would lay down the treatment regimes nearly every week, and more or less treat us like a bunch of soldiers, if not school-kids. On one occasion he said: 'As you know, I believe in treating doctors like responsible adults.' Andy Crookes doubled up in silent laughter, only saved from Joe's eyes by the fruit bowl on the table.)

Julie had a dry Australian sense of humour. She took a photograph of the local Party office, with its Orwellian slogan prominent outside: UNIP IS IN POWER FOR EVER: (OBOTE STREET BRANCH). The point being that Obote, the tyrant of Uganda, had been recently deposed (and now UNIP is no longer in the driving seat). She did not realise, nor did I till later, that this was a risky action. She might have been arrested as a South African spy, which would have been a bitter fate for Julie. What's more, some forms of humour don't travel as far as Julie: the idea of trying to make an African court see the joke boggles the mind.

I took Julie out to the Catholic mission. We went in my car and made a picnic of it. There were two lovely black nuns there. I said it was a waste for them to be nuns. Julie frowned: 'I don't believe in what they stand for, but I don't know -' I could see the warning lights of feminism ahead (though too crass a word for Julie, as I said) and dropped it.

We sat and had lunch by the dam. A butterfly settled on Julie's knee. 'He thinks you are a flower.' 'Gee! Thanks, Warren.' Of course, I was half in love with her. She used to say, 'You're the only person I can talk to here, Warren.' Which was surprising, as I was pretty conservative. 'Have you always been as right wing as this, Warren?' 'More so in the past.' 'Christ!'

When I told her I was a Christian - though not in an orthodox sense - she protested: 'O, you can't be a Christian, Warren! There's so much going on in the world.' I suppose she viewed Christianity as an otherworldly religion. I could have pointed out that many Christians thought there was enough to do in the world. And most important, that Christianity was the basis of everything *she* 'stood for', which was Western liberal democracy. But I did not think of these things till long after, so did not say so.

At the mission we saw a dog lying on its side, under the wooden steps of a ward. It was salivating profusely and panting, its staring eyes unblinking. They thought it had been bitten by a snake, and Brother Joseph was going to shoot it.

Later I heard of an outbreak of rabies in the district - mainly among pigs. One woman died. We had seen our first case of this disease. I have seen many more since, animal and human.

I took Julie up to Lubumbashi (the old Elizabethville) in the Congo, which was famous for its restaurants. It was an older city than Kitwe and looked Continental - I remember the old Belgian sets in some of the streets. Julie liked the Continental atmosphere. I told her how the British nearly got Katanga, and she said thank God they didn't! So then we had a furious argument. We had several, though most of the fury was on my side. I told her about the two systems: the indirect rule of the British, which worked through the native institutions; and the Franco-Belgian system of direct rule, which treated the Africans more or less like apes, and ran everything down to ground level through the notorious *agents de postes,* who practically cut out the African headmen, ie, abolished even their NCOs. And look at education! British Africa wound up with five universities. The French didn't have secondary schools till after the Second World War; and what about the famous 'twelve graduates' of the Belgian Congo at the time of independence? As for the famous 'multiracialism' - that was best summed up by one British district commissioner as 'sleep with them, but don't shake hands with them!'

In all this I had the advantage of a greater knowledge of Africa, where Julie confessed, the British beat the Aussies. I would not have that advantage now.

Then came a famous scene in a restaurant. Teasing her of course, I said Hitler was a socialist. 'That's what he called himself - a "National Socialist", didn't he?'

Julie turned white. I thought she was going to bring up the frogs' legs I hadn't enjoyed much seeing on their way down. She got up, trembling, and walked to the door. There she paused. It would be unworthy to suggest she wondered how she was going to get back to Kitwe - 150 miles away. I prefer to think she chose to 'master herself' (if that is the word); and she returned to the table.

Julie did not get on well with most of the whites on the Copperbelt. There were many Rhodesians and South Africans, who had (with some exceptions like the Millers) fixed racialist attitudes. But they were not half as virulent as the shoals of little Andy Capps and Alf Garnetts from UK, who greatly outnumbered them, and to whom racialism was then a new religion, which they embraced with all the fervour of the convert. At least one of these annoyed Julie with his attentions.

At a party - one of those boozy all-white affairs Julie hated - Len sat next to her and 'fancied' her right away. Len could have been Alf Garnett's son and (unlike his disappointing lefty Liverpool son-in-law) the apple of his father's eye. Len knew about Australians, or at any rate, knew of them, for he would not have met many at that time, even in his East End. If he had, he might not have taken the risk he did with Julie. But he did know they were 'colonials', like Rhodesians and South Africans, with whom he had discovered much in common.

Learning that Julie was a doctor, he decided on the philosophical approach.

'Don't you fink, Julie, it'd be better to leave these Kaffirs jist to die orf of all their 'orrible diseases? I mean, the world'd be a better plice wivout 'em, wouldn't it? We could even run the mines wiv machinery.'

After about ten minutes of this, in which Julie's frozen silence failed to register, Len reckoned he had earned a kiss. He slipped a hairy paw round Julie's neck.

His suit did not prosper.

'Git off me, you colonialist fascist pig!'

Now given Len's understanding of Australians, this was like collecting a belt from Father Christmas.

(Well, that is the usual way I tell the tale. But, of course, Julie would never call anyone a pig in earnest - unless he was hurting a child, or something. I think she gave a shrug and a kind of snarl, but the reaction was certainly surprising to Len.

As the Irishman said, 'What do you want: a story, or the truth?')

Before dismissing Len from these pages, it is worth recording that even Andy puzzled him. Andy was giving a plangent rendering of Carrickfergus -

I wish I kne-ew a handsome boatman
To carry me o-over the sea to die.

When he had finished, Len asked: 'What was that? "A 'andsome boatman?" Is that meant to be a bloke singing that song, Andy?'

Julie was brilliant. Later she got the Himalayan MRCP (specialist degree) in one go, and a public health diploma. Thereafter, she returned to Africa, where she has remained ever since, working mostly among the blacks. She can speak at least two African languages fluently, and must know the customs through and through. I urge her to write her memoirs. They would contribute far more of solid knowledge at any rate than these ramblings of mine. Compared with her I am Bertie Wooster in the bundu.

Sister Steadie lived up to her name (at any rate, her husband's name: whether he did I do not know), and she would have no nonsense on her ward - and this is no old battle-axe I am talking about, but a small pretty woman of thirty.

We were at the head of men's surgical on the morning ward round, she and I, she pushing the little trolley which carried the case notes. Three policemen entered the ward, comprising a big-booted sergeant and two plain clothes CID characters in pork-pie hats and dark glasses like Tonton Macoutes. They bore down on one of the beds, and the Tonton Macoutes grabbed a prostrate patient and pulled him up by the shoulders.

'Sergeant!' rang the clear bell-like voice of Sister Steadie, as she stared not at them but at the wall in front of her.

'Yes, madam?'

'Come here.'

The Tonton Macoutes dropped the body and the trio trudged up the ward. All the patients capable of doing so sat up in their beds and began to take notice.

When they reached teacher's desk, Sister Steadie, now looking the sergeant steadily in the eye, demanded quietly:

'Would you like me to come into your office like that, unannounced?'

'Yes, madam.'

'What?'

'No, madam.'

By now the patients were beginning to wriggle, as if they had all discovered ants in their beds.

'What can I do for you?'

The sergeant fumbled for a scrap of paper in his breast pocket.

'We got dis name, "Boniface".'

'Well, you've got the wrong man, haven't you?'

'No, madam.'

'What?'

'Yes, madam.'

'For your information Boniface is too sick to be interviewed.'

'Yes, madam.'

'And you won't get much information out of him when he is better, because he is a boy of eight.'

'Yes, madam.'

'So I think you had better return to the station, don't you?'

'Yes, madam.'

'Good morning, sergeant.'

'Morning, madam.'

They turned about and trudged back again down the ward. By this time, the patients, who did not feel free to laugh in the humanistic democracy of Zambia, were all in epileptic convulsions, and every bed the trio passed beat like a tribalistic drum. The sergeant stared ahead of him like a frustrated rhinoceros, while the Tonton Macoutes eyed each patient in passing, as if they were trying to remember every one of them.

It was about this time that Billy came to share house with me. He was an instrument technician at the hospitals. His wife had left him, taking the children, and going off with another man, who had even taunted Billy in the club with his achievement. 'Ay, lad, and ye're welcome tae her!' retorted Billy, telling me he was glad to have the answer on the tip of his tongue then and there instead of in the back of his head a day later.

He was a small Scot. To describe him, I have only to say that he was the physical image of Beethoven, whom he resembled also in dauntless character, if not quite in genius (which is no sarky way of saying he was a fool - he was a member of MENSA); and I have

117

only to see the defiant features of the great composer on an LP sleeve, and mentally give him a Glasgow accent, to have Billy before me again.

Incidentally, he loved classical music, though I do not think he had gone into it much, and I was able to enrich his experience with my large collection of LPs. With unaffected good taste, he soon put Mozart at the top of his pops, closely followed by Beethoven himself and Brahms. For the emotionalism of Tchaikovsky he had no time. 'What's he trying tae prove?'

If Billy was dauntless in spirit, physically I have never known a more courageous man. One night, coming out of the club, we were too late for the mine restaurant - it was Wednesday and we had given our cook the evening off - so we decided to go for take-aways at a place bearing the interesting name for Central Africa of the 'Eskimo Hut'. We hung about, waiting for the queue to shrink, when Billy noticed a small black boy, who had seemed to make more than one appearance at the end of the queue. It became plain that every time he reached the hatch where the food was served, someone bounced him aside. Billy approached the lad.

'What's going on, son?'

'Please, sir. I want some food.'

'Come with me.'

Meekly the bare-foot child followed the sturdy Billy, like the page of Good King Wenceslas. At the head of the queue was a black giant who must have stood seven foot in his socks, with lateral dimensions to match. The boy pointed him out as the latest of his tormentors.

By some movement like a practised chess player, which I hardly saw, Billy replaced the large black piece with the black pawn on the same square.

'Give this lad what he wants, Papadopoulos!' he commanded.

Meanwhile, the black giant looked around for the cause of this sudden change of gambit, which seemed as irregular to him as it must have done to Capablanca, and saw only a small chunky white man as the possible agent. He looked discontented.

Now Billy had not been brought up on the streets of Glasgow not to recognise the first signs of discontentment and know how to allay them. He faced the black giant, or rather, he directed an evil stare upward to meet the discontented downward one: and when Billy wanted to, he could look very evil indeed. I was reminded of the honey badger/elephant situation described earlier in these pages; and besides being the fiercest animal in Africa, the first thing the honey badger goes for is the pudenda.

The black giant seemed to become uncomfortably aware that his own were about on a level with Billy's teeth. Thereafter, he seemed to grow smaller by the minute.

'So what's the matter with you, then?' spat Billy.

'O, nothing, sah!'

'Then take that dirty look off your face!'

'Yessah!'

'AND GET YOUR HANDS OUT OF YOUR POCKETS!!!'

'YES-SAH!'

By the time he sprang to attention, the black giant looked no bigger than Billy.

One day there was a 'card sale'. This meant all the Party bullies were out on the streets selling membership cards in the Party at fifty cents each. Needless to say, the sales were not unpressured.

They were often shameful. People parted with their fares at bus stops, even mothers taking their children to hospital, who had to walk long distances instead. And they blockaded the supermarkets, where they supplemented the work of the checkers. To be exact, they did this outside the doors, not because of anything to do with legality, which was exclusively the Party's affair in Zambia anyway, but because it needed less workers to cover one or two doors than half-a-dozen check-outs.

Outside the OK Bazaar they had placed a school desk, where a couple of bully officers sat with a ledger and a cash box. They rarely accosted Europeans, but these were some of the more ardent spirits. As Billy entered the store, they asked him in a tone Billy did not like if he wanted to buy a Party card.

'No!' snarled Billy. 'I do not. Do I look like an effing Zambian?'

They were about to let him pass, but Billy had not finished with them yet.

'I am going into this store to make my legitimate purchases. When I come out, I do not expect to see you or this desk here. If I do I will throw it and you into the street!'

When Billy came out, the desk and its handlers had disappeared.

A famous institution in Central Africa is the 'long bar': needless to say, exclusively male. The long bar at the mine club was as long as a cricket pitch. It was of course multiracial, but the whites used the left end and the blacks the right. As the place filled up, the two groups would meet at an uneasy conjunction somewhere between.

One evening, at sundowner time, Billy was the last man on his side of the border. He had had a hard day, and perhaps had taken too much on board. At any rate, it was not his first brandy and coke which his black neighbour knocked over.

In the ensuing altercation, Billy used the fatal word, 'Kaffir'.

He hardly had time to think about it, still less regret it, when he felt a tap on his shoulder. Turning round on his stool, he found himself facing a po-faced individual with notebook and biro.

'I have noted the things you have been saying to this comrade, comrade, including the offensive word in question. I should inform you that I am a member of the area committee of UNIP, and I can assure you that you will shortly be leaving the country.' With which the individual put up his notebook and pen and left the bar.

Hardly noticed by a somewhat crestfallen Billy, a small group of Africans drinking at a nearby table put down their glasses and left also.

Presently, one of them, a respectable little grey-haired *madala*,[1]returned and approached Billy in what appeared to be a spokesman capacity. Touching his crinkly forelock, he addressed him.

'O, Mistah Doughty, sah, you don't have to worry about our friend with the notebook. You see, Mistah Doughty, sah, we know you, sah, and we know you are a good chap, and when you are saying these things about "Kaffirs", we know you are not meaning them. Anyway,

---

[1] Old man. WD.

when we got our friend outside, we beat him up and burned his notebook.'

Billy and I gave the first (and last) multiracial parties on the Copperbelt. We had the nucleus of the hospital staff to build on, where race relations were easier than in most places. One of these parties was invaded by a group of drunks, encouraged, no doubt, by the unusual racial mix, who invented an instant African custom to justify their intrusion, to the effect that anyone is welcome at any party in 'African culture'. They were led by one 'Tembo of the *Times*' (a title Billy later recalled with derision). As they were being rejected enthusiastically by both black and white participants, they had the cheek to call us 'racists' and 'colonialists', etc, in the usual knee-jerk way of Rentamob, and vowed to return with their friends next day. Tembo even threatened us with the hammer of the press.

   After they had gone, Sister Chitambo reassured me: 'They were talking nonsense, Dr Durrant. That is not an African custom. We call them "gate-crashers".'

As a result of our initiative, Sister Chitambo invited Billy and me to the engagement party of her niece, with a very decorative and persuasive invitation card.

   We turned up at the time requested - about 4pm - and found the happy couple welcoming the arrivals outside the house. The fiancé was in a morning suit, the girl in a long white dress and long gloves. Both looked about as animated as tailor's dummies. Thank God, Billy and I had decided at least to wear shirts and longs instead of our usual week-end shorts and whatever.

   After shaking hands we went inside. We found ourselves in the usual enclosed veranda of such an old house, where a number of other guests were sitting. Europeans in such a situation would have split up into groups, each group exclusively male or female, unless the numbers had been small enough to oblige them all to get together. In African society togetherness is inescapable, and the chairs were lined round the walls facing inwards, like some kind of tram car. All were in their Sunday best. Beer (for the gentlemen) and Coke (for the ladies) were being taken in small paper cups. Billy and

I took our places, and were similarly accommodated. Conversations of excruciating politeness were proceeding.

'And how are you, Mr Longo?'

'O, I am very fine. And how are you, Mr Bongo?'

'I am very fine. And how is Mrs Longo?'

Mrs Longo, who did not presume to answer for herself, stared bashfully into her Coke, leaving her husband to speak for her.

'Mrs Longo is very fine. And how is Mrs Bongo?'

After about half an hour of this, Billy and I crept into the sitting room.

Such a room has no exterior windows and is in more or less darkness, on some days even aided by electric light. Here more chairs lined the walls. Some younger people sat about, no less formally dressed. Music was playing quietly from a record player.

Billy, nothing if not a spreader of joy, approached a solitary girl, who also wore long gloves.

'Would ye like tae dance, miss?'

The girl nearly choked, then seemed to emerge from some kind of trance, looked wildly about her and stiffly replied: 'O! I don't seem to be dancing.'

Billy resumed his seat. It was not often I saw him deflated.

Little cakes on paper plates were passed around. The light faded in the swift tropical twilight. The formality continued relentlessly. Billy and I felt ourselves slipping into rigor mortis. Then like a good fairy, Sister Chitambo appeared before us.

'O, Billy!' she pressed. 'Why don't you go and get some of those nice LPs you played at your last party at your house?'

Leaping at this chance with almost indecent alacrity, Billy replied: 'Certanly!' and to me: 'Can I borrow the car, Warren?'

Then he was gone. He was gone a long time. Night came on. I plied the paper cups as hard as I could, but nothing changed. I realised I had reached that grey stage where even alcohol has failed. And like Mariana's boy friend, Billy cameth not.

About eight o' clock I made some excuse - a case at the hospital. I got a lift from someone. Take me home first - I have to do some study. Someone else will fetch me. O, what a tangled web!

Next day when I woke, I got the rest of the story from Billy as he sat up in his own bed in the next room. He had got the records but, as I had guessed, got holed up in some bar and did not rejoin the party till nearly midnight. The whole scene had changed.

- Tae begin with, they had got rid of the paper cups and were drinking the stuff straight from the bottle. They must have got through fifteen crates by the time I got back. Mr Bongo and Mr Longo had discovered they supported different political parties. 'How can you support that man?' 'I thought this was a democracy!' 'You must be stupid! -' [This was almost as bad as 'Kaffir', and was meant to be.] 'Who are you calling "stupid"?'

- The music was now shaking the building, and that little floozie that wouldnae dance wi' me came flying across the floor, wrapped hersel' round me and screamed: 'SOCK IT TO ME, MISTAH DOUGHTY!!!'

- The next thing, I felt a heavy paw on my shoulder, and when I turned round, there was a bluidy big bloke like Idi Amin staring doon at me out of his smoky eyes. He said, 'You put her down! She has a boy friend and he is my friend. I will beat you!' -

Billy decided it was time to leave.

Lazarus was well-named. A creeping, cross-eyed creature who knocked on our door more than once asking for 'work, baas!' We had two servants: little old Peter, the cook, and Elias, the gardener. It is true that Elias had a spell put on his stomach by someone and had to return to the tribal lands for specialist treatment, and we never saw him again. The winter was coming on, and we decided to leave our garden, which never amounted to much, to lie fallow. In any case, we didn't like the look of Lazarus.

Billy had a dog, some kind of collie bitch, called 'Shereen', and she liked the look of Lazarus even less than we did. One day, when he crept up to the house looking for work, Shereen saw him off the premises. Peter saved Lazarus with a timely closure of the gate, but that did not appease the evil creature.

According to Peter, Lazarus then began to 'throw stones at doggie, bwana!'

Billy's Caledonian blood turned black with murder at this news. 'The next time that black bastard comes near the house, Peter, you tell me! D'ye understand?' 'Yes, bwana!'

It must have been shortly after that Shereen died. Nothing to do with the stone-throwing, but the loss affected Billy deeply and did nothing to soften his heart towards Lazarus.

Lazarus had the sense to keep away for a bit. Then one Sunday morning, while Billy and I were sitting up in our beds reading the Sunday newspaper, a tap came on the door. I went to open it. Outside was Lazarus. 'Work, baas?' 'No,' I said quietly. 'You better not come here. Bwana Doughty know you throw stones at dog.' 'No, baas, I never,' pleaded the shameless creature. 'You go quick!' I urged, and closed the door.

'Who was that, Warren?' came Billy's mild inquiry from his room. 'It was Lazarus.'

It was enough. Billy flung aside newspaper and bedsheet. He was dressed only in his pyjama shorts. He shot out of bed like a cannon ball, paused only to rattle open the door and bawl 'Lazarus!' just as the latter had reached the garden gate.

Lazarus then achieved a speed I would never have credited his twisted body with, streaking down the avenue with Billy in his pyjama shorts streaking barefoot after him.

After a minute or so, Billy became aware of a number of well-dressed Europeans also progressing down the avenue at a more leisurely pace on their way to church, many of them probably liberals who wondered, no doubt, what that indecent-looking white man was doing chasing that poor little black man. The pyjama shorts also did nothing for Billy's self-confidence, and before he reached the railway line, he gave up the chase. At least, Lazarus got the message and we never saw him again.

One night that winter, I was wakened by the 'music of two voices' in the house some time after midnight. I recognised Billy's tones, somewhat thickened by the 'hard stuff'. I also recognised a male African voice. This turned out to be a trainee manager Billy had taken under his wing at the club.

After doing the honours, Billy took on the didactic tones of Dr Livingstone improving his black congregation. Billy had evidently got out a record and started the record player.

'Now you listen tae this, Boniface, ma boy. This is Beethoven. I mean that's the man who wrote the music. Now listen weel, 'cause ye never had naething like this in your culture!'

'Thump! Thump!' I recognised the opening bars of the *Eroica*.

The first movement surged to its end after fifteen minutes or so. Another fifteen took us lurching through the funeral march; at least, it did Boniface and me, as subsequent events showed.

When it reached its dying fall and the end of that side of the disc, I heard only a persistent clickety-click. Of course, I well knew what had happened.

I got up. An embarrassed Boniface introduced himself, somewhat unnecessarily, and I de-activated the machine. Billy, of course, lay slumped in the arms of Morpheus.

It was a cold night. I spread a blanket over him, put some clothes on myself, and drove Boniface home.

Life with Billy had never a dull moment. He was due to go on long leave - to UK, of course. We threw a party the night before. Billy's plane would leave Ndola at 7am: an internal flight to Lusaka, the international airport, but a vital link in the chain, whose strength lay in its weakest link, etc. At any rate, Billy had to be at Ndola airport at 6.30am or all was lost.

The party was the usual such party, and sank in the same drunken stupor and chaos. I woke up next day with the sun - which was rather too late. Billy's alarm clock had failed, or not been heard, or more likely not been set. For Billy was none of your sober, taking-thought-for-the-morrow type of Scot. He had more of the wild Hielander in him.

The usual wreckage lay around me: bottles and dirty glasses, dirty plates, the remains of food scattered about, the furniture all over the place, the record player still clicking, a number of bodies that had fallen at their posts, a pair of legs sticking out from under the sofa, doors and windows left open - and no dog to guard us now. Yes! -

we discovered a burglar had been and lightened us of a few watches and wallets.

When I returned from the toilet, I glanced at my own watch which fortunately still lay at my bedside - 6am. We needed an hour to get to the airport. Should have left half an hour ago at the latest - up at most at five to pack. And there was Billy, still snoring like a pig.

I shook him. 'Billy! Billy! Wake up! It's six o' clock!'

'What! What! What's happening?' Then it dawned on him. 'O, my God! What went wrong?'

'Never mind. Let's get cracking!'

Billy leapt out of bed. We both threw on our clothes, for I had to take him to the airport. Billy packed his suitcase as fast as he could, looking for passport, money, etc, crying out all the time, with a sob in his voice like Gigli. Finally we were in some state to travel.

'Gimme the car keys, Warren!'

He thought my careful driving would never get us there.

'You're never driving any car, Doughty,' I insisted. 'You're too emotional.'

Suffice it to say that we got to Ndola airport about five to seven. We could see the plane on the runway, with the doors already closed, and some men about to remove the steps. The propellers only had not started to turn.

Billy leapt out of the car with a rapid 'Thanks! Good-bye, Warren! See ye!' He was aye the gentleman! Then he tore into the airport building.

God! I thought. How long would it take him to get through there? I was rapidly enlightened. Billy simply smashed through all the barriers, and immediately after, I saw him charging out of the other side of the building like a runaway bull in the market, clutching his suit-case, with two little men in peaked caps and smart uniforms running after him.

Then Mwari, the Rain God, clapped his hands. There was a sudden tropical downpour. This did not deter Billy - Mwari had done this for him! The two little officials thought about their smart uniforms and ran back for umbrellas. And that was their big mistake.

By the time they re-emerged, still struggling to open their umbrellas, Billy was at the plane. But the men there had removed the steps.

Billy dropped his suitcase, shoved the handlers aside and pushed the steps back to the aeroplane door himself, grabbed his suitcase and ran up the steps, where he banged on the door so hard the surprised people inside opened it for him - and the props already turning, for the pilot, naturally, was unaware of these events. Such is the force of personality!

The last I saw of Billy was when he disappeared inside the plane and they hastily closed the door.

I once said to Andy, 'Billy has all the passionate virtues.' The remark reached Billy who reflected, 'Ay, and nane o' the ither kind!' I don't know, but if we can't have everything in this world, I know which set I prefer.

I compared us to David Balfour and Alan Breck: Billy, of course, in the character of the dashing, if erratic, swordsman. One night, we sat on either side of the fireplace, reading; Billy re-reading *Kidnapped* from the Kitwe library in the light of my statement. He looked up. 'He doesnae gie me a very guid write-up, Warren!'

I last saw Billy when I left for UK at the end of my contract. I wrote to him, but never got a reply. This was no bad sign. Correspondence was not one of his virtues.

I heard later he had become a pastor in the Church. Best wishes to him! He would make a bonnie fechter for his Master.

2 - On Safari

In August 1971 I went with Piet and Margriet on a car journey through East Africa for one month.

They were a Dutch couple, he a doctor with the mine, she perhaps a nurse, I do not remember: at any rate, she did not work in Zambia. They were both tall and blond, and there the similarity ended. Piet was a thin, highly-strung type, liable to panic attacks, or, at any rate, bouts of excitement, like a disaster on a submarine. Margriet was a buxom, pretty girl of cow-like placidity (if the comparison with such a beautiful creature is permissible, which I do not see it is not) and was the perfect counterpoise to Piet.

We went in an old car of mine: a ten-year-old Victor. (I reckon the Vauxhall people should pay me something for this.)

This was not the first car I owned in Zambia. I started off with a BMW, second-hand, it is true, but still the most ambitious car I ever had in my life. Then one night I lent this car to Billy, like Davie Balfour lent the money to Alan; and like Alan, he blew it all in one night.

Coming home along Second Avenue, the great suburban artery of Kitwe, at five in the morning, Billy fell asleep at the wheel. At least, that is what I told the insurance man, and I am sure I was right. In fact, he must have been or he would never have survived the next series of events, even if he had been a professional stuntman.

First he jumped a ditch, missed a concrete lamp-post by six inches, knocked down a tree, did a somersault into another tree, slid down it, landing upside down, and after taking a short breather, crawled out with a small scratch on his face.

Somehow he got himself to the management hospital, and there I found him later in the day, sitting up in bed and looking as sorry for himself (or me) as Alan on the said occasion.

'Sorry about the car, Warren!'

I remember being worried about him, about a party we were supposed to be giving that night, and about the car not at all.

After making sure he was all right, I asked: 'Did you remember to order the glasses from the club?'

128

'Listen to him,' chuckled Billy, for other friends stood round the bed. 'The show must go on!'

Meanwhile, Piet drove to work down Second Avenue, recognised the wreckage of my car at the roadside and believed that Warren could no longer be in the land of the living. He ran into the hospital with tears streaming down his face, the dear boy, crying: 'Vere's Varren? Does anyone know vot has happened to Varren?' He was pleasantly surprised to find Warren in one piece, happily at work.

I had a look at the car in the garage. It was a write-off. The garage owner informed me that when he found the vehicle, the radio was missing. He was an Afrikaner. Most of the garage owners on the Copperbelt at that time were Afrikaners.

I called in to see Billy again later and told him about the missing radio. Billy was furious.

'I don't believe him, Warren. The lying bastard! The bugger's pinched it himself. That's just the kind o' trick those Japie bastards are up to. Ye're too soft, Warren! Let me handle it. I'll soon have it oot the bugger.'

I do believe he would have left his hospital bed there and then and caused a very unfortunate incident, if another visitor had not timeously arrived and informed us that he had found the radio missing before the garage people got to it.

'By Christ! These black bastards are like ants,' commented a somewhat mollified Billy. 'They're on ye afore ye're even deed.'

(It will be seen that Billy was politically incorrigible, thank God. His stock was humanity, not correctness.)

As soon as he got over his fright, Piet's mind, which moved as fast as Billy's in its own way, jumped to the next question.

'Vot about our safari, Varren?' Piet had done all the planning, but my car was to be used. I had to find another one quick.

And so it came about that a person in the Long Bar, a smooth-talking little man from Newcastle, negotiated the sale of the Victor, which belonged to a friend of his, for 400 dollars. (I got 2000 dollars on the BMW.) He said it was an old car, not a fancy car, but as a mechanic himself, he would guarantee it was a sound car. With the cosiness of an old family doctor he assured me: 'That car will take ye onywheer in Africa ye want to go!'

As the reader will discover, in a manner of speaking, he was right.

We loaded up the old Victor, an estate model; or rather, I put my suitcase in and Piet proceeded to load it. There was going to be no British muddling through: we had Dutch muddling through instead. Half the mysterious boxes Piet loaded in (I wondered if he was doing some gun-running on the side) were never opened. We had no room for extra drinking water, and the overweight caused eventual shipwreck. But I run ahead of my tale.

We drove down to Kapiri M'Poshi, where we found the Great North Road. This was the most notorious road for skidding in the rainy season and losing your bearings. At least it was well metalled but otherwise the most boring road in the world, unless the Sahara or the steppes of Russia have something to offer in competition. The same low Bushveld for hundreds of miles. Eventually we came to Chilonga mission, near Mpika.

Piet had been a flying doctor (full time) in East Africa, so knew many missions. They took guests without charge, but one was expected to leave a donation: two dollars per person per night was usual. A country hotel would have cost five dollars. But there you would have got a hot shower. The servants of the Lord spurned such luxuries, or could not afford them; so we coined a phrase: 'as cold as a mission shower'. We got plain beds in plain rooms, and three square meals a day.

We must have covered about 400 miles first day. And same next day, which carried us over the border into Tanzania, where the tarmac road immediately disappeared and the 'hell run', as the lorry drivers called it, began.

It knocked hell out of our old car, at any rate, and we barely limped into Mbeya. Here the mission was full, so we stayed at the hotel. Piet got the mission mechanic to work on our car, which they kindly allowed at voluntary rates.

The hotel was the usual lovely African inn: large airy dining room, lounge ditto, with battered armchairs and old magazines, thatched roofs and a wide veranda for drinks and chat, which in itself is one of the best pleasures of Africa.

When he heard at the mission of our arrival, Father Philippe Morin turned up and joined us in the sitting room. He was an old friend of Piet's. A tall lean sunburnt French Canadian, he looked more like a white hunter than a priest, and in fact told us with gusto about a buck he had recently shot. He invited us to join him at his own mission station, fifty miles away over the hills, at Lake Rukwa.

I think it took Brother Thomas a day to fix the car, so we killed time in the hill town of Mbeya, and after another night at the hotel, set off for Saza next day.

Here we saw for the first time the strange baobab trees, basking like fat giants in the hot sun. Someone described them as 'upside-down trees, with their roots in the air', for the bare crazy branches, hung with heavy fruits, are like that, and their bark is the grey hide of an elephant.

Philippe took us out on the lake in an outboard motorboat. We landed at an island where fishermen were camping. Their canoes were drawn up on the bank. They were curing barbel over a slow fire. Some of the barbel (which can live a long time out of water) were still writhing. Margriet made the fishermen knock them on the head, to the surprise of the fishermen, and Piet vigorously backed her up. Even then, some were still writhing, so Margriet kept them at it. Philippe and I said nothing. We weren't about to change Africa that day. And I do not know what fish feel: these were half-dead, already. I was getting harder since the fish eagle business at Ndola.

We visited the hospital, where there was a young Dutch doctor and his wife. Piet, the pig, persisted in speaking Dutch to his compatriot, who courteously insisted in his turn on replying to Piet in English for my benefit. It was a one-sided conversation as far as I was concerned, but I appreciated the other doctor's attempts to drop heavy hints on Piet.

While we were in the doctor's house, a young man in a bush-shirt and a hat with a leopard-skin band knocked on the door. He looked liked the blond hero of a South African film. He was not any kind of African. He came from Russia. He was an engineer working on some project in the neighbourhood, and was making a friendly call.

After we had all sat down with drinks in our hands, I raised mine to the Russian and said: *'Shchastlivo, tovarishch!'* I had learned some Russian in the army. Now I am a born mimic. People think I am good at languages. I am not, but I can get accents perfectly. And by the look on his face, I knew this young man, for a second at least, wondered if he was listening to a foreigner.

A shadow fell across his bronzed features, in which you could practically read the letters: 'K-G-B' - 'the shadow of the autocracy', in Conrad's words.

'Vi russki?'

'No, I am English,' I reassured him, unnecessarily, in view of my next stumbling sentences in the same language. 'I learned Russian in the British Army in Trieste, after the war. There were many Russians in Trieste at that time.'

'Tourists?'

'Refugees.'

He looked solemn. I explained to him about the 'victims of Yalta' and how those in Yugoslavia were not returned to Russia. (These people were the original refugees of 1917 and their children.) Feelings between the two tyrants had already soured, and Tito was only interested in killing his own people. When they fell out altogether in 1948, Tito indeed expelled the Russians, but to the West. All this of course was complete news to Sergei. Much of it was news to other people too.

We had planned (or rather, Piet had planned) to move on to Tabora, where there was another mission. This meant crossing the Pora - a hundred miles of desert. They got a young seminarian, called Oswald, to go with us as a sort of guide. One was recommended to carry five litres of water per person in case of breakdown. We had one squash bottle between us. In the event, we got through without difficulty, though we were stuck in deep sand several times and were glad to have Oswald to lend muscle, as well as for his company and knowledge of the country. Then, as we approached Tabora, the road 'improved' to rock-hard corrugations - the typical dirt road of Africa, wrinkled by the sun.

Piet had a theory, derived from the practice of the East African Safari drivers, he told me. Instead of limping along at our usual

132

twenty miles an hour (when the going was good), you should drive at fifty over these ribs, while rocking the steering wheel from side to side. This way you 'skated' over them. I tried this, and it was a very rough skate. Whether it helped the car, I do not know.

After staying at Tabora, we ran across the Highveld of Tanzania, wide, hot and open. For miles we passed hundreds of baobab trees, which looked like Don Quixote's windmill giants. This was the country where Williamson, another Don Quixote, but a sadder one, found a diamond and became thereafter the prisoner of his treasure, immured in solitary confinement for the rest of his life at the nearby mine, which bears his name. We did not try to visit this place, not wishing to be shot on sight.

We came to another mission near Mwanza, where we stayed with another young Dutch doctor and his wife. One night here and we moved on, catching an unsatisfactory glimpse of Lake Victoria. This lake is so surrounded with marshes that I have never had a decent look at it except from the air. And in the same day, we entered Serengeti.

When we were well and truly inside the great game park, there was a tremendous bang, and the car started taking a series of great leaps on its hind legs, like a giant kangaroo, as if it had completely forgotten what continent it was on. After about three such leaps it came to a stop. Piet, who was driving, went into his submarine disaster routine, and even Margriet said: 'O!' I, as usual, said nothing. Nobody can beat the British at a time like that.

When we got out, the car's guts seemed to be hanging out, from what we could make out by peering under it. We had thoughts of a night among the lions. It was about four in the afternoon: not the best time of day for a breakdown in Serengeti.

Just then a Land Rover drove up from the opposite direction, and a guardian angel in the shape of an Indian garage owner stepped out. He quickly diagnosed the complaint. The U-bolt on a back wheel spring had snapped (under the weight of Piet's kitchen sink or whatever), dislocating the prop shaft, which had acted like a vaulting pole. He could send his men out from his garage in Mwanza, now 100 miles away, to fix it next day.

We locked the car and got into his vehicle. We dropped off Piet and Margriet at the entrance lodge, and he invited me to stay the night with him in Mwanza, to pay the bill next day.

So I went with him, and after a substantial Indian supper, bed and breakfast, and paying the bill, I returned next day in the Land Rover with two of his workers.

Piet and Margriet were no longer at the lodge. The warden informed us they had spent the night there and got a lift in the morning to the main camp.

It was after four before Susi and Chuma (the ghosts of Livingstone's last bearers?) finished the job, and you can be sure I tipped them handsomely. I drove on to the main camp. The swift tropical night overtook me on the way. I spotted two headlights following me. People were supposed to be out of the park before dark, and these were escorting me to safety.

I found my friends at the main camp: Margriet slightly worn, Piet hopping up and down, complaining about a most awful sleepless night in a rondavel at the gate: 'bitten by rats and pissed on by bats'.

We spent a few days in the park. The usual animals: a black rhino out on the plain, a giraffe in the woods, a pride of lion lazing in the afternoon. All this from the official vehicle. Then on the road again.

And a terrible road! I described it in mental letters home as 'like a dry river bed'; then we saw such a river bed running alongside the road, which looked in better condition than the road, so we used that for a few miles until it parted company out of disgust with the dreadful road, which we were forced to resume.

Then out in the lonely landscape, we came upon a branch road with a sign: TO OLDUVAI GORGE 9 MILES. Sure enough, it ran down into a valley. We were sorely tempted to visit that cradle of mankind, but the road looked so terrible we despaired of getting back.

Soon we came to another great place, the Ngorongoro crater: a strange Garden of Eden, left by an enormous spent volcano, millions of years ago. An impossible road ran down here also, but the warning, FOUR-WHEEL DRIVE VEHICLES ONLY, was only too real, and we had to let it go. We got a limited view from the top of the road, but I was eager to climb the thirty-foot rim of the crater. Prudent Piet said, 'Look out for lions!', and he and Margriet remained in the car. I was nervous, but this did not hold me back. A short scramble up the grassy bank and I was looking into the great theatre below - the Greatest Show on Earth: 2000 feet deep and ten miles across. (If we had known then quite what a wonderful place it was, we must have taken a guided tour.) From my distance the wildebeest were like ants and the elephants like mice, the lions invisible. In fact, Piet's warning was unnecessary: the lions had everything they wanted down below.

And at my back the bulk of Oldeani filled a quarter of the sky - a landscape of the giants!

Next we entered the Manyara park, by underhand means I had not suspected in Piet. On the way we had come across a party in a Land Rover, calling themselves the United Nations Hydrometric Project. They were based in the park. Soon after, Piet told me: 'The locals only have to pay two dollars a day to stay at these game parks, and foreigners have to pay five, vich I think is a svindle.' I was not sure if his reasoning was just, but said nothing. 'Leave it to me,' he added.

We came to the gate lodge of Manyara park. Piet got out and announced to the warden in an important-sounding voice: 'I am Professor Von Glockenspiel, of the United Nations Hydrometric Project. I believe some of my boys came this vay.'

'O, yes, bwana,' confirmed the warden, and next thing they opened the barrier without extracting a single dollar from us. What's more, we spent two free nights in the lodge of the hydrometric men, who even seemed to think we had something to do with them, and treated us to a day's guided game-viewing into the bargain.

As I said, we were in the land of the giants. Next day we reached Arusha, where Meru greeted us, and later in the afternoon, the queen of them all - Kilimanjaro.

We must have been twenty miles away when on the north-eastern horizon a curtain of cloud began to lift, like the curtain of a theatre. What met our eyes was incredible. Step by step a vast green wall grew before us, filling the north-eastern sky and barely contracting to reveal the snowy crest, gleaming gold in the evening sun: Kilimanjaro, 19,000 feet high, fifty miles across, one of the most dramatic and majestic sights on earth.

We called at another mission, not to stay, but for Piet to look up old friends. Everyone was out except for a small African brother. Piet asked after the others.

'How is Father Francis?'

'He is very fine.'
'And how is Father Joseph?'
'He is very fine.'
'And how is Brother Martin?'
'O, it was very sad about Brother Martin.'
'Is he dead?'
'No. He is married.'

On the way to the coast, something fell out of the sump, and we had to fill up with oil every ten miles. Piet started moaning again.

'Varren, I don't feel I am on holiday. Ven vee set out vee vere spending von day in the garage and two days on the road. Now vee are spending two days in the garage and von day on the road. I think that guy svindled you ven he sold you this old car.'

'Think of Stanley and Livingstone, Piet. They didn't have it too easy.'

'But they veren't on holiday!' protested Piet. 'They vere doing it for a job!'

We stayed at a holiday camp on the coast called Kanamai: sort of Club Mediterranée, full of young people.

One day I went swimming. The tide was out beyond the coral reef, but I pressed on, climbed over the reef and plunged into the surf.

Then I noticed with alarm that I was drifting out to sea. The heavy wave carried me towards the reef, but the undertow drew me outwards, and the undertow was stronger than the wave. After each wave I found myself farther out. I vaguely remembered stories of people drowning in the surf. This must be the reason.

I turned and began desperately swimming towards the reef. The waves helped me, but the undertow that followed was a battle. Finally, a wave cast me onto the reef, where I grazed my legs badly and began to bleed. Happily, the next wave did not pluck me off again, or the sharks might have got scent of my blood.

I limped bleeding into camp, where Piet gave me a lecture about swimming beyond the reef.

We visited places on the coast. Mombasa, where we explored Fort Jesus. One of the Portuguese sailors of three centuries ago had made a beautiful carving of a caravel on a wooden lintel. Modern sailors would have carved something different, no doubt. *Autres temps, autres moeurs!*

We visited Malindi, with its narrow Arab streets and lovely white buildings. Here I parted company with my friends, who had taken two weeks more leave than me, and made my way home alone.

Down to Tanga, then Dar, where something happened to the gears, and I was forced to drive through the teeming city in first gear, with traffic building up and protesting behind me, until I could find yet another Indian garage.

Then back along the hell run. Morogoro only on the first day; the lovely hill town of Iringa on the next, like one of the hill towns of Spain or Italy. And another lovely African country inn to stay at: the White Horse.

Now I was among the Southern Highlands of Tanzania; not the giants of the north, but beautiful too, like the Highlands of Scotland, with the same rivers running in rocky beds in the valleys.

And so to Mbeya. I asked to stay at the mission, but the bishop had banned guests, except for their own people. Too many people had failed to make the customary donation. So I was glad enough to stay at the good old inn.

Back down to Chilonga, which was still taking guests. At supper a jolly clerical conversation took place.

'Doctor comes from just near me in UK,' announced Father Harrison. 'He comes from Liverpool. I come from Manchester.'

'I have heard of Liverpool,' commented Father Schmidt, 'but I have never heard of Manchester.'

Father Harrison eyed him narrowly. 'Cheeky booger!'

And so, after another boring 400 miles, I was running up the drive of my house, just after dark. All lights were on; music sounded; people everywhere; drinks, food: Billy had prepared a party to welcome home the weary wanderer.

In that old car I had covered a distance of 4000 miles, including some of the roughest roads in the world.

3 - Through the Congo

When I came to the end of my contract in Zambia at the end of May, 1972, I decided to make my way home through the Congo. Various men whose contracts were ending at the same time or who were going on long leave promised to go with me, excited by the romantic name, usually in their cups in the Long Bar. Next day, the now dreaded name made strong men blanch and remember previous commitments. One ex-Congo mercenary offered to accompany me - 'in a Ferret car' - but he was not free at the time anyway.

So, in the end, like the little red hen, I did it myself.

The Congo was then enjoying a rare period of calm in the years since its independence, and in the event I had no trouble at all. Most of the crooks in a country like that are in uniform, and robbing travellers by means of dubious or misused regulations is their main source of income. I did not realise it at the time but it later occurred to me that I had probably been taken for a priest, and as everyone knows, a priest is not worth robbing. For I was not travelling in the ancient Victor (which I had sold to Billy): the Congo being too ambitious altogether even for that resilient vehicle. I was entrusting myself to public transport: rail, river and air.

I looked like a priest for two reasons: my sole luggage was a battered suitcase, and I was wearing a black safari suit with long trousers - the only one left in the shop. Under the jacket, as it was winter, I wore a grey polo-necked sweater, which enhanced my clerical appearance.

Some effects I sent home in a box. I had given away a canteen of cutlery to old Peter, my cook. I had no books to send - those I had borrowed from the Kitwe library, and two I took with me to read on the journey: Barnaby Rudge and Martin Chuzzlewit, which I intended to post back when I got home. That left only my LPs, which I had not trusted to the box.

I took the LPs along to the post office, and asked for them to be sent by surface. 'Five dollars,' said the clerk. This sounded high to me. I asked: 'Is that surface?' 'No,' replied the clerk. 'Surface is two dollars.' 'And what's air mail?' He looked in his book. 'Ten dollars.'

'So what is this five dollars?' 'That's special post.' 'And what is special post?' 'That means we don't knock them about.'

I had been mistaken for a priest already in this ensemble at a party at the bowls club in Kitwe to which Billy and I had been invited. (And in Umtali before, if the reader remembers.) Mr and Mrs Gallagher from Glasgow were running the show. Mister was officiating behind the bar: Missus was looking after the eats and moving about, making sure everyone was happy. I got up to find the toilet.

Mrs Gallagher, a good Catholic herself, asked: 'Can I help you, father?'

When I got back to my seat I told Billy: 'Mrs Gallagher thinks I'm a priest. I suppose it's this black safari suit.'

After he'd got over his laugh, Billy called out: 'Mrs Gallagher. Would ye step over here a minute, ma'am?'

'Cool it, Billy!' I said, rightly suspecting some mischief.

'No, no, Warren! This is too good to waste.'

When she came over, Billy announced: 'I want you to meet Father Durand - White Fathers - doon from the Congo on leave.'

'Pleased to meet you, father,' said Mrs Gallagher; and I swear she dropped a curtesy. Then she rejoined her husband and had a word with him.

Mr Gallagher came rapidly to our table, wearing an apron. What followed surprised me in view of what had gone before.

Addressing me, he announced in a rough voice: 'Ony more trouble from you, mate, and ye're oot!'

His wife, who had been trotting behind him, quickly grabbed his arm and led him aside. Mr Gallagher came flying back.

'I'm terribly sorry, father!' he exclaimed. 'It's been a most unfortunate misunderstanding. The wife was telling me afore aboot some feller that was causing trouble, and I thought she meant you. Please forgive me, father!'

'That's all right, my son.'

I was given a lift as far as Lubumbashi by two friends, Pierre and his wife, Anne. Pierre was a Belgian doctor, Anne an English girl. Pierre was a small fiery chap with sandy hair. His pretty dark wife looked more Belgian than him.

He was normally the most good-natured little chap you could wish to know, but his fiery outbursts were famous. Once he had such trouble getting a line out of the hospital, I found him working the exchange himself, sitting in the box with the headphones on. The operator, about twice his size, was lying on his back in the corridor, like an immobilised beetle, where Pierre had thrown him.

We stayed at the Leo II hotel, where the Licops intended to make a week-end of it. At the bar we met another Belgian doctor, Dr Briac, who was district medical officer at Dilolo, 450 miles to the west and 24 hours on the train. He had come up to Lubumbashi (which was the provincial capital of Katanga, a province as big as France) to try and prise his salary out of the authorities. He was a tall lean man with, not surprisingly, a world-weary appearance.

We all had supper together. Dr Briac inquired of me in a lugubrious tone:

'Do they still eat mint sauce in that country of yours?' This required some explanation for Pierre's sake.

When I said, yes, Dr Briac continued: 'When I am in 'ell, I shall know it, because they will be eating mint sauce.'

Next day we met Pierre's uncle, by arrangement, who was also up in town. He was a priest at Manono, 400 miles to the north, and still in Katanga. He showed us the beautiful cathedral. And he expounded his interesting theory on the new name, 'Zaire', which Mobutu had thrust on his country, in place of its genuine African one, in the cause of something he called, in unblushing French, 'authenticité'.

When the Portuguese arrived off the mouth of the Congo river, 500 years before, said Pierre's uncle, they asked the locals what it was called. In the immemorial African fashion of answering a silly question with at least a simple answer, they replied: 'That's a river, bwana,' using the Kikongo name for river - 'nzare', which the Portuguese heard as 'Zaire' and printed on the ancient maps which had misled the good President Mobutu into imagining was the original name of his river and country.

I have said that most of the crooks in countries like Zaire are in uniform. The police especially were pests, stopping cars every five minutes and demanding international driving licences or other nonsense, and fines in default. I would get very hot under the collar, a reaction I realised later was fear. However, I never submitted to the indignity of paying a 'fine'.

Piet on such an occasion, when I was in Lubumbashi with him and Margriet, waxed more indignant than I did and demanded to be taken to the police station, a rash request which was fortunately refused and we were left alone: fortunate for if we had once got into a Congolese police station, it might have been a costly business getting out again in more ways than one.

Pierre had a smooth way with these people. He would step out of the car, call them *'mon capitaine'*, slip a dollar bill into their breast pockets - 'for the police ball' - and end by inquiring the way to save faces all round. Big smiles and old pals by the time we drove away.

I left my friends at the station, where I took the train for Kamina: again, 400 miles and 24 hours away. The Congolese trains then had four classes. Twenty years before I would have gone fourth class with the common people and their animals, struggling with my French and trying to learn Swahili; but as one of my old professors said, one does things at twenty one does not do at forty. I took a first class compartment, which I had mostly to myself. My main companion on the journey was Barnaby Rudge.

African trains (except in South Africa, which is another place) move slowly, covering about twenty miles in an hour, stopping at every halt. Here women sold food and drink to the poorer passengers through the windows. I used the dining saloon.

Katanga is Highveld, about 4000 feet, and the winter nights are cold. I slept fully clothed on my bunk. A blanket was not necessary. At one stage, when I was lying on my front, an attendant woke me to inform me that my wallet was sticking out of my back trousers pocket. Honesty!

The following afternoon I arrived at Kamina, the usual wide-open dusty small town of Central Africa. At the station a small boy with a handcart presented himself. This type of vehicle was later called a 'Scania'. It was practically a charity to employ him. I placed my suitcase in solitary state on his cart and followed him to the Hôtel de la Gare.

I stayed here a couple of nights, waiting for my next connection - to Kabalo. Round the bar after supper there were Greeks, Indians, and some of the posher Africans, enjoying their evening at the local. The first two groups spoke English, and made racialistic remarks in the freemasonry of the language about their black neighbours.

There were also two (non-racialistic) Americans present. One was a teacher making his way home: the other was a medic who was engaged in machine-gunning the villages with a vaccine gun.

Next day I walked about the town with Wayne, the teacher, while Hank was at work. We sat in the taverns, pulsing with the rather charming Congo dance music on the radio, and drank the famous Simba beer, the only beer I know (with the others in the Congo) so strong its bouquet hits you before it reaches your lips.

Next day, in the afternoon, Wayne and I took the train to Kabalo, another 400 miles; or rather, he was moving on to Albertville. Hank saw us off. The gates were closed until the train arrived so we stood about in the crowd outside. Then we were borne through in a mighty crush, and when we emerged from the bottle-neck (there is no platform) I found I had been painlessly relieved of twenty dollars and a biro from my breast pocket. I had taken the precaution of buttoning my back pocket. Thereafter, I placed my wallet in one of my socks and my travellers cheques in the other.

Twenty-four hours later, in the early afternoon, Wayne and I parted company at Kabalo, just after the train had crossed the mile-wide breadth of the great river - the Lualaba, the Upper Congo.

The great rivers of Africa, winding their mighty courses through plain and forest, stir me as few things can. The land opens and there it is, the great thing on its way. Dear God! I'd rather be a pagan suckled in creed outworn, so I could sing aloud.

Instead, I found myself in the wide dusty square of the seedy little town. The usual 'Scania' appeared and we proceeded across the square to the hotel. This looked very dubious and throbbed with rather too much Congo music for my taste as well as being full of drunks and tarts at three in the afternoon - where did they get the money from?

I needed some myself, after having been relieved of my small change, so directed the taxi to a Greek store, where I knew I could change a travellers cheque at a better rate than the bank, if such a thing existed in this place.

I found the owner half asleep over his counter. He brightened up somewhat at the sight of a white face and readily cashed my cheque. He was mightily amused when I removed the book from my sock. I told him how I had been robbed at Kamina. I asked about the hotel.

'L'hôtel, c'est merde. Vous feriez mieux rester chez moi.'

And so I did, for three days and nights. He had a small guest room and gave me most of my meals. When I came to settle up, he told me I could pay him on my next time through. To say that a fresh white face in such a place is payment in itself is not to depreciate his generosity.

After leaving my suitcase in my room, I went for a stroll around the town. I found a sign: *"Hôpital'.* I often dropped into district hospitals on my African travels: the sort of place I was aiming for myself, and where I was to spend most of my African career. I found the place, the usual small hundred-bed affair, a larger edition of Samreboi, and introduced myself to a medical assistant as a doctor from Zambia.

'Où est le docteur, s'il vous plait?'

'Il n'y a pas de docteur ici.'

He found me instead the person in charge, a European nun. When she discovered I was a doctor, I found myself doing a two-hour ward round.

I asked questions. Did they have a theatre? (In many African countries nurses perform major operations.) Yes, but the instruments were stolen during *les événements* (the troubles of '64) and never replaced.

Now I knew this hospital covered an area as big as a large English county and a population of 100,000. The nearest hospital which could operate was Albertville, twelve hours away (if the patient was rich enough or lucky enough to find transport), which is a long time for most emergencies. And that was on top of the time it would take them to get to the local hospital. It was obvious that for many the situation was hopeless.

I returned to the store. Before sundowners Spiros took me for a drive around town in his Land Rover. The swift twilight was falling. *'La prostitution s'allume dans les rues.'* Spiro called to a young white man on foot: *'Tu cherches la femme, mon ami?'*

Spiros told me of a mine disaster, where I had come from, he had heard about on the radio. It was not exactly where I came from: it was the Wankie Colliery disaster in which 400 died.

Before supper we sat with his French wife on the balcony overlooking the river, sipping our sundowners. They had no children. They spent as much time as they could in Europe.

'La vie est triste ici,' sighed Spiros.

I asked if they had television (which was available then in Zambia, though Billy and I never bothered with it). *'Ah, si seulement il y'en avait!'*

Next day he took me to meet another Englishman in the town, a large man from Newcastle who was working on the railways. He was living alone. He in turn took me to the house of a doctor. So there was a doctor in the town! The railway doctor, a little African from the Ivory Coast, whom we found sitting in his clinic.

Alas, the clinic was bare! He had a small patient with him, a little boy with a greenstick fracture of the forearm. The doctor had not even a sling to offer him. Now I knew what few European doctors get the chance to know, as fortunately what is known as the 'natural history of disease' is rarely observable in Europe (except in incurable cases): I knew that such a fracture would reduce itself by natural forces and the boy's arm be as straight as ever in a month. Small consolation to our doctor in his empty clinic!

I thought it would not have been beyond the wit of man to unite the empty-handed doctor with the doctorless hospital, which were both government property, but did not broach the subject. Besides, that would have meant re-equipping the hospital. The African hopeless feeling was beginning to get to me.

The doctor took me home with him for lunch, where I met his wife and baby girl. I told them about the Copperbelt, where I felt sure they could get a job. This seemed to bring a ray of hope into their lives.

After three days, Spiros's friend, the stationmaster, told me the train for Kindu was expected that afternoon. This was news to him as much as to me. He had not consulted the time-table, which was merely an academic document: they had told him over the telephone - at least they had that. So at three o' clock in the afternoon I found myself alone in my first-class compartment with Barnaby Rudge, waiting for the train to make up its mind to start. Through the window I could see a plaque, announcing to all who ran and read that the station was opened in 19-- by *Son Excellence, le Président des Colonies.*

Incidentally, as we got more and more up country, the trains became rougher and rougher, and this one was exceedingly rough indeed.

We got moving, and after dark, before I fell asleep, I was joined by one silent fellow traveller on our bunks, when the train stopped in the crowded station of Kongolo.

It was no more than my fancy, no doubt, but there seemed an aggressive air about the lamp-lit crowd. This was the town where the sixteen Italian airmen were murdered at lunch during the troubles. There was nothing unique about Kongolo. Kolwezi was to gain the prize for the biggest massacre of whites in Africa ten years later. Old, unhappy things, etc! And it is only the murder of whites we remember.

Next morning, when the sun rose, I found myself in *La Grande Forêt:* the high forest I had not seen since West African days. The same giant trees, the same fin roots, the same tangle of greenery, the same hot, wet air. When I moved to the dining saloon for breakfast and lunch, the windows lay open in the heart of the green grotto. There was good food and lager to be had on a clean table-cloth.

Then towards 6pm the train took a long high curve and below us was the town of Kindu, burning red in the evening sun.

I caught a 'Scania' which led me up the high street to the hotel, Le Relais. Here was a pleasant Belgian host and another English traveller, a young man, a teacher I think. After supper we wandered down to the river and found a couple of rather disconsolate-looking Indian traders sitting gazing at the water on what was evidently their evening constitutional. They brightened up at the chance to speak the tongue that Shakespeare spake.

Kindu was the railhead. My next journey would be by river. And sure enough, the boat was there next morning. I packed my bag, paid my bill, and without benefit of Scania, made my way to the quay where lay the boat.

And what a boat! A dirty little tramp, its lower deck stacked high with the logs which were its fuel; some palm oil drums and a single white man on the upper deck directing the loading. A smaller vessel interposed between boat and quay, and a perilous bridge of duck boards ran over all. The boat had side paddle-wheels and two barges in tow, and on her funnel proudly bore the letters: CFL *(Chemins de Fer des Lacs)*.

Presently I boarded with the usual crowd. We all paid two dollars, but as soon as the black captain saw me, the Great White Man, he installed me in a cabin on the top deck behind his own, which I could share with the engineer at no extra charge. He ordered a deck chair for me so I could sit outside under the awning. He and his family occupied the front cabin, and there was a bathroom between us. This was the extent of the first class accommodation, and I was the only white to travel on the ship: the other was a checker and would not come with us. After making sure I was comfortable, the captain joined the checker in busily stacking the black passengers into the bowels of the ship like sardines.

I asked about food and discovered none was provided. I flew back to the hotel and mine host seemed to find this amusing: the blighter! - he might have told me; or perhaps he was an absent-minded type like me. He hastily prepared a stack of sandwiches - enough to last three days, which was the duration of the journey to Ubundu. I ran back to the boat, but need not have panicked. I was to sit on my deck chair observing the scene for another hour before we moved.

Finally, after a lot of hooting the boat moved off, making a great curve across the mile-wide river to change direction to the right side. Now this surprised me considerably.

Up to then I had been convinced that Kindu lay on the east side of the river and the boat was pointing north. The opposite was true. Not for the first time, I had experienced the strange impression to those

146

born and bred in the opposite hemisphere of inversion. I had noticed it in Kitwe. Ask me to point to South Africa, or for that matter, merely Ndola, and I would point north to the Congo: ask me the opposite and I would do the opposite. For me the north was south, and vice versa.

(The same thing happens to our opposites. When years later I brought a Zimbabwean wife to England, and she went shopping with our small son in Liverpool, when she wished to return home to our flat in the south of the city, my wife insisted on boarding a bus for the Pier Head. My son tried in vain to get his mother to cross the street until she was at last convinced by the words on the bus. She may have been convinced but she was not reassured: in fact, she thought she was going crazy.)

I think this is because, as far as we northerners are concerned, the sun passes through the southern sky, and that is where we are aware of the light: in the south it is the opposite way about.

By afternoon we were sailing up the broad brown river, past the monotonous green wall on either bank. There were many islands in the river and, although the boat kept to the right bank, sometimes coming so close that we looked into the heart of the forest, like a green wonderland, the channel presented difficulties and a man crouched on a pontoon, dropping a plumb-line and calling the depth to the captain on the bridge; and like railway trucks, veering from side to side, the barges trailed behind. We saw canoes with men fishing. Otherwise, mostly the empty river and the blank forest. At one point, another river joined ours from the west, in the great drainage system of the Congo basin. The sunlight slept on its southern bank as it wound out of sight, incredibly remote, making the heart faint with loneliness.

People grew bold and came up onto the upper deck. Ladies sat in chairs while other ladies modelled their hair into balls, spikes, linking plaits, according to fashion or fancy. I sat in my deck chair with Martin Chuzzlewit (Barnaby Rudge parting company on the last train), and had already joined Martin and Mark on their similar voyage on the Mississippi. And as often I left off reading and gazed on the scenes around.

Before night we came to our first landfall - a palm oil station. The clearing hove in sight on the left bank and we swung across to reach it. It was a simple square half-mile or so cut out of the forest, with some works and simple company housing. On the bank stood masses and masses of drums of palm oil, like an army of black beetles or armoured Samurai; and beyond them a more intriguing sight. This was a mass of boxes piled up with a man leaning on each side like book-ends. These were the crates of beer and Coke bottles - the empties of the previous week, waiting with the palm oil drums to be loaded and replaced (except in reverse - the drums full and the bottles empty).

We drew alongside with the usual hooting, and I looked into the large crowd which had gathered for this weekly event. The thought crossed my mind that this would be a good place to escape one's creditors. In the crowd I saw a small blonde girl, about eight years old. She stood out among the black faces like a light or a lemon on a tree. Her skin alone was brown. She was not an albino (who are fairly common in Central Africa, more so than in West Africa), or she would have been as red and sunburnt as me: more so, in fact. She was a half-caste. But how so in this region where whites were almost never seen? I reflected, she could have been fathered by one of the mercenaries *(les affreux)* who fought through these parts (the dreaded Manyema) in '64.

I became thirsty. Was there water? There was a large tank with a tap. This was full of river water. Fortunately, I had a cup with me, or rather, a copper tankard presented *To Dr Durrant from his Colleagues at Kitwe, 1972.* I filled my gift, hoping that the water had been taken on away from human habitations, as I did not wish to die of typhoid in these remote parts and have my tankard (my familiar article) left on my grave instead of flowers, in African tradition.

Then the unloading and loading began. Men like ants bearing the large palm oil drums along the duck boards, up and down, to and from the boat and the barges behind. This went on after dark by the light of kerosene lamps. They were still at it when I fell asleep in my cabin. Some time in the night I woke to see the engineer creep into the bunk on the opposite side.

Next day the sun came up on the right bank, blazing white among the trees. I ate some of my sandwiches and visited the water tank. The captain asked me if I wished to take a bath.

I entered the bathroom and shut the door. Immediately, I was in complete darkness except for streaks of sunlight which entered round the door and through the cracks in the walls. I got used enough to the obscurity to run the water into the huge bath from its mighty tap: the water was cold so there was no need for two. The bath was plugged with a most curious device, a large hollow cylinder which fitted into a simple drainage hole. Strangely enough, I was to see another such bath plug later on my leave in a hotel in Aviemore, which has long since, no doubt, been tarted up out of recognition. And soon I was in my deck chair with Martin Chuzzlewit, the river and the forest.

And so it went on monotonously. Suns rose and set like fires among the trees. There were one or two more palm oil stations, with the same crowds and activity as before. At other spots, we stopped where people could buy food. I stepped ashore to stretch my legs but found nothing I could eat. At a larger place, Lowa, there was a tavern where one could get beer. A large lady sat beside me and tried to engage me in friendly conversation, but as she spoke no French and I had no Swahili, we made no progress. In fact, the only conversation I had was on the third and last day, when a plump girl who could speak French told me about Kisangani (the old Stanleyville, next stop but one) and recommended the Hôtel Stanley.

At one point on the second day, a gang of about thirty soldiers with FN rifles scrambled onto the boat, bound for some place downriver. They came onto the upper deck. As well as myself, there were the usual strays from the lower deck whom the captain seemed prepared to overlook, but he drew the line at these soldiers. He boldly ordered them below, rifles and all, telling them that the upper deck was reserved for first-class passengers, and they meekly obeyed. He was a tough little character, a sort of black Billy Doughty, equally fearless, if stouter. When one considers that a few years before, the soldiers would probably have shot him, thrown him to the crocodiles, taken over the boat themselves and run it into the bank, one could see that things had improved (for the nonce, at any rate) in the Congo.

On the third day we reached Ubundu, the end of the stage. After that, the river became unnavigable at Stanley Falls. One took a train from Ubundu to Kisangani. It was night and the captain recommended me to the home of the priest, the only white man in the town, and the usual 'Scania' led me there. Here I found a small Luxembourger in his white cassock. He was very pleased to welcome me, explained that he had already dismissed *'le boy'*, but prepared me some food himself. The last of my sandwiches were going green after three days and I had thrown them overboard and gone without lunch.

The father sat beside me while I ate. He talked as if he would never stop: how long since he had last had talk with a fellow white? I had difficulty following his eager stream of French. He told me about *'les événements'* of '64, and described with unChristian glee how the mercenaries had whipped the Simba rebels - *'paff! paff!'* I could understand his feelings, when one remembers what the Simbas did to the missionaries.

He showed me to my bedroom, complete with mosquito net. (Yes, they had provided one on the boat in my 'first-class' cabin, and, of course, I was taking antimalarials.) I offered to pay for my keep but he refused. In any case, I left the customary two dollars by my bedside next morning, but afterwards realised that *'le boy'* no doubt appropriated them. (Ah well, ye who now do bless the poor!) The father drove me to the railway station in his Land Rover, where I caught the train to Kisangani.

The train arrives at Kisangani on the left bank of the river, and to cross one has to take a canoe: not the small canoes I had seen in West Africa or on the river so far, but sixty-foot vessels with seating on either side facing inwards for as many as a hundred passengers, driven by an outboard motor. In one of these I sailed across the mile of water.

Kisangani (or Stanleyville as it was called by the people who built it) was the loveliest city I saw in the Congo. It was admitted on the West Coast, even by the Brits, that while we built shanty towns, the French and Belgians built European cities (I was to discover later the same was true of the Portuguese); and while this aspersion is not true of our people in East and Southern Africa, it must be admitted that

Kisangani was a small piece of Paris, planted 1000 miles up in the jungle. As well as the handsome Continental streets with their pavement cafes, there was a lovely promenade along the riverside. I found the Hotel Stanley and booked myself in. And when I unpacked my case, I discovered I had left Martin Chuzzlewit on the train.

It was sundown and too late now to re-cross the river. I did so next day. I noted the train was still in the station: these things do not move about Africa in the restless spirit of Europe. I went into an office where the usual bored clerk sat behind a large desk.

'Pardonnez-moi! J'ai laissé un roman anglais dans le train.'

He opened a drawer and pulled out the book in question. He studied the title.

'Comment est-il appelé?'

'Martin Chuzzlewit, de Charles Dickens.'

I signed for it, he handed it over, and the property of the Kitwe library was saved.

I had meant to take the next river boat: a considerably posher one, I understood (and hoped) for the next stage of 1000 miles (ten days) to Kinshasa, but through some confusion I missed the connection and had to travel by air. Otherwise, I could wait two weeks for the next boat to arrive: too long, I felt, to hang around Stanleyville.

So the following afternoon found me taking a taxi (not a 'Scania') to the small airport, a mile out of town, where the Belgian paras landed in '64, too late to save the hostages in the city.

As we flew out, I looked down on the Grand Forest: the ocean of tree-tops, clearings which contained small villages of thatched huts, the great rivers that glinted like reptiles. Then the swift tide of night ran in and all was swallowed in blackness.

At Kinshasa I stayed at the famous Memling Hotel. I strolled about for a day but found it a less lovely town than Kisangani. The planners had taken no aesthetic advantage of its site on the great Stanley Pool, which was lined only by docks and warehouses.

After two nights I boarded a Sabena jet, which flew overnight to Brussels, and got a connection next day to London. I had been abroad two years.

PART THREE - RHODESIA

1 - To Rhodesia

I now knew that Africa, or rather the African work, was my vocation, and as the reader will have gathered, I was aiming at permanent settlement, by which I mean wife, home and family. For reasons already outlined, I decided this was not possible in the expatriate situations north of the Zambezi. This left only the true settler countries of Rhodesia and South Africa.

South Africa seemed to me too 'civilised'. In work, I was a loner: at least I wanted to take on as much responsibility as possible. This may not sound like the altruistic motives we attribute to Livingstone and Schweitzer (who in truth were the most monstrous egoists), but as Schumann said: nothing of value is achieved in art without enthusiasm; and he might have been talking about medicine too.

Now, South Africa struck me as being suspiciously overdeveloped for my purpose. Hadn't Dag Hammerskjöld exclaimed: 'This is not Africa: this is Europe!'? I could see the place over-run with specialists, and the bush doctor like a GP in England. This is not to say that British GPs are not excellent people in their way; but their way was not my way. In fact, there were some wild parts in South Africa - notably among the 'homelands'; but they were not 'countries', where I could settle, more black backwaters. Besides, South Africa is rather a foreign country to an Englishman - very tight and Teutonic. Rhodesia, I felt, was altogether more relaxed and British. For to realise my complex ambitions, I needed people of my own kind. If I had been by nature a monk, work alone would have satisfied me, and nothing would have suited me better than an up-country mission hospital in the Congo. But I wasn't and it wouldn't. So I decided Rhodesia it was.

Rhodesia was then in a tricky position: an international pariah, after the Unilateral Declaration of Independence of 1965. I decided that as a doctor, I could stand aside from politics, and this I mostly managed to do. I was there as a settler, a serious person - no longer a sojourner. This, as with the other settlers of those countries, seemed to me its own justification.

People advised me to take a car as they were hard to come by in the country. In my ignorance, I chose a Fiat, which turned out to be unlucky as the most popular models were French and Japanese, and gave rise to difficulty in the matter of spares. Taking a car meant going out by sea, so I booked a leisurely twelve-day passage with Union Castle, and left on the Oranje from Southampton.

The voyage out was certainly more commodious than air travel, even steerage. There were all the usual facilities of such a voyage: swimming pool, deck games, bar, dancing in the evening, spacious dining-room and lounge, and no more then two to a cabin. And three good meals a day.

Each table seated about a dozen people, and at mine we had two unofficial entertainers we came to call 'Old Bill' and 'Young Bill'. These two were English South Africans: I think Old Bill had spent his early years in London but was otherwise as South African as Young Bill, a curly-haired young fellow of about twenty-two, who was born there.

And both Bills were rebels.

Your English South African rebel, as I have hinted, was not as fierce as the kind the Boers produced themselves, but was probably more entertaining. Old Bill and Young Bill spent every mealtime winding each other up over the shortcomings of their country and its system, and as much time in between as they found themselves together.

I first came upon them at it in the bar during sundowners when Old Bill was going on about their own prime minister, John Balthasar Vorster.

'The bugger wanted to drag us in on the side of the Nazis when the war broke out.'

'They put him in prison,' commented Young Bill.

'Prison! They should have shot the bastard.'

Some of the people at our table found this sort of thing less amusing than I did: one young English girl especially, who was emigrating, and did not want to be put off; wanted to judge for herself, as she said.

'They won't let you,' sneered Young Bill. 'You'll be brain-washed in six months.' He seemed to overlook his own remarkable exception, as well as his ancient companion's. Old Bill was about sixty.

At breakfast some sort of news-sheet was delivered to each place, which, besides world news, was heavily loaded with tidings of South Africa. Young Bill would peruse this as soon as he had secured his fruit juice and corn flakes, eager for more fuel for his revolutionary flame. So did old Bill, but he was slower off the mark, being incommoded by age and a fumble for spectacles. So Young Bill was usually first with the latest outrage. His style was satirical rather than angry: he laughed while Old Bill growled from his deeper disillusion.

'Ha! Ha! Listen to this one!' from Young Bill. 'Betsie Verwoerd says white parents should stop letting black nannies carry white kids on their backs, as they get used to the smell and break the Immorality Act when they grow up.'

A few mornings later he nearly choked on his cornflakes and had to extract one from his nose before he could share the fun.

'O Christ! What next! They are going to introduce apartheid donkeys on Cape Town beach.'

Now all this was very jolly, but the table next to ours seemed entirely booked up by the South African rugby team, to judge by its heavy Teutonic-looking occupants who, although they could not catch every word, seemed to be picking up unwelcome vibrations from our table. Electricity built up amongst them like a thundercloud, and one morning came a warning flash.

The most articulate of them (the rest seemed more devoted to deeds then words) growled at Young Bill. He ignored Old Bill as either beyond redemption or, being rather behind us in social advancement, they were not in the habit of molesting old men.

'We know what you're up to, Bill.'

Young Bill looked superior. 'I thought I was enjoying a private conversation,' he drawled, retracing the ship's course, so to speak, in his accent a few thousand miles towards Oxford, the more to annoy his interlocutor. His appeal for privacy was also a new departure for him.

'You're trying to put them off our country.'

Young Bill ignored them. It says something for South African standards that he came to no physical harm and was still on board at breakfast each morning.

I danced with a rather lovely Greek-looking girl who had been in Rhodesia. She described Gwelo (which was my destination) as a 'blink wunce tahn' - ie, blink once as you drive through and you don't see the town. There were such towns in Rhodesia (and in South Africa); but if Gwelo did not measure up to her Johannesburg, I do not think that is a true description of the capital of the Midlands Province.

(Incidentally, a 'town' in those countries is anything down to a garage, a hotel and a couple of houses, as long as it is occupied by whites. A 'village' is something with mud huts.)

And one morning we were in the magnificent harbour of Cape Town, viewing Table Mountain through a forest of masts. I looked over the gunwale at the quay below. I could hardly believe my eyes. In West Africa and Zambia I had seen whites, blacks and Indians. Here were men of all colours; and even when I got ashore I saw 'white' men in whites-only bars with crinkly hair, 'white' men with flat faces, and 'white' men with thick mouths. (I was seeing, of course, 'Coloureds', people of mixed race, but the mixing seemed to spill over the official boundaries.) In my first letters home I was writing that apartheid was not only immoral and unworkable: it was meaningless. This was a naive first impression, no doubt.

In the customs they inspected my modest suitcase. On top of my things lay a copy of *Cancer Ward*, with a bold hammer and sickle on it. 'I'll have to check that book, sir, with that sign on it,' said the customs man. I explained. 'It is an anti-communist book. It has been banned in Russia. It would be an unusual distinction to be banned in South Africa too.' He went behind the scenes to consult his 'Index' and presently returned with more out-going vibes. 'Yes, that's all right, sir.' By the time I had with difficulty re-packed my suitcase, he was postively friendly. 'You'd better buy a bigger suitcase with your first pay cheque, sir.'

I stayed at the Mount Nelson Hotel one night, and was off north in my Fiat in the morning. Jimmy Lennon told me how he had passed the same way many years before. After a hearty breakfast he inquired the way to Salisbury, Rhodesia. 'Just drive down that road for a week,' he was advised. By my time the period was shortened to four days: otherwise the advice held good.

I picked up a young white couple who were going to Johannesburg. Companions are usually an asset on the long and sometimes problematic journeys of Africa, though nowadays I imagine picking people up is more dangerous than it was. Pity!

Cape Town was ringed by fantastic mountains towering into the sky. I thought how my hill-walking friends in England would envy me such breath-taking sights under the glowing blue heaven. The road climbed quickly and I was among the green slopes and vineyards of the wine-growing country, which looks like the south of France, and where the Huguenots brought the first grapes; but before midday I had reached a very different country - the Great Karoo, a country of stone and coarse grassland, semi-desert, stretching 700 miles to the north-east and 500 miles north to the Kalahari.

I made the small country town of Victoria West by nightfall. My companions had a tent and went to a camp-site. I told them to meet me next day at the hotel, where I put up for the night.

After supper I took a short stroll. The sky was clear and starry overhead. This was October, the hottest month, but the Highveld was cool at that hour. One sensed the vast clean distances of the country.

Next morning the sole other occupant of the breakfast room was a middle-aged man: the clean, intelligent-looking type of the best Afrikaner. He looked like a schoolmaster, maybe. We had a word or two between separate tables then got together on the veranda after the meal. He was something of a 'liberal'. He said, 'There are white men in this town who cannot sign their own names, who have the vote, which is denied to an African professor.' He drew the line at some things like intermarriage as the offspring, he believed, suffered a loss of identity. I wonder how he found the new South Africa, if he lived to see it.

I paid my bill to the manager who first greeted me in Afrikaans: *'Gooie more, meneer!';* but switched readily enough to English when he heard he was dealing with a *Soutie.*

I picked up my friends, and on we went to Kimberley; after which the Karoo became more barren than ever. But soon we were on the wide grasslands of the Transvaal. The land rose to the cool of the Rand, and as night fell I got a photo of the moon rising beside a candelabra tree. I left my friends in Johannesburg and put up at the Celeste in Hillbrow.

Next morning I got a picture of that hustling, towering city from the top floor of the hotel: more like America than anything I had yet seen in Africa.

The third day found me in a country of strange hills, some cone-shaped, some hump-backed, called *kopjes* (pron, 'copies'). Then the road descended into the hot, steamy Lowveld.

Here I gave a lift to a young black woman, an educated woman, probably a teacher or a nurse. We did not have much conversation. She was very shy, and I was wondering if I was breaking the Immorality Act: just wondering, I don't mean I was afraid. Of course, I was not breaking the act, but it would have been regarded as strange and a little suspicious by the whites in South Africa and Rhodesia in those days, rather like two men sharing the same house, to say nothing of bed, in England since the homosexuals literally queered the pitch. I had the soft look of a missionary, besides being British, both of which would have excused me, as an object rather more pitiable than suspicious in local white eyes. However, much of the black girl's silence would be due to her own embarrassment, as people might have mistaken her part in the situation, not to her credit. I may say the lift was unsolicited and I dropped her in due course with, I felt, some relief on her part, and came after dark to Louis Trichardt, where I spent the night.

Next day I found what looked like a small French town, with its church spire rising among small wooded hills in the mists of morning. It was Sunday and strolling about I passed a small Afrikaner boy and girl, dressed in a kind of folksy style, on their way to church: their Sunday best, rather like something in Germany or

Austria. I longed to take a snap of them, but felt it a violation of their privacy.

And the same day I crossed the 'great, grey, greasy Limpopo' into the country that was to be my home for the next eighteen years.

On the Rhodesian side I met two young white men, who asked for a lift to Salisbury. They were from Zambia, and were looking for work in South Africa, but had been refused entry for some reason - perhaps their Zambian passports. One sat beside me, the other behind.

Presently we came to the Bubye river, a river of pure white sand now at the end of the dry season. It was so remarkable a sight I got out to take a picture. I wondered about leaving the keys in the car, but thought, perhaps quixotically, that it would be insulting to the honesty of my passengers to remove them. Besides, I reflected, they would not get very far in a country like Rhodesia, which although the size of the British Isles, was socially and economically speaking more like Wiltshire. The highly developed car-stealing industry which has grown up since independence did not exist then. My act would not have escaped the notice of two such sharp lads, and I wondered what they thought of me. Probably an old fool. It was not till many years later that I rediscovered a greater authority to support me, which I had forgotten: *'Il est plus honteux de se défier de ses amis que d'en être trompé.'*

We came to a motel, the Lion and Elephant: the usual lovely spread-out African inn. We ordered sandwiches and lager on the wire tables outside. I told the boys how it was impossible to get anything less than a five-course meal for lunch in South Africa, through which the Boer farmers and their wives worked their way with steady industry. The boys said, 'You're in a civilised country now, Warren.' They seemed to have it in for South Africa, after being refused entry.

On the road, as I got tired, I let the boys take a turn at the wheel; and did those lads enjoy driving the new Fiat! The needle stood at the top of the clock most of the time. As it grew dark, after Fort Victoria, they asked me if they were driving too fast. I requested, modestly, if they would stick to 80mph. If I had known about the stray cattle and kudu one could meet on that road, I would have kept them below that.

We parted in Salisbury, and I booked into the Selous Hotel. Next morning I stood on the top balcony and viewed the lovely garden city around me.

I reported to the personnel officer at the Ministry of Health. He had already recruited me from Zambia. On the wall was a map of the country with all the hospitals, including the district hospitals which most interested me. There were thirty-six at that time, and the name of the district medical officer was attached to each - the sole doctor on the station, though the larger towns might have one or more private doctors too. I noted that some of the posts were unfilled.

But first I was destined for Gwelo, the provincial hospital of the Midlands, as doctors new to the country were both vetted and given such extra training as they needed to equip them for their duties, especially those who had opted for district service, as I had, who were going to work on their own.

I spent another day 'in town' where I bought new safari suits, among other things. Next day I set off for Gwelo, where I arrived at midday.

2 – Gwelo

'Gwelo' was the Matabele name for what is now called 'Gweru', the Shona name. When the pioneers arrived in 1890 and established the modern country, they put the Matabele names on their maps (when they did not introduce English or Dutch ones), I imagine because at that time the Matabele dominated the country: the Midlands province lying in the Shona area.

Gwelo was a typical Central African town, built on a central grid pattern, with the oldest suburbs nearest the centre, then somewhat dilapidated and occupied by Coloureds and Asians. Further out lay more opulent and leafy suburbs where the whites lived. Here were two cathedrals, no less: Anglican and Catholic, and a large boarding prep and secondary school. And well beyond all were the African townships, which were sprawling and far from leafy, though the little houses each had a plot of maize and fruit trees - bananas and paw-paws. There were primary schools full of boys in khaki shirts and shorts and girls in cotton frocks (there were two African secondary schools in Gwelo); clinics with waiting crowds, mostly women and children; stark churches with tin roofs; and beerhalls pulsing with music day and night.

On arrival, I met first the superintendent, Dr Plato Mavros, who gave me lunch. 'Mav', as he was known to all his friends, including his wife, was then half way through a distinguished career. He was a man of medium height and build, and of Greek extraction, as showed in his regular features and dark, curly hair. His invariably calm, gentle manner contained a considerable force of character. His wife, whom he called 'Boo', was a tall, distinguished-looking woman of pioneer stock, and her husband's equal in character, although considerably more out-going.

There were about six doctors at the hospital then, only one a specialist: David Taylor, a consultant physician; though Mav was a skilled surgeon, in fact, a good all-rounder - the best type of African country doctor, the model I aspired to myself. David was also Rhodesian, about Mav's size, lightly built, fair and incisive.

The medical services of the country were then well-established on a model which, except for important developments which came later, which I will describe in due course, has remained unchanged, so it is appropriate to describe them here.

Then, as now, there was a state sector and a private sector. Then, as now, the state sector served ninety per cent of the population and comprised a quarter of the country's doctors. The private sector served ten per cent of the of the population and comprised three quarters of the doctors - a situation which has remained unchanged to this day, except possibly to the disadvantage of the state sector. This is the same throughout Africa. The reasons for this disparity are no doubt personal as well as economic; but the governments could neither match the incomes nor maintain the numbers of the private sector.

As far as other services went, I must not forget the mission hospitals which lay more or less in the state sector. Other hospitals were industrial or private - both in the private sector. Private doctors had access to private beds in the larger government hospitals, which had a separate section for Europeans. The government doctors had some white patients, such as police and the 'pioneer pensioners' - the impecunious descendants of 'pioneers', who were defined as persons settling in the country before 1900. There was also a public health service which came under the state and municipalities.

Gwelo hospital had then about 300 beds. It covered the Midlands Province, which was as big as Scotland and had a population of about 750,000. The province was divided into eight districts (including Gwelo itself), each of the others having a hospital of about 100 beds and one doctor, covering an area as big as a large English county and an average population of 90,000. These figures will stagger anyone familiar with European medical services: for instance, in UK, one GP serves 2000 people, and has access to complete specialist services. And Rhodesia was the most highly developed country south of the Sahara, bar South Africa. How was the impossible balancing act performed?

I have already limned the great African principle of elevation of responsibility, and how it works from the grass roots upwards. The grass roots in this system - primary health care, where the patient

161

makes first contact with the service - were the medical assistants, the mini-doctors heretofore described. These people did the work of GPs and hospital house doctors in England in the district and provincial hospitals: not forgetting the maternity aassistants, who were rather more than British midwives. And alongside them worked the nurses and general hands.

In charge of the medical assistants (MAs) and nurses were the state registered nurses (sisters). These were usually ward sisters and acted as administrators. They existed in delicate, and sometimes invidious, relationship with the MAs. The sisters were 'officers', the MAs 'employees'. The sisters received more than double the salaries of the MAs, but lacked many of the skills they asked them to exercise.

The MAs formed the filter in which major cases were separated for the attention of the general doctors, in district or provincial hospitals, who were trained to deal with most of them, in medicine, surgery, obstetrics and gynaecology, paediatrics, etc, at registrar level in England; but across the board, not separately. Few cases would be referred by the doctors to the specialists: a difficult hysterectomy, perhaps, but certainly not a caesar.

The provincial hospital was supposed to have a full complement of specialists: that is, one in each of the core specialties, but rarely did. At the time I joined there was no gynaecologist, so I was given the job, under Mav's wing, which was a broader one than mine as far as obs and gynae went, and all other things besides.

In the townships and out in the country were clinics and small rural hospitals (run by nurses - a term I shall use in future to include MAs and ordinary nurses), which dealt with patients like general practices and cottage hospitals in England, and could refer cases to the district hospitals (including Gwelo in its own district). These represented the primary health care level. I shall have more to say about them later.

Small charges were made at government hospitals and clinics for outpatients and admission, which could be waived in cases of indigence at the discretion of the superintendent. Private services were covered by private insurance.

I was given a house in the hospital grounds at nominal rent (a married man with lively youngsters would have paid four times as much), and a cook recommended to me. Anderson was a Malawian who was retiring from the hospital kitchen. In his servant's jacket and trousers and bare feet (in the house), he was a cheerful little soul. He lived in a *kaya* at the bottom of the garden. His wife lived in one of the townships to secure his base there. His grown-up children had long since left home. Stove and fridge were provided. It wanted only to furnish the house at my own expense.

'Boo' offered to go shopping with me, rightly suspecting that a woman's guidance was needed. She took me to a good but moderate store and proceeded to equip my house with practical sense and lively good taste. After dining and lounge suites, carpets and curtains, we came to beds. I eyed a monastic cot. Boo said, 'O buy a double bed. You're bound to get married, and anyway, it's much nicer sleeping in a double bed.' Sheets. I fingered some white shrouds. 'Don't be so British!' commanded Boo. 'Candy stripes!' she ordered, from the attentive Mr Saddler. She brought me luck: through her orders and her prophecies, in one way or another, I have slept in a bed of roses ever since.

Mav put us in various departments and moved us around every six months to save us from the ruination of specialisation. And each night two doctors were on call: a junior with a senior to fall back on.

One night I was on call with David Taylor, when a man walked out of a beerhall under a train, which went over both his legs. He was going to need a double amputation. Neither of us had done one before but we were not going to drag Mav from his much-needed rest: that is not the way of Africa, as the reader will have gathered by now. I volunteered to mug up the operation from the bush doctor's surgical bible: Hamilton Bailey's *Emergency Surgery,* while David resuscitated the patient with a view to giving the anaesthetic.

The patient had of course taken his own 'premedication' at the beerhall and a good deal of the main anaesthetic besides, so in fact, David kept him comfortable with intravenous pethidine and Valium, an invaluable tool in Africa.

I took off the first leg below the knee, a proceeding which took me about an hour. Then I changed gown and gloves and returned to the theatre, saying to David: 'Now for Henry the Fourth, Part Two.' (The seeming frivolity which sometimes affects surgeons about their lawful occasions is, of course, a cover for emotions which are by no means frivolous.) I amputated the other leg above the knee, which took me even longer.

All went well and I saw the patient in a wheelchair a few days later, with the undefeated grin of Africa on his face. He was of course no longer my responsibility, being surgical. I think they fitted him up with something in the way of peg-legs and crutches.

We were joined by Willy and Kate, an English couple. Kate was a small dark, very pretty woman with a special knowledge of anaesthetics. Willy was half way to being a gynaecologist. Nevertheless, Mav let me work out my six months in the maternity department, true to his system.

Willy was a short stocky man with a black fan beard, who looked more like a trawler skipper than a doctor, and had chronic difficulty in looking 'presentable'. He did his best for a court appearance - in sports jacket and flannels, a black shirt which might have been discarded by Mussolini, and a rustic-looking tie. The prosecutor took one look at him and addressed the magistrate: 'Excuse the doctor's appearance, your worship. He has just come out of the operating theatre.' As Willy had done no such thing and the prosecutor had no right to say so, Willy was rather ruffled, but recovered enough to tell the tale against himself afterwards.

We worked hard and were on call one night and one week-end in three, but had leisure to get around. I explored the surrounding country with Willy and Kate. We did a round run to Bulawayo and Shabani and back, via Selukwe - three hundred miles, which shows what can be done in Africa in half a day. We had supper in Shabani in the big bare hotel. After the meal we took a stroll in the dark empty main street. My heart sank as I thought how lonely it would be as a bachelor in a dorp like this. Little did I know that within a few years I would be district medical officer here, come to call it a 'sweet little town', and find a wife there.

I went fishing by myself. There were some lovely dams around Gwelo and though I caught little, it was very pleasant to spend an afternoon among the sights and quiet sounds of the high open country. Sometimes little clouds sailed across the hot sky of summer, and I had recourse to an umbrella to save my skin. Other days were as grey and cold as Yorkshire (or seemed so), under the peculiar drizzle or Scotch mist of the country, called *guti*. But always lovely places alone with space and nature.

Coming home from one dam along a dirt road I skidded (something one can do as easy as on a wet road, which I did not know), and after a few turns, ended up in the ditch. Typically, I had lost my bearings. It was night. I found the Southern Cross and quickly reorientated myself. The car was bent and undriveable. Some passing Africans told me I was fifteen miles from Gwelo, too far to walk, and directed me to the farmstead of Mr Pringle, whom I found watching his Sunday night telly. He kindly took me home, and we even got a garage man to rescue my car, which they assured me would otherwise be minus wheels by morning. They had to send to Italy for spares, and for five months I was 'without wheels' anyway.

That year was a drought year, and one burning morning succeeded another as I showered and breakfasted and enjoyed the equally sensuous monotony of Delius's Cello Concerto on my record player. Very pleasant for me, but I little knew what a threat to life it was to the poor people in the tribal lands. The country was well-managed, and there was 'corn in Egypt' for the dry years, but even in Gwelo I saw the effects of malnutrition: a little boy on the verge of blindness from measles, whose sight I was able to save with a single dose of vitamin A.

I noted, not for the first time, the originality of African parents in naming their children. In Zambia, one 'Disgusted, Bongo Bongo' had complained to the Times of Zambia about 'this practice of giving our children these ridiculous names derived from the culture of our colonial oppressors. How can anyone achieve dignity in life with a name like "Motorcar"?' Needless to add, 'Disgusted Bongo Bongo' was a name conferred on the writer by himself and not by his parents.

These names would be plucked at random, it seemed, from the hedgerows of experience. A simple visit to the supermarket might result in such christenings as 'Weetabix' or 'Fairy Liquid' (the later a rather lovely name for a girl, though it was mostly the boys who were the subjects of such exotic experiments: the girls, as the carriers of tradition, I suppose, usually bearing such old favourites as 'Dorcas' and 'Rebecca'). A mechanic visited northern Zambia, left his handbook behind, and returned a year later to find a number of little 'Carburettors', 'Chokes' and 'Big Ends' - all boys, of course. In West Africa I met a 'Keyboard' Ankrah, and, in Zambia again, Andy Crookes collected a 'Durex' Musonda: acquired accidentally, perhaps!

Popular names for boys were 'Hitler' and 'Stalin'. Knowing nothing of the details of those distant squabbles of the white men, African parents of the time yet recognised that these names represented powerful figures in their own circles, and the God of Africa is the God of Power. It amused me later, in Shabani, to greet my clerk each day with: 'Good morning, Stalin!'

But top of my own collection were the three little boys I found before my desk one morning in Gwelo clinic, all in Balaclava helmets, for it was one of those cold days you can get even in summer on the Highveld: each one smaller than the last like Russian dolls. Their mother, who sat behind them, presented their cards. I could hardly believe my eyes. 'Are these their names?' 'Yes,' replied Mother, simply. They were: 'Anyway', 'God knows' and 'Breakfast'.

3 - Marandellas

One day, after six months at Gwelo, Mav told me I was wanted at Marandellas, as acting superintendent, no less, as the senior doctor there was on long term sick leave. Marandellas was a 'general hospital', a breed now extinct - really a glorified district hospital, augmented with an extra number of European beds, to be found in small towns with a larger than usual white population. These white beds were used by private GPs of whom there were a number in the town, apart from those occupied by the white government patients already mentioned. The hospital had an establishment of two government medical officers, including the superintendent. I made the journey with Anderson by train (my car being still in dock) - I first class, he fourth class: myself at government expense, Anderson at my expense. Not that I was too mean to buy Anderson a first class ticket, nor was the section banned to Africans. I knew where he would be most comfortable.

When I arrived at Marandellas hospital, I stayed in the nurses' home for two weeks until I was able to find a cottage nearby to rent. There was no servant's accommodation, so Anderson found a bed in the township and came to my house on his bicycle. I was to stay at this hospital for twelve months, though when the super returned I reverted to number two. In the meantime, a succession of locums helped me.

Three Scottish sisters arrived at the same time, but like the girl in *The Nun's Story* they were not happy to be assigned to the idle European hospital where they felt, quite rightly, they were under-used. They all moved later to Bulawayo where they more active and happy.

Marandellas was always my favourite town in the country. At 5500 feet it was the highest, with the possible exception of Inyanga in the Eastern Highlands. It was on the crown of the Highveld, with vast sunlit views of fine grasslands and distant avenues of tall blue gums on the white farms. The landscape was broken by many stony *kopjes,* and winter and summer, the air was clear and bracing.

167

The town itself was small - I called it 'Stow-on-the-Veld', for a number of reasons, not least because it had the largest percentage of Britons in the country: around the bar in the club they outnumbered the Rhodesians. They were mostly old, and I used to say it was a sort of elephants' graveyard where all the old 'Poms' went to die. It even had something in the town centre called the 'Green', which was usually brown, and most of the shops were built around it, apart from those on the main Salisbury road. But it was the usual spread-out African town, far more spacious than anything tucked up in the Cotswolds. There was a number of leafy avenues in the town itself, but houses spread out to a distance of seven miles - each fifty or a hundred yards apart, in up to ten acres of land. Even the township, Dombotombo, looked cleaner and more picturesque than most.

Marandellas was famous for its schools, both government and private, all of which were modelled on the English prep and public school system, and mostly European. There were good African schools in the country, but not one tenth as many as were needed. Beyond all spread the European ranches for about thirty miles, and beyond them, the African tribal lands.

In those lands the hospital covered two 'rural hospitals' - another Rhodesian peculiarity: more than a clinic, as it had beds, as many as fifty; but was run by medical assistants. The doctor visited weekly, and saw cases. Emergencies were sent to the main hospital, after calling the ambulance from that place.

And scattered throughout the district were small clinics run by the local authority, which were supervised by the provincial medical staff. These could refer patients to the main hospital with free bus vouchers. Emergencies at night had to find their own way usually in the car of the local headmaster, unless the clinic had a telephone and could summon an ambulance from the main hospital.There was a clinic also in Marandellas township, run by the local authority.

At Marandellas I did my first brain operation, having assisted Mav at them before: a man with a head injury with signs of internal bleeding. These cases can last a day, and they can succumb in an hour. Potter of Oxford had written: 'Some emergencies are relative: this one is absolute.' And as to the surgeon to do the operation - 'the

168

first one competent to do so' - a principle long abandoned in specialised Britain, with some notorious disasters as a consequence.

I could have sent this case to Salisbury, an hour away by ambulance, except that I had found you must add two hours to the time of the journey to include the preparations at either end. And the man could well have died in that time. Fortified by Potter's philosophy, I ordered the patient to theatre.

This did not please Sister Fleet. Sister Fleet was a highly competent nurse, and a very pretty girl besides (though no doubt that has nothing to do with the matter), but she was the type who would argue with the doctor. No African nurse would do anything so unwomanly (with one or two exceptions I have met, and pretty unsavoury specimens they were). Now I was never too proud to take advice from any quarter, high or low, (or in between), but I simply did not agree with Sister Fleet, quite apart from her manner of delivery, which was sharp.

I drilled the necessary hole, evacuated the blood and sutured the bleeding vessel, and had the feeling I was winning, when Sister Fleet poked her head round the theatre door.

'He could have been in Salisbury by now.'

To this nobody replied. Besides myself they were all Africans in the theatre, and Africans are not in the habit of making unnecessary remarks.

'Besides, you're using the wrong instrument.'

She was wrong. I was using a burr. Perhaps she was thinking of a trephine, an instrument I saw even specialist surgeons use later. I tried it myself, but found it a clumsy tool. At the time, I was not sure, so said nothing. Besides, it was not the time for a debate on the subject.

Sister Fleet and I got over our tiff and became good friends - especially after I left the hospital. And most important, the patient made a good recovery.

Then disaster. I was doing a caesarean section, when the nurse anaesthetist put the breathing tube down the wrong way. I got a live baby, but the mother died two days later from brain damage. In cases like this, the senior carries the main responsibility. Unless one knows one's staff very well, one should always check their work - a principle I was to learn here the hard way.

There was an inquest before the district magistrate, when I and the nurse appeared, and I, of course, had most of the explaining to do. The courts were always very understanding towards medical people, and the matter was not further referred. Patients and relatives would show equal indulgence.

This is not to say that the guilt/blame nexus is absent from African culture. As I have said, nothing is supposed to happen by accident, and some source of spiritual interference is sought for, either a witch or an offended ancestor. But the doctor is rarely blamed or suspected - an attitude, I suppose, we owe to its careful cultivation by the witch doctors themselves over the centuries; whose business, of course, is to impute (or deflect) the blame. Witchcraft was never a crime under colonial law (which did not recognise its objective existence): to accuse anyone of witchcraft was - a position all African countries, to my knowledge, retain to this day. So a discreet witch doctor would stick to ancestors.

Where a wife was lost, a husband would quickly find another; African reasons for marriage being more practical and less romantic than ours. (The man who danced round the theatre in Ghana found a new wife within months; nor was this a reflection on the sincerity of his grief. Among the poor, love - and hate - comes through propinquity rather than inspiration.) When a woman is widowed, it is not so simple.

Sometimes her brother-in-law is obliged to marry her and take over her children. In other customs (conspicuous in Rhodesia/Zimbabwe, where there are pressures to change them), the widow is stripped of everything by the dead husband's family - house, property, children - and sent back to her own people.

A woman was run over by a bus at the terminus. Her leg was crushed below the knee. I thought it impossible to save and said I would have to amputate. She cried and refused. The nurses worked on her and she dried her tears and bravely accepted.

When she was resuscitated and under the anaesthetic, I felt a pulse in her foot. That and a nerve are usually all that is necessary to save the limb. I went to work with a medical student on attachment to the hospital (David Hurrell). We cleaned up the wound and even managed to close the skin without tension. We set the leg in plaster. (Later, I would learn how to apply traction through a pin in the heel.) Imagine the woman's joy when she came round! It was cases like that which made me glad I had come to Africa.

One night an old man was brought in with a distended abdomen, vomiting and absolute constipation - nor gas nor faeces. I knew what this was before the X-ray confirmed it. Not only the intestinal obstruction, which any British surgeon would have recognised by this point, but the special African kind - primary volvulus, either single or double. The first type is rarely seen in Western Europe: the second never.

A volvulus is a twist in the large or small bowel: a double, or compound, volvulus is both together, in one enormous knot. Why the latter is so common in Africa (the district doctor sees two or three a year) nobody knows.

I could, of course, have sent this man to Salisbury, where there were specialist surgeons; but I knew I was going to be in remote places, where it would behove me to be confident. I decided to do the operation myself, with David assisting.

When I opened the abdomen, I could see nothing but a pool of black gangrenous bowel, and felt like closing it again there and then in despair. I explored and found healthy bowel. Then I went ahead.

First one excises the affected section of large bowel, then the same for the small bowel. All this I did, and the nurses measured twenty feet of black small intestine, leaving about six feet behind. People can live after such a loss, though they never again have a weight problem! I joined the healthy small bowel to the large bowel, and then I turned my attention to the gap in the large bowel.

The proper thing to do next is to bring it out to the surface in a double-barrelled colostomy, and come back in six weeks when all is clean and healthy, and close it. In my ignorance, I closed it there and then.

Next day, the old man was leaking faeces from his wound. Something had obviously broken down inside. I sent him to

Salisbury, where the surgeon saved him with the colostomy I should have done in the first place.

I went up to Salisbury to see my patient, and met the surgeon, who gave me a friendly and instructive talk on the subject. This surgeon was a brilliant if fiery young fellow from South Africa. I later learnt that he fell out with the anaesthetist during an operation. In true colonial spirit, they doffed gowns, etc, and settled it with a punch-up in the corridor outside, before returning to finish the operation. Of course, they were carpeted by the 'headmaster', but kept their jobs, which I doubt they would in England - or even Ireland nowadays!

And once a week, as I said, I visited the rural hospitals, a hundred-mile morning run in a van, and in my car, when I got it back: the dirt roads in that district being in good condition.

First stop, Chiota, with a great crowd of patients standing outside, or packed on the veranda if it was raining. I would see only selected cases, then do a ward round. So on to Wedza. The little town of Wedza looked like a Mexican village in a spaghetti Western, complete with the Happy Hotel, a two-storey shack. The hospital lay outside the town, and in the distance, Wedza mountain, a large *kopje*, glowed like an amethyst in the fresh morning air. Wedza provided no food, so the grounds were always full of relatives at their cooking fires.

And as in Ghana, I considered the first purpose of my visits was educational. This principle ran through the service from top to bottom, and from bottom to top, as the doctors could learn from the nurses about local customs, etc.

So the doctors attended annual refresher courses at Salisbury or Bulawayo, staying two or three nights at good hotels at government expense, and getting pumped full of information every day: and given protocols. There were protocols for everything from obstructed labour to meningitis. And the district doctors made up their own protocols for the simpler activities of the rural hospitals (not forgetting the splendid auxiliaries' handbook produced by David Taylor): though those 'simpler activities' included the management of typhoid and malaria. And all maternity units, rural and urban, used that wonderful invention, the Rhodesian partogram.

Many practical contributions to modern medicine have been first developed in Africa: such as the rehydration salts, now familiar to every British mother; and the under fives' road to health chart (less familiar because its main use in Britain must be keeping children's weights down). But the partogram is the most ingenious.

It consists of a large chart which records the progress of labour, and is crossed by a warning line which prompts the midwife to seek medical aid if the graph line reaches it. It contains much more information, such as the foetal heart gradings, which were all explored for the first time in Rhodesia, sometimes in tragic circumstances, when the mother refused caesarean section, and the doctors sadly discovered every milestone on the baby's road to death. This chart is now used throughout the world.

When a mother, transferred in prolonged labour from one of the clinics, arrived at the hospital at night, the sister on duty had only to read out the chart to me over the telephone and I could order a caesar if necessary and snatch an extra hour's sleep while they got ready.

Only by such rules of thumb could the system be run so efficiently with non-specialist staff. And by broad standards, efficient it was.

One morning I arrived at Chiota to find a lad of sixteen on a stretcher, rocking himself up and down, moaning and holding his head. Before I did the lumbar puncture which proved it, I guessed he had meningitis. I filled in a head-sheet and told them to call the ambulance from Marandellas. When I got back from my rounds in the afternoon, the lad was on treatment, and in a few days made a full recovery.

We saw meningitis commonly: say one case a month; though never the massive epidemics of the drier regions to the north in Africa. It was most satisfying to treat: this killer disease, which, a generation before, left the doctors helpless; though we sometimes got cases brought in too late, which we were unable to save; or were left with some defect, the saddest being a little boy who turned out to be blinded.

And in Marandellas I had a case rarely seen in Europe - a full-term abdominal pregnancy, where the baby grows to full size outside the womb - obviously, an ectopic which survives. I saw six cases during my twenty years in Africa (only one of them my own), when six gynaecologists in Britain would hardly see one between them in their whole careers.[1]

The midwife called me to a case of foetal distress (baby's heart slowing) in early labour. It needed a section. When I opened the abdomen, the first thing I came down on was the baby itself, a full-grown healthy girl. I could not understand it. I thought I had cut too deep - into the womb itself. Then I thought she had a ruptured uterus, and the baby had escaped through the tear and was luckily alive. At any rate, I extracted it, cut the cord and handed the babe to the midwife. Then I followed the cord. It ended at the placenta (afterbirth), which was stuck to the outside of the uterus, itself enlarged to thirty weeks' size and contracting as in normal labour.

Now this case I had studied in Lawson and Stewart *(Obstetrics and Gynaecology in the Tropics)*. No ordinary British textbook would have helped me. And Lawson and Stewart, as I remember, said: 'if the placenta is attached to uterus or adnexae, it should be removed, *together with these structures'* (my italics) - otherwise it should be left inside, to be absorbed naturally. The sight before me bore out their advice. The placenta had made a deep erosion in the uterus, which itself, as it contracted, was shedding the placenta and pouring blood from the erosion. I remembered with gratitude the subtotal hysterectomy Andy had taught me in Zambia, and instructing the nurse who was assisting me to apply a towel to the bleeding area, performed it there and then for the first time. It was the mother's first baby. She would never have another, but she had one healthy child, and her life was saved.

Then a sadder case. A little boy of about ten, with a perforated typhoid ulcer and advanced peritonitis. As he lay back on the pillows, his face sunken with the disease, his mother and father sitting in silence on either side of the bed, I knew the case was hopeless. Nevertheless, I resolved to try.

---

[1] The first ever in UK was seen in 2008. WD.

I resuscitated him as best I could and ordered him to theatre. I started the anaesthetic myself, but it was too much for his heart, which was affected by the poisons of the disease. He went out like a light as soon as I injected the Pentothal.

I walked back to my house. I passed the parents, sitting on a rock, the mother silently weeping. I did not approach them: it seemed intrusive. But I broke down myself. I had to remove my glasses to wipe my eyes. They saw my tears. I hope they got some comfort from them.

Among all his other commitments, the district doctor was also the police surgeon. Our duties were defined by the request forms the police presented to us: assault, rape, postmortem and drunken driving. For reasons of economy, the first two were included on the same form, and to the question: 'Weapon used', in cases of rape, the simpler African constables would faithfully enter, 'Penis'.

Postmortem requests were mostly for suspected murder. These murders would follow the most trivial causes, as recorded on the police forms: 'He knocked over somebody's beer'; 'He picked up somebody's change'. A stabbing would follow and a postmortem on Monday morning. At Gwelo, Willy received a simple report: 'Found on her way home from a beer-drink with her head cut off'. The PM did not take him long.

Although so forgiving in most ways, the people seemed to have no forms for propitiating offence (or perhaps it is something they have lost, as we British seem to; and moreover, as indicated, these murders usually took place under the influence of alcohol). One saw this daily in the clinics, where there was often trouble with doorways. Sometimes the pecking order was clear: women gave way to men; lower gave way to upper classes. Age was no privilege (or no longer, perhaps), especially if joined to poverty. More often the issue was obscure, and an ugly scuffle would result, which never failed to irritate me.

And for my part, I got so used to African nurses, male and female, standing aside for me in doorways, that I sometimes forgot myself and preceded white sisters, which gave rise to comment. Then a Belgian female specialist, who was by way of being a feminist, confused everything by refusing my deference and standing like Balaam's ass in every doorway.

Capital punishment existed, but for premeditated murders only, which never in my experience involved Africans (except later, as the emergency developed).

And one day I had a postmortem with very strange connections.

I always referred to it as the '*muti* murder', meaning one committed to obtain *muti* (medicine) from the corpse, for purposes of witch-craft. The victim was usually a child (presumably for its purity), and the medicine was made from the internal organs by the *n'anga* (witch-doctor) to bring luck, usually to someone's business venture, such as a new store.

This murder was not of that kind: indeed, it did not begin as a *muti* murder at all.

The police brought in the body of an elderly man, which had been 'found in the veld' and had been dead about forty-eight hours. It was winter time, or even by then, decomposition would have been far advanced in those latitudes, and the postmortem difficult, as well as distasteful.

The most conspicuous injury was that the face had been removed. I thought it might have been torn off by an animal: a hyena will do this to a sleeping victim. But the policeman said they suspected foul play; whereupon I set about performing a meticulous examination: the only way of avoiding a bad time in the witness box in due course.

Sure enough, although there was no other external injury and no fracture of the skull, on opening the cranium, I found a bleeding around the brain. This was a sure sign of head injury, and allowed a presumptive diagnosis of death from brain laceration.

A few months later, I was called to the High Court in Salisbury. There were two prisoners in the dock: an old woman and a man of about thirty. After hearing my evidence, the judge invited me to inspect exhibit A, which was a wooden stick.

'Could that object have caused the injuries you found on the body of the deceased, doctor?'

'Yes, m'lud.'

Thereupon he ordered the male prisoner to be stripped to the waist. He asked me to walk over to the dock and inspect the prisoner's back. There I saw a vertical scar, about a foot long.

'How old would you say that scar was, doctor?'

I made an uneducated guess. 'About three months, m'lud.'

'Show the doctor exhibit B.'

Exhibit B was a large knife.

Could the injury you see on the male prisoner's back have been inflicted with that knife?'

'Yes, m'lud.'

I noticed another exhibit, 'C', a bloody shirt with a long gash in it. I was not asked to comment on this.

I got the full story from the local police the following week. On the night in question, Father, Mother and Son had been sitting round the fire outside their hut, very cosy, talking, telling stories and drinking doro (maize beer). Evidently, they took too much of the latter, as a quarrel broke out between Father and Son, in which Son picked up a stick and hit Father over the head with it. Father fell down. Mother hurried to examine him and found him to be dead.

Now Mother was a *n'anga* and told Son, we are going to have trouble with Father's spirit. She took a knife and carved off most of Father's face, put it in a pot and boiled it. When the soup was ready, she made Son drink it as a prophylactic against any postmortem operations on Father's part. When Son had taken his medicine, the ever-thoughtful Mother said they had better make it look like Son's action was self-defence against Father's previous attack. 'Turn round!' commanded Mother, and using her all-purpose knife, gave Son a great slash down his back.

These actions seemed to account for all the evidence. I think Son got eight years and Mother three as an accessory.

At Marandellas I visited the prison, a duty of government doctors, to be described in more detail later.

Marandellas was an open prison, devoted to farming, where the better behaved offenders were kept. Two of my patients there were the notorious 'terrorists', the Chinamanos, a husband and wife team; though anything less terrifying than Josiah Chinamano, a bespectacled little schoolmaster who read Dickens, would be hard to imagine. He became a minister in the post-independence government. His wife was more formidable (though always charming to me), and became a powerful voice in the same parliament, to whom the term 'independent' applied more aptly than to the institution itself.

The superintendent was 'Taffy' Darnley, a little Welshman, who will not object to his name appearing *en clair* as his cover has already been blown by an even more famous terrorist, Judy Todd (as she then was). Taffy stands as a dreadful warning to authors. Even compliments failed to please Taffy: quite the opposite.

I have not read Miss Todd's book, but I understand it refers to the time when she was Taffy's prisoner, and she describes him as a very decent man who mitigated to some extent the horrors of the Smith regime - that sort of thing.

Now Taffy did not see himself as a 'decent man'. He saw himself as the terror of the earth. Saddam Hussein was less well-known then or Taffy would have placed himself in that league, way past such bland figures as General Pinochet. He voiced his indignation long and often in the bar of the Three Monkeys hotel in the town.

At Marandellas I experienced my first real African winter. Winter in Zambia is a few cold nights in June/July, and in West Africa, the fresher breath of the harmattan. Winter in Rhodesia was the real thing: temperatures down to zero, but so dry I described it merely as 'sports coat weather'.

But first came the autumn: the grasslands growing tawny and then white, the woodlands grey-green; migrating swallows gathering in thousands on the telegraph lines, the departing white storks flocking on the veld.

And then, almost in a day, a strange change in the light. A poem I wrote at the time will serve better than my memory.

The mellow autumn sunlight of southern Africa
Stands like champagne on the land, bringing the exhilaration
*   of champagne,*
Charging the blood with soft electricity, making it race and tingle,

Filling the lungs with soft fire.

The snowy light is like silk on the skin,
Blanches the rooms within the houses:
Light with a touch of snow, so one feels the country leaning to
  the Pole.

'A 'diamond light', as Ransford calls it:
Certainly, the soft burning of a diamond,
Veiled with a touch of gold, causing dense bronze smoky shadows.

The air is changed,
The brassy sky of summer gone high and soft, standing like
  water behind the emerald hills.
The earth stands still and clear like a heaven:
Almost one could touch the leaves on the distant trees.
The dainty feet of the donkeys and the wheels of their little carts
  scarcely ruffle the white soft powder of the roads.
The evening air is sharp with the scent of wood fires.

So, even Africa pauses!
Even she receives this cleansing bath!

And so into winter, when the soft light hardens into the 'dry white season', and sometimes the south-easter brings grey weather and even a drizzle of *guti*, and it is very miserable. The men huddle in their greatcoats and balaclavas, the women in their blankets and woolly caps. And the children in similar headgear and such extra rags as their parents can give them.

But the winter is mercifully short. In the single month of September the brief spring has exploded in the high summer of October.

First, in the cold days of August, the scarlet flowers of the kaffirboom appear on the bare branches. Then the white clouds of the knobby thorn, the yellow shower of the wild pear. And then the whole country changes as the msasas 'burn red to green'. Yes, the commonest tree of the Highveld does the opposite of its northern cousins. The new leaves are red as an English autumn; but they are not about to fall: they soon turn green, and the false autumn to spring.

In the towns the exotics bloom: the red fires of the flamboyants, the mauve clouds of the jacarandas, the ivory petals of the frangipanis; in all the avenues and gardens.

And then the long anxious wait for rain: the thunders and torrents of November.

Always in Africa one was close to nature. The hot smell of the earth. The rain crashing down like Victoria Falls, after a preliminary bombardment with atom bombs. Once I was caught in my car on a dirt road and had to stop with visibility down to zero in the downpour: at least one is safe from lightning in a car. The thunderbolts fell around me like depth charges round a submarine.

And above all, the sun. I was returning in the small hours from a late night party in Salisbury, when the sun came up quite suddenly over the veld. I stopped for a leak: when I finished I walked towards it. It was so glorious, I found myself in tears. It was like an ultimate revelation. I had companions in the car, or I would have opened my arms and breast to him and cried aloud, like an Aztec or Inca of old. But it was enough: I had seen the glory of the sun, and it stayed with me many days.

By November I had been employed by the ministry for twelve months and was entitled to leave. I decided on a safari to South Africa and Mozambique.

I set off on one of those cold grey days which even in the Rhodesian summer could remind an Englishman of home, and by late afternoon had come to Fort Victoria, where I put up at the hotel.

Here some horrible woman was abusing the old waiter. 'You are stupid! You 'ave always been stupid! What are you?' The waiter said nothing but went on with his brushing. The other people in the lounge looked embarrassed, but buried it in their newspapers or their conversation. This was definitely not the Rhodesian way: or at any rate, the Anglo-Saxon way. The Affs came in for more of it from the Dutch breed, to which this woman probably belonged.

It was a folksy belief among both Anglo-Saxons and Afrikaners that the Africans preferred the Dutch brutality to the Anglo-Saxon hypocrisy; and indeed, an African once told me so himself. I don't think the matter is as simple as that.

There is a bond between master and servant, as there is between husband and wife, which will take a lot of abuse; but if there is no bond, or it is betrayed, then real hatred can fill the gap. It was these cases that got targetted later in the Civil War. But again, life is not so simple. A lot of good people got targetted too. But I must not run ahead of my tale. I will only say, one felt no such bond in the present case.

Next day, across the border, and to a town in the northern Transvaal, called Warden. This was solid Boer. I booked into a hotel. I put my foot in it right away when I thought the barman had an English accent, and with all the simplicity of Noddy, asked him if he was English. He served me without another word.

After the usual hearty supper, I retired to the lounge, which was soon taken over by a lot of men and women in their best clothes, who proceeded to execute an ungainly sort of folk dance to a record player, in which I was not invited to join. If a sore thumb can take an armchair and pretend to read a book, that was me. I took myself off to an early night with Churchill's *Second World War*: that other prisoner of the Boers!

Next day, Johannesburg, where I stayed in a small hotel, and the day after, had great difficulty getting myself off the famous ring road that runs round that city. I was heading for the Drakensberg. I ended up in some Coloured area. Thank God, it wasn't Soweto, or I might not have got out alive.

Then I came, on a dark wet afternoon, to the Wagnerian mountains of the Berg, and put up at the hotel Mont au Sources under the shadow of the Amphitheatre.

This magnificent terrace of the giants was glowing in the evening sun as I contemplated it with the young man who worked at the hotel as guide.

'What about doing it tomorrow?' I asked brightly.

'How far away do you think that mountain is, sir?'

'About five miles.'

'Actually, it is twelve miles, and takes two days to climb it; that is, if you are young and fit:' with a glance at me. 'Otherwise, more like three, or even four days.' One loses all sense of scale in the vastness of Africa.

'What I suggest, sir, is a gentle walk up to the foot of the cliff and back. That makes twenty-four miles, and will take us all day.'

Which we did. A party was made up next day, and he led us up the valley of the Tugela river, higher and higher, with the landscape opening up, with its enchanting views, wider and wider around us, in the glowing light of the summer morning. And soon it was hot work. We were happy for the cool of the gorge, where we had lunch by the river. Further up, we swung on a chain ladder across the gorge. Until finally, we were under the towering crags that sailed in the moving sky. Then the long, pleasantly tired slog homewards.

I spent a few more days here on the lesser slopes, then on to Durban, from where I took the road to Swaziland and on the way picked up a young Englishman, Rufus. He was an agricultural student who had been gaining experience on a South African farm. He was a big country-bred lad and a public schoolboy.

We saw little of Swaziland, before coming to Mozambique, where we crossed the Motola river and were in a different world: the lazy, decadent, Latin world of Portuguese Africa.

Lourenço Marques was a beautiful Mediterranean city with handsome streets and pavement cafes. We also noticed the astonishing beauty of the mestizo women: one in a government office, behind her typewriter, I could not take my eyes off and thought about for days: sort of Sophia Loren, only more tropical. And I introduced Rufus to the *fado*.

I had heard records myself, but never the real thing. There were many *fado* clubs in the city, and we went to one every night and heard the plangent singing, with its incomparable blend of nostalgia, gallantry and consolation: *saudade,* in the Portuguese - one of those untranslatable words.

Up the coast to Inhambane, where we stayed, took an evening stroll and found a small obelisk in the square; and on a plaque, set in the ground: *Aqui é Portugal.* I wonder if it is there now.

The Portuguese were there for four centuries, and always called themselves 'Portuguese'; never suffered a sea-change into 'Rhodesians' or 'Australians', etc, as the British do.

We came to Beira, where we stayed. In the evening, Rufus and I sat in a cafe, waiting for the *fado* to begin at nine o' clock. That was on the upper floor, and we waited meanwhile in the bar, where were a number of tarts. One sat alone on a stool, advertising her wares, when a gang of Portuguese soldiers came in. They surrounded her, while the corporal questioned her - evidently about the price. It rapidly turned to the third degree. A slap across the face. Too much! Think again! The girl sat sullenly, saying nothing. More slaps, more demands, until finally the corporal grabbed her beads and twisted them until he nearly choked her. Still too much! Finally, he ripped the beads off and flung them across the room.

All this was too much for the English public schoolboy in Rufus. He got up, walked over to the corporal, took him by the scruff of the neck and marched him under his brawny arm to the door, where he threw him into the street.

I quietly removed my glasses and watch, anticipating trouble and making ready to go to Rufus's aid.

Rufus returned to his seat. The rest gathered round us and let off a lot of steam. We stared through them with cold English stares. Presently, they gave it up and marched out after the corporal.

Meanwhile, the girl sat like an Egyptian statue. What she made of Rufus's action, I have no idea.

After a night in the Eastern Highlands, I took Rufus to Salisbury on his way to England. Then back to Marandellas and work for me. Anderson had taken a holiday at the same time.

4 – Umvuma

I had been a year in Marandellas when early in 1974 I saw that the post of district medical officer at Umvuma was advertised in the customary notice circulated to all stations. This was an established post and therefore one applied for it: government medical officers, or GMOs (the term here used in its specific sense, like second-lieutenant), were simply ordered about. I applied. As usual, I was the only applicant and was appointed. I was to stay here a year, before fate (or something) moved me on.

I had been doing the work already at Marandellas and have sufficiently described the duties, but now I had the official title - for me, the finest medical job on earth: in that position, I would not have envied the most famous specialist in Harley Street, nor did I.

I walked into the bar of the Falcon Hotel at sundowner time and announced myself. I was to stay there two weeks while they got my house ready. After I had been shown to my room and deposited my bag, I joined my new friends and patients in the bar. For I was the only doctor in the town and was monarch of all (medical) I surveyed.

To be more exact, many of those present would attend private doctors in Gwelo or even Salisbury. As there was no private doctor in the town, according to regulations I could establish a private practice myself, which would have augmented my income considerably. I couldn't be bothered. They could come to me anyway, and many did for the usual government fee.

The hotel was for whites only, like most hotels in the country then; but if race was a problem in Rhodesia, social class was not. Round the bar, which was crowded with the Friday night regulars, I found myself and Jamie, the agricultural officer, representing the professional classes; Jock, from the Gorbals of Glasgow; Bill, from the Falls Road; and Tony, the scion of a noble English house, who died recently a peer of the realm: all British and all on first-name terms, when we would probably never have met in our own country. For when in Rhodesia, the Brits did as the Romans (or 'Rhodies') did, and all white men were literally and metaphorically members of the same club.

As well as Africans, there were Indians in the town, who owned many of the shops in the arcaded streets - the usual grid pattern being here reduced to its minimum of two streets crossing two others - and lived around the secret courtyards behind them. There was also a Portuguese cafe, whose owners kept to themselves as, like the Indians, they were not invited to do otherwise. The Greeks had made it by then to the white man's club, but not the 'Porks'. They did so later when their own colonies collapsed and Rhodesia needed them. Already, the government had scraped the slums of Naples and Barcelona in 1973 for ' a million whites by the end of the year', and had not found them. And after the war, they had sent home thousands of Italian prisoners of war who wanted to settle, because only British were wanted.

These things you could discuss with people like Mav or David Taylor, who were part of the twenty per cent liberal vote. Most of these lived in Salisbury. Few of them lived in Umvuma, so the discussion would have been unprofitable there, to say the least - and I've hardly mentioned the black question. It serves no purpose to rub people up the wrong way: I meant to live in this town and you got on best with people by approaching them on their positive side.

Beside the Falcon Hotel, the town boasted the district commissioner's office, the police station, post office and telephone exchange, two small churches (English and Dutch), and a swimming pool (whites only). There was the club (ditto). There was a backyard gold mine with a tall defunct chimney which could be seen ten miles away, and served as a sort of symbol of the town, which lay off the main Salisbury road to the south on a branch road to Gwelo, fifty miles to the west. There was a small leafy suburb and a small African location. There was a small ramshackle Coloured township, called Blinkwater. And there was a small railway station.

This lay on the Fort Victoria-Gwelo single-track line. The train left Fort Victoria one day, via a 'blink-once town', Chatsworth, then Umvuma: another 'blink-once', called Lalapanzi; and so to Gwelo by evening: next day, the same in reverse order. At each of these places everyone, including the crew, got down for drinks, tempered by a bar lunch at Umvuma. One could see why the trains were restricted to a speed of twenty miles an hour, quite apart from the many dry halts in between. At Umvuma, the stationmaster himself was by no means standoffish, and while he usually received the train in his official capacity on its arrival, it was frequently flagged out by his fourteen-year-old daughter on its departure.

The hospital was small - 100 beds - but had the usual facilities, including operating theatre, as did all district hospitals. It lay below the tracks near the location. It admitted Africans only, but had a European clinic. The only other white on the staff was June, the secretary.

June was a tough little spinster of about fifty, with a tanned, cheery face, who lived with her old father in an old house near the hospital. She had been born and bred in Umvuma and was a pillar of local society, especially at the club where she played bowls. She was an independent spirit and was afraid of no one.

Too independent sometimes for my comfort. She handled the mail. One day I received a letter from head office which began: 'Your offensive letter of 25 ult refers', and went on to deal with matters I had never heard about. I took it through to June, whose office lay outside mine. 'What's this about, June?'

'O, that's some nonsense I thought you couldn't be bothered with. I just wrote back and told them if they wanted to know they should get off their fat butts and come down and see for themselves' - all over the subscription: 'Squiggle, pp District Medical Officer'.

I would see the European patients in my office, where I had installed a couch. They waited on the veranda outside June's office and she called them through. The previous doctor had given them a very different service.

I suppose he had engaged in private practice because he was a family man; but Dr Blood, in spite of his formidable name, was a very nice man who lived in terror of his white patients. June told me how the week-ends, when they were most likely to have their road accidents, were a nightmare to him. I would cut up a white man with as much relish as I would cut up a black one (and I hope I treated both like the Queen of England). I positively looked forward to a juicy road accident, black or white; and to have to send a patient to a specialist was like cutting off a finger to me. I even talked of opening up a windowless store-room as a 'white ward', as if any of them would have stayed a day in that prison. But I can understand Pete's fear, as the whites were more likely to bite the hand that cut them (so to speak) than their black brethren. Years later, I went through a bout of litigation fear, myself, and I know how unpleasant it can be. Then I decided that the only thing a doctor has to fear is his own conscience, and that is bad enough, in *all* conscience. So I was able to separate the two, and dismiss the other. But far be it from me to give poor Pete, or anyone else, a lecture - even if I have done, as the Irishman said.

But Pete ran a clinic at his house, which I could not be bothered with, especially as I was not charging for my services. The DC had a quiet word with me about this in the club. 'People much happier with Dr Blood's arrangement. Didn't feel at ease in the African hospital, etc.' I explained politely the inconvenience to me, and forgot about it.

June was aware of these feelings: she knew everything that was going on in the little town. Fortunately for the DC, this particular complaint never reached her ears or she would not have hesitated to give him a plainer explanation than mine.

Like the case of the police reservists. As the emergency developed, the local farmers entered the police reserve - voluntarily at first, I think. Wholesale conscription came later. They had to have vaccinations, so June marched them into a convenient room and instructed the black MA to get on with it.

At the club the following Saturday night, one of them complained to me about this: 'Serving the country, etc. Expected the doc to do it.' This time the complaint did reach June's ears: she was standing nearby. I didn't have to say a word: I might have been a West African chief with a 'linguist' to do the job for me.

June planted herself between me and the complainant: a number of fellow complainants were standing behind him, and all got the full treatment.

'What sort of a bunch of bloody pansies are you lot then?' she opened up. 'Do you think no one can touch your lily-white skins except the doctor? Do you think the doc's got nothing else to do? The medical assistants do the vaccinations; are perfectly capable of doing them; always have done them; and always will.' And that was that. June could have been the matron, and a formidable one too.

As Hermanus was the next to find out. Hermanus was a farmer, who called the ambulance out for a sick worker. Fair enough. But when the ambulance driver arrived at Hermanus's house, he found the 'sick worker' lying down on the ground outside, very dead. And obviously dead since some time before Hermanus telephoned. The ambulance driver explained that it was against regulations to carry a cadaver in the ambulance. Hermanus retorted: 'I'm going to check with the doctor. 'He walked into his house, walked three times round the table and came out again. 'The doctor says it's OK.' The perplexed ambulance driver felt he had no choice, but he complained to June. He knew who to complain to.

Suffice it say that Hermanus got a very plain lecture in the club next Saturday on the uses and abuses of ambulances, and June didn't care how many other people got the benefit of the lecture at the same time.

Another thing that 'got June's goat' was when whites, especially women, asked her if she didn't feel 'at risk', all alone in that 'Kaffir hospital', with the doctor not always at her side and sometimes out on his rounds. '"At risk"!' June would snarl in contempt. 'Why the hell should I feel at risk? They are perfectly civilised people. I've known them for years and I trust every one of them.'

Astute as she was, even June could be deceived by the serpent of rumour. Japie van Blerk was the only Afrikaner I knew who looked like a leprechaun. He was red-haired, skinny and small. His sharp eyes stood closer to his thin nose than most other people's. His portrait may be seen as 'Sly', the goblin, in the sanitised (de-golliwogged) editions of Enid Blyton's Noddy books. He was a district officer cadet, and supplemented his slender salary by giving lifts in government vehicles to Africans at fifty cents a time: a concession to African custom (among them lifts were always paid for) in which his professional obligation to educate himself would not have excused him, because, needless to say, it was clean against regulations.

Although born and bred in the country and fully aware of its peculiar ways of thinking, when he took over his small government house, he installed a female black cook instead of the usual male one. This led to a good deal of ribbing at the club and the bar of the Falcon.

One night, at the latter place, he turned on his latest tormentor, a large policeman, and punched him on the jaw. Instantly regretting his rash action, he turned tail and fled from the pub. The enraged policeman followed.

It had been raining. The policeman slipped in a puddle outside and continued his journey feet first before nearly knocking himself unconscious on the pavement; Japie meanwhile making good his escape.

An imperfect version of this story reached June's ears, and next morning she informed me: 'That little Japie van Blerk is tougher then he looks. Did you hear how he knocked out Bertie Kriel outside the Falcon last night?'

My house was on the edge of the town, on a hill, and overlooked the town and the green ocean of the veld beyond. Once again, as I sat on my veranda with pipe and drink and book, I thought I was looking south, until I took a look at the map and found it was the opposite.

The house was probably the largest DMO's house in the country. It had been built for a former mine manager. The government bought it during a depression, and now the present mine manager lived at my feet almost in a mobile home, while they were building him something permanent. The front veranda, which went round a projecting front, must have been thirty yards long. There was a large dining room, sitting room and three large bedrooms. Anderson had a *kaya* at the back. The garden was large and I soon employed a gardener. It had a fine collection of aloes and cycads. And I wandered about in that house like a lost soul. A little white boy told his mother, 'I'm never going to be an old bachelor like the doc when I grow up and live in a big lonely house like that.'

I had my books sent out from England for the first time. I had my record player and a good collection of LPs. Wednesday, I gave Anderson a half day and took sundowners and supper at the Falcon. They had got me playing bowls, so Saturday afternoon and evening I spent at the club, where a light supper was served. Sunday, I had drinks and a bar lunch at the Falcon. Sunday afternoon, I usually spent fishing with friends, ending with sundowners and supper at the hotel. A regular life but, as the little boy said, 'lonely' - and in the celibate way he meant.

The reader may wonder how I had reached the ripe old age of forty-six without getting caught. All I will say is, I had met women I wanted to marry, and women who wanted to marry me, but until I met my wife, a few years later, they were never the same ones. And I would have been a less melancholy soul if I had known about the bright day that was not too distant.

As I say, I went fishing - first with George. He was often to be seen at the bar of the Falcon, or with his wife and sister at the tables outside. He always wore an old shirt and pair of trousers held up with braces, a punched-out trilby hat like the Africans and again like Africans, sandals made of old car tyres. He was then about sixty. Like June, he had been born and bred in this little town - called a 'dorp' by those who did not live in it, and by some who did. He had worked on the mine and lived all his life in Umvuma except for five years away in the army in East Africa during the war. Now he was retired. He was short and fat. He and his skinny womenfolk lived in a dilapidated house near the station, which smelt of the sixteen cats they kept. In South Africa, he would have been called a 'poor white'. Nobody thought that way in classless Rhodesia or used that term.[1] He would buy the future earl a drink in the bar, and the earl-to-be would buy him one. And George had wealth of another kind, which I envied him.

He had an encyclopedic knowledge of the veld: every tree and flower and their seasons, every bird and animal, every fish in the rivers. And he could speak fluent Shona, the main African language of the country. Most of the white people spoke Fanagalo: 'kitchen Kaffir' - a sort of corrupted Zulu which is the native lingua franca from Cape to Congo and very useful. Africans, however, find it degrading and 'colonial' (though they would use it among themselves

---

[1] Not quite true. WD.

when they had to, as in the mines): white Shona speakers are rare and respected by the Africans because they imply respect. Shona is a difficult language. George never learnt it from books - which is practically impossible anyway, say I, after a dozen failed attempts. George learnt it by running about barefoot in the veld as a child with the black children: something not so uncommon among the white countryfolk, at least for the boys. The girls were kept away from the black children in case of 'moral contamination'. Nevertheless, the farm language tended towards Fanagalo, and as I said, true Shona speakers were rare. Town whites barely spoke either.

George showed me all the local dams, where we caught bream and the universal barbel; and the Canadian bass on the specially stocked farm dams. There was no angling society in Umvuma as there were in the larger towns, but we were welcome to the farm dams and that at the Catholic mission at Driefontein. George always gave notice of our arrival, nevertheless, to farmer or father: a polite but not strictly required formality I and my later friends usually dispensed with. George was very particular about Ian McArthur's dam, which according to George, had problems with the 'railway people'.

'Ian doesn't mind his own workers fishing in his dam, doc; but he doesn't want those railway people coming here.'

The 'railway people' lived on the siding where the railway crossed the main road to the south at an almost imaginary place called Fairfield. One day, George spotted some railway children, distinguishable only to his knowledgeable eye, fishing with bent pins. He pounded bawling across the veld towards them on his bare feet, in imminent danger to his heart, which was not sound. The ragged little brats snatched up their primitive gear and easily outdistanced him, leaving him panting and sweating, pulled up at the end of his puff, while they danced up and down and cried: 'Fat man! Fat man!'

One morning at seven, I got a call from George's wife. He had a pain in his chest and looked very ill. 'Would I come and see him?'

When I got to the house, it was as she said. George was sitting in a chair, looking grey. When I took his blood pressure, I found him in shock. I asked him how long he had had the pain. 'Since three in the morning'. Why didn't they call me earlier? 'Didn't want to disturb you, doc'.

I gave him a shot of pethidine, and within seconds he said: 'The pain's gone, doc.'

Those were the last words he spoke to me. I ordered him to bed. At eleven o' clock his wife rang me at the hospital to say he had died peacefully in his sleep.

I attended the funeral. I was held up at work and too late for the service in the tiny church. I waited in the little cemetery on the edge of the bush, and presently the coffin and procession arrived. There, among other obscure colonial souls, they buried George, under the msasa trees, and the blue sky of Africa, he loved so well.

Beyond the town lay the white farms for twenty miles, and more in some directions; and beyond them the tribal lands (now called 'communal lands'). We covered a number of hospitals and one clinic over an area as large as North Wales, which has since been rationalised to form two districts. There were two mission hospitals, as large as Umvuma; and one of them (Gutu, sixty miles out) was later made into a de facto district hospital.

Gutu marked one boundary between white farmland and tribal land. We had a rural hospital there, where an ambulance was based to cover two further rural hospitals in the tribal lands themselves. Once a week I would visit Gutu and take in one of the other hospitals, except for the week I visited a hospital in the opposite direction - Chilimanzi. Once a week, on another day, I visited our clinic at Lalapanzi, which will be remembered as one of the railway 'watering points'.

I travelled to Gutu in my own car along a metalled road. After the usual clinic and ward round, I would be taken in the Land Rover, banging and snapping like a biscuit tin over the rough dirt roads to the outer hospital: Chinyika or Chingombe, each twenty miles further on. Now we were in the typical tribal lands of Central Africa. We passed villages: not the large villages of West Africa, but small family affairs, often bearing the family name: Moyo; or the family totem: Gudo (baboon), Garwe (crocodile), Tsoko (monkey). There was the family hut, made of mud and wattle and thatched, each in its tribal manner; and round, so that evil spirits would have no corners to lurk in (unlike the rectangular huts of West Africa), though richer people had brick houses which were rectangular with tiled roofs. The women built the walls and the men the thatched roof after. People from neighbouring villages cooperated in the building.

Beside the hut were the granaries, also of mud and wattle and thatched, like tiny huts themselves. There would be the cattle kraal made of wood stakes and woven with branches, to protect the beasts at night. There were overhead holders for storing grass feed. Outside the huts were racks for pots and pans. Everything showed the shapeliness of skilled hands.

Women hoed the fields and reaped the meagre crops of maize and native corns. The men did the ploughing and planting. Young children minded cattle and goats out in the veld all day. Older children walked to school, sometimes ten miles each way, with no food from breakfast till supper, sometimes crossing fords where crocodiles lurked.

Evening was a time of much activity. Women and older girls fetched water from dams and rivers, which they carried in buckets on their heads, cushioned with coils of cloth. Older children watered the beasts at the same time, while boys ran about hunting a hare for the pot with their half-wild, skinny, whippet-like dogs. Women fetched firewood which they carried in bundles on their heads. Women pounded corn outside the huts in mortars with pole-like pestles, sometimes two together in rhythm. Cooking fires were lit before the hut. In winter the fire was carried inside and left to smoulder all night in the middle of the floor, while the family slept around it. And people fell into it - drunks, children, epileptics - so that was our main burns season. The huts were so smoky, it was our asthma and bronchitis season too. The toilet was the bush.

The cattle were too many. They were hardly eaten, except on ceremonial occasions, and gave little milk. They were not exactly the sacred cows of India, but they represented a man's wealth and status. They were also bride price. Young men went away to the mines or factories to earn money to buy them for a girl's father. A girl with O levels came very expensive, to say nothing of a teacher or a nurse, though among the middle classes, money was accepted in lieu of cattle. The custom was instituted in the hope that the wife would be cherished.

The cattle wasted the grass, and the goats finished it off, eating the roots also. The goats were eaten with rather more regularity than the cattle. Chickens also ran around the huts and were eaten, but not their eggs, which were thought to cause sterility.

Looking always for sources of protein, I asked my driver once if the people drank goat's milk.

'What, docketa! Do the people drink the milk of the goats?'

'Yes.'

'O, no, docketa. The people cannot drink the milk of the goats.'

'But the Magriki and the Ma-italiani drink goat's milk.'

'O, docketa! They do not drink the milk of the goats?'

'Yes. It makes them strong.'

'No, docketa. The people cannot drink the milk of the goats!'

As in England, every two or three years we had a measles year, and smaller outbreaks at any time. Measles is a serious thing in the undernourished children of Africa, causing chest infections and worse (unless they are fatal), blindness.

At one outer hospital I found three little brothers with measles and their eyes in a very bad state, with keratomalacia, or softening of the eye, on the brink of blindness. I ordered them a teaspoon of vitamin A each, and when I returned in three weeks' time, found that each child had one blind white eye and one clear healthy eye. Meantime, I had reiterated instructions to all our medical units to give vitamin A to all cases of measles.

And we saw cases of kwashiorkor and marasmus: the former swollen and water-logged, due to protein deficiency in children fed on maize alone; the second thin and wasted, due to simple underfeeding, especially in drought years. So I had fresh protocols made out for feeding children with nourishing local foods; though even so, in drought years these were unobtainable.

And with the rains in November came first malaria, as the mosquitoes were able to breed again; and typhoid, when everything in the unclean villages was washed into the rivers and dams.

I came to one outer hospital and found a large number of people sitting around outside, huddled in the wet weather in great-coats and blankets. After the clinic I did my ward round. Most of the patients had typhoid. The nurses were handling them as I had instructed. If someone had fever, treat first for malaria, as this was more urgent. If the fever did not go down in three days, when indeed the tell-tale 'step-ladder' temperature chart of typhoid would have shown itself, treat for the second disease.

I did my ward round, males first, and all seemed under control. The nurses knew how to recognise complications - the commonest, perforated typhoid ulcer, producing severe abdominal pain - or pneumonia; and would send these to the district hospital by the Gutu ambulance straight away. I was about to pass on to the female ward when, as at the Last Day, all the patients able to walk rose from their beds and went outside. Then their places were taken by another lot from the waiting people I had seen. At the end of my second ward round, the same thing happened again. On the female ward it was the same story. One hundred and twenty patients, mainly typhoid, sharing forty beds, God knows how, many on the floor, no doubt. I wondered how many of my old chiefs in Liverpool were ever asked to repeat their ceremonious ward rounds twice in an afternoon, and what they would have said about that.

The rains were heavy that year - good for crops, not for diseases. I realised something would have to be done about the hygiene of the district. I wrote an agitated letter to the Gutu DC, Mr Menzies, asking about the possibility of making the people dig pit latrines, with fines for non-compliance. I said, if cholera appeared, the district would go up in flames. The DC must have thought, we have a right stirrer here!

He wrote back and invited me to drop into his office on my next visit to the district. Next time, on my way home, I did so. He gave me tea. He was courteous and sympathetic; had noted my concern about the district 'going up in flames'. First he said he understood public health came under the provincial medical officer of health (correct), but could see my point of view as the chap on the receiving end. He agreed that pit latrines were the obvious answer, but there was no question of coercion. I quickly retracted this gaffe. He said he would do what he could - no doubt, what he had been doing long before I came on the scene: the ungrateful task of Jenny's in Ghana of trying to stop Africa from back-sliding. But now he was preoccupied with the security situation. The bush war had already started in the north-east - the 'sharp end'. The first rumours were reaching our part of the country.

But between us, we had hit on certain principles which were to bear fruit in more propitious times, as I shall relate in due course.

One week in four I would visit our hospital in Chilimanzi, which was in the parish of Jamie, the agricultural officer. I had a standing invitation to supper and would usually arrive before he was home. The cook would give me a beer and I would settle down with one of Jamie's extensive collection of P G Wodehouse, in the Penguin edition. And in due course, Jamie would arrive.

He was a large ebullient Scot with a florid face and shock of dark hair. His father had worked in India and Jamie had been sent home to prep and public school in UK. When the Rhodesians asked him if he was really 'Scotch', which he did not sound like to them, he would explode: 'You mean "Scottish"; and why on earth does a Scot have to have a Scottish accent?'

He had a party line which seemed to be permanently blocked by the local Boer farmers. Jamie would get engaged in crossed-line arguments with these people, with most of the heat on Jamie's side (which is saying something), in a perfect natural antipathy which nothing would change.

He was a member of what we called the 'Diners' Club': which existed among the bachelors, each of us giving supper in our houses to the other members, once a week. These were rowdy affairs which progressed to the town swimming pool, where we would throw a switch to light the place up and all plunge in in the buff. If Jamie was the last, with his huge body he would create a tidal wave which almost left the rest of us on the bank. Jamie was thirty: except for myself, the oldest. I sometimes wondered if I was in the right age group.

After the swim, into the Falcon, where more booze was consumed and we played darts; when Jamie, who had a Scottish pedantic streak, would argue heatedly about the rules, to the exasperation of the easy-going Rhodesians. 'It's the same rules for everyone, Jamie.' 'Yes, but it isn't logical!'

He got into an argument one sleepy Sunday afternoon in the lounge of the hotel with an Afrikaner miner, which ended in a brawl among the *Illustrated London Newses* and the *Wild Life Rhodesias,* of which I believe Jamie got the worst. Altogether, I think he was a little too hot for the climate and I feared for his blood pressure, though he never asked me to take it. But I was in tune with my fellow Brit and got on splendidly with him.

In Umvuma that year I did seventy caesarean sections and thirty symphysiotomies. This last operation is limited to developing countries where it has a special application. Briefly, it consists of splitting the pubic joint in the front of the pelvis, under local anaesthetic, to widen the pelvis and allow delivery of the baby in cases of moderate disproportion. When conducted by the correct rules it is an excellent operation: which can be said for any operation in current use.

It is not as drastic as it may sound. The mothers complain of no pain at any time: nor are there any subsequent ill effects. I asked them to return after six weeks (the only postnatal examination we bothered with), and got them to perform a simple test - an African dance, which all performed with ease and gusto. The joint fills with fibrous tissue and is indeed, stronger than before, so that the operation can never be repeated (which would be inappropriate, anyway). It was usually performed on first-time mothers and next time round, in most cases, they would deliver naturally.

It has a place in primitive countries, where communications are poor and a woman not always able to get to hospital in time; for a previous caesar - a woman with a scar in her womb - might in those circumstances rupture, to say nothing of those prejudiced against hospital after that operative experience, who might be tempted to go it alone with possibly disastrous consequences. These circumstances were aggravated as the emergency developed and travel by night became impossible. The previous caesars often ruptured: the symphs did well.

I must have done more than a hundred in my time with consistently good results. When services and communications improved in later times, the operation was less appropriate and I abandoned it.

I first heard of it in Ghana from Des, though did not practise it myself until I had learnt the principles and technique from the Rhodesian maternity handbook. Des mentioned it, in a spirit of Irish mischief, to Sir John Peel, the President of the Royal College of Obstetricians and Gynaecologists, at a dinner of the College to which Des had somehow got himself invited. Sir John was horrified - had never heard of such a barbaric proceeding in all his days.

He would not have been mollified by an article which appeared in the *Central African Journal of Medicine* which stated that, from the evidence of skeletons, the witch doctors had practised the operation in Central Africa long before the coming of the white man.

I did a hernia operation on a little fat man. As his blood pressure was high and difficult to control, I did the operation under local anaesthetic. In fat people, the landmarks are less clear. I accidentally nicked his femoral artery. This is not the disaster it sounds: it would have been more serious to nick the femoral vein, which is more difficult to deal with. A single stitch repaired the damage. Meanwhile, a spurt of blood had hit the ceiling.

'Is that my blood up there?' the little man mildly inquired from behind the usual screen.

'Yes, *madala*,' replied one of the nurses. 'You had too much, so we took some away.'

'Does that mean I am a blood donor?'

I had two compound (double) volvulus cases at Umvuma. One was an old man brought in by the nuns one night from St Theresa's Mission Hospital. Their own doctor was away. It was a carbon copy of the Marandellas case.

The nun anaesthetist did a good job and kept the old fellow up to the mark. Again, I took away twenty feet of gangrenous small bowel, as well as the affected large bowel (sigmoid). It was a hot night and half-way through I felt exhausted and wondered if I could make it. And this time I did not omit the double-barrelled colostomy.

The old man made a good recovery, though he never had a weight problem again, if he had one before, which looked unlikely. After six weeks I sent him to Mav to close the colostomy, though soon I would pluck up courage to do this myself. I must have done nearly twenty such ops in my time in Africa and lost very few patients. I got my operation time down eventually to two hours.

Another case was hopeless from the start. A young man who collapsed in the fields. He must have been ill for some time before that and carried on in the stoical way of the African. When I opened him up, as well as the affected sigmoid, his entire small bowel was black. I took out as much as I dared and left behind as much as I dared, which was little. After two days, in spite of copious blood transfusion, he passed a massive melaena stool (of altered blood) through his colostomy, collapsed and died.

One night, I was called to the labour ward for a retained second twin. Two fat little midwives were in attendance. I had hardly finished, with a happy result, when one of the midwives, who had been hovering about the open door, informed me: 'Doctor, something is at your car.'

I went outside in my apron and boots. The two fat little midwives stood beside me in great curiosity. In the darkness, I made out a large grey shape just beyond my car, which seemed to be making a strange noise: *Raah! Raah! Raah!* I said, 'I think that's an elephant.'

The next second - zapp! zapp! - without a word, the little midwives shot back inside the labour ward, incontinently slamming the door after them, leaving me to contemplate the menace outside.

Presently I made out the large object as the water tank. The noise was coming from my windscreen wipers which I had left on, it being raining when I got to the hospital.

I got my first cases of pelvic abscesses in women. One young lady who erupted several litres of pus as soon as I opened the abdomen. Another in whom I attempted to remove a tubal abscess but failed, and worse, severed a ureter: the tube that carries urine from the kidney to the bladder. I was able to repair it satisfactorily and the patient made a good recovery on antibiotics.

In the Falcon at sundowner time, where I used to unload, I said: 'I hate it when things go wrong.'

'You should try farming, matey,' replied Ian McArthur. 'Things are always going wrong.'

Another night at the bar, I suddenly remembered I had forgotten to tie the tubes, as requested, of a woman at caesarean section that afternoon. I was foolish enough to blurt this out. Big roar, and drinks all round on me! It required a second operation next day; which might have cost me (or my defence fund) more than a round of drinks in some other places I could think of.

At Umvuma I first met Gareth, who has remained my good friend to this day. He was a Welshman, who farmed a thousand acres (a small-holding in Rhodesia), twenty miles out of town. He supplied vegetables to the hospital and would arrive once a week in his pick-up: a short, sturdy, dark man with a florid face and heavy moustache, rather like an Italian peasant. In his youth he had been compared to Anton Walbrook, and in later life to Joseph Stalin. I thought he looked like Cecil Rhodes. He finally expanded to Sir John Falstaff.

He had gone to earth in more ways than one in Rhodesia, having left his second wife spitting venom at him in a Canadian divorce court. His opinions on the unfair sex were a legend. Over the years he had polished a number of sardonic aphorisms on the subject, which I called the Maxims of the Duc de Baker, and even tried my hand at rendering some of them into French, in which language they seemed to find a natural home. 'If God ever made anything dirty, it was a woman,' was one; and another, more subtle: 'The only thing a woman cannot forgive a man is the thought that he can live without her.' *'Si le bon Dieu a jamais fait une chose sale, c'était une femme,'* and: *'La seule chose qu'une femme ne peut pardonner un homme c'est la pensée qu'il peut vivre sans elle,'* were the best I could do for the French edition. But he refused to be described as a woman-hater, and indeed, retained his eye for a pretty face. He simply said, he wanted nothing more to do with them.

Gareth had been in Bomber Command during the war, and had survived sixty missions over Germany (nearly half with the Pathfinders): the average survived being fifteen out of thirty. After his first tour of thirty, Gareth was awarded the DFM and commissioned by a grateful sovereign. He volunteered for a second tour, in what he described as the madness of youth, and was duly awarded the DFC, having shown both classes of courage. After that little lot, he put his name down for the Dam Busters, but was wisely turned down by the medical officer, who evidently thought that Gareth had done enough, and duly reported to his CO.

He seems to have been an enlightened doctor for his time. Lord Moran's theory about the quantitative nature of courage - it is like capital: it can be depleted and must be replenished - was unknown then. It would probably have mystified Gareth's CO as much as it did Winston Churchill when he refused to write a preface to Moran's book. Gareth's CO obviously did not know how to break the dreadful news to Gareth: the terrible letters, L-M-F (lack of moral fibre), no doubt hovering in his mind. His attitude therefore puzzled Gareth. He accused him of 'trying to hog all the glory to himself' and 'not letting the other fellows have a go', and more in the same strain, as if they were talking about children's motorboats. It was not till years after, with a little help from me, that Gareth was able to understand what was going on.

Gareth came fishing with us but never caught anything. We used to say his pessimism communicated itself down the line to the fish and put them off. He played golf at the club and was a regular Friday-nighter at the Falcon, but not a member of the Diners' Club, having, no doubt, a more accurate idea of his age than I did of mine.

Gareth had a most mellifluous voice - officerly, with a touch of Welsh - but assured me he could not sing.

Besides his accomplished fourteen-year-old daughter, Ted, the stationmaster, had a younger son, David; and one day Ted and I and Gareth took David and one of his little school friends for a week-end's fishing at the Zimbabwe Ruins Hotel.

The boys came half-price, which, I suppose, was meant to accommodate family custom. What it did for the hotel's profits is another question, as the boys ate twice as much as we did.

In the late afternoon, after our arrival, we strolled beside the Kyle dam, our fishing venue of the morrow. The two boys accosted Gareth. 'Can you take us fishing at four o' clock tomorrow morning, Uncle Gareth?' We did not know that they had already failed with Ted.

In the warm glow of the end of a tranquil day, with the comfortable prospect of his sundowner and supper before him, Gareth said, 'Yes, my boys,' and probably meant it at the time.

At four o' clock in the small hours, a telephone rang in the room next to the one I shared with Gareth, boring through the thin wall like a dentist's drill, waking both of us. It stopped. A woman's angry voice bawled: 'Get lost!'

A few seconds later, the telephone rang in our room. Gareth wearily picked it up and a piping little voice asked: 'Are you ready to go fishing, Uncle Gareth?'

I had not been long at Umvuma before I received a visit from David Taylor, the physician at Gwelo. He told me it was his custom to visit the district hospitals once a month, something which became a regular policy later, but was then a matter of individual enthusiasm. And very welcome such visits are, and very helpful and instructive: just as important as the DMO's visits to the rural stations. And one day, he arrived in the nick of time.

I had a middle-aged female patient who had been puzzling me. For a week she had had general pains and a low-grade fever (blood smear was negative for malaria), and now she was developing weakness in the legs. Already she was confined to bed. Just as we entered the ward on David's monthly visit, she stopped breathing.

Quick as a flash, David diagnosed Guillain-Barré syndrome: ascending paralysis of unknown origin, probably infectious - the first time I had heard of it. I have seen several cases since, and have been able to take pre-emptive action in time, thanks to David's most opportune visit: otherwise, I would have had a very mysterious death on my hands and would probably have called it polio.

We had no mechanical respirator in the hospital. We wheeled the patient quickly to theatre, me pumping her midriff on the way, got her onto the table and a tube down her windpipe, connecting it to the Boyle's anaesthetic machine, which, of course, can deliver oxygen. Then we loaded patient and machine onto the ambulance and drove the fifty miles to Gwelo with me sitting in the back, pumping the bag. At the hospital, they got her connected to a Manley machine, and I left.

Next day, I heard on the telephone that she had already recovered respiration and was off the machine. The paralysis disappears in reverse order to its onset, from the head downwards. She left hospital fully recovered, a month later.

I was on the bowling green one Saturday afternoon when a car stopped in the road beyond the hedge. Two young white men got out and then helped a friend, whom they brought up to the hedge in a four-handed lift. There were calls for the doctor, so I went over to have a look.

I recognised Jan van der Merwe, a young local farmer, who had fallen off his horse, playing polocrosse, and had an injured ankle. They had removed his riding boot and the ankle was very swollen.

I scribbled some instructions to the nurses at the hospital on a cigarette packet - morphine, X-ray - and asked his friends to take Jannie down there, telling them I would follow shortly. Then, like Sir Francis, I went on with the game.

When I got to the hospital, I found Jannie, more comfortable after his morphine, sitting on the X-ray table. I studied the plates, looking hard at the malleoli - the knobs of the ankle, where most fractures occur - and could see no fracture. (The degree of swelling and pain in an obviously stoical patient should have made me more suspicious.) I diagnosed a sprained ankle. I thought Jannie might be more comfortable in a plaster, so ordered one.

On Sunday evening I was in the bar of the Falcon when Jannie's wife came in. Jannie was in great pain and wanted the plaster off. I scribbled another note to the people at the hospital, asking them to remove it and replace it with a crepe bandage.

Next morning Jannie telephoned the hospital, still complaining of pain. June received the call, and believing (with the rest of the town by now) that he had only a sprained ankle, was less sympathetic than she might have been otherwise. She asked Jannie to send his wife up to the hospital for more Panadols.

Not surprisingly, Jannie's wife did not appear, and next Saturday evening, I was surprised to see Jannie in the club on crutches with his leg in a fresh plaster. He was telling his friends (who by then did not include me) all about it. He had been, he said, to see a 'decent doctor'. To my concerned inquiries, he informed me that after June's (innocent) rebuff, he had got his wife to take him to my colleague, the DMO at Enkeldoorn, thirty miles away. I gathered that the doctor there had taken more X-rays and (to my selfish relief) had seen no fracture either, but having the advantage of the previous history, had sent him to a specialist in Salisbury. The specialist, according to Jannie, had said he had a fracture which might need a screw.

At the earliest opportunity on Monday morning, I got out Jannie's X-rays again and, with the help of Crawford Adams, re-examined them very carefully. Finally, I discerned that two of the bones in that Rubik's cube of the upper foot, whose names nobody remembers after medical school, were really one, divided by a line which looked less smooth than the articulating faces of the other bones. I was seeing the first (and last) fracture of the talus (the bone which forms the tenon to the mortise of the ankle) I was to see in forty years of practice. And instead of happening to some uncomplaining black African, it had to happen to the unforgiving white African, Jannie van der Merwe.

A few days later, David Taylor came out on his monthly visit. Over a cup of tea I told him the story (I had to unburden to some colleague), and, before I got to the solution, tested him with the X-rays (which was probably an unfair thing to do to a member of the Royal College of Physicians - whose specialty is not bones). To the satisfaction of my ego, he also failed to recognise the fracture.

By now, Jannie was going about the district blackening my name to all who would listen. Not everyone approved of this attitude, including his own wife; but being conscience-stricken and feeling sorry for him, I sat down one night and wrote him a letter. (This was not as mad a proceeding as it might have been in a more litigious country than Rhodesia.) I explained that I had taken another look at the X-rays and could now see the fracture, which was a very uncommon fracture, and apologised for any lack of sympathy I may have shown when under the impression that he had simply sustained a badly sprained ankle.

I received no reply to this, or any verbal acknowledgement. In the event, Jannie did not need an operation and made as good a recovery as he would have made in any case. But he never had a civil word for me after that.

At a place like Umvuma in those days, there was only one government doctor, who was on call all the time, day and night, week in, week out, for years on end. He could only escape by leaving the station - a long way behind. Then emergencies would be sent to the next suitable place - usually the next district, where one's colleague would also stand in for weeks or months while his neighbour went on leave, and vice versa. In the case of Umvuma the matter was simpler, and emergencies were sent to the provincial hospital at Gwelo, a mere fifty miles away.

Otherwise they called me by telephone or they sent the ambulance out for me, if I went fishing say. Sometimes I would play bowls at Enkeldoorn. I would tell them to telephone me there, knowing that they would never drag the doc off the bowling green on a Saturday afternoon for anything less than a caesar or a major road traffic accident (RTA).

I was fishing at a river pool once, a little distance from my friends, and started pulling bream out like rabbits from a conjuror's hat. After I had about half a dozen, I was about to call my friends to share the lucky strike, when a black face appeared through the reeds and the ambulance driver said they wanted me at the hospital. I packed up, fish and all, and followed him in my own car. I found a woman with a ruptured uterus - labouring out in the bush too long, perhaps, with an old caesarean scar (I forget) - and performed my second subtotal hysterectomy. 'Another life saved,' as Howell in Birkenhead used to say, to the fury of the theatre sister (both of them Welsh), every time he did a circumcision.

One night there was a sing-song at the Falcon. Somebody brought a guitar, and I was one of the strummers. The old Southern African favourites were bawled out over the cups: *Sarie Marais, Come a Rookie, Marching to Pretoria* - there was nothing effete about Rhodesian singing; in those days, at any rate.

Billy Campbell and Phil von Lilienfeld (yes, another Umvuma aristocrat) left early - ie, about midnight - in Billy's pick-up. Soon a report was brought that they had been involved in a road accident.

The two young cops (whose departure usually signalled closing time, giving the rest of us plenty of scope), who had a remarkable gift for sobering up at a moment's notice, took off. The ambulance went out, and I went to the hospital to prepare for casualties.

They had hit an African bus, almost head-on, knocking off its outer wheel and sending the bus plunging into the ditch, with no one hurt. Billy had been killed on the spot. John Holland, the owner of the Falcon, remarked philosophically: 'He knows it all now.'

Billy's truck was crumpled up. Phil had a fractured ankle. He had, of course, provided his own anaesthetic. I put a plaster on it and sent him off to Gwelo: I was not up to screwing ankles at that stage.

In the early hours one morning, a young African man, a teacher, crashed his car into a train at the Fairfield crossing and was killed instantly. His brother came to the hospital to identify the body. I met him outside the little mortuary.

The brother was a fellow doctor, Dr Mazarodze, who later became a minister of health in the post-independence government, before his own untimely death after only a few months in office.

I had made sure the face was washed and the body covered with a blanket. I simply said to my colleague: 'I am very sorry.' I led him into the mortuary. The attendant lifted the blanket from the face. Dr Mazarodze sobbed: 'O, my God! Stephen!'

I put my arm round his shoulders and gripped him firmly until he had recovered himself. Then I led him outside. I asked him if he would like a cup of tea. He said quietly, 'No, thank you,' and left.

After a week I received a letter from him. 'Thank you for your kind sympathy on the sad occasion of my brother's death.'

My touch had not gone unnoticed.

A medical student came to stay with me. He was a friend of one of the policemen and still in second year. This was earlier than usual for an attachment, which comes in the clinical years ahead. But Graham was very keen, and I have always had a bit of the schoolmaster in me, so I was glad to have him and his company.

While at my house he became addicted to a certain drug. It did not affect his studies, as he shortly after passed his second MB, gaining gold medals in every subject: he was the brightest student in his year, and many other years too.

The certain drug was Russian literature.

He was a reader. He was a pale dark lad and, unlike most Rhodesians, not interested in sport. But he had never met Russian literature before, of which I had a fair collection.

He devoured *War and Peace* in three weeks, *The Brothers Karamazov* in a fortnight. Then he started on Chekhov.

He read the Russians morning, noon and night. He took them to the toilet. He sat at the side of the bowling green and read them when I dragged him off to the club. In the Falcon he sat with Raskolnikoff in the taverns of St Petersburg while the darts flew over his head.

Trying to vary his literary diet, I offered him Dickens and Hardy. He gave them ten minutes each, before silently replacing them on the shelf and taking down another Russian.

While at Umvuma, I attended the annual bush doctors' refresher course at Bulawayo, where I met 'Jock' Scott for the first time: a man who was to play a big part in my life later. He was then DMO at Belingwe.

In spite of his sobriquet, which like Mav's was used by all his friends, including his wife, Jock was a Londoner. He was then about sixty: a tall, swarthy man whose remaining hair sprouted rather wildly from the sides of his head. Altogether, he looked as much like a gipsy fiddler as a doctor.

The musical appearance was not inapt. Jock had a teacher's certificate from the Royal College of Music, and played both violin and piano. He had considered a musical career but decided, in his own words, 'he would rather be a second-rate doctor than a fourth-rate musician'.

We had some chat about music. I took an instant liking to him and was glad, as the narrative will show, to find him my neighbour some years later.

The circumspect DMO at Enkeldoorn was succeeded by an Australian, Dr Sadd, who was rather less so. Unfortunately, the poor man was rarely sober: only, in fact, in the morning, before the pub opened, when his work was impaired by his hang-over. He did not last long, and was dismissed the service after a few months.

I met him in his local one Sunday afternoon on my way home from Salisbury. Dr Sadd sounded as unhappy as his name in Enkeldoorn. He complained about what he called 'young Rhodesian lay-outs'. Moreover, most of the whites in the town were Boer farmers, who reminded him every other day about who started the 'bloody concentration camps', which was pretty hard on an Aussie. (My younger readers must not imagine his persecutors were referring to the Germans.)

He invited me to his house for supper. About four o' clock, we went to his place in separate cars. We sat down in the sitting-room with more beers. His wife strode in. Without a glance at me, she started in on her husband in an abrasive Australian voice. 'Where have you been till this time, you drunken bum? As if I didn't know! You told me this morning you were going to the bank. Mrs Oosterhuizen tells me the banks don't open in this country on a Sunday, you lying bastard! If you want your lunch, you can scrabble for it, 'cos it's in the bin.'

There must have been some conversation of a more general nature in the course of the afternoon, because I was introduced to the lady and their two young sons, before, under another assault from his more sober half, Dr Sadd slid out of his chair and into the arms of Morpheus. The visit ended with me taking the wife and the boys back to the hotel for supper.

A few days later, I got a call from Mrs Sadd at the hospital. 'Tell me, Warren. Is there such a thing as an alternator in a motorcar?'

'I've never heard of it,' I answered, truthfully. The internal combustion engine has always been a closed book to me.

'I thought as much. That lying bastard told me I couldn't use the car this morning 'cos the alternator needs fixing. Just wait till the bum gets home for his lunch!'

I picture the little man, innocent for once, coming home to this welcome: 'Warren says there's no such thing as an alternator in a bloody motorcar!'

Dr Sadd was not long for this world, let alone the service. After his dismissal, his wife left him and returned to Australia with the boys. He went into private practice in a small town near Salisbury but, not surprisingly, did not prosper. Soon after, I heard that he had crashed his car in South Africa and killed himself.

5 - Back to School

After a year at Umvuma I saw the post of medical superintendent at Sinoia advertised. This was another general hospital like Marandellas but larger. I was beginning to feel the limitations of the little backwater of Umvuma, not least in the direction of marital prospects. The Scottish sisters from Marandellas had called on me on their way to Bulawayo, sat outside the Falcon and declared they would go mad in a week in this place. I had my work to keep me occupied but I was human too. So, with 'the cries of unsatisfied love', I applied and was accepted for Sinoia.

There were three or four doctors there, including a consultant physician. It was a busy hospital and emergencies came thick and fast. I thought I was doing fairly well, when an old doctor (then a part-timer) drew me aside one day and told me he thought I needed more surgical training. What is more, he had written to the secretary for health[1] expressing the same opinion. This was a shock and a blow to my pride, as surgery was my strongest suit and my leading interest.

The secretary came down, had a chat with my colleagues and another one with me. In the event, I agreed to go back to school again at Umtali, the main hospital of the eastern province of Manicaland; incidentally taking two steps down the promotional ladder to simple GMO again. As I was not a married man, that was the least of my disappointments.

Umtali was a hospital the size of Gwelo and had three specialists. Henry, the surgeon, was a South African of French extraction with the stern, dark looks of a South American dictator and an authoritarian manner to match, best described by one sister (white, of course) as, 'God has entered the ward!' Ian, the superintendent, was an orthopaedic surgeon, a tall, dour Scot, who was 'not one to suffer fools gladly', as they say: which I have always regarded as an ominous expression. Ivor, the physician, was a Rhodesian, like David Taylor; and that was all they had in common. Ivor was a tall,

---

[1] In Rhodesia/Zimbabwe this means the permanent secretary. WD.

dark man of Welsh extraction and excitable temperament, who would throw the notes across the ward at the slightest provocation - with or without the clip-boards. He had a saving sense of humour - at least, he laughed as heartily at my jokes as he cursed my shortcomings.

At Gwelo, I had worked exclusively with ladies and gentlemen: at Umtali, I was to get the abrasive treatment. Which was the more efficacious, I have never been able to decide.

And at Umtali, I met up again with Jimmy Lennon, the schoolmaster from Liverpool. He had now moved from Brown's Hotel to digs. I asked him to share house with me, and he gladly accepted. We were to have a happy year together, the period of my tutelage at Umtali.

Jimmy had had a sad life. He first came to Rhodesia during the war, under the Empire Air Training Scheme, based at Gwelo, and met and married a Rhodesian girl. He took her home to England with him, found a teaching post in a Liverpool suburb and a house in Wirral, 'over the water', not a very convenient arrangement. He returned home on his first day, after a long journey by bus and train, to find his Rhodesian wife, now deprived of servants, sitting weeping in the dark, and no supper ready. They struggled on for as long as they could before Jimmy decided his wife was a little tropical flower, plucked from its native soil and unlikely to flourish in the unkinder latitudes of Mersey. He found a post in Rhodesia and took her home again, Kathleen (though, in fact, her name was Rosemary).

They had three children, but the marriage still did not prosper. Jimmy went home on leave to England alone and on his return found that his wife had left him, taking the children, and gone off with a communist: adding insult to injury as far as Jimmy, a devout Catholic, was concerned. Moreover, through some sort of influence, she had got him transferred to Wankie, the remotest and hottest part of the country, in the hottest month, October - the 'suicide month'. (This part of the story seems to require further explanation.) For Jimmy, it was the lowest point in his life: he told me how he cried himself to sleep at night and wished he would never wake again. Or rather one of the lowest points. The second came just before he joined me at Umtali, when his two daughters were killed in a car crash.

He would get to Salisbury when he could to see his children. His wife seems to have got her hands on his money for he was very poor. He told me how he would hitch a lift down to Bulawayo in the guard's van (300 miles), and the same to Salisbury (another 300 miles), and back, over a week-end. Finally, his wife divorced him - a position Jimmy, for religious reasons, never recognised, despite the advice of more 'advanced' priests of his church to the contrary. To complete his desolation, the communist was expelled from the country, and took Jimmy's family with him.

I was introduced early to Henry's style after an operation one night. Their teaching method there was not very good. Henry and Ian did all the operations, even the minor ones: the GMOs gave the anaesthetic and learned what they could by watching the masters. This was still useful to me: I had had my hands on already and could learn much by watching; but it was no good for tiros, and to do them justice, before I left, they were beginning to change it for more practical methods.

I had prepared a case of ruptured ectopic for Henry - or thought I had. I had needled the abdomen and got blood. Thinking to kill two birds with one stone, I sent this blood to the lab for the usual business, including matching stored blood for transfusion. When Henry arrived, I gave the anaesthetic and watched him as best I could while still watching the patient.

After the op, in the changing room, instead of changing, Henry sat sombrely in a chair. I was about to change when he stopped me with a question.

'What was the trouble about that woman's blood tonight?' he asked in the tone of a Victorian headmaster on 'your record this term'.

'I don't understand.'

'That I can well imagine.'

He paused, then continued: 'How did you obtain the blood you sent for grouping and cross-matching?'

'I sent the paracentesis specimen.'

'And did you expect that specimen to clot?'

I wasn't sure, so said nothing. Besides, I have always considered the Socratic method unneccesarily patronising.

'Of course, it wouldn't bloody clot!' shouted Henry, unable to contain his natural choler any longer in the cold judicial manner which did not suit him. 'And how was the man going to group and cross-match the blood if the specimen didn't clot?'

What he meant was, the technician had to test both cells and serum, which would only separate in a clotted specimen. The blood I sent had already clotted in the abdomen, and was simply a kind of soup, which would never settle out. This, Henry could have explained in two sentences, as above. But that was not his style: his style was the rhetorical style.

'First prrinciples man!' he bellowed, rolling his 'r's' like a Dutchman, which he was not, although he came from the Orange Free State. By now he was pacing up and down like Hitler on one of those days his generals used to hate. 'I'm talking about first prrinciples! Not your bloody *Brritish Medical Journal* wrritten by intellectual twits and show-offs, trrying to get ahead in the rrat-rrace!' (I agreed with him about the *British Medical Journal,* or rather, for practical value, preferred the more basic publication, *Tropical Doctor;* but this did not seem the occasion for discussing the various merits of the medical press.) 'I'm talking about the things you were supposed to learn as a medical student!'

Well, that covered a multitude of forgotten lessons, and I was not going to learn them from Henry that night. I had to sit down and work them out next day, which I suppose is one way of teaching.

Next, I got it from Ian. Admittedly, a shameful case on my part. A young soldier came to outpatients who had lost his nerve about military operations - the bush war was spreading further, and had now reached all the eastern districts. I had no idea how to deal with this case. I knew nothing of Moran's theories of the 'anatomy of courage', as indicated before, though his book was obtainable then. I had heard of cases of airmen involved in crashes, who were sent straight up again, *before* they lost their nerve. This was, of course, inapplicable in the present case, which I would have seen if I had given the matter more thought. But on the spur of the moment, I told him about this method and suggested he try and carry on.

Fortunately for the lad (if not for me), the case reached Ian's ears: most things did. He sent a message for me to await him in his office. When he came in, he berated me at the top of his voice. At least, he told me what I should have done: namely, put the poor fellow off duty on tranquillisers; for which I was grateful, if not for the way he said it. I felt like asking him if this was his usual way of addressing his colleagues - the short answer to that was 'yes', as far as the GMOs were concerned, and I later learned I had shared the dubious honour with his own son-in-law; but I lacked the necessary confidence and missed the opportunity.

At least I was not lacking in cold courage, and decided to have it out with Henry, who had given me the rough treatment more than once. I arranged a meeting with him.

'Yes, Warren,' he smiled, as soon as we were alone. 'What can I do for you?' He could be charming when he wanted: he was unfailingly charming with women, and I have to say he was kindness itself to children.

'Mr Denard,' I began, falteringly. 'I am afraid that you bully me sometimes.'

He said it was entirely unintentional, and asked me to give an example.

'Well, the first time was the case of that ectopic, when I sent the paracentesis specimen to the lab. I thought the way you spoke to me then was not very friendly.'

'Please understand, old chap,' he pleaded. 'I do not claim to be a gynaecologist.'

This was pure flannel, and Henry knew it. A brilliant career in politics awaited him any time he chose to take it up.

There was more pleasantry of a similar sort, and the meeting ended on a friendly note - as they say in Belfast.

Two days later, he was as bad as ever again.

I have already mentioned Ivor's discus-throwing performances. I was rapidly becoming the whipping boy of the hospital.

I can joke about it now, but at the time it caused me some distress, and I even lost sleep over it. Jimmy was most indignant, being a fiery Irish type himself, and was all for having a word with Ian about it, who was a personal friend of his, but I restrained him. He did not know Henry, but took the opportunity to observe him at a wedding reception. He came to some Celtic intuitive conclusion, and assured me: 'You'll get nowhere with that man, Warren. He's made of concrete.'

Of course, it would have been better to catch them on the wing, so to speak, in the middle of their rages, with a sharp protest; but I lacked the confidence.

In time they softened towards me. As men get to know one another, mutual confidence grows, and I am glad to say it did in this case. Before my time was up, I was enjoying good relations with them, which endured after I left.

Moreover, I was not guiltless of these crimes myself. I bullied the nurses, especially the Africans, whose cultural respect for authority impeded them from protesting. (Henry, of all people, reproved me for never saying 'please' and 'thank-you' to them; and I can't say he wasn't justified.) This is the cowardice of the bully, who always senses the soft target - and leaves the other kind alone. This was true of my tormentors, and it was true of me. Once I bullied a sister, a Zulu girl of delicate beauty, as sensitive as a gazelle. She burst out in tearful protest at the end of the ward round. I led her outside and apologised profusely, promising her (and myself, inwardly) it would never happen again. I hope I kept my promise.

Jimmy was a great champion of the Africans, and, indeed, the poor the world over. He was much troubled by some statistic that most of the wealth of Britain was owned by ten thousand people, but admitted the strength of my argument that the important thing was that nobody should go without.

We took a holiday at Kariba over Christmas. At breakfast one day, Jimmy was dilating on the miserable wages of the African waiters. He called one over.

'How much do they pay you at this place, my friend?'

'Sah?'

'How much money do you get every month? *Malini?*'

'Thirty dollars, sah.'

'And how many children do you have?'

'Five, sah.'

'Listen to that, Warren! How do they expect a man to support a wife and five children on thirty dollars a month?'

The waiter went away. He spoke to other waiters, and a delegation of waiters approached the manager. (Shades of me and the latrine boys of Ghana!) The result was the manager granted them a rise of five dollars a month - miserable enough at that.

The revolution spread, and after we left, the hotel managers were no doubt asking one another, who was the funny little man who looked like Father Christmas, who had been stirring up the waiters that festive season?

Towards the end of my time at Umtali, we were joined by a young doctor from Argentina, who shared house with me and Jimmy. His wife was to follow him later. This was Carlos.

Jimmy soon found reason to reprove Carlos, who had spoken of the 'stupidity' of the Africans.

'Carlos, you must realise that that is a very offensive word to Africans. Besides, they are *not* stupid. Just because they are different from you, does not mean they are stupid.'

'But they *are* stupid, Jimmy.'

'Carlos, did you hear what I said? These people are your patients, and you will never be a good doctor unless you learn to respect your patients.'

'Yes, Jimmy. You are like my father. You *look* like my father, Jimmy.'

'I am not your father. I am just thinking of your good, Carlos.'

'Yes, Jimmy. You are my father.'

One day, Carlos came running into the sitting room with a soapstone head some man at the door was trying to sell him.

'Look at this head, Jimmy! It only costs ten dollars.'

Jimmy rose from his seat, went to the door and closed it in the face of the pedlar outside. He returned and spoke to Carlos.

'Now, Carlos. Just because that man asks you ten dollars for that thing, does not mean it is worth ten dollars. Ten dollars is a lot of money in this country.'

'Yes, Jimmy. You are my father.'

'I am not your father,' replied Jimmy, taking the head and leading Carlos by the elbow to the door. 'Come with me.'

Jimmy opened the door and said to the man outside: 'Now, my friend, how much are you asking for this head?'

'Ten dollars, sah.'

'Ten dollars!' retorted Jimmy. 'Tell me, my friend, which school did you go to?'

The man was taken aback, but, in true African fashion, quickly concealed it. 'St Michael's mission, sah.'

'St Michael's mission!' exclaimed Jimmy, who had taught in, or knew, nearly every school in the country. 'That's Father Flanagan's school, isn't it?'

'Yessah.'

'I know him well. And what would Father Flanagan say if he knew you were going around the country robbing people?'

'Yessah.'

'What?'

'No, sah.'

'He'd give you a good hiding, wouldn't he? *Maningi shaya?*'

'No, sah.'

'What?'

'Yessah.'

'So how much do you want for this head?'

'Nine dollars, sah.'

'Did you hear what I said? Do you want me to write to Father Flanagan?'

'Yessah.'

'What?'

'No, sah.'

In the end Jimmy got the head for two dollars.

About this time (early 1975), we got our first war casualties. The first three were shot by a white farmer on his own land when he thought they looked suspicious and they refused to stop when he called them. The country was getting very trigger-happy and nervous. Soon the notorious Amnesty and Indemnity Act came out, waiving prosecution in cases of action against 'suspected terrorists', which Mugabe found very convenient in his turn, and which remains on the statute books to this day.

The three men had been shot in the abdomen - the worst cases to deal with. Even head and chest shots were easier: they either died on the spot or required comparatively simple surgery. Limb shots had their own problems, but were still simpler than abdominal shots, which were like firing a bullet through a television set: there was so much to damage, and sometimes so hard to get at.

Henry had been involved with the Lumpa troubles in Zambia, a decade earlier. Ian had spent busy holidays with the ski-slope surgeons of Austria, where he would have learnt much about injuries. Certainly, they were both on top of modern war surgery, and in the next few months I was to learn much from them - and use it within a couple of years myself, as the war spread until it involved the whole country.

These three cases they tackled between them, swiftly, expertly and successfully, working in two theatres at a time. Then an even bigger order, when an African bus ran over a land mine, and Henry and Ian did eight rapid amputations between them in an afternoon.

Why the guerrillas (I shall use the BBC term as the most neutral: though I questioned its accuracy at the time), why they planted mines in the tribal areas, where the most likely victims were going to be African buses and other vehicles, I do not know; except to try to exclude the security forces. I asked an African doctor about it, who was sympathetic to the nationalist cause, and he simply said: 'the people accept it'.

Life went on despite these dark clouds. One night a man of about fifty was brought in. A leopard had taken his eye out. This turned out to be an occupational injury. The man was a leopard-killer. He went about his business with a knobkerrie, hanging about the affected kraal until the intruder appeared. On this occasion, the man took the opportunity to announce his retirement, while he had one eye to guide him through his old age.

As the 'war situation' developed, the DC started recruiting district assistants to supplement his personnel. These people had medical examinations at the hospital. In Africa, delegation is an important and necessary principle. The doctors did the main business and filled in the relevant sections of the forms, which they then signed. As doctors are unworldly souls who do not read small print, few of us studied the previous entries made by the nursing and clerical staff.

The DC was used to taking a closer look at things, and presently returned the first batch of forms, in which he remarked in his covering letter, some men were marked down as ten feet tall and others as three feet tall, who appeared to his untutored eye to be within normal limits.

When we re-examined the forms (if that is the right expression), we found that it was true. Matron investigated and discovered that the great principle of delegation had in this case been pushed too far. The boring business of measuring heights had been passed on to a little old man from the kitchen. When asked to demonstrate his working method, he showed us on the machine how, when he got a measure of 5' 10", he marked it down as ten feet, and for 5' 3", he put three feet.

In my last months at Umtali I did some locums, which I might say are a luxury in Africa: for the recipient, I mean, who, as I have earlier indicated, more usually shuts up shop and leaves everything to the nurses, with instructions to transfer anything they cannot handle to the next person who can.

First I went to Inyanga District Hospital, in the mountains. Inyanga was the only white-occupied place in Rhodesia which I heard described as a 'village'. It was a spread-out sort of place, like some places in the Scottish Highlands, nestling under the shadow of World's View, as the nearest big mountain was called. I stayed at one of the small local hotels.

The DMO was Harry Knight, then about 80, who had already made as many retirements and come-backs as Gigli; and I had a couple of days with that delightful man before he went off on leave. He was a cherubic figure, like Mr Pickwick, and I noticed that he had taken to driving round his district, which was already infiltrated by guerrillas, with a sub-machine-gun beside him in his car, looking like a country clergyman with a fixation on Al Capone. I did not bother with weapons at that stage.

Inyanga in those days was a quiet station. (It got busier later, with the growth in population and the influx of refugees from Mozambique.) I used to call it an 'old man's station', and certainly Harry managed it happily enough. Most afternoons I was free, after an hour at his house, conducting the private surgery to which more than one patient rarely came, and I spent most of the hour reading a book from Harry's library. Then I would take a boat and go trout-fishing on one of the dams. The ambulance driver, of course, could always get me for an emergency.

The operating theatre must have had the loveliest view of any in the world (most have no view at all), overlooking the mountains - a solace to the straining surgeon when he looks up from his work.

There were two rural hospitals to visit. One lay up the lovely Inyanga North Valley - a wide, flat valley with conical hills on its floor, like the mountains of the moon: one of Kipling's 'great spaces washed with sun'; which looks so like the Great Rift Valley of East Africa that I wonder if it is not the lost tail of it.

One week-end Jimmy came out to see me and shared my room at the hotel. And I was to discover that Jimmy's charm was visible to more than myself, especally as far as the ladies were concerned.

As we sat with our fellow guests round the fire one evening, that 'winter in July', Jimmy was his usual ebullient self; sprinkling his out-going personality around him like a life-giving fountain. And one who bathed in it more than most was a dark lady of mature charms sitting beside him, who seemed to be with a large surly man. We thought nothing of this until next morning.

As the sun rose, so did Jimmy, like another sun himself, and stood at the door of our room in the spread-out motel. Across the cheerful beams of both the sun and Jimmy, hove the shadow of the large surly man. This did not prejudice Jimmy any more than the larger sun above him. 'Good morning!' called out Jimmy, in his warmest tones.

Whether the response was unexpected from such a source, I will not say. It certainly shook both of us.

'Are you looking for a punch on the jaw?'

The large surly man took his shadow elsewhere, without waiting for a reply. Jimmy worked it out this far, at any rate: 'Warren, I believe that man is jealous.'

It did not take long for Jimmy's suspicions to be confirmed. He had not been back at Umtali two weeks before he received an interesting letter.

'I've got rid of YOU KNOW WHO. The coast is clear. Love, Anita.'

We met a number of army officers at the bar of the hotel, who had been taught by Jimmy. Jimmy had taught about half the people in the country, white and black. When some politician appeared on television once, Jimmy commented: 'I know that man well, Warren. I taught him. Thick as two short planks!' He also received political pronouncements with a device of his own which I called 'Lennon's corrector'. Eg, when Smithy or somebody told the country he would not increase taxes, Jimmy would reply smartly: 'He means he will!'; and the contrary to positive statements. Lennon's corrector, of course, is a useful political tool beyond the borders and times of Rhodesia.

One of the officers recalled how Jimmy would mark exercises while supervising prep - at lightning speed. Refusing to believe in the efficiency of this speed, one boy inserted in his exercise the message: 'I bet Eggy Lennon doesn't see this.' Jimmy's flying pencil came to a sudden stop. 'Stand forth, Perkins minor!'

Jimmy left before I did. In some parts of the country, convoys were already in operation on the roads between the towns. At first, just numbers of people getting together with their own weapons. Later, more formal convoys were formed as the towns became islanded by the spreading bush war: a police reserve pick-up leading with a Browning machine-gun mounted on the back, another in the middle in a long convoy, and one bringing up the rear. These convoys assembled at fixed points, and left at fixed times. And sometimes came under ambush and returned fire.

People had not started forming convoys to or from Inyanga yet (never did, I believe), but Jimmy was a prudent man and on the day he left, organised one himself. The local police chief, returning to the village, was surprised to see the first convoy in his district coming round a bend, led by a stern-faced Jimmy.

After Jimmy got back to the house, he got his name in the local newspaper. Rhodesian schools worked from 7am to 1pm. Every afternoon there was sport, which Jimmy, who was now 60, was excused. He would return to the house exhausted, he told me, physically and emotionally. He would throw himself into his work whole-heartedly. He was then teaching at an African school. He took as much as he gave, he told me. 'When I look at your happy faces,' he would tell the children, 'I am not teaching you; you are teaching me!' But by one o' clock, he had had enough, and the first thing he did on getting home was to lie on his bed for a couple of hours.

He was lying back one day when he heard music coming from the sitting-room. He had seen no one there when he entered. Carlos would be at work. Warren was not expected back till next day. He got up to investigate, and found the record-player playing one of Warren's records to itself. Then a noise from the bathroom. Maybe Warren back a day early, taking a bath and listening to music. He glanced through the open door, and saw a black man treating himself to a hot bath, as free as you please.

Jimmy's first thought was one becoming fashionable then: terrorists. (He did not seem to associate burglars with music and hot baths.) He put his hand round the door and extracted the key, closed the door and locked it; then telephoned the police, who, of course, came rushing in with all their artillery. At least they didn't kick the door in, but what they found inside was no terrorist, just a frightened black man, who turned out to be one of the poor lunatics who haunted the bins of the hospital, competing for food with the dogs. This one at least got a bed for the night. All duly reported in the *Umtali News*.

The reader may wonder what food was doing in the hospital bins in 'starving Africa'. And well he might, for by the time they were emptied, say, once a week, they not only overflowed but lay on their sides, where the dogs had pulled them over, scattering food like the horn of Ceres.

I thought at first it was because the stuff was unappetising: it was certainly coarse enough to delicate white palates, especially the wretched ration meat. Once, in Zambia, I had a lady patient who was reluctant to leave hospital. This was unusual: as a rule they were into their street clothes as soon as I gave the word. Although cured, I expect she needed rest, the poor thing, which is not surprising among the women of Africa. I jokingly suggested she was staying for the food.

My joke misfired. The woman took me at my word, silently rose from her bed and began to change her clothes. Thank God I was able to perceive my gaffe and urge the sister to persuade the woman I was joking! What was hard tack to me was a banquet to her.

But the prodigious waste of food was universal. When I had my own hospital later in this story, my northern English frugality rebelled against this extravagance. The plates were certainly loaded: overloaded, I thought and ordered the rations to be cut. It made no difference: still the bins overflowed. Fortunately, someone explained the mystery, or I might have gone on till the patients actually went hungry. It is good manners in Africa to leave some food on one's plate. 'Licking the platter clean' might seem to imply an insufficiency, and insult the munificence of one's host.

A few days back at Umtali, then another locum at Rusape, where the 'Baroness' was going on leave. Rusape was another general hospital, with two doctors. The Baroness was a large German lady: her number two was a tiny, black-eyed Polish girl, whom I called the 'Princess'. The Rusape Club had their own names. The Baroness, who must have weighed twenty stone, they called 'Twiggy': Stephanie, the Polish girl, they called 'Ipi Tombi', which sounds like a fetish doll.

The Baroness gave me supper on the day of my arrival. (Stephanie was not present.) We were neither of us conversationalists, so the evening was in the words with which Trollope modestly (and unjustly, in my opinion, as regards him) described his own performance: 'comfortable, but not splendid'.

The Baroness, I believe, was the doctor who performed the postmortem caesarean section referred to in Part II of this book. She was a Bavarian Catholic. She was an outdoor woman and once sustained a two-foot gash in her leg when out shooting. She *bopered[1]* herself (in the Rhodesian phrase) and got herself back to the hospital, where she calmly requested the nervous senior medical assistant to, 'stitch me up, please, Mr Moyo.'

She was said to have played a part in the German resistance during the war. She was a formidable lady, and I can well imagine her putting Hitler, 'that commonest little blighter' (in Chamberlain's phrase), in his place, if she ever encountered him.

A third locum at Marandellas, while the new superintendent was on sick leave, brought me to the end of November. It was pleasant to be in this lovely spot again, but I was already listed to go elsewhere.

Harry Knight had informed me that Shabani was going. This was a district hospital, plumb in the middle of the country, in a mining town. It was over a hundred miles away from the nearest specialists, so a good place for an independent spirit like myself. I applied and once again, as the only applicant, and presumably passing muster, got the job.

I left Marandellas and went to Shabani via Umvuma, spending the week-end there en route. The previous DMO Shabani had left three months before, and my old friend, Jock Scott, at Belingwe, was covering; but in the leisurely way of Africa, a week-end between friends made no difference.

I put up at the Falcon, met the old Friday night crowd, and had supper. I sat up in the hard bed in the plain room of the old hotel, with *Phineas Finn,* and was as content as our imperfect nature can be.

Next day, I played bowls with my old companions. One of them turned out to be the uncle of Ivor, the fiery physician at Umtali. The uncle asked me how I got on with him. Being, like Samson, my 'small boy' of Ghana days, too childish simple for the diplomatic evasion, I told them about the way he threw the notes across the ward - with or without the clip-boards: a touch June, especially, relished; at which the uncle laughed heartily, which told me what I knew already, that humour was not lacking in that family.

Next day, at nine o' clock in the evening, I drove into the quiet streets of Shabani: an action which, as I was to say in my annual report the

---

[1] Tied up. WD.

following year, would have been madness at the later date, when the tide of war had engulfed the whole country.

6 - Shabani

In the main street I asked the way to the hospital. I rang at the front door which was opened by a pretty white sister. She called a maid who took me to my house in the hospital grounds - or rather, a temporary house until my house was ready. (Meantime, and during my locums, I had given Anderson leave.) Deborah said, 'Be sure to lock your door, doctor. There has been a lot of pinchings from this house.' This was because it was unoccupied: burglary was not a problem in the town.

I had a good feeling about this post from the first, which was not disappointed by trials ahead, including those of increasing war: a feeling which was to find romantic fulfilment not too far ahead.

Next morning I woke to find myself surrounded by little hills, like the many breasts of Diana, glowing emerald in the strong light of summer. Shabani lay where the Highveld descends into the Lowveld, and, at a height of 3000 feet, was already 1000 feet lower than Gwelo. It was an up and down place, being not only surrounded by hills, but built on them, and the usual grid pattern was missing. The main street ran downhill into the town from Bulawayo and uphill out of the town, past the mine hospital, on the way to Fort Victoria. A branch road ran north to Selukwe and Gwelo, and the government hospital lay off this to the left. From these roads ran many smaller roads, up and down, round suburbs and townships, as well as the mine itself. There was a large township called Mandava, which came under the council and had a clinic under me. The mine, which was for asbestos, ran a hospital for their own people, who lived in four smaller townships with their own clinics; besides the management, who attended a clinic at the mine hospital, and were admitted, if necessary, to the white section of the government hospital, under their own doctors.

The town had then a population of 27,000, and the whole district (including town), about 75,000. The mine had three doctors, who looked after their own employees and families, and private patients from the general public (10,000 people in all). All the rest came under the single district medical officer.

The government hospital had 150 beds, thirty of which were for Europeans, who were treated by the mine doctors. There were some government whites, such as pioneer pensioners (before mentioned) and police. All road traffic and other police cases came under the government doctor.

The white ward had been built first, so the hospital (although now overwhelmingly black) was still called by the people, the 'White Hospital', or simply the 'White'. Out in the rural areas there was one rural hospital, which I visited once a week, and a number of council clinics, which were then visited by the provincial medical staff. The township clinic (Mandava), I visited every morning, referring patients to myself at the hospital (a mile away), whom if necessary I would take in the back of a van, delivering them to the clerk with a cry of: 'Mandava Tours!', which he heard with an indulgent grin.

I had a number of these stock jokes (which I would explain, if necessary, not wishing to take advantage of anyone). When I saw the radiographer in the corridor with one of his creations, I would ask, 'What have you got there, Rembrandt?' All of which, I hope, added to the gaiety of nations, or, at any rate, the hospital.

My district was as big as Cheshire: 50 miles by 30, and was the smallest in the country. I managed this seemingly impossible situation by the system and methods already referred to in the chapter on Gwelo.

And next to me lay Belingwe, Jock Scott's district, which was as big as say, Norfolk, and contained about 100,000 people. It is fair to say that Jock's district was also served by a number of mission hospitals - 'was', but not then, as will emerge.

I knew Jock was my neighbour and looked forward to meeting him again. I did not do so until the Christmas party at my hospital. All government departments gave Christmas parties and invited one another's personnel and the mine management. All these parties were whites only. The African sisters, who lived in a sisters' home adjoining and symmetrical with the white sisters' home, also gave a Christmas party, to which whites were invited, and I and the matron would attend. But the compliment was not returned in those days, I am sorry to say, not through any fault of myself or the matron: it would have been socially impossible.

At the Christmas party, Jock and his wife, Joyce, gave me a standing invitation to Sunday lunch, which I soon and often took up; and occasionally (self-centred bachelor) reciprocated. Jock had been at Belingwe eight years. He had a public health diploma and had previously worked as assistant medical officer of health in Bulawayo. He had served in the RAF in the war, which had first introduced him to Africa. He abhorred the cold, so when they asked him where he would like to be posted, he said, 'somewhere warm'. They sent him to the Gold Coast: something else we had in common.

The actual microscopic 'town' of Belingwe was only fifteen miles away, and from the first it was a delightful occasion to sit on Jock's veranda with him while Joyce prepared the lunch. We sat with our beers and watched the louries dropping down from a big wild fig tree in his front garden, and flapping up again, now and again uttering their cry: *'g'way! g'way!'*, for which they are also called 'go-away birds'. And Jock and I would talk work, books and music.

After lunch, I would bash his piano: a concert Bechstein, no less. I found it a heavy instrument to play: like driving a heavy lorry without much in the way of power-assisted steering. Jock said all grand pianos are like that. I don't believe it!

He never played to others himself, either on piano or violin: too self-critical, I think. He had a record-player and a fair collection of LPs, and the house was full of books. Jock's musical taste was pretty catholic. If he had a blind spot (or deaf ear), it was Mahler, whom he regarded as a dangerous lunatic, and was amused that Mahler had consulted Freud. At that time, I was developing an enthusiasm for Mahler, which was to become incurable (as Jock might have put it), but we never came to blows on the subject.

I was now carrying a heavy revolver and a cowboy belt full of bullets on my journeys out of town, in the received wisdom that if you ran into an ambush you drove through it, but if you were brought to a stop and showed no evidence of a weapon, they would come in and finish you off. Jock never carried a weapon, and here I think he was wise - at any rate, as far as his own district was concerned. Doctors were rarely attacked where they were known, and with a weapon, one might have got into an avoidable disaster. Outside one's district it was another matter.

Some doctors were killed, it is true. The guerrillas raided the clinics for drugs, which the staff readily supplied. Perhaps those doctors actively interfered and got into trouble: others turned a blind eye or, like Jock and me, were unaware of what was going on.

Jock had a sardonic turn of humour, which he was presently exercising on the Swedish missionaries in his district - or rather, not in his district. These people had been advised to leave by their organisations and had gone, leaving only the African nurses. Jock assumed the self-imposed task of supervising their medical establishments. And Jock was a devout atheist.

The task was self-imposed because so far from it being expected of him, various people were becoming anxious about the way he continued to drive all over his district as if it were not only as big as Norfolk, but Norfolk itself. I confined my outings to his place and our rural hospital at Lundi, seven miles out of town. Sometimes Jock would take Joyce with him in the battered Audi when she felt like a breath of fresh air. Joyce was a typical Cockney sparrow. Together they embodied the expression: 'London can take it!'

When questioned, Jock would reply that nobody was going to put him off his job; and add, he had had a good innings, anyway. Incidentally, as to his prospects thereafter, whenever the subject arose, he would smile sceptically and say: 'Dr Scott's carbohydrates, fats and proteins will melt back into Mother Earth.'

First the police, then the DC advised caution. Finally, the latter wrote to the secretary for health, who wrote to Jock in similar terms. Jock kept this letter to produce for the diversion of his friends. He did make some concessions. He submitted for a time to a police escort, but this was impracticable: Jock and the escorting vehicle seemed to come unstuck, or never meet - not, I fancy, without some contribution on Jock's part. Next he agreed to check with the police if the road was safe. Once, after receiving this assurance, he came upon a bridge, recently blown up. It was only a short walk further to the clinic, so Jock completed his journey on foot. When he returned to town, he told the police: 'I've got news for you!'

Finally, he got warnings in uncertain English from the guerrillas themselves, which he told me about but kept secret from his wife; as I discovered when I blew the gaff, fortunately when it was all in the past. After the war, the local guerrilla chief told me: 'We used to see Dr Scott every day, but we never shot him because we knew he was working for the people.' When I retailed this to Jock, he laughed in unbelief. More plausible to his cynicism was another explanation I got from one of his clinic nurses, also in the 'aftertime' (in Churchillian term): 'We needed Dr Scott to sign the drug requisitions' - on which, of course, the guerrillas also depended.

This does not explain the warnings from them. I can only say that many of their actions seemed arbitrary. The most rational suggestion I can make is that such policies as they had evolved through trial and error.

Jock and I stood in for each other on leave and other times when one was off station. Long leave (90 days) overseas must have been a trial for him, when he had the burden of both districts: I mean, he was then over sixty. When I was away, he would visit my hospital once a week. If they had an emergency, he would come over, as Shabani hospital was larger and altogether better equipped than Belingwe, which was little more than a rural hospital. How he managed to do caesars there, I do not know: and yet Mav had done massive bowel resections there, years before Jock; though, in the absence of a mortuary, he used to do his postmortems under a tree. No connection, of course!

But I used to feel for Jock as my long leave drew to an end. From Edinburgh once, when I had still two weeks to go, I sent him a card: 'Hold on. The Campbells are coming!' (Heaven knows what the Scottish postal people made of that.) He preferred me to take my leave first, so he had something to look forward to and keep him going.

When he was away, I would drive out to his place once a week and do a clinic and ward round and, of course, they would send emergencies to my hospital.

Jock had a 'thing' with the police, whom he called the 'Gestapo'. There was nothing political about this: he called Smith's police the Gestapo, and later, he called Mugabe's police the Gestapo.

In 1976 Jimmy retired. He stayed on in the house at Umtali with Carlos, but things got difficult when Carlos's wife, Maria, arrived and Jimmy felt in the way. They had furious Latin rows which sounded to Jimmy, lying low in his own room, like murder in the house. Moreover, Maria had a phobia of cats and I had left behind two.

The cats, brother and sister, had been given me by a policeman in Umvuma after a cobra walked into my house one night, but fortunately left when it saw me. Cats are as good as mongooses when it comes to snakes - and less antisocial. (Les Cady in Ghana had a pet mongoose which tried to eat his guests.) Maria had driven the cats out of the house and Jimmy did not know what to do about it. I told him they would look after themselves. They would find forage in plenty round the hospital bins, along with the dogs and the lunatics. One learns to be a bit heartless in Africa.

The last straw came when Jimmy wrote to me: 'The Antoninis have discovered tea-bags. Now, Warren, you know how I love my tea - but if there is one thing I cannot stand, it is tea-bags!'

I told him to come and join me in Shabani, and as soon as my house had been repainted and my furniture was installed, he came. He brought his few possessions with him, the largest after his car being his desk, which had gone with him everywhere for many years, to which he was greatly attached.

We planned a holiday over Christmas - a safari to Victoria Falls. Gareth came down in his pick-up, bringing a couple of rifles, and we went in my car.

The more you enjoy your work, the more you enjoy your holidays. Dull work, I suppose, makes for dull holidays and a dull life altogether. I don't know: that is one trial I have been spared, thank God. So it was always with the greatest zest that I sat behind the wheel and hit the high road on the first day.

If Barchester was 'always afternoon', Africa was always nine o'clock in the morning; that was its most characteristic hour: the eternally young continent, raring to go.

We passed the sign to Balla Balla, and Jimmy for the umpteenth time told us about the English public school man he met who called the place 'Blah-Blah'. We stopped at the hotel there for a drink. Over the bar was a notice: 'FREE BEER TOMORROW'. After independence, when the clientele broadened, the notice disappeared. Some humour is simply not transcultural.

At Essexvale we stopped for a bar lunch, and Gareth got his first experience of the Lennon effect on the ladies. When we left, they all kissed Jimmy good-bye, as if they had known him sixty years instead of sixty minutes.

Jimmy crackled with Liverpool humour. 'That lot were all right, fellows,' he said. 'But I have noticed - perhaps you can explain this, Warren - I have noticed that the older I get, the younger are the women I am attracted to. Mind you, I suppose I'm like a dog chasing a car: I wouldn't know what to do with it if I caught it!'

It was not ofter Gareth wept, with laughter or anything else: he was the phlegmatic Welsh type, which does exist, after all; but he wept now.

At Bulawayo we stayed at the old Selborne Hotel. Jimmy retired early to bed: early to rise. Gareth and I took a stroll in the quiet streets, had a night-cap, and followed him, long before midnight.

Next day, we took the Falls road. Jimmy took a turn at the wheel. We came to a cross-roads. The car stalled, and Jimmy could not get it going again. He went red in the face and started cursing so loud that a man in a car diametrically opposite, about fifty yards away, got out and called: 'Who are you swearing at, mate?' Jimmy shouted back: 'I'm swearing at this bloody car!' The man shrugged: 'O, that's all right, then,' and got back into his seat. When shortly after, Jimmy stepped out for a packet of cigarettes, Gareth remarked to me: 'He's a fiery old beggar, isn't he?'

Indeed, Jimmy's temper was legendary, though when I knew him the legend was mostly in the past, as legends would be. He had become teetotal, not because he was an alcoholic, but for the same reason you don't throw petrol on a fire. I believe a spectacular fight in a Merseyside tavern, followed by a rueful confession, led to this decision many years before.

When he entered a water-hole with us, he always ordered a pot of tea. In the five-star Montclair Hotel, on the road to Inyanga, the waiter asked him if he was a resident. 'A resident!' retorted Jimmy, rather wasting his Liverpool humour on the waiter. 'Do you think I would stay in a crummy joint like this? I only come here for the tea.'

We lunched at the Half-way House, and stopped in the afternoon at the Baobab. The African barman told us about a guerrilla who walked into the African bar (perhaps he wished to discourage his fellows from patronising the white establishment), opened up on the line of drinkers, missed everyone, and killed himself with his last bullet, which bounced off the wall. 'It served him right,' commented the barman, in a Sunday school tone of voice.

Then, in the late afternoon, as the wide, monotonous Matabeleland Bushveld begins to dip towards the Zambezi valley, we saw the spray cloud of the Falls, rising in steam from the bush, fifteen hundred feet: *Mosi oa Tunya,* the Smoke that Thunders. Soon we were in the ambit of that thunder, which continues in the background, in the pauses of the day, in the watches of the night, powerfully but unobtrusively, like the engines of a great ship.

We put up at the Casino Hotel, and walked to the Falls next day. Christmas is a good time to see them, just after the rainy season has started. By April, the spray cloud is so dense, they are practically invisible. In October, at the end of the dry season, they are at their lowest and though always beautiful, not at their most impressive. Livingstone first saw them in November, which is a good time after fair rains. I have seen them a dozen times, at all seasons. Nothing can stale the hypnotic power of the massive white waters, plunging for ever into the abyss.

At the hotel swimming pool, we met Japie van Blerk, the cheeky DO cadet from Umvuma. He had since gone into the army and was now demobbed. He was staying at the cheap chalets in the town. Then on Christmas Day, a sad thing happened.

Jimmy became afraid at the expense of our holiday. We proposed to go on to Kariba, down the great lake, and stay at further expensive hotels there. Jimmy was now on an exiguous pension, but he had, in fact, secured another post to go to at a Catholic boys' boarding school, near Wankie. Nevertheless, he was afraid, and wished to turn back. He was quite prepared to make his own way, and was not going to disturb us in any way.

We had planned to take Christmas dinner in the evening at the Victoria Falls Hotel, no more expensive than the Casino, but older, with its own Edwardian charm. Jimmy got cold feet and took his Christmas dinner by himself at the Wimpey.

Young Japie, whose heart was as light as his pockets (but he was forty years younger than Jimmy), was glad to join us for dinner and for the rest of our holiday. We had a merry supper, and even made jokes about poor Jimmy. 'It was Christmas Day in the Wimpey. The tears were falling fast.'

Next day, Jimmy secured a lift to Balla Balla. That still left him 80 miles to Shabani. He told me later, he stood at the side of the road while car after European car drove past him. Finally, one stopped and he was rescued from the boiling sun. I asked him if he had had his hat on. 'Of course I had my hat on! D'you think I was going to give myself sunstroke into the bargain?' I explained that under his broad hat, his face was as dark as an African's. His limbs were burnt dark too. Not many Africans wore shorts, but that was a minor point. Whites rarely stopped for Africans. Prejudice apart, they left them to their own kind, who made a charge for the service. Africans would rarely pick up a white man because they would not expect a fee. At the lucky moment, perhaps, Jimmy took off his hat to expose his famous 'eggy' head.

But for ever after this incident, Gareth, in his deep Welsh way (I mean an Englishman would not have taken it so personally), felt profoundly disappointed in Jimmy: in a sense, never forgave him, as if he had let him down in some way. Myself, I was indifferent. Jimmy was an old friend, and I felt that somewhere in his life, in his Liverpool childhood, perhaps, he had been infected with the deadly fear of poverty, which men can harbour even when they have grown rich: something I have missed, and I suppose Gareth too; although Gareth had never had life handed to him on a silver platter.

We left the Falls and drove to the Mlibisi ferry on Lake Kariba, 60 miles across some very wild country: a dirt road. I must have seemed nervous, as that little devil, Japie, actually read my thoughts: 'Are you worried about land mines, Warren? I wouldn't worry about land mines: you won't know anything about it if you *do* hit one.' The confidence of youth!

We stopped a couple of nights at Mlibisi, and tried to catch tiger-fish. The African ghillie first caught two or three bream, to use as bait, with an ease that astonished us and provoked our envy after the many fishless afternoons we had spent beside the dams and rivers of Umvuma. Then he drove a motorboat while we trawled for the fish. Japie caught one wretched thing, barely half a pound: he must have foul-hooked it. Later, I was to catch them easily off Fothergill Island from an anchored boat.

One night we boarded the car ferry and set sail down the 170 mile lake. Next afternoon, everyone was ordered below decks as we went through Chete gorge, where a Canadian tourist had been shot dead on the upper deck from the bank. When we came to the midmost part of the lake, the boat stopped to let people jump into the sparkling clear water and bathe. We old men, including that young old man, Japie, were too lazy. The crew assured us the crocodiles never came into the middle of the lake. Later, I read in the paper a letter from a Wild Life official who said this was a fond illusion: crocodiles moved all over the lake - no doubt, when they saw the car ferry coming!

We spent two nights on the boat and arrived at Kariba town in time for breakfast. The town and its situation rather resemble the same in Switzerland or North Italy, except that, with a population similar to say, Locarno, it is scattered over a much wider area, and Kariba lake must be ten times bigger than Lake Maggiore.

At Makuti, we picked up a young Englishman who had joined the Rhodesian army: a mad type with ideas about the Master Race and the survival of the fittest. Even the Afrikaner, Japie, thought him barmy. A number of outsiders joined the Rhodesian forces, mostly

Americans who had been in Vietnam, and very strange people some of them were: not all, but definitely some.

We dropped him at Sinoia, where we spent the night. We dropped Japie in Salisbury, next day, and went on to Umvuma, where we arrived in time for the DC's New Year party. The early-nighter, Gareth, gave this a miss and went home to his farm. Ted, the stationmaster, had accompanied him to Shabani and brought his pick-up back to Umvuma.

Jimmy stayed with me about three months and in the New Year went to Wankie to take up his new post. In April, I got a message from a friend that he had died - suddenly, according to the friend, who was in the house at the time. Jimmy was singing in the bathroom. Suddenly the singing stopped. The house fell very silent. When the friend went to investigate, Jimmy was dead on the mat.

He was cremated, and a memorial service held in the Catholic cathedral at Umtali. I attended. I had to travel from Shabani the day before to catch the dawn convoy from Fort Victoria. (No convoys out of Shabani then, but soon after.) I was surprised that few people attended the service: Jimmy was so out-going. I realised that essentially he was a very private person: the few friends he had were true friends, and what man can say more?

I wrote to his sister in England: 'Jimmy was one of the life-givers. He was like nine o' clock in the morning. He was like the first day of the holidays.' And he was.

I suppose the cliche, 'gay bachelor', refers to men under thirty: there may be gay bachelors over that age, but they never included me. After the age of thirty, until I met my wife, my life was a grey desert, relieved by the occasional oasis, which invariably turned out to be a mirage - as the Irishman said. However, a mirage is better than nothing: 'tis better to have loved and lost...! Indeed, it is more than nothing, for any love, even unrequited, is a treasure and advances us in spirit.

I first saw Katie across a crowded floor - in the cricket club, in fact. I had been in Shabani a year. I asked the man I was with: 'Who is that beautiful woman, over there?'

He smiled. 'That's Katie Woolfson. She's a widow. Her husband was killed by a land mine two years ago.'

I did not lose time in introducing myself. 'I don't think we have met...'

'Yes, we have. You gave my baby second prize in the baby show last year.'

'Only second prize!'

She was tall and slender, she was blonde and green-eyed. She had a face of classical beauty. She was alive and intelligent. She was as strong as steel and as soft as honey. And I believe I saw it all in the first ten minutes.

I don't mean she was superficial. A diamond is not superficial: it is clear and true to its depths, and a lifetime will not exhaust its interest. And that was Katie.

Next day I said to a woman in the office: 'I met a lovely woman last night, Katie Woolfson. What do you know about her?'

Sue was excited. 'Yes, she is lovely; and she is a super person. But I must warn you: she has a boy-friend, and I think they are pretty steady.'

Well, they all have boy-friends. I made it a principle to ignore them.

The day after, Sue was standing on the steps, waiting for me.

'Good news! No. Good news/bad news! Katie Woolfson's boy-friend was killed in an ambush last night.'

Well, reader, how would you have taken that news? I leave my feelings to your imagination.

I thought I had better give it a decent interval before approaching her. Six months? Someone else might approach her before then. After two months I rang her up and asked her round to supper. She put me off with some excuse. I rang her once or twice later. She accepted once but discovered a PTA meeting at the last minute: she was a teacher at the local white primary school. She had five children of her own.

Then I sent her a book for her birthday, with a gushing letter, like any schoolboy. She wrote back a serious letter, saying she did not want to disappoint me, but she had resolved to form no further romantic relationships with men. She dreaded another tragedy - her heart just could not take it.

So I bided my time.

I saw her occasionally about the town: the clubs, at the hospital, and we chatted in a friendly way. I would not say we had nothing in common: we had plenty. But it was plain, on some fundamental level, I was not her type.

Then, after about eighteen months, I saw her with a tall dark handsome man. And it wasn't long before Katie renounced her vows.

Of course, it was inevitable. She had lived, not only in grief, but dread for over a year; but life and courage come back, and the heart of her nature was love.

And soon after that, I met my wife, and within a year we were engaged.

'I am glad,' said Katie. 'I am always glad when something nice happens to people I like.' She was a good person.

My fiancée and I became friendly with the Marais. Danie was the nicest chap you could wish to meet: a gentle giant. I played their piano. I had invited Katie to hear mine at one of the candlelight suppers that never came off. It would have been a disaster.

I played Spanish music, which enchanted Danie, who had a romantic streak. Katie had romance as wide as the plains of Africa, but it did not stretch to Spanish music, which she called 'jerky'.

'That's rhythm,' I protested.

'It's not,' insisted Katie. 'It's jerky.'

She did not want anything 'heavy' either, which seemed to rule out the rest of my repertoire.

Danie attracted me as much as Katie. Not only was he gentle and sensitive, he had great strength, and I respected him enormously. He also had a killer instinct, which I never had, except in desperation, which is not the same thing. One night, at the bar of the police club, I was telling him about the delights of war surgery - how after I had fought for hours in the night, saving a life from a gunshot wound, I felt too exhilarated to go back to bed before I had had a beer and music on the record-player.

Danie leaned back and laughed in his beard. (He was in the police reserve.) 'It's funny you should say that, Warren. What you have been describing is the way I feel after I've shot one of the buggers.'

Katie and Danie had something elemental about them. They belonged to Africa and always would. They were made for each other like the night and the day, like thunder and lightning - but I hope they did not have too much of that in their marriage.

In 1977, Gareth decided to retire, at an early age, and devote himself to enjoyment; like Rossini, whom Gareth resembled in appearance and sanguine temperament, as well as loving his music. He sold his farm and bought a place outside Marandellas in ten acres of land. He kept sheep at first: the lean African things, of course, which look like greyhounds (fat English sheep would have starved), but eventually found it too much trouble, and settled for fruit-growing and bee-keeping. And I had a standing invitation to stay. I returned the compliment, and Gareth came one week-end to my place, but country mouse as he was, preferred to stay at home, so I was able to visit him every six months with a clear conscience.

And after the heavy and sometimes harrowing work of the hospital, there was nothing more relaxing than to arrive at Gareth's place, after the 280 mile journey to Marandellas, finding myself bowling down the Igava road, which dipped to the vast distance of the Highveld, on whose crest Marandellas stood. And I had hardly put my bag away and washed my face before I would get it into a pint of Gareth's home brew - the only beer I know which shares with the Congo beers the power of a strong bouquet.

We talked. I talked more than Gareth, Welshman as he was; unloading myself, as he had a peculiar power to induce. He would have made a good psychiatrist. The best psychiatrists are made of such earthy stuff - not the intellectual weirdos of popular imagination. Though Gareth would talk often about bombing Germany, not in any boastful way, but because that seemed to be the high point of his rather disappointing life: not that he ever used such terms, and a more imperturbable and philosophical chap you would go a long way to find.

He read much in his lonely days, mainly non-fiction: war, exploration; though his days were solitary rather than lonely, as that is how he preferred them. He was a miller of Dee if ever there was one, though while it would not be true to say he cared for nobody and nobody cared for him, the numbers were limited and highly selective, at any rate, on his side. Otherwise, he played golf once a week and enjoyed a drink afterwards at the club.

Gareth loved music, especially the more melodious and romantic kind. He loved opera, but his favourite was Tchaikovsky. We listened to records much while I was with him. He had a peculiar aversion to Chopin, which I could not understand. Years later, he admitted that Chopin had written some good tunes: he had been put off by the wimpish way Chopin let that Sand woman push him around. A curious foundation for musical criticism!

In the daytime (for I would stay three nights), we went fishing one day and played golf the other. Gareth would have a nap in the afternoon, while I sat with a book on his veranda, which gave a lovely view across a *vlei* to a rocky *kopje*, about a mile away.

Gareth had two dogs, both English bull terriers. Joker, the elder, was becoming a social menace, as he noisily fumigated any room he was in; but Gareth loved him more than the pretty young bitch, Sally. The two dogs ran about the country together. One day, while I was there, only Sally returned, with a four-inch gash in her leg, which I stitched up while Gareth held her down. We thought they may have disturbed a leopard or baboons on the *kopje*. Gareth hated baboons with a black Welsh hatred which surprised me. Gareth was a good friend and a bad enemy. Joker never came back. I tried to console Gareth, saying that he had gone down fighting and would feel no pain. Better, too, than a painful old age; though Gareth would have spared him that, hard as he would have felt it. And he felt Joker's loss hard then, for all my words.

As for Sally, she soon got tired of Gareth's dull company, and took to wandering off to the African township, where eventually she decided to remain. 'Just like a woman!' growled Gareth. 'Serve her right! Soon she'll learn how the Kaffirs treat their women!'

Gareth never had a servant: did everything for himself, except for a girl who came in to wash and clean once a week. He never had another dog after Sally left, male or female. I warned him about security. Even he left his place sometimes, if only for the club or an occasional run up to town, to buy brewing requisites chiefly. Then he took to going away for holidays, and leaving his place alone was a worry. His nearest neighbour was a hundred yards away. For longer periods he put the dogs into kennel anyway.

Indeed, he had some break-ins: nothing much stolen; there was nothing much to steal, and that more of sentimental than material value, though the former would weigh more with Gareth. I advised him that the next best thing (better) to a fierce dog was a fierce houseboy. Gareth had a *kaya* on his land, so he leased it out for nothing, except the security of the place, to a strong honest fellow called Armando, who settled in with his family. What is more, I was surprised to learn that Armando's pretty little wife, who certainly did not look the part, was a witch-doctor. It certainly strengthened Gareth's household insurance: he never had another break-in after that!

On his little breaks, Gareth had discovered the delights of the Troutbeck Inn. This large, comfortable hotel, all in one storey except for the Lake wing at its feet, lies beside a lake in a valley of the Eastern Highlands. It has a delightful nine-hole golf course, all up wooded hill and down dale, with a closing shot across the lake. There is trout-fishing, tennis, etc, and indoor games like snooker. It also had a piano in the vast lounge which I played to Gareth and such other guests as cared to listen. In the foyer is a log fire which is kept burning all the time, winter and summer, and is always a welcome sight in the fresh and sometimes keen air of the mountains. For it was not long before Gareth introduced me to the place and we had the first of many holidays there, starting in the cold of winter.

Meanwhile, the bush war was spreading. The white farms between Marandellas and the Highlands were still free, and remained so till the end, so we had to join no convoy, despite Jimmy's enterprise in the matter. The infiltration from Mozambique was proceeding, north and south, and the guerrillas were beginning the permanent occupation of the tribal areas, which eventually they would complete throughout the country. Nevertheless, on the night of July 14, 1978, fireworks were added by Comrade Mugabe to the other entertainments of the Troutbeck Inn.

Gareth and I were sitting up in our beds at 10.15pm, reading our books, in the East wing of the hotel. Everyone else was in the bar. On our arrival, we had left our weapons at the desk, to be locked up in the manager's office, as was the practice in hotels in other parts of the country. Suddenly we heard what sounded like a fireworks display from the direction of the golf course, across the lake. Very soon I recognised it for what it was. I said to Gareth: 'That's an attack!'

First, the irregular crackle of automatic rifles, then the steady hammering of a machine-gun, then the *boom!, boom!* of mortars and rockets, solemn and sinister in the night. I knew you had to get two walls between yourself and a rocket-propelled grenade, which burned its way through the first one and exploded inside. I told Gareth, we had better crawl into the corridor.

We doused the lights and got down on the floor, or at least, I did. I was about to reach up for the door handle when, glancing over my shoulder to see if Gareth was following me, I saw his stout form silhouetted in the window. He had actually opened the curtains, and said: 'It doesn't seem to be coming this way, Warren.'

Then all the lights in the hotel went out, as the manager raced for his office and threw the master switch.

Meanwhile, firing was coming from the hotel itself. The people in the bar (who had *not* put their weapons in the manager's office) had broken the windows, and were firing back, Wild West fashion.

When the shooting started, two 'bright lights' had been patrolling the front of the hotel. These were police reservists, sent to guard hotels and farms and suchlike exposed country places; so called because they mostly came from the bright lights of the city. They had crossed beneath the large globe lights of the hotel's central steps, and were as exposed as could be. They hit the ground and started firing with their rifles across the lake. When the lights went, they somehow broke into the Lake wing, whose french windows stood behind them, and fired back from some cover.

The guerrillas, a party of about thirty, were ensconced in a pine wood, across the lake. They had got a mortar on the tenth tee - a long-range speciality of the course, for stronger players, crossing the lake - which gives the range to the ninth hole: 350 yards. Add another fifty and they had the range of the hotel. They got one bomb on the terrace in front, and another in the car park behind, nicely 'bracketing' the building. Then they got a third one on the roof, which blew a hole in it over the foyer. The rockets all flew over the hotel and landed harmlessly in the open ground beyond.

The people in the bar and the bright lights aimed for the flashes of the guerrillas' weapons, including the mortar. The firing grew too hot for the mortar-handlers, who, after three shots, decamped. The evidence of all this we saw next day: the flash burn of the mortar on the tenth tee,[1] the scores of the bullets within feet of it, the pine trees gashed with high-velocity bullets, discarded AK magazines, and even an RPG left in the little wood.

Meanwhile, Gareth's bulky form filled the window. Suddenly he exclaimed: 'Good God, Warren! Why haven't we got our weapons? It will all be over without us!'

Pausing only to don dressing-gown and slippers, he shuffled into the corridor, and I followed him likewise. We got to the foyer and saw the starry sky through the big hole. Someone with a rifle challenged us. I answered nervously: 'Dr Durrant and Mr Baker.' Gareth wanted to find the manager and retrieve his .303. Like Dr Watson, I had brought my revolver, which would not have made much contribution, even if I had Gareth's enthusiasm, which I did not. I was not afraid, but neither was I interested in gun-fighting. But the manager was too busy firing himself, and Gareth and I had to sit in the smoky corridor.

And in ten minutes, it was all over. No one was hit on either side. The guerrillas suddenly stopped firing and made their way back over the hills. Smoke continued to fill the corridors. It was coming from a mattress, smouldering in the Lake wing. The manager had it pulled out on to the lawn.

The lights came on and everyone gathered in the bar, in the euphoria which follows a happy issue on such occasions. The bar was riddled with bullets. Most of the bullets had gone high, as is

---

[1] Probably a recoilless rifle. WD.

common in such exchanges. All the windows were shattered from the activities of both sides. The ceiling was scored all over. The big mirror behind the bar was shattered, and many of the bottles in front of that. Every room in the Lake wing was riddled, but the East wing, out of the line of fire, escaped. Wire furniture on the terrace was smashed by the first mortar bomb. The second had done little damage in the car park. All this, too, we discovered next day.

Meanwhile, the bar opened for drinks on the house, and a party started that went on till two in the morning. A pretty Australian girl, who was holiday-working at the hotel, found herself the excited and exciting centre of attention from bearded men with smoking rifles. She would have a tale to tell when she got home. She did not wait to tell it. She quit her job and left the country next day.

Otherwise, the only cloud rested on Gareth, who was fuming. 'I've never felt so frustrated,' he spluttered, 'since I was looking the wrong way when that German night-fighter flew past us over Berlin.' Gareth was a forward gunner at the time.

When we got back to Marandellas, we told our tale at the bar of the Three Monkeys Hotel, expecting to be kings of the pub and bought a round, at least. But such tales were two a penny by now, and most of the drinkers, being younger than ourselves, were spending half their time in the security forces, one way or another. We did our stuff, like dual announcers on the television. When we finished, there was a pause. One man put down his glass, and remarked reflectively: 'Troutbeck! I lost three golf balls in the lake there once.'

The following Christmas we went up to Troutbeck again. As we entered the foyer, Gareth brandished his rifle and said to the manager behind the counter: 'Here we are again, David! All ready to shoot a few terrorists, what?'

David received this greeting with a certain coolness. 'Things have changed, Gareth. We have our own guard force now.'

Both coolness and information failed to register with Gareth, who carried his rifle to our room and propped it lovingly beside his bed, like a favourite teddy bear. He carefully laid a bag of ammunition beside it on the floor, in case it got hungry in the night. He was not going to be cheated of any sport going this time. I had my cowboy outfit with me, which I put away in a drawer. After that, we went for sundowners and supper.

At supper, a white youth of about nineteen in a T-shirt approached our table. This was the captain of the guard force. He had no difficulty making out whom he wished to speak to. David had probably described Gareth in terms of the Galloping Major, which would certainly have picked out Gareth in a crowd.

'Excuse me, sir,' he began. 'I believe you have a rifle in your room.'

Gareth put down his soup spoon. 'Yes, my boy,' he replied, rubbing his hands together. 'Expecting a spot of trouble, are we?'

'If we do have any trouble, sir,' replied the youth, 'we would prefer you to remain in your room.'

'But you see,' replied Gareth, anxiously, 'we are in the Garden wing. You don't have a very good field of fire from there.' The Garden wing lay behind the main building. 'Shouldn't I report to an assembly point or something?'

The youth looked at the ceiling. He looked down again.

'Look, sir,' he concluded. 'If we want you, we will send for you.' With which he walked away.

'Don't ring us, we'll ring you!' mocked Gareth, bitterly. He looked at me earnestly. 'Why, Warren! I was seeing action when that child's nappies were on the line!' He looked away, engaged in some mental arithmetic. He looked back at me. 'Dammit! When his *father's* nappies were on the line!'

Something aged in Gareth, almost visibly. Between spoonfuls of soup, he went on bitterly: 'Not wanted! That's it! Not wanted! Too old!'

Now that the shooting has started in these pages, 'liberal' readers (lock up the spoons!) may be asking what I was doing toting a gun on the 'wrong side', with which I might have killed someone old Mr Gladstone used to describe as 'struggling, rightly struggling, to be free'. Quite apart from the chances of hitting anyone with my ancient Webley, carried for self-defence, or simply deterrence (as previously explained), while pinned down in a ditch, under a hail of bullets, I suppose it still implicated me in the situation; and even if I had been as defenceless as Jock Scott, I was still committing the 'sin' of risking my precious hide in a 'wrong cause', even if I did have a romantic idea of death in Africa, under almost any circumstances, as carrying its own crown of glory: all of which may call for some explanation.

I had hoped to avoid politics in this book, as I had in my position as a doctor in Rhodesia; but perhaps they will not avoid me.

Frankly, I did not see right or wrong on either side; at any rate, in simple terms. I knew that Comrades Mugabe and Nkomo were 'on the side of history' (if not each other's), and that Smithy on his blasted heath was as mad and wrong-headed as any old Greek defying the wrath of the gods. But this situation, I saw, not in moral terms, but as tragic. Both sides were right and both sides were wrong, and there was nothing anybody could do about that: which I take it is the essence of tragedy.

I must confess that if I had had sons of military age, I would have done my best to get them out of Smithy's clutches: not for them to bear the sins of the fathers. But, for myself, I saw these as the last days of the Empire, which, with all its faults, I regarded as one of the great creative enterprises of mankind; in which I found my own fulfilment, for I was not in Africa for any empty philanthropic ego trip.

I hope there is some moral interest in the above. The sensible reader may wonder why I bothered to justify myself.

For a year or two, some spirits had been advocating combining districts in certain cases, so that the doctors would have the benefits of two heads and time off duty. Meaning they should choose the superior hospital and run both their districts from there. At Umvuma, David Taylor had already suggested that I should join with Enkeldoorn, but being too independent, or cussed, I had resisted the idea.

Now I found myself approaching Jock with a similar proposal, based on my hospital, which was larger and better equipped than his. I had broached the idea soon after my arrival at Shabani, but he was as reluctant as I had been at Umvuma: I discovered that other doctors at Shabani had made the same proposal without success. However, in time, I did succeed where others had failed, due partly to our growing friendship and mutual confidence, and, perhaps more forcefully, to other events: the most important being the Wall.

As the security situation worsened, the authorities erected a wire fence around the small town of Belingwe, with a gate, to be closed and guarded at night, like some medieval town. And Jock's house and beloved hospital were left outside the wall.

There was some talk about expense, which did nothing to appease Jock. He was not afraid, at any rate, for himself. But he was certainly not happy about Joyce. Besides which, there was the insult of the position.

The final indignity represented by the wall and the gate emerged when Joyce had to knock on the latter for permission to enter after dark to attend her bridge parties, to have the muzzle of a rifle thrust in her teeth.

That clinched it for both of them. But there remained one problem: Jock's nine-foot Bechstein. The available house at Shabani was a two-storey one, near the main gate, called the 'bottom house', as the internal hospital road sloped down to the main road. The doors and rooms of this house would never have admitted or accommodated the concert grand. I lived in the 'top house', a single-storey house above the hospital, among trees, altogether more spacious. I had a Steinway upright, but this would fit comfortably in the bottom house. So, it was agreed that I would give up the top house to Jock and Joyce, and move into the other one.

This was done, and the Bechstein and the Scotts comfortably installed, to begin a happy association between us for the next six years, until Jock retired.

Every Wednesday the Scotts gave me supper - taking pity on the lonely bachelor. Radio Rhodesia broadcast a concert that night - on discs, though there were, in fact, two amateur orchestras in the country: Salisbury and Bulawayo. Jock had played violin in the Bulawayo Symphony Orchestra. The man who ran the radio concerts was a Mahler enthusiast, so we got a Mahler symphony about once a month, which was a trial to Jock, but fortunately sufficient

Beethoven, Brahms, etc, most other weeks. Then I would bash the piano before departing.

Once, when I was called to the hospital from my own place, not on a Wednesday night, I heard Jock playing. The Chopin studies came cascading down the hill with a technique almost at professional level. 'You didn't hear the wrong notes,' said Jock, when I told him next day. Once only did he play to me: his technique was of a high level, but his performance lacked finesse.

Jock had perfect pitch. Not only would he name any note I played at random on the piano. One evening, a tree frog was trilling its single note after the rain. I asked Jock if he could name it. 'E flat,' he answered, without hesitation. When I checked him on the piano, he was correct.

He could recognise the make of the more famous violins or pianos by their tone, he told me. I never asked him about orchestras, but I expect he could recognise the more famous ones too.

The mine had a surgeon when I arrived in Shabani - a chunky little Pole in his fifties, called Marek. He gave me a lot of help and instruction. He could be brilliant, and sometimes less so: which can be said for most surgeons. I have seen no surgeon more dextrous. Henry, at Umtali, was a virtuoso; and Ian was a sound craftsman. But Marek could open the abdomen with a single slash, without touching anything within, which I never saw anyone else do. He did this when I called him in to a man with a ruptured spleen - a case I had seen only once before - in Ghana, and failed with in my early days. Marek was into the abdomen and had the pedicle ligated in seconds: the organ was completely avulsed and it is a wonder the man ever reached the operating table.

I had a gunshot wound - a man shot in the throat with an enormous haematoma (bleed) that so distorted the anatomy I could not find the windpipe to insert a tube; for the man was choking. Luckily, Marek was in the hospital at the time, and I called him. He took the knife from my hand without scrubbing up, found the windpipe in seconds, and got the tube in.

But alas, in other matters, his reach exceeded his grasp. A guerrilla was brought in with his jaw smashed by a bullet. The police wanted to question him. 'Maybe vee can do somesing viz vires,' said Marek. I thought: 'we have ways of making you talk'. Alas! there was nothing to be done with wires - not then, or by us, at any rate; and I sent the man to Bulawayo.

Unlike Henry, he also fancied himself as a gynaecologist. Certainly, he could do a good caesar and hysterectomy, but he thought he could do the highly specialised business of repairing vesico-vaginal fistulas - the hole, so many African women develop between the bladder and the vagina after obstructed labour. After a failed attempt of Marek's, which I had to transfer to Bulawayo, a gynaecologist sent me a cautionary letter referring to him. When I passed the message on to Marek, he retorted: 'Who eez zees boy? I voz doing VVFs before he knew vot a vagina voz!'

Later, came another surgeon to the mine. Their establishment was simply for three medical officers: if they had specialist degrees, so much the better. They all did general practice, anyway. Percy was a retired British Army surgeon, an old-fashioned debonair type, rather like Noel Coward. From the first, he and Marek clashed like rival prima donnas or the editors in Eatanswill. It was an elemental antipathy, unequalled by nature since her last experiment with the cat and the dog.

Percy's opinion of Marek was unutterable - or should have been in the eyes or ears of the Medical Council - but that did not stop Percy uttering it; nor did he care whom he uttered it to. At an open air luncheon of a fishing party, which must have included half the local angling society (needless to say, lay people all, except Percy and me), Percy aired his views of Marek. 'Did you hear what he did to poor, dear, old Mrs Blenkinsop? Bless my soul! I felt positively ashamed for my profession!'

Marek could hardly have sued him for slander, even if litigation was popular in Rhodesia (which it was not), as he would have been hampered by the usual handicaps existing between the pot and the kettle. He had no hesitation in criticising Percy's work, even when it was wide awake and listening to him. 'An outdated operation! Nobody does it now.' I have seen him more than once spread Percy's notes and X-rays round the duty room to demonstrate Percy's

249

supposed shortcomings to all who ran and read, or merely listened, including the cleaners.

I had a feeling that Percy was Jewish, although he never said so. Jock agreed when I put it to him. 'He has all the Jewish touches,' he said. Jock and Joyce played bridge with Percy and his wife, Marguerita. 'He'd lend you a thousand dollars as soon as you asked him, but he'd fight you for five cents at the card table.'

One night, the police brought Percy to me for suspected drunken driving. The case was completely irregular: they had got him out of his bed three hours after the incident in question. But he was so emotional, like a ham actor overplaying an outraged Shylock, that I feared for a horrible few minutes that he *was* drunk. 'Don't talk to me, you scoundrel!' he shouted at a black police constable. 'I'll report you to your superiors tomorrow. I'll report the lot of you. Just see if I don't! The magistrate is a friend of mine. I play golf with him. Just wait till he hears about this, damn you!' I went through the prescribed routine: even without the blood test it was obvious that he was cold sober. They let him drive his car home: they had let him drive it to the hospital, just to botch their case completely.

Another, more tangential clue, I thought I saw when I told him one morning: 'I was saying to my mother - I mean, my wife!' Percy chortled at the Freudian slip with what seemed an ancient wisdom, more than Anglo-Saxon. He would have chortled deeper had he heard my wife the other day call me 'son', and I twenty years older than her.

I have a talent for improbable friendships, as the reader may have noticed. Koos was a mine captain, a big Afrikaner, by common consent the strongest man in the town, white or black. His moustachioed face was like Bismarck's Pomeranian grenadier's: I even think he had a touch of the Zulu in him (one can never tell with those people), of which he would have been more proud than otherwise, for he had not a scrap of racialism about him. He had had a hard life - brought up in some South African orphanage - and he drank too much. But he had soul.

He painted. He spoke several languages, including African ones. He played guitar and sang a little, and had a good collection of books, mainly of the scientific encyclopedia kind. And he was a music lover. The first record I heard in his house - he had a place with a bit of land outside town - was the *Hammerklavier*. And then I gave him Mahler.

Talk about Chapman's Homer and the road to Damascus! Mahler's music rolled through the big soul of Koos, as he said, 'like the surf at Cape Town, crashing over me', and reverberated like thunder from the African heavens. '*Ag*, man! Why didn't you introduce me to Mahler before?'

In the widely-spaced houses of Africa, you can make as much noise as you like. (Among the closely-spaced houses of most of the blacks, they don't care, anyway, and sleep through anything.) So, black or white, it tends to be a noisy culture. In the pubs and clubs, the white Rhodesians would bawl at one another across twenty yards. Even their private conversations could be heard that distance. You could tell the Pommies by their conspiratorial whispering groups in corners. So there was never any problem about raising Mahler at three o' clock in the morning over a crate of beer, as Koos and I did more than sometimes.

Koos spent half his time in the TA, as did all the whites under 56, who were not actually in the army or police reserve. Out in the bush, he did his duty as bravely as any, but his heart was not in it.

His wife owned the main garage in town. She was a Cockney, name of Byron, and claimed descent from the poet, which I suppose a lot of people could. Over the garage, they had one or two flats, one rented by Sister Mutema, from the government hospital.

Most of the African staff were either sympathetic, if not actively involved, with the nationalist cause, though we hardly suspected it at the time. Sister Mutema was a key worker.

Koos, who knew the Africans better than most, must have guessed this. Once, he saw a trail of blood leading to Sister Mutema's door. 'Harbouring terrorists' and 'failing to report the presence of terrorists' were serious offences. Koos got a mop and washed it up. It was all in character with the man. He could face his enemy in the bush: shopping people was not his trade.

He must have been a difficult husband. Every now and again, he would throw up his job and take off: once to a mine in the north-west, once to South Africa. He would return to town in strange moods: one time raging on a fishing outing about God knows what; once, sitting in my house, where he confessed: 'Sometimes I wish I could die in my sleep.' I remembered Schubert said the same thing.

On his South African excursion, his wife, an Italian-looking, passionate woman, herself, who really loved him for all the terrific rows they had - Anita told me, Koos was working with a couple of blacks, unloading steel pipes from a lorry, when the blacks suddenly pushed one of the pipes into Koos's stomach - for no reason, just the white man. 'And there's no one less racist than Koos,' cried Anita. Koos ended up in hospital, but not before he had put his two assailants in *their* hospital as well.

Sister Mutema had a secret lover. The most unmilitary specimen you ever saw in battle fatigues. He sat in his camouflage at my table on the veranda of the Shabani hotel and poured out his sad story to me over his beer.

This was Cecil, about thirty, some kind of office worker, trapped in the police reserve. Part of his duties was guarding the government hospital at night. This was simple enough. Mostly they sat in the sisters' common room in the European hospital, drank tea, flirted with the white sisters a bit, and slept. The black sisters also used this common room, where Cecil must have met and fallen in love with Sister Mutema.

Sister Mutema was a handsome woman. She was a nicer person than Winnie Mandela, but fell little short of her in force of personality: in other words, she could have eaten Cecil for breakfast. And, needless to say, she was totally unaware of his existence.

The rabbit-like Cecil appealed to me. 'I think Sister Mutema's got something against me, doc. I can tell by the way she looks at me. I think it must be this uniform. Honest, doc, I never asked to be given this uniform. I've got nothing against the bloody Kaffirs. I only wanted to be left alone. Do you think you can make Sister Mutema understand, doc? I'd like to get to know her, really.'

I finally had a word with Sister Mutema - *after* the civil war. At an earlier date, she might have had him slain, like one of the old queens of Ireland, when their subjects looked too high. I'm sorry to say, she did not even laugh.

In 1979, Smith held his first one man one vote election (when Muzorewa became prime minister, or something, under Smithy's control), in which even foreigners like Anderson and me were allowed to vote. I filled in the forms. Anderson's wife was living with him then. 'What is your wife's name, Anderson?' Anderson was then polishing the floor. He straightened up on his knees, smacked his forehead, and exclaimed: 'Ah, *bassie*!' He scuttled off to the *kaya* and after a few minutes came back.

'Sarah!'

There is a love which *need* not speak its name.

Rhodesia was always an easy-going place. It was in this year, I think, that the secretary for health telephoned me one morning with the question: 'Dr Durrant, are you aware that you have not been registered with the Medical Council for the last five years?' It was a rhetorical question: of course I was not aware. The reminders had followed me around a number of changes of address and then lost me: my own part in the disaster need not be gone into. I had been practising illegally for five years. He told me I had better get on to the Council soonest and send them fifty dollars. I don't know what happens to one in UK in such a case: it would certainly make a British doctor tremble.

Jock also was off the register for two years. A Dr Scott had died, and the Medical Council buried the wrong man. I never inquired how it took them (or Jock) two years to discover the error.

It was not long after his arrival in Shabani that Jock and I did a combined operation. I was wakened at daybreak by a telephone call. The night sister told me someone was on the line from the JOC (Joint Operational Command - military, of course, not surgical). But it was not a war casualty. A man's voice came on. 'There's been a derailment on the Buchwa line, doc. There's a guy trapped in the wreckage, and they reckon you'll have to amputate his leg to get him out.'

We were to meet at the small airport outside the town, where they would pick us up in a helicopter. 'We' would include Jock, whom I called to give the anaesthetic. We arranged to meet in theatre.

There I got an amputation pack from the night sister, and Jock collected syringes and Pentothal. I planned to do an emergency guillotine amputation under tourniquet and finish the job at the hospital.

We drove to the airport, and there was the chopper. We climbed in with the pilot and the gunner, who sat beside a large Browning cannon. The helicopter was modified to disembark troops rapidly. It had no seat belts and no sides. I am not very good on altitude. I sat on a box seat and clutched it with sweaty hands. Jock, the old RAF man, sat unperturbed. I never knew anything make Jock nervous, anyway.

We lifted off and sped like a flying carpet across the tawny earth, already vibrant with the morning light. Below we could see women outside their huts, about their household chores, and little naked children. Faces looked up at us.

Then, about thirty miles ahead, loomed the great iron mountain of Buchwa, with its mine. It looked as big as Snowdon from our angle. Soon we picked up the railway, which led to the mine on its way to South Africa. By following it we should come to the wreck we were seeking.

Then, there it was, in a cutting. A mass of trucks, which looked as if a giant, or a petulant child with his toys, had thrown them into a heap. It was not sabotage, we learned. There had been a fault on the permanent way.

We landed and were met by other people. About twenty police reservists had been called out to guard the wreck, and were sitting on top of the cutting, in their camouflage, holding their rifles.

Jock and I climbed over the tumbled trucks, following a guide. And then we found him. A young white man. He had been taking a shower in the caboose, when the crash caught him. He was hanging in the wreckage in the crucified position, in nothing but his drawers. His head was on his chest, and he was quite unconscious. He had been hanging there all night. The sister from the mine clinic had come out and given him pethidine and set up a drip. It was this that must have saved him from death by crucifixion.

When we climbed down to him, I saw that he had a compound dislocation of his right foot. His left leg was buried up to the hip in the wreckage.

I realised this was going to be tricky. For a start, I was worried about giving him Pentothal, which I feared might finish him off. Nor could I see how I was going to get at his leg. I thought I would try and get him into a handier position.

I asked the railway people to lower a rope. They found one and did so. I got it under the man's arms and round his chest, and made a bowline, as I still remembered from the Boy Scouts. Then I told them to lift.

They did so, and his leg came free without a mark on it!

Surely, we must be told somewhere in our medical training, never to take a third party's word for granted!

We got him onto a stretcher and into the chopper, where there was now less room than before. The gunner kindly let me have his seat in the forward bubble. He sat on the edge of the floor, and swung his legs in the air. They told me cheerfully, you can't fall out of a helicopter, because of the upward thrust, or something.

As we sped towards Shabani, I told the pilot on the intercom that we could land at the hospital, as we had a helipad there. He asked me, where was the hospital? We were then flying west, towards Bulawayo. 'On the Selukwe road,' I shouted.

He banked the machine to 45^0, and swung north. I found myself staring down the chimneys of the Nilton Hotel.

We landed in front of the hospital, and I was grateful for terra firma and my own familiar operating theatre. The foot did not present much difficulty: a good wash-out, and the tarsus slipped together like a Rubik's cube. I closed the skin without tension.

A few days later, he went out with a plaster and crutches. He lived in Salisbury, so I referred him a with letter to his own doctor, and never saw him again.

Nor did I tell him about the amputation he so narrowly escaped.

7 - War Surgeon

Early in 1977, the war came to Shabani. I heard for the first time the shattering roar and whistle of a helicopter, bringing in the wounded, or 'casevacs', as they called them: a sound that my stomach never got used to over the next three years.

The first was a civilian (they were mostly civilians), 'caught in the cross-fire'. A man of forty, shot through the thigh: the bone smashed and the artery severed. I had not then learned how to do a vein graft, or I would have attempted it. Later, a surgeon was to teach me, verbally - at the annual bush doctors' refresher course at Bulawayo.

(In Africa, the old adage, 'an ounce of practice is worth a ton of theory', is reversed. The man with the knowledge in his head can do something: the man without it, nothing.)

I took the man's leg off with eleven centimetres to spare: I could barely get the tourniquet above his wound. He needed nine pints of blood, but he lived.

(By now, as the risks of hepatitis became better known, we drew our blood supplies for transfusion exclusively from the National Blood Transfusion Service.)

I was sitting in a friend's house one Sunday afternoon. I got a call from the hospital: a woman with a gunshot wound of the arm. My friend was a medic with the TA, so I took him along for the experience. The upper arm bone was shattered, but nerves and arteries were intact: a relatively simple wash-out, debridement and packing, and application of a U-plaster and sling. My friend, a mechanic, was most impressed. When we got back to his house, he told his wife: 'Warren just did his job like I do mine.'

Some doctors in Africa show their friends operations as a form of entertainment. Needless to say, this is unethical, and although I may have done it in my earlier days, I soon realised this and stopped it. People like military medics, Red Cross, etc, I regarded as students, and would allow them to watch. It was well understood that all government hospitals took students.

However, one Saturday night, I was in the mine club with Koos when a call came: another gunshot wound.

'Man!' pleaded Koos. 'I've always wanted to see an operation.'

Well, I reflected, he sees active service in the TA: gunshot wounds are his business. I decided to bend my rule. 'But you'd better pretend you're an army medic.'

On the ward, I studied the X-rays: a forearm wound this time. I showed them to Koos. 'You can see the joint is not involved. That's very important.'

Koos took the X-rays from my hand. He pointed them out to the nurses who were present. 'You see, the joint is not involved. That is very important.'

I said, 'Cool it, Koos. You're supposed to be an army medic, not a visiting consultant.'

Koos donned boots, mask and gown, and stood well back in the theatre, like a good boy, very interested. When it was over, we met Sister Feldwebel, outside the theatre. She was a German lady of the 'old school', meaning the ram-rod type. Koos greeted her in what he thought was German, and got a cup of coffee for us in the duty room.

The telephone rang. It was Koos's wife, Anita, cooling her heels in the club.

'Is my husband there?'

'Yes, he's been watching an operation with me.' Something innocent, of course.

'Just remind him he's got a wife, will you. I've been sitting here like a sausage for the last two hours.'

I passed the message on to Koos. Sister Feldwebel said, 'I'll unlock the front door for you.'

She had trouble finding the key. She need not have bothered. Koos had left the room. When we got to the front doors, we found them swinging in the breeze. Koos had opened them like any other rhinoceros would have done.

'Just look at that!' shouted Sister Feldwebel, who knew Koos of old. 'And you call that your friend? You, a doctor - an educated man!' She stomped away. 'As for him pretending to speak German!'

By now I had learnt (theoretically, as I said) to perform a vein graft, and I got my opportunity: a little girl of eight, shot through the upper arm. The bone was intact, but the main artery was severed. There was no pulse at the wrist.

The operation has to be done within six hours of the time of injury. If I transferred her to Bulawayo, this time, already short, would be lost. Also, we had a rule not to transfer cases after four o' clock in the afternoon, as that was when the shooting season started, when the guerrillas could mount an ambush and have the rest of the night to get away. In the early days of the war, the security forces would pursue by night, but in the total African darkness of moonless nights, they got lost and sometimes fired on their own members.

I debrided the wound and trimmed the ends of the artery. Then I dissected out a section of the long vein of the leg in the lower part, carefully tying off all the little branches. I flushed out the graft and the distal (outer) section of the artery with heparin/saline solution, and stitched in the graft. I released the tapes and a column of blood pulsed down the graft - and stopped half-way.

To my despair I realised that I had forgotten to reverse the graft. A vein has valves opening towards the heart: a vein graft must be reversed, as an artery conducts away from the heart. I had even marked the graft with large and small forceps - north and south. In removing them, I had still failed to reverse the graft. I had been at work two hours. I was nearly dropping with fatigue in the hot night. I must get a grip on myself. Now I had to start the whole business again, taking a graft from the other leg.

First, I cut out the original graft. Good job I did so, for, to my relief, blood spurted from the distal section of the artery. The collateral circulation was intact. Resuscitation and the anaesthetic had restored the flow of blood. The wrist pulse was now palpable. I had no more to do than ligate the ends of the artery. The little patient made a good recovery.

I had a good excuse for my absent-mindedness. As I walked back to my house, I felt a pain in my groin. When I got home, I found a scab on my thigh and tender glands. My temperature was 38 ^{0}C. I realised I had contracted tick bite fever (African typhus). I must have been near to collapse in theatre.

A thing like that would not stop me working. I gave myself a short course of tetracycline, and in a few days was better.

But I reckoned I could chalk up my vien graft as a theoretical success. And if I could do it on the tiny vessels of a child, I could do it on an adult.

That was my first (and last) vein graft; but I nearly had another.

One Sunday afternoon, I was getting a book out of the white hospital library, when I saw Jock (who was on duty) examining a patient in one of the wards. I looked in out of interest. It was a white soldier with a gunshot wound of the thigh. I had heard no helicopter because the man had been brought in by road by his friends. It turned out the femoral artery was severed. It needed a graft, and most of the six-hour 'golden period' had been lost. Jock meant to send the man to Bulawayo. I debated in my mind whether to offer my services: I had to balance my slender advantage in time against the superior skills of the surgeon in the Central Hospital.

Colleagues who have worked together as close as Jock and I have an intuitive relationship. This was Jock's case: I knew he wanted to send the man away. There was no point in arguing, especially in front of the patient, even if I felt that sure of myself. So, with uncharacteristic modesty, I said nothing.

In the event, the man arrived too late. The surgeon operated, but the graft did not take, and the leg had to come off next day. The man was very bitter about it, but the surgeon wrote to his lawyer (for it had come to that) that Jock had done well to keep him alive, and so he had.

Later, I learned from one of his friends how the man had come by his injury. They were 'bounty-hunters'. Not satisfied with their statutory duties in the TA, etc, these desperadoes went in for the sport of man-hunting, which, apart from the pleasure Sir Garnet Wolseley so enthused about in West Africa, was here profitable. In short, if they brought back a communist weapon from their expeditions they got $1000 for it. And no doubt it was an exciting substitute for the other shooting and fishing they used to do, which the war had curtailed.

So, on the Saturday afternoon, they drove out into the countryside (a party of half-a-dozen, or so), left their vehicle, and marched off into the bundu, arriving under cover of darkness at a spot they had marked beforehand: a *kopje* overlooking a village. There they fed and watered, and lay up till next day.

After sunrise, they watched the village for any sign of guerrillas. The sun mounted to its furious zenith in that part of the country, bordering the Lowveld: and they ran out of water.

They got thirsty. Around midday, our patient (I will call him George), to the astonishment of his comrades, and before they could stop him, staggered out of cover and down the hill to the village, carrying his rifle and his water-bottle.

Whether he found water, I did not ask. The guerrillas, the seemingly ordinary peasants, sitting around, found him and knew he had not come from nowhere and alone. They let him walk back again up the *kopje*. Then they pulled their rifles out of the thatch and did a bit of field-craft of their own.

They took up a position on another *kopje*, higher than the first, and the first thing George and his companions knew about it was when they were fired on from above - an indefensible position.

George was the only one hit as they evacuated, and it says much for the devotion of his friends that they got him out alive.

One night, a police reservist was brought in, shot in the chest in an ambush. I noted he was the same age as myself then - 49. He was nearly bled out. He was still conscious and said he could not move his legs.

We transfused him. The chest X-ray showed the left side full of blood and a foreign body in the spine. The communist bullet had a copper coat and contained lead and a gun-metal cylinder, called the tumbler. The bullet would shatter on hitting bone, but the tumbler would penetrate deeper and fly anywhere. The FB in the spine was the tumbler.

The patient needed an immediate operation.[1] This was going to be a tricky anaesthetic. I called one of the mine doctors who was a skilled anaesthetist. He got a tube down the windpipe and I opened the chest.

I evacuated the blood and reached my hand deep inside. I could feel the tip of the tumbler buried deep in the spine, impossible to remove; nor would that have served much useful purpose.

I debrided the wound and inserted a water-sealed drain - a tube that goes into a bottle of water to release air and blood from the chest and prevents air returning. I closed the chest and the anaesthetist re-inflated the lung.

There remained the problem of the paralysis. There were two possibilities: one probable, the other just possible. Most probably, the spine was severed. On the other hand, perhaps it was merely compressed by a haemorrhage into the spinal canal which might be relieved by the operation of laminectomy - removing some of the spinal arches: something beyond my judgement, if not my skill. It might be done even by a general surgeon at Bulawayo, but no time should be lost to avoid progressive paralysis, even death.

As I have explained, our policy was not to transfer people by night, because of the risk of ambush. I never required this of our ambulance drivers, to say nothing of exposing the patients.

I put the matter to the man's comrades, and a gallant police officer volunteered to take him in his car. In the event, I learned many years later, the ambulance driver got to take him, with the police officer riding shotgun.

As it happened, next day, one of the country's two neurosurgeons, based on Salisbury, was on his regular visit to Bulawayo. He took one look at the X-rays and decided that further operation would be profitless.

But we had the satisfaction of saving the man's life, and for ten years he pursued a courageous and useful career in business and civic affairs, before succumbing to his injuries.

What seemed the bitter irony of this case was that someone left open the back door of the armoured personnel carrier they were

---

[1] On second thoughts, all he needed was a chest drain. WD.

travelling in, and our patient received a bullet through the fatal gap. Later, I learned that these vehicles were so intolerable in the hot weather that the door was invariably left open. Very human, and very sad!

The brave police officer who escorted him came to a sad end. He survived the war, but in the disturbed conditions which followed, was killed by a bandit when attempting to arrest him. And it was so much later that I learned about his gallantry, that I was unable to thank or even identify the plucky ambulance driver. Let me do so now.

I had five brain shots in the three years of total war, three of which I saved.

The first was a white corporal, shot through the forehead, just above the right eye, which was shattered also.

This case was also admitted at night. I called the mine anaesthetist, Ben Theron, to this case too. It was a parlous case in a white man, and I knew that the African nurse-anaesthetists, for reasons which the reader may appreciate, were nervous of such: it was unfair and unwise to expose them to something they were not happy with. In other European cases, where I was confident myself, they gladly obliged.

After resuscitation and intubation, I opened his head and washed out most of the right frontal lobe of the brain. I instructed the scrub nurse to stem the copious haemorrhage with a surgical towel, while I prepared a muscle graft. This is simply a piece of meat taken from the patient's thigh, beaten flat, and applied like a dressing to the bleeding area. It sticks like a postage stamp in ten minutes, and effectively arrests the haemorrhage, before becoming eventually absorbed. I have saved many lives by this method in cases of head injury from what used to be called 'uncontrollable haemorrhage'. I then closed the scalp without drainage. At the same time, I removed the shattered eye.

I sent the man to Bulawayo next day, where no further intervention was found necessary. I never saw him again. He was discharged from the army, and returned to his home in Salisbury; but I heard from his friends who told me that he was well enough but his personality had changed. He never became depressed and he never became excited. The frontal lobe is the part of the brain used for worrying. The bullet had inflicted a pre-frontal leucotomy, an operation which used to be performed in cases of intractable anxiety, but has since been abandoned. I hope he suffered no worse after-effects.

Another case was a carbon copy of this one, except for the eye injury, in which I operated on an African with a satisfactory result.

The third was an African lad of about sixteen, shot in the side of the head: the motor area. He survived, but was left with some lameness of his right leg and a paralysed right arm. His speech was affected, but mercifully, not much.

I did less well with abdominal shots, of which I had about half a dozen. There is a lot to go wrong in a television set. One succumbed to thrombosis, and at least two others to infection. I had only one clear success: a man whose bowels were riddled with mortar-bomb splinters. It was a simple matter of sewing up all the holes, followed by a wash-out. I was barely learning the abdominal trade when the war ended.

The most piteous case was a lad of seventeen, 'caught in the cross-fire'. When I appeared he looked at me hopefully and cried, 'Docketa!' Alas, I was unable to save him, and that was the last word he spoke.

My last abdominal shot came a few days after the cease-fire. A white soldier fell out with his companion on the veranda of the Nilton Hotel. He drove home to get his rifle, came back with it and chased the other man along the veranda, before shooting him in the back. It was night, but there was no problem now about transferring him to Bulawayo, where the surgeon was able to save him. Good job for his assailant, as, if I had failed, he would probably have hanged for premeditated murder.

A certain Greek trader went up from Shabani to Gwelo. He had no car (but he carried four hundred dollars), so he hitched a lift from a white man who was going to the quarry, seven miles out of town, opposite my rural hospital at Lundi. The man warned him he would have to put him down at the roadside, where he would have to take his chance - in more ways than one. They probably thought little of it - a mere seven miles out. The man went regularly to his quarry, as I went to my hospital.

The little trader was unarmed: which re-opens my previous discussion about carrying weapons. For it was not guerrillas he fell among; who might have shot him on the spot, or even taken him prisoner and carried him to Mozambique (especially as he was not armed), like the remarkable cases of the white road-maker and the white farmer, who were decently treated and even spoke appreciatively of their captors, when they were later released, even before independence. One never could tell. A party of black road-workers was shot down on the spot, and thirty black tea estate workers were led out of their compound one night and massacred.

Our trader fell indeed among thieves - a rat pack of *mujibas* - young lads, described in the courts as 'running with terrorists': generally scouting, sitting on *kopjes* while about their normal avocations of minding cattle and goats in the tribal lands. Sometimes they formed packs, armed with imitation rifles with which they imposed on the simple people in order to rob them and gain favours from their womenfolk; no doubt, in imitation of their masters: otherwise, they would have no weapons but sticks and stones.

They did not strip our certain man of his raiment, but they robbed him; nor did they leave him for dead. God knows how they killed him, but his rags and bones were found in an old mine shaft three months later and brought to me in a box.

And as in any war, there were the funny incidents. Even at Inyanga, the police told us about an African farmer who drove over a land mine in his pick-up, fortunately hitting it with his rear wheel, or he would never have survived. Incidently, there was an innocent idea to begin with, even among the whites, that if you drove fast enough you would be away before the thing went off. Of course, that only ensured you made a higher journey through the air.

After rising the usual twelve feet, our farmer came down with a bang and sat half-stunned in his vehicle. When the police arrived, they asked him how he was. He replied: 'I think I had a very bad blow-out.'

A mission was attacked in Matabeleland. All hit the floor except Father Murphy, who ran to his room and came out firing an automatic rifle, with which he drove off the attackers. (He, at least, had no scruples about killing people rightly struggling to be free.) The newspaper report concluded: 'None of the other fathers knew Father Murphy kept a rifle in his room' - like a packet of joints or a girlie magazine.

But the biggest comedy of the war was the Great Battle of Shabani. Historians are divided over the cause. The most popular theory was that it was started by a Portuguese (still not fully admitted to polite society) firing a revolver at a cat in his garden. The town, by now completely surrounded by the guerrillas in the countryside, entered and left in armed convoys by all three major outlets, was in a nervy state. Like the famous shot in Sarajevo, this one ignited a powder-keg. It was night. The DC's people, the rawest and most nervous, began firing on the police camp. The police fired back at the DC's place, and the army, which had a camp outside the town, fired on both. Soon all three were firing on one another without prejudice. I stood on my balcony and watched the tracers crossing the town in all directions. Then the *boom!, boom!* of mortar-bombs began. The whole thing went on for about three hours. The matron rang me and I asked her to clear the front bays of the wards, which was our usual preparation for mass emergencies. I did not bother calling in extra staff as I was sure they were all under their beds in their homes and wouldn't budge. Otherwise, I decided to adopt an expectant policy. With one final *boom!,* all the lights in the town went out, meaning that they had hit the power station; when all at once the firing stopped, like little boys who realised they had gone too far. Needless to say, there was nary a guerrilla involved. Moreover, there was nary a casualty on any side, which was regarded with what I suppose was mixed relief.

Next day, an aeroplane, carrying a high-ranking officer, was seen to fly into our small airport, and a lot of awkward questions were no doubt asked.

The war produced other indirect medical consequences. Public health programmes were disrupted, including rabies control - the vaccination of dogs in the tribal areas. And we began to see cases. One was a little boy, bitten by a dog in the leg about a month before. Rabies virus travels up the nerves to the brain, and in an adult takes about two months from a bite in the leg and one month from the arm; and correspondingly less in a child. The case was obvious when the little boy's mother offered him water, and he literally barked like a dog - hydrophobia (the old name of the disease), fear of water, the very sight of which provokes the painful spasms in the throat. I set up a Valium drip, and gave him an initial injection of the same through the tube. The little boy slept mercifully and peacefully for two days before he died. I was glad to see that the dreadful effects of the disease could be so easily controlled (more easily, in fact, than in tetanus, where the activity is in the spine, less readily reached by the drugs), though the outcome in the established case is universally fatal.

Another case was a woman. As the ambulance brought her in, she went into choking spasms in the vehicle as it splashed through puddles on the road. Nor was she controlled with a Valium drip, but continued to stagger aimlessly round her bed. Obviously, the dose was too low. Rather than waste time adjusting it, I started large doses of Largactil, and she settled and also died peacefully after two days.

Then a rabid puppy attended a European children's party. Its condition was discovered when it died a few days later, and the veterinary laboratory found the tell-tale Negri bodies in the brain. It had been vaccinated, too, but was obviously already infected at the time of vaccination.

Europeans tend to make more fuss about these things than Africans, even the colonial types of Rhodesia, whose anxiety threshold is much higher than in other places I had better not mention. So I organised a meeting of the parents concerned. This sort of thing, again, fell under the government medical officer.

I had already consulted with the animal health inspector and the secretary for health, and had formulated a policy. No one, as far as we knew, had been bitten. I did not go into the controversial business of licks in the face, thinking it an unnecessary alarm. I proposed vaccinating all the children under five, as unable to give an account of themselves, and offered it to any others concerned who wished it for their children or themselves. In the event, everyone opted for the fourteen-day ordeal of radial injections around the navel, which was the regime then. A telegram was even sent in pursuit of a woman who had gone to Israel, and altogether the government was set back a tidy sum. No cases developed.

As the war developed, nothing moved by night in the tribal areas except the guerrillas themselves; and we began to see other medical consequences - especially for the women in labour. In short, I had about a dozen cases of ruptured uterus brought in, after a night of obstructed labour. All of these I dealt with by subtotal hysterectomy, and lost only one - a woman who had been ruptured more than twelve hours and succumbed to infection. One might imagine there were others who never made it to hospital. I never saw any at postmortem, but it was not usual to report natural deaths occurring in the tribal areas.

One day, about half-a-dozen people were brought in, suffering from strange symptoms: abdominal pains, mostly, and some developed paralysis. Some rapidly died, while others began to recover. They told a story of eating tins of meat they had found in the bush. I suspected botulism, and reported to the provincial medical officer. The DC seemed to regard the cases as more suspicious.

After a few days, I received a telephone call from the secretary. By then, the recovered cases had gone home: the dead had been buried. I probably wrote food-poisoning on the death certificates. The secretary requested exhumation of the dead for further investigation.

After a week, he rang me with the news that thallium had been found in the bodies. No further explanation was available.

After the war, I got the answer from one of the Selous Scouts. I was wrong when I said only the guerrillas moved in the bush by night. The Selous Scouts were a body of desperadoes, black and white, who lived in and off the bush for months at a time: tracking, engaging, and even infiltrating the guerrillas as spies. And they got up to dirty tricks. Leaving booby-trapped radio sets around was one of them, and so were the thallium-injected tins of meat. These things were aimed at the guerrillas, as the guerrillas' land mines were aimed at the security forces, but in each case trapped more civilians than either.

For years after the war, guerrillas returned from Mozambique, reported stomach pains and stories about poisoned meat, which must have mystified doctors ignorant of these events. I encountered no more cases among civilians, though no doubt they occurred.

Before breakast one morning, I was called to a gunshot case in the European hospital. A local farmer and his wife had been taking their son and his friend to Gwelo to report for conscription. The younger brother, a lad of about fifteen, went too. All the men were armed. Call up was eighteen for all white males. Even so, eighty per cent of the security forces, police and army, was black.

The white party ran into an ambush, just outside town. It was most unusual at that hour. This was the last year of the war, and the guerrillas must have been getting very cheeky, or rather, they knew how thinly stretched were the security forces by the increasing demands made on them. The Land Rover was brought to a stop, and in the ensuing gun battle, father was killed and mother got a bullet in the belly. The others were unhurt, before the guerrillas, who never hung around for longer than ten minutes, made off.

As I walked to the hospital, I passed the young lad on the path in tears. His father was already in the mortuary.

Mother was a fat little woman. Although she had entry and exit wounds, she seemed to be comfortable, and the X-rays showed no free gas or other signs of injury. I decided to watch her. After a couple of days she began to leak faeces from the entry wound, but was otherwise still comfortable. Percy agreed that this was a fistula or track which had sealed itself off and would heal itself. We put the lady on a liquid diet, and so it did. Another abdominal shot that did well, thank God. The family even joked that Mother was so fat she was bullet-proof.

The war ended, not with a whimper, but a bang. Mandava, the large African township - never the leafy European suburbs - used to get hammered now and again by the guerrillas with mortar attacks, usually with little effect; though my one successful abdominal operation followed such a demonstration. For that is what I suppose they were - sort of gunboat diplomacy, to show the people who was boss - the kind of thing Richard Dimbleby used to say the natives (or whatever he called them) had learned from their colonial oppressors.

And at least one night, it was rather more than a demonstration, when the guerrillas entered the township itself, dragged the Muzorewa supporters from their beds, and executed them in the street, before the over-stretched security forces could turn up, an hour after they had gone.

Just before New Year, it happened again. I stood on my balcony, observing the flashes from the hills, and hearing the bangs in the long-suffering township, and nerving myself for casualties, which happily never came. But the peace treaty had not long been signed at Lancaster House. It wanted but two days to the ceasefire, and here they were, trying to kill their own people yet again.

I reflected that the post-independence elections were not far off. Shabani, near the border with Matabeleland, was by way of being a marginal seat. This must be a shameless electioneering ploy to persuade the waverers with the only kind of persuasion that counts in Africa; for the voters well knew, from the direction of the firing, which party it was coming from. I wondered what they would say in Britain if Mrs Thatcher mortared a marginal seat in the Tory interest.

Two days later, peace broke out.

8 – Romance

I met my wife because, like Maria in *The Sound of Music,* I did something good.

It began on the veranda of the Nilton, when Jock and I were having a sundowner. Jock said: 'You'll have to do something about that matron.'

The matron in question was Lilian, a middle-aged lady of charm and ability, but from what Jock was telling me, she seemed to be succumbing to that disease, fatal to Europeans in the tropics, of idealism.

I had not noticed it myself. I was a poor judge of matronly performance, as I didn't take much notice of matrons, as long as they left me in peace. But Jock seemed to think it was serious. As I seemed nonplussed, and no doubt recognising that administration was not my strong point, he offered to get in touch with the secretary, and I rather weakly acquiesced.

A few days later, the secretary rang me up. He said he would be delighted to come down. (I presume Jock had invited him.) He told me, himself, he had been 'gunning' for Miss Harrison for years. I did not take this as a reflection on her competence, which even I could see was unquestionable. I rather got the feeling of Ted Heath on the subject of Maggie Thatcher.

And a few days after that, he arrived - by air, at our little airport. I went to pick him up in my car. He was a dry little man in a grey suit, accompanied by a brawny official with a submachine-gun. We were still in the last year of the war, and if they had come down in the bush, they might have had to defend themselves; but after the secretary's words about 'gunning', it made me think twice about his intentions towards Lilian.

They got into my car: the secretary in the back, his shotgun beside me. By the barrier stood an unprepossessing individual who looked like the Hunchback of Notre Dame, whose business it was to raise it. This person had a medical complaint, and someone had told him there was a doctor in the car.

After raising the barrier, instead of standing back and minding his own business, the man approached the vehicle. He must have been new in town, as he did not recognise me. Between myself in a safari jacket and the person in a city suit on the back seat (which is well understood in Africa to be the place of honour), there was little doubt in this person's mind as to which was the doctor. To make sure he addressed the secretary.

'Are you a docketa?'

'Er, yes -' murmured the secretary in a guarded tone. He hadn't handled a stethoscope in years.

'I got dis tooth.' Whereupon, the man put his head through the open window, and placing his fingers in his mouth, thrust his open jaws and his halitosis under the secretary's nose.

The secretary said: 'I am sure, if you apply to Dr Durrant at the government hospital, he will attend to you.'

'Are you a docketa?'

'Would you drive on, please, Dr Durrant?'

The secretary was closeted with Lilian for some time, during which she tendered her resignation from the service - that drastic!; though I don't know what Jock and I had expected.

The secretary re-emerged, gave us the news and took a cup of tea. Then he left, declining our offer of lunch.

Next day, Lilian had sufficiently recovered to telephone me at my house before breakfast. She said she realised it had 'all been her fault, and would I give her a second chance?' I said I would speak to the secretary about it. I need not repeat what I have said more than once in these pages about myself and administration, except to wheel on the old adage that good doctors make poor administrators, and good administrators make poor doctors; which I suspect got its start from doctors who were poor administrators.

Anyway, when I rang the secretary, as the reader may imagine, he hit the roof - at any rate, he fell silent for a few seconds.

'Dr Durrant!' he snapped. 'I thought we had arrived at a decision about this matter. Now the matron can plead the indulgence of a superior officer. You have hopelessly compromised the situation, and put me in an impossible position!'

I said nothing. The secretary said he would have to re-think the question. What he would do, he did not know. He would let me know in due course, but it would not be soon.

Then it occurred to me that I had known Lilian of old - at Gwelo, where she had been a deputy or something. I remembered her there as pleasant and relaxed. It seemed to me that she might be easier in a position where she was not the boss. I duly rang the secretary again with this idea.

The secretary may not have expected to welcome any more suggestions from me, but he saw the merits of this one. In short, Lilian, in due course, was given a lateral transfer to a deputy post in a larger institution, where I hoped she would be happy, as well as those around her.

(Now I ask myself: did I mean she was not fit to be 'in charge'? In fact, the question did not occur to me: I have merely described the expedient that did occur to me to get her out of her scrape. Now I like to think I was sending her 'back to school', as I was sent back to school, from which I hope she emerged as happily as I did.)

But if Lilian had gone when she would have gone but for my intervention, she would not have been replaced by the person who replaced her at the later date, whom I would never have met; and that person was Terry, my future wife.

As The Boy in the folk play said, in my Ghana days: WHEN YOU DO GOOD, YOU DO IT TO YOURSELF.

One day, Lilian told me she had heard from the new matron on the telephone: 'A nice young voice,' she said. And a few days later, Terry arrived.

It is a widespread belief among men that women are materialistic little marital calculating machines from the age of two, thinking of only one thing: the great prize, Man; while men, the poor things, are innocent as the wild deer, until the luckless day they are brought down by the huntress. Bernard Shaw has written a lengthy play on that very proposition. I don't know about other men, but my own thoughts were as marital-materialistic as the proverbial frustrated spinster's.

I was due to go on long leave soon after Terry's arrival. Quite shamelessly, before she came, I calculated that if this new matron looked like promising material I would postpone my leave and concentrate on her.

I first set eyes on her when Lilian brought her to the duty room of the European hospital. She was a tall dark woman of about thirty, no particular looks, and rather shy. Over the next days and weeks, I studied her. She had intelligence and force of character, but I did not fall in love with her.

I did, however, show her operations: I took her to Jock's hospital (he was then on leave) - things I had not done for previous matrons. But I did not postpone my leave.

When I was in England, I sent her postcards (which I had never done for matrons before), but while I climbed the hills of my beloved Lake District or swam in the coves of my beloved Cornwall, and sojourned in all my other habitual leave places, including the bricks and mortar of my native (and more mundanely beloved) Merseyside, I did not think often of Terry.

When I returned, I thought it would be polite to call on her at her house. I did not have a gift: there was no reason why I should, but I took her crumpets and a pot of jam, which my Cornish cousin had given me.

Terry gave me tea, but had little time to linger, as she had a squash date at the club. The scales fell from my eyes: I saw her beauty, and felt sure then and there that I wanted to marry her.

Then I got a shock. She said: 'I'm leaving, Warren.' And she didn't mean for the club.

My heart fell. I didn't ask her where she was going. I asked her what she was going to do. I hope I don't have to explain what I meant by that.

She said she was going to Salisbury at the beginning of the new year to study for the matron's diploma.

I almost laughed with relief. It was now October. That gave me three months to do my stuff.

I gave her supper. We sat on my balcony with sundowners. A flamenco record was strumming on the record player downstairs. Terry liked this. She had made a long tour in Europe with a girl friend, and worked in London for a time. Otherwise, she was a second generation Rhodesian, brought up on a farm near Gwelo. She had three older sisters, all married. It was not a big farm, and her parents had never been rich. Terry had been brought up quite hard. But she had been to a good state boarding school in Gwelo. She had trained as a nurse and midwife in South Africa.

We talked about marriage - I mean in a general way. Terry said: 'It's not a tragedy, Warren, if you don't get married.'

This struck me with the force of a revelation. I hated my celibacy and thought about marriage with the obsession of the proverbial old maid. Yet here was a vital young woman who seemed to regard the subject with indifference. What she showed me was a freedom of the spirit, without which true love is impossible.

I exploited the limited resources of the little town. Fishing and country walks had been curtailed for some time by the war. There was the mine club and the golf club, where I enrolled Terry in the hackers' section, where I already belonged. We gave each other supper and we had music: LPs, or when I played the piano. It was the music that softened her most. Her eyes would grow liquid, and I thought she was beginning to love me. After three weeks I had told her I would marry her.

Long ago, I used to write poetry. Now I broke a silence of years for Terry.

Softly as a leopard, you come down
The path behind my house,
Your feet pausing, balancing on the ground.
I look, and you are there, where the path was empty
*   just before:*
Electric as a leopard in the evening.

How often shall I stand on my balcony, after you have gone,
And look for the leopard presence, and see the ghost of it:
The electric, silent presence in the garden?

Terry's feelings for me fluctuated, I could see it, between involuntary tenderness and a fearful withdrawal. For there was one barrier, or rather gap - the gap of twenty years between us.

One night, as I left her house, I took her in my arms and kissed her for the first time. She said, 'O, Warren, don't let's get too involved!' I took no notice. As I walked home, I felt again the joy of youth after years in the desert.

The time came for her to leave, and it seemed I made no progress:

I get ready
For your going away.
My soul sinks
In resignation,
Then rouses up
For one last fight for you.

Some memories will be hard to lose:
Your way of looking at me sometimes, with all your
Sweetness on tip-toe, as if
You half began to love me.

No matter, it is written somewhere,
One way or another,
And will soon enough be read.

Terry went away. In her first letter, she said she would never be so foolish as to marry a man so much older than herself. But other letters sounded different, and in one: 'Come if you want'.

So, of course, I went up to Salisbury, and stayed in a hotel near the nurses' home, where she was convented. I went up as often as I could, at least once a month. But Terry was wayward: to and fro with me, caught between attraction and fear. We must have parted and come together half a dozen times.

Then one day, it seemed final:

In the fair modern city where you live
Are lodged my last lancing memories of you:

The purring handsome cars in the luminous evening,
The wide streets clouded with blossom-dripping trees;
And the new day opening like a flower in the city like a flower,
The great sun standing in the panorama of the sky,
Between the tall flashing buildings that rode like ships above
*   the trees;*
Evenings with you in velvet restaurants,
On terraces above the streaming-lighted street:
City where you never felt at home
In your alienating flat, where the traffic banged outside;
Where yet we spent
Afternoons in a cell of curtained light like a yellow flower.

Feminine city, with a glamour of living, which was you!

I was back at home in Shabani. I had not heard from Terry for two weeks. Then one evening, I was sitting on my balcony, reading, when the telephone rang. It was Terry. 'Warren, we *could* get married...'

That was September. We planned to get married next year, when Terry had finished her course. Even then there was a difficulty. She was committed to give them three years' service in return for her grant. She decided to give them six months. That meant she had to pay $5000 reimbursement. As that was by then practically from our joint account, I always told everyone I paid $5000 bride price for my wife: *lobola,* as the Africans call it - about fifty cows in those days, and mightily were the Africans impressed. Alas, if only her poor father could have received it!

Terry proposed a Christmas holiday for the two of us, after her studies. This was now October. Terry wanted beaches and the sea. I made enquiries. Everywhere was booked up - Mauritius, Seychelles, Kenya, even South Africa. Then I remembered. In Ghana there were beautiful beaches. No chance the white man's grave would be booked up. In fact, booking didn't seem to be on the cards at that time. I made plans to get there on our own.

I discovered that to get to West Africa, one had to travel through Kenya - much further in all and more expensive than Europe. It would have been cheaper and easier to go to Greece; but who wants Greece with the barbaric splendour of Africa to choose from?

So to Nairobi we went, spent a night, and took another flight for Ghana via Lagos. Once again I saw the green ocean of the rain forest, and we were soon above the round green tops as we dipped into Port Harcourt. Terry, the daughter of Africa, was thrilled.

It was December, the dry season; but something was different. A lot of dust, or cloud, in the air. I realised I had seen nothing of the forest for cloud over the Congo; nothing, until these tree tops emerged from the yellow fog below. We might have been dropping into London in the days of the pea-soupers.

On the ground they told us. We met a white man on his way to Lagos, who came with us on the next leg. It was the harmattan, the north wind off the desert. Tens years before, this had been a breath of fresh clean air: now it was something foul and sinister.

In that ten years, the Sahara had marched a hundred miles to the sea: the harmattan now brought a smog of sand. When the plane landed at Lagos, the passengers (the previously half-empty plane having filled up with Nigerians at Port Harcourt) all cheered, as if we had had a perilous deliverance. And on the ground, visibility was down to a hundred yards.

At Lagos, we asked for the transit lounge, telling them we were on our way to Ghana. We found ourselves in a large hall, with our luggage beside us.

Huge crowds in all the colours of the rainbow. Southerners in smocks and caps, with fat wives draped in gaudy dresses and turbans. Fulanis in jelabas, with trains of veiled wives. All milling for tickets and struggling through the entrances. Terry was stunned by what she called 'culture shock'.

I spotted our friend from Port Harcourt with some expats at the bar and joined them, soon quaffing beer and swapping Africa talk. I turned to ask Terry what she wanted.

For she was dragging behind, her face now clouded with more than culture shock. 'Warren,' she urged, 'this isn't the transit lounge.

277

Where *are* we?' She was always more switched on than me, which may not be saying much.

It was the arrivals hall. 'We haven't had our passports stamped,' insisted Terry.

I thought no more about it. I enjoyed my drink and the chat. Terry sat with us, not joining in the conversation, looking more and more anxious.

Then it was announced that as the conditions at Accra were even worse than Lagos, the onward flight there had been postponed until next day.

Our new companions invited us to spend the night at their place. They worked for a dredging company, and had been at the airport to see off one of their friends to UK. We went off with them. They gave us bed and board at their hostel, and next morning, dropped us off at the airport - rather hastily, I thought, like hot potatoes. By then, the news of our illegal entry had got through to them.

We approached the barrier and asked for the transit lounge, as we were en route for Ghana, etc. We spoke to a little woman who kept us waiting at the barrier while she went in search of her superior. Presently, a male official in a grey uniform and peaked cap returned with her.

We explained again. He was not impressed. 'I don't understand. What are you doing here? I see you have no stamp in your passports.'

No, we were in transit to Ghana. A certain woman had led us to the entrance hall. It must be a mistake.

'I know nothing about that. You had better come this way.'

They opened the barrier. But help was not at hand.

'You see, I find you here in an illegal situation. You could go to jail.'

He let that sink in.

'Unless I fix it.'

West African memories flooded back. I said to Terry, 'He wants a bribe.'

Terry had all our Nigerian money, about seven pounds. Now frightened, she thrust it into my hand. 'Give him all of it, Warren.'

I wasn't disposed to be so liberal. Official was now walking away in a contemplative mood, while we meekly followed him. I selected five notes and handed them to him. He continued his contemplative walk, without looking at them.

'I thought you were going to offer me something reasonable.'

What he meant by 'reasonable' was a hundred pounds - a quarter of our joint holiday money.

Terry recovered her courage with her indignation. 'Tell him, Warren, we want to see the airport manager.'

Official did not wait for my intervention as a 'linguist'.

'The Big Man!' he laughed. All this time he walked and looked ahead. 'He will want three hundred pounds.'

So we had to go to the exchange. 'Tell them to put it in an envelope,' added Official.

'Aren't they vile!' I exclaimed to Terry, as we walked away. She made no reply. She was white and trembling. Well, there was nothing for it: we were over the proverbial barrel.

All the time this was going on, they were giving us *Hark! the Herald-angels Sing* on the piped music.

When Official received our present, he stamped our passports with a seven-day visa for Nigeria, as our flight was still postponed. He became positively friendly, led us to the airport entrance, and secured a taxi. He wished us a pleasant stay in Nigeria. We did not reply. Terry looked as if she could murder him.

After that, we needed a drink. In a bar, I consulted with some more British expats. The tale did not surprise them. I asked them to guess the 'dash'. 'About fifty pounds.' I felt doubly swindled. 'Don't worry,' they said. 'The price doubles during the season of good will.'

Autres lieux, autres moeurs! I expect he spent our money on Christmas presents for his kids.

After a night in a Lagos hotel, we decided to try and get to Ghana by road. We took a three-tier Peugeot, a popular form of transport, crowded in with about seven other people, at £5 (naira) for 100 miles. We passed the mangrove swamps of the coast, and reached our first hurdle: the border with Benin.

This used to be Dahomey, where life was played out, in Conrad's words, like 'a sordid farce acted out in front of a sinister back-cloth'. After the days of the slave trade, Amazon warriors, etc, the tradition of sick humour was carried into independence with the annual institution of the Christmas Coup. Every year, in the festive season we were then enjoying (in its special West African form), the president of Dahomey would be sitting in his office, writing his Christmas cards to what he thought were his friends, when the door would be kicked open and his successor to be would burst in and knock him off with a Tommy gun. Next year, the successor would be sitting in his office, writing his Christmas cards, etc, when *his* successor, etc. This comedy ran for about nine successive years. I cannot remember how or why it was taken off.

At any rate, the next comedy for Terry and me was when the border official informed us that we would need a visa to get into Benin. If he stamped us out, we would be left in some dreadful limbo between the two countries - and he didn't even add 'unless I fix it'. We had actually stumbled on an honest Nigerian official. I even saw him refuse a bribe for some purpose from a Dutch priest. I expect the poor man (I mean the official) is there yet, at the bottom of the promotional ladder.

So we had to take a taxi back to town, which cost us more than the Peugeot, which was going on. Incidentally, I noticed that the traffic in Nigeria was now driving on the right. It must have been changed on the Devil's birthday. It would not have required the old expat joke: 'in order to break you in slowly, for the first week, only the buses will do it'.

By now, we despaired of the beaches of West Africa. I suggested to Terry we use our return tickets for Kenya, and complete the rest of our holiday there.

After another night in Lagos, we repaired once more to the airport. We now had a lot of useless Nigerian money to get rid of. We went to the exchange in the arrivals hall, and while the man was half-way through changing our money into pounds sterling, Dutch guilders, and whatever else he had in his piggy bank, he informed us that he had run out of foreign exchange and the office was closing down for the duration, which left us with ninety useless Nigerian pounds as a souvenir of the country.

But we were luckier than a young Englishman we met. Not only had he failed to convert his money; he had had his air ticket thrust back at him at the barrier - not once, but for the third time in as many days. He wanted to get back to England in time for his wedding, no less. Now, the planes for Europe were fully booked; nay, they were overbooked - systematically. In order to secure a seat, it was necessary, not only to purchase a ticket in the usual way, but to bribe some official to kick someone out of the seat. 350 into 300 won't go, even on a jumbo jet, and the surplus 50 was the staple of a thriving local enterprise. The 'dash' could rise to £1000: it was like a game of snakes and ladders, with loaded dice; and unless you were prepared to pay for the dice, which our proud English friend was not, you slid down a snake, and he had already slid down three. The poor fellow was still trying to get married when we left him.

We had no difficulty getting into the transit lounge, thanks to Official's stamp and the low demand for planes to Kenya. We duly declared our wealth, including the ninety naira to the grinning officials at emigration. With such plentiful sources of humour, no wonder they are a laughing people. But our adventures in this fabulous country were not yet over. In the transit lounge, yet another official approached us. Nothing threatening about this one, not even his smile. And his first words were: 'Aren't you Doctor Durrant?'

There were even then eighty million people in Nigeria, and it was ten years since I was on the Coast. But this was Timothy, the former barman at the Samreboi Club, now working at the airport.

We told him our adventures. The trick with the transit/arrivals lounge, he told us, was a regular one. The 'certain woman' was working with Official, who must only have been surprised at the time we took to resurface in his net.

Timothy offered to change our naira for us. In the afternoon, he met us again, with a secretive-looking friend who, in some obscure corner, took our naira in exchange for forty American dollars, then quickly slipped away.

Our plane was due to leave. We passed a policeman. Terry had no money to declare. She was walking to the plane while the policeman, with a surly face and a pistol on his hip, searched my wallet.

'Have you declared all this money?'

'Yes,' I lied. I was getting acclimatised to Nigeria.

'Because if you haven't, I will arrest you.'

Pointless remark. I said nothing. He would have to drag me back to emigration to prove anything, when I would have offered him the forty dollars, like Pierre in the Congo, 'for the police ball'. No doubt, he was trying to shake me, and his remark was not so pointless after all.

At any rate, we breathed a sigh of relief when the Pan Am jet took off for Kenya.

Terry and I had ten uneventful days in Kenya, which after our Nigerian adventures, was all we wanted. As neither Dante nor Milton succeeded in making Paradise as interesting as Hell, I will not try to surpass them.

Terry got her DNA diploma and was now a matron grade III, which was too high-powered for Shabani. She therefore applied for and received the matron's post at Chiredzi, in the steaming south-east of the Lowveld: another long hop from Shabani - 200 miles.

We planned to marry in June, when she would retire from the service. We shared many delightful week-ends together at one or the other's places.

A girl friend of Terry's came to my house. Terry came to me in the garden, where I was taking the evening air. 'How would you like to get married in Que Que?' she asked me. That (pronounced Kweck-Kway) was where her friend's husband had a farm.

And so we were. It was a small wedding, limited to our hosts and Terry's immediate family. I had met my new parents: now I met my new sisters and brothers for the first time. At last, the lonely exile was a member of a large and happy family again, and the country of my willing exile I was invited to call home.

We all foregathered at the farm, and Terry and I were married in the church of St Luke in the town, whose were, of course, the proper auspices for a medical couple.

We had a week's honeymoon at the Troutbeck Inn. This time, we ran to the Lake wing, the most luxurious. One of Terry's friends had advised her to 'get Warren to spend his money' (Terry, as I have explained, had already spent hers, and paid husband-price rather than bride-price), and from the start, I discovered that two cannot live as cheaply as one.

We woke in the crisp winter air of the mountains every morning, with hoar frost on the ground, and on the heather - for the African heather, taller than the Scottish kind and always white in frost and flower, covers the hills not planted with pine trees.

We did all the usual things, and one afternoon climbed Mount Inyangani. This is 8500 feet, but as the veld at its foot is 7000 feet, it rather takes the rise out of it, so to speak, and so the climb itself is but a pleasant afternoon's stroll.

But the mountain has an evil reputation, and few Africans will climb it, even if most of them saw any sense in climbing hills at all, except for some practical purpose. It is the abode of spirits, and it is true that people have disappeared on it without trace.

I had climbed it once before, on another winter day, with Graham Lee, the medical student. We reached the summit easily enough: it is a long hill, standing like a long barrow or ship against the sky, an easily recognised landmark from all quarters, and makes a fine ridge walk. But when we tried to come down this seemingly simple mound, we lost our way. We had to return to the summit no less than three times before we could find the way down, and then only got off the mountain as the swift tropical night descended. Tropical or not, it would have been a bitter spot to spend a winter's night, well below freezing.

But now, this day, the path was clearly marked with cairns, no doubt, by the Mountain Club, and we had no trouble - at least, about direction. But Inyangani had another trick up his sleeve.

When we neared the peak, which stands alone at the head of the ridge, we found it occupied by a troop of baboons, who got very excited when they saw us. They began running about among the rocks, barking, and seeming to organise themselves.

Which they did. For the next thing, we confronted a cavalry charge of the barking brutes, as they came across the heather towards us.

I clasped my new wife with rather more courage than I might have felt on my own, and we instinctively stood our ground. Which was, of course, the right thing to do. To run away might well have been disastrous.

Suddenly, all together, they came to a stop, about fifty yards away. Their leader gave a final bark, and they all ran off to the left, leaving the peak vacant to our possession.

We climbed the last few feet, and found ourselves on the top - under the violet sky, in the blinding white winter light, looking a hundred miles to the west, across the veld, the 'great spaces washed with sun'; and to the east, on the valleys plunging into Mozambique. A world of the eagles.

We came down easily, following the conspicuous cairns. We found a rock pool - a small perfect bath. I stripped and slipped naked into the icy water. Terry contented herself with sitting on a rock, watching my gambols.

At the end of our week, we left for home. On the way, Terry made me stop while she gathered some of those dry flowers from the roadside, that stay in the house, seemingly for ever, like artificial flowers, but natural and wholesome.

We stayed with Terry's parents in Salisbury, and went on to Shabani next day.

When we arrived, we found a surprise party prepared for us by the staff, in African custom, to which we as great folks had to foot the bill for much food and drink. First, we had to change into our wedding clothes and appear on the balcony like royalty, to the hearty cheers of our loyal and loving subjects. We had to sit in state in the same costume on the veranda below, taking part in the feast, while our subjects proceeded to tear the house apart and smear it with mud (sic).

This is all part of the custom. The resulting wreckage is supposed to break in the new bride to her duties, and stop her straying for the next few weeks.

In the midst of the festivities, a Land Rover drew up outside - not the police, but Koos Bezuidenhout, the only other white in town besides ourselves who would have attended an African party. When he had eaten and drunk, he stood on the wall of the veranda and led the crowd in a rousing rendering of *Ishe Komberera Afrika,* the great southern African hymn, which even the British reader must know by now.

Then came a crash as Anderson, who was supposed to be waiting, fell over with a tray of drinks, whose sources he had obviously been conscientiously testing. He could not be roused. Koos threw him over his shoulder and carried him to his *kaya,* where he tossed him on to his narrow bed, and he was no worse in the morning.

By the time all had gone, we were left to contemplate our new nest - emptied of food and drink, completely knocked about, and filthy from top to bottom.

PART FOUR - ZIMBABWE

1 - Independence

The year before I married, Gareth and I took a New Year break at Inyanga, just after the cease fire, 1980. Jock had taken the Christmas holiday. We were driving home when we saw files of guerrillas trekking to the assembly points, manned by British and Commonwealth troops. The guerrillas were loaded with weapons and festooned with machine-gun belts. They looked half-starved, as lean as whippets.

'Look at that!' crowed Gareth. 'They've been fighting for nothing.'

African politics was not one of Gareth's main interests. I knew very well they were not giving themselves up for nothing. (They were not giving themselves up at all, for they retained their weapons in the assembly camps.) But no whites in the country and few people outside knew what Mugabe and Nkomo had up their sleeves; because for as many of the guerrillas as came to the assembly points, as many more stayed in the tribal lands to complete the political education of the people in preparation for the forthcoming elections. And most whites were surprised and horrified at Mugabe's victory, having expected Muzorewa to win, after his sweeping victory in the elections of twelve months before. But Muzorewa was unable to stop the war: how many divisions had he got? So deluded were we by the internal propaganda of the country, that these consequences, which were obvious to everyone outside the country, surprised us.

Then came the elections, 'monitored' by the British bobbies, who must have felt like Alice in Wonderland. Most of them returned home without their helmets (through no fault of their own), which still grace many a Zimbabwean wall, like other trophies of the chase.

In the new year, we admitted two cheeky characters, calling themselves 'freedom fighters', who had each received a gunshot wound of the forearm, some months before. Their forearms looked very bent indeed, and as there was no urgency and the cases might have presented difficulties, I decided to transfer them to Bulawayo on the next ambulance in due course. Any sympathy I might have felt for them, they rapidly forfeited.

To say they treated the place like the Ritz would be inaccurate. The Ritz would soon have asked them to leave. They allotted themselves a private ward without reference to doctor or matron, and treated the staff like their slaves, ordering fancy meals at any time they fancied, etc. They drank beer and smoked with I imagine more freedom than was usually allowed (though I was always vague on points like that). At any rate, under pressure from the nurses, one day I gave them a telling off.

They complained about me to Comrade 'Soft Guy', the political commissar of the local brigands. I received a message from Sister Mutema that he would like to discuss the matter in the duty room.

Our two guests were present, still smoking energetically. I opened the proceedings myself by telling them to put their cigarettes out. They glanced at their superior, who nodded, whereupon they pinched out the offending articles and dropped them out of the window. 'Soft Guy' was the so-called *chimurenga* name of the officer: all who joined the 'armed struggle', or *chimurenga,* gave up their original names for the duration for *chimurenga* names, for all the world like entrants to a religious order. He was a tall thin man with a quietly-spoken manner which seemed to justify his sobriquet.

He asked me why I did not treat our two 'comrades' with more respect. 'They don't deserve respect,' I burst out, as much from nervousness at my entirely novel situation as anything else. 'They've been nothing but a nuisance to everyone since they've been here.'

Comrade Soft Guy glanced at Sister Mutema who was with us. Sister Mutema nodded and Comrade Soft Guy sharply ordered the two culprits out of the room. He assured me he would look into the matter, and the meeting broke up.

A few days later, Comrade Soft Guy's luck ran out. He developed toothache and needed an extraction. I entered the ward one morning to find Jock dealing with him just inside the door. I have said Jock's piano-playing lacked finesse, and I think the same was true of his dentistry. At any rate, Comrade Soft Guy was rolling about on a chair, under Jock's head-lock and an evidently imperfect local anaesthetic, bawling like a sick cow, while Jock was saying, 'No wonder they call you Comrade Soft Guy!'

There was nothing vindictive about this. I am sure Jock had as much simple faith in his local as he had in his dental skill.

Then I got an invitation to an independence party at the house of one of our sisters, about five miles out of town. When I told Terry over the telephone I was going (she was then in Salisbury), she said I must have rocks in my head. I was the only white present. Sister Mushaya's husband ran a store and tavern, attached to their house, and sitting on the bar was the local guerrilla capo, Comrade 'Bee-Gee'.

It was then he told me how they had spared Dr Scott. Comrade Bee-Gee was built like Mike Tyson, and moreover had the cold eye of one who knew how to aim a rifle, instead of waving it about, as his subordinates were cheerfully believed by the whites to do. All this made me glad for Jock's sake that Comrade Bee-Gee approved of his activities; though he could have looked like King Kong and shot like Dead-eye Dick for all Jock would have cared.

Comrade Bee-Gee also told me that the two naughty boys had been 'dealt with' - which made me feel sorry for them for the first time and hope they were still above ground, or that Comrade Bee-Gee had not anticipated the surgeon in the matter of re-setting their fractures.

Comrade Soft Guy was also present - with a towel wrapped round his face, for some reason.

A succession of youths came in, carrying home-made imitation rifles, which they handed over to a stern-eyed Comrade Bee-Gee, which he dropped on a growing pile behind the bar. These were evidently the *mujibas,* previously described. They looked very sheepish, but were allowed to join the party.

Then a privileged number of us were invited into the house itself to watch Prince Charles on the telly lowering and raising flags (lowering anyway). And suddenly there was a call for the doctor.

A man in the tavern had had an argument with another man, who had struck him. The first man had a friend who was a deaf-mute, as devoted to him as a dog. The deaf-mute, a skinny little creature, possessed surprising strength, or spirit, because he sprang to the aid of his friend and knocked down the second man, who was much bigger than him, with a single blow. The second man fell backwards and hit his head on the concrete, just outside the door. When I examined him, he was unconscious with fixed but constricted pupils.

We threw him into the back of my car and I took him to the hospital, where I ordered the usual half-hourly observations. After three days, he was the same. There were no indications for surgery, but I ordered him to Salisbury for specialist management. There, after a few days, he died.

There was an inquest at Gwelo. I spoke my piece. Then the pathologist's report was placed before me - brain laceration - and I was asked to elucidate. No verdict is reached at a magistrate's inquest in Zimbabwe. The matter was not further referred.

It was a year or two before the new order made itself felt in the health service. I have said the hospital was divided into white and black, the white section (with the exception of the pensioners) being private and used by the mine doctors for their private practice. In 1979 (before independence), when Muzorewa became prime minister, the last official racial barriers fell away throughout society. The private wards were now open to all races, and educated middle-class Africans (as in hotels and other places their tastes inclined them to use) were no longer subjected to insulting exclusion: something which most whites by now realised should have happened years before. It would not have solved the country's main problems, but it would have done much to help.

But the new government was still in the first flush of its Marxist-Leninist enthusiasm. It was not only concerned with race: it was concerned with class.

To be sure, the boss class took good care of itself: the first practical (as opposed to theoretical) principle of a Marxist state is, of course, the *Nomenklatura* - which is Russian for jobs for the boys.

But private beds in government hospitals were out (except maybe in the capital for the more equal animals).

I was sitting in the dressing-room of the theatre with Percy, when I received a telephone call from the secretary for health - not the one who arranged my marriage, who had gone long ago - but a black socialist one.

'I hear you still have private beds in your hospital.'

'Yes.'

'Didn't you know that private beds had been abolished in government hospitals?'

'No' - nobody had told me. Our wide-awake hospital secretary, a little highly conscientious old man, called Peter Reynolds, would certainly have shown me any such directive, if only out of high indignation, even if I had missed it myself, which was more probable.

'Are there any private patients in your hospital now?'

I reflected. As it happened, there were two - two little old ladies who happened to be pioneer pensioners.

'Yes, there are two pensioners.'

'What sort of pensioners?'

'Pioneer pensioners.'

'What are you talking about?'

I explained. The bit about people whose ancestors arrived before 1900 may have peeved him, but that was not my fault.

'Get them out!'

'Shall I wait till they are ready to be discharged?'

'No. Get them out today!'

Well, by regulation, they could and should have gone to the old African ward, which would have been a cultural hardship, to say the least. It was a cultural hardship, as I said, to people like the secretary himself, and was not the sort of thing he was used to in Salisbury.

An order is an order. I put the telephone down.

'What was all that about?' growled Percy, whose antennae, as well as his ears, were in good working order.

I explained. Percy was now superintendent of the mine hospital. He offered to take the pensioners under his wing. In anticipation of such changes, the mine had built a new managerial and private

290

hospital, small but gleaming. Percy offered the pensioners permanent accommodation there.

Well, these two old ladies were under Jock's care, and he didn't appreciate their premature discharge and transference to other hands on non-medical grounds at neither his nor their expressed wish. Nor was there any reason why he should, or reason why he should not be furious - which he was. Needless to say, his fury in no way included Percy, to whom he was duly grateful.

This still left the problem of outpatients. The 'white' hospital had a small outpatients department, still used by 'government whites' - ie, police and pensioners. Jock continued to see the pensioners in this outpatient department. (By now there were few Europeans in the police service and they had all gone private - as had the African police officers.) I could see trouble in this. (I should say that the previous secretary sanctioned the conjunction of our two districts on the condition that each of us should have the last word in his own area.) Of course, I sympathised with Jock. It was outrageous that a doctor should be separated from his patients, or they from him, against the wishes of both. But I had a family to raise in this country, and it behoved me to keep my nose clean.

I explained this to Jock, and pointed out that Percy had undertaken the total care of the pensioners. It really would be better for them that way: if Jock wanted to admit them, he would have to surrender them to the mine hospital, anyway, unless he intended to treat them in the 'African' wards.

'We have no right to expect Percy to take them,' protested Jock, with an irrelevance I did not choose to argue with.

Then he took to seeing them in his own house. As this was government property, he was still breaking the rules; but I was not going to make an issue of that.

Now I had thirty empty beds to dispose of. In fact, we needed them. The 'black' maternity ward was overcrowded, so I moved these ladies into the old white hospital, and formed a new lying-in unit (this, in fact, was the solution adopted in similar situations throughout the country), where they were delighted with their improved accommodation. The old maternity ward became a children's ward: the children previously being admitted to the female ward.

And now also we had an empty outpatient department, which itself became a source of bitterness. I proposed to turn it into a secondary outpatient department for patients referred from the clinics, including the township clinic of Mandava. (I hope the reader is still excited by all these administrative events, which I wish I could make even half as interesting as Trollope made the similar invidious business of *The Warden:* indeed, I was beginning to feel like the Reverend Septimus Harding, myself, and Jock was beginning to loom like Archdeacon Grantly. At any rate, if the reader is not excited now, he soon will be.)

For the Mandava clinic had long been a sore. When I arrived, there was not even a waiting room. The patients stood outside in the hot sun and the rain and the cold of winter. After several years' battle with the town council, I got one built, before independence. But the clinic was still hopelessly small for a township of 16,000 people. I had long ago applied to have it enlarged to at least twice its size, or a second clinic built in another part of the sprawling township.

My wishes were overtaken by events.

Some restless or embittered souls took it into their heads to stir things up against the hospital, which was hardly to blame for its own inadequacies: but hospitals make convenient whipping boys throughout the world. Who has not heard murmurs about their local hospital, even in paradisal England? And the restless souls had two restless groups to work on: the Women's League and the Youth League - both branches of what we now knew as the 'ruling party'. The women had the traditional trials of women in Africa to keep them on the boil, and the youths had found their expectations of independence bogged down in massive and growing unemployment.

The first I learned of the gathering storm was when I was informed that the mayor of Gwelo was waiting in outpatients and wanted to see me.[1] The mayor was a figure who added much colour to local public life, mainly through his personal style, which chiefly consisted in knocking people down - at any rate, if they were smaller

---

[1] He was a union leader. WD.

than him, or female, and preferably both. He was a chunky figure with the face of a Stone Age boxer, and I went to meet him, bracing my spirits, as I imagine our forebears in the service of empire went to meet the local cannibal chief.

In the event, he exuded oily charm. He was accompanied by two surly companions: the combination of oil and threat being a well-known one in the more rebarbative political systems. One of the surly companions I recognised as the district administrator, the new form of the fatherly old DC, who was now a political person.

The immediate matter in question was about a mini-bus load of party workers who had been overturned while about their self-appointed business and been admitted by Jock over the week-end. Jock was not the most congenial host the workers could have chosen; but that was the least of their complaints.

I went to the ward with the trio, and they interviewed the comrades in their beds. The African deputy matron was also present. The comrades waxed bitter about conditions in the hospital - tea cold, meals late, cheeky nurses: quite unprovoked, of course - all of which did not please the deputy matron, or a number of nurses who were discreetly listening.

After we had heard the complaints, we repaired to my office, where a map, still bearing the guilty title, RHODESIA, was pointed out by one of the surly companions as the sort of thing the people were objecting to. Another was the absence of what he called the 'Party flag' from the pole outside, which had stood empty since independence for the simple reason that nobody had sent us anything to decorate it with - a deficiency he gracefully promised to repair. By the 'Party flag', he meant of course, the national flag, and seemed to think (perhaps not without cause) they were the same thing. The mayor interrupted this fascinating discussion to inform me that a demonstration had actually been planned to take place at the hospital that morning, and he was off to try and turn it back. He got into his car with his two friends, and drove away.

He did not succeed. Shortly after, a column, mostly women and youths, came prancing and chanting up the hospital road towards the entrance, where Jock had now joined me along with the white matron, now a nice little Welshwoman, called Liz Jones. We all felt like General Gordon on the steps at Khartoum, and hoped we would not share his fate.

The mood of the crowd was good-humoured, but a crowd can change unpredictably, especially an African crowd. They mostly danced about and chanted. Some ladies wiggled their bottoms in our faces. A number of banners was displayed, of which not the most encouraging was GIVE US OUR OWN DOCTORS.

Presently, the mayor and his chums returned in his car. They got out. The mayor stood on a wall and harangued the crowd, no doubt with great promises for the future. He seemed to satisfy them, for they soon turned about and galloped and chanted back to wherever they had come from.

After which, the mayor took a cup of tea, and looked forward to happier relations in the future - the cheeky blighter! The glum companions drank their tea in silence.

I had to report on all this, and our superiors soon demonstrated the power of the profession even in socialist Zimbabwe. The district administrator was cooled off in the provincial office for a year or two. The mayor became such an embarrassment, even to his party, that he soon fell from office and was more or less forced out of its ranks.

It remains to be said that the mayor underwent some kind of reform. At any rate, he turned into a doughty fighter for political freedom in Zimbabwe; even if, not the less, perhaps, because he had been diverted out of the main stream.

As to practical causes and results, I can only say that I shortly after opened the new outpatients, as I had intended, and we had no more trouble thereafter.

In 1978, the World Health Organisation held a conference devoted to the development of primary health care. This means the point and level at which the patient or public makes first contact with the health services; or otherwise considered, the grass roots of medical care. In a country like Zimbabwe, in terms of personnel, this means nurses (or medical assistants, the two now becoming blended in fact as 'nurses'), and public health workers. Even general doctors function at secondary level - the specialist or hospital level of Europe.

When this conference was held (abroad, of course), and its policies emerged, Zimbabwe was still in the throes of civil war. Existing health programmes were curtailed: there was no question of developing new ones. But in 1983, the thing happened.

It started with workshops. These were not very welcome at first to working doctors, who do not like being pulled out of their practices or districts, having a feeling that everything will collapse without them, especially in a country where locums are rarely available and one has to leave colleagues with a double burden. But soon I came to appreciate them. In Africa, the general doctor feels very much in control: he is that unique thing, a big fish in a big pond. In Europe, he is a small cog in a large and complex machine. Most of the machine does not even touch him: his interest in it is largely academic, and academic interest tends to atrophy. In Africa, the country doctor, as I have repeatedly shown, is vitally involved with every part of a machine which has been admittedly simplified by what is called 'appropriate technology', but which stimulates his learning interest in every area. In short, never before or since did I know the joy of learning my trade as I knew it in Africa.

The workshops introduced the new programmes. The first was the Extended Programme of Immunisation. Then followed others on diarrhoeal diseases, tuberculosis, management, and more. The first workshops would take place at national level, and were attended by the provincial officers, who in their turn, organised provincial workshops to instruct district officers and staff, who finally organised district workshops to instruct their own people. A simple and enthralling example was the devolution of the total management of Tb to the district staff, again, by the traditional method of protocols.

Moreoever, curative and public health services were at last combined at district level, so the DMO became his own medical officer of health, and supervised, at any rate, the public health programmes - shades of the 'latrine boys' of Samreboi! But here was a highly structured system, with full national support, not the haphazard and limited efforts of those days. Even in Zimbabwe, where decent public health systems already existed, these were energised considerably by the involvment of local agents.

We discovered clinics in our districts we did not know existed, which had been managed before with difficulty by the provincial staff. Now I would visit them every month. In my district, there were ten - again, the smallest number in the country. I would take in two or three a week - on a Friday - and so get through them all in the month. I used the same methods at them as I did when visiting the rural hospitals. But first we had to find them in the network of dirt roads that ran round the tiny fields and rocky hills of a countryside very like the west of Ireland in the old days - even to the donkey carts.

And we discovered the old-world manners of the country people, who lived in a world where people still had the leisure for good manners; indeed, where being in a hurry was considered the height (or depth) of bad manners.

The community sister (a new appointment) and I were looking for a clinic for the first time. We saw an old woman gathering firewood. We stopped, and the sister leaned out of her side of the Land Rover to ask the way. But not so simple as saying so.

'Good afternoon, grandmother,' said the sister, in Shona, who well knew what was expected.

The old lady straightened her back and greeted us with a sweet smile that lit up her leathery face.

'Good afternoon, young lady.'

'Have you spent the day well?'

'I have spent the day well if you have spent the day well.'

'I have spent the day well.'

'Then I have spent the day well.'

And only then:

'Is this the way to Mutambi clinic?'

Among other duties, I would inspect the clinics and note their requirements. In time, all got telephones, which were a great boon: the ambulance could be easily summoned for emergencies which had previously depended on local means for transport - usually the local headmaster, who was the only one likely to own a motorcar. For less urgent cases, bus warrants were issued, but that charity went back to pre-independence days. Incidentally, then and later, the waiting time for, say, a hernia operation, in that country of one doctor for 50,000 people, and one specialist surgeon per million people, was two days. Explain that, 'developed' Europe! The patient would present himself to the clinic, be given a bus voucher by the nurse, arrive at the district hospital within twenty-four hours, and be operated on that day, on my afternoon list. The provincial anaesthetist advised that a patient should enjoy at least one night's rest after his journey, so the waiting time shot up to three days.

I would take note of such requirements as new chairs for Murowa clinic - the most remote, the poorest, and most beautiful corner of the district, in the wide open country under the shadow of Buchwa mountain. There was but one chair, which the doctor was honoured with. The nurse-interpreter stood by, and the patient sat on an old cooking oil tin. Alas, the services of the council (or the system) were slower than those of the hospital, and moved at the more traditional pace of Africa. Month after month, year after year, the request for chairs would appear in my monthly list; and month by month, etc, the cooking oil tin sank lower and lower, like a concertina, until it was level with the floor, and the act of sitting on it became a mere ceremony, whose original meaning was lost in the mists of time.

On the road out of this clinic, I had to cross the 'Devil's Bridge' - a name I gave it myself, which soon passed into local usage. This, and the road itself, came under the railways; and a sign, RHODESIA RAILWAYS, survived unnoticed many years after independence. The bridge was of concrete and passed over, or more often, through, a small stream, for its back had broken long ago; maybe even blown up in the war. I had to inch the Land Rover gingerly down to the fracture, manoeuvre it across, then scramble up the other side, in imminent danger of overturning the vehicle into the river. Monthly letters went to the railways about this matter, but for all I know, bridge and tin are the same to this day.

The clinics had consulting and treatment rooms, and a few beds for short-stay patients and deliveries. They were staffed by two nurses and a nurse aid (unpaid, in line for nursing training); a general hand, whose main jobs were fetching water and tending the garden;

and the sanitary assistant, who looked after the wells and latrines, Tb programme, etc.

The clinic was supposed to serve a radius of five kilometres and 10,000 people, but it usually covered much more of both. It was, in fact, an African country practice. As well as curative services, it conducted maternal/child health clinics, including family planning, immunisation, and educational sessions - simultaneously, on what was called the 'supermarket system', so people did not have to travel more than once for all their requirements.

The general hand fetched water in a donkey bowser (two drums drawn by a pair of donkeys) from the nearest dam or river, sometimes miles away. The newer clinics had wells or bore-holes. None had electricity. Vaccines were kept in a gas fridge. Non-disposable instruments were boiled over open fires, and there were disposable syringes and needles. From time to time, a wicked nurse (in town and country) was caught conducting his (or her) own private practice with a stolen (and unsterilised) syringe. This happened only once in my own bailiwick, and that was at Marandellas, during the early years of the civil war. The culprit was not dismissed the service (not my business, anyway), but sent, like Uriah the Hittite, to the 'sharp end', where at least he survived, and his sentence soon became less meaningful as the war engulfed the whole country. But on the whole, they were devoted folk - local, most of them, who lived at the clinics with their families.

The garden fed the staff, and also served to educate the people in what foods to grow. Western people have pious ideas about African diet, which is supposed to prevent most of the diseases we suffer from. It could do, but they are learning bad habits, especially in the towns. The diet of most towny child malnutrition cases was 'buns and Coke', which was thought very 'smart' by their young unmarried mothers. Even the staple maize meal can now be refined out of existence, and the 'super' forms are preferred by the city folk. The rough 'straight run' is sold anyway only in 50kg bags, which become weevily before they are a quarter used, and is fed only to cattle. The country people grow their own maize and take it to the local mill, where they get the good stuff.

But only in Africa is white maize still grown, and the people are very conservative in their habits. In the drought years of the eighties, maize was imported, and, of course, it was yellow. The starving people complained like finnicky children about this; although the doctors pointed out that it contained vitamin A and would wipe out xerophthalmia (dry eye disease, which was the principal cause of blindness); and the commercial farmers pointed out that the yellow maize was drought-resistant, and some brave ones even grew some themselves - and lost money by it. Still the people were not persuaded: the government even had to mix the yellow maize with what remained of the inferior white stuff.

Now Zimbabwe is growing oil palms. But will the people use the oil (loaded with vitamin A) for cooking, as in so many parts of Africa, where xerophthalmia is rarely seen? I doubt it. The stuff is produced to make soap, anyway.[1]

And with independence, the Swedish missionaries returned to Jock's district, like the swallows (who had, of course, been back several times), and inspired Jock's naughty humour again. There was some confusion over the jurisdiction of the clinics; these missionaries being a new lot. Jock described how 'I was doing a clinic at Jeka, when this Scarwegian bint came in and said it was *their* clinic. I said, "Look, mate, where have you been the last three years?"'

The devolutionary changes did not please everybody. I was driving home from a workshop on Tb with Mr Kazembe, the health inspector. He told me that he had noted looks and murmurings of discontent among the provincial health assistants, whose previous duties took them on quarterly visits to Shabani at government expense, including spending money of ten dollars a day. 'And I happen to know that there are many unattached young ladies in Shabani, which these chaps used to stay with. Now they will have to stay in Gwelo with their wives.' Mr Kazembe was such an obviously solid family man himself, it gave the lesson added force. I was also intrigued to learn that what I had taken as the one-horse town of

---

[1] I have since learned that the scheme failed, the climate too dry. WD.

Shabani was seen on another plane of existence as the Paris of the Midlands. In fact, it suffered (or enjoyed) the usual social consequences of an African mining town with a large migrant labour force.

Not all Africans exhibited the charming manners of the old lady (or, for that matter, the community sister). One such was Mr Chipembere, who was as cheeky as his namesake, the rhinoceros. He succeeded the dignified Mr Kazembe as health inspector in the district. Under the new system he was supposed to send his reports through me, so that I should at least know what was going on in my parish. (Incidentally, this included the building of the special pit latrines and protected wells I had seen the need for in Umvuma days, and were evidently in the pipe-line even then, only awaiting the conditions to install them: both local inventions which represented yet more of this country's contributions to world health.) Mr Chipembere continued to send his reports up the vertical channels of the old system. To my request, he replied that I would not understand them anyway.

He also appropriated one of our precious vehicles to his own personal use. This he was entitled to use for his work, but was supposed to park in its proper place outside the hospital at the end of each day. The van was more usually parked outside Mr Chimpembere's own house, and on Saturday mornings could be seen outside the stores, as his wife did her weekly shopping. I had to bring in the guns of the provincial medical officer to get Mr Chipembere to conform, sometimes for as long as a week together, before he reverted to his old ways again.

Then came the school health programme. It was planned to appoint a 'health officer' in each primary school, and one of the staff was selected for training. First aid kits were supplied by the pharmacist, but unfortunately, on the opening day, the kits were not ready. Mr Chipembere recognised my departmental responsibility in this matter, at least, and informed me on the telephone that such shortcomings 'created a bad impression'.

Finally, he compromised in the matter of his reports to the extent of sending me copies, at least, affording me the pleasure of collecting his most priceless effort in my experience. This one went to the secretary for health, no less, not only over my head, but that of the PMO. Its contents showed that Mr Chipembere was no more overawed by the head of the service than he was by a mere DMO. He had been to a conference of his kind in Zambia, and informed the secretary that arrangements at the Zimbabwean end 'left much to be desired' and 'compared unfavourably' with those at the Zambian end (and may well have 'created a bad impression', for all I remember). I wondered how the secretary (who was the man who ordered out the pensioners, and was not known to be deficient in a proper sense of what was due to him) received that on his desk. I was reminded of the 'educated expressions' of Mr Cudjo (another health inspector), in Ghana, and wondered whether the secretary took them as coolly as Amos.

Committees sprang up like mushrooms overnight, which held meetings - too many of both for my liking. First was our own little government, the district health executive, of which I was prime minister, which included the district nursing officer (another new appointment), as well as the redoubtable Mr Chipembere. This met once a week; and once a month, or less often, as time went by, we called a regular little parliament: the district health team, which drew members from all over the district, including from other government departments, and even little old men of rural functions, who had to have much of the proceedings interpreted for them. All this at government expense, of course, under the formula, T and S: transport and subsistence, which with the workshops was all very good business for the Nilton Hotel. Indeed, hotels throughout the country were doing very well out of the government at that time: whether they are still, I do not know. And the minutes of all meetings were taken by the hospital chief clerk, Mr Sibanda, who always concluded his record with the ambiguous formula: 'Having nothing to say, the meeting closed.'

And the next level up the pyramid was the provincial meeting, which was called every three months or so at Gwelo, and included an overnight stay for delegates at the Midlands Hotel, where the conference was held. This began in generous and inclusive proportions - up to a hundred people - but was later scaled down to DMOs alone and the main provincial officers, and held in the PMO's office: a much duller affair than the earlier occasions, which had given scope to some colourful characters, including the American lady, a sister from some remote mission, who seemed not to have used the English language from one occasion to another, to judge by the extent she indulged in it, like a thirsty traveller at an oasis, at the provincial meetings. On one occasion, I heard a stage whisper from the platform, addressed to the chairman: 'Can't you shut her up?' But most colourful of all was Dr Rossi of Gokwe.

Dr Rossi was a priest as well as a doctor: I believe he was priest at Gokwe until he decided to be of more practical use to his flock, and returned to his native Argentina to train as a doctor. Now Gokwe was the largest and poorest district, not only in the province, but in the country. It must have been the size of Yorkshire: certainly a hundred miles across in all directions; and the population even then must have been nearly 300,000. I once visited Gokwe, when looking for a likely district, and I must say it cowed even my independent spirit. The Tb officer at the time, who read my mind only too well, informed me: 'There's lots of marriageable girls at Gokwe, if you like them with rings in their noses.' After my visit, I described the 'town' itself as 'a scout camp on the moon'.

None of this frightened Dr Rossi: this was what he had come to Africa for. Even the absence of electric light in the whole town, with the sole exception of the operating theatre, did not affect the noiseless tenour of his way: like the locals, he got up with the sun and went to bed with it. If he wanted to read - and I imagine his reading was confined to his medical books and his breviary, or something equally devout - he used the operating theatre, when he was not using it for its usual purpose, which I am sure was pretty often. There was a club in Gokwe, used energetically by such ordinary mortals as Internal Affairs and police, but not by Dr Rossi, who neither smoke nor drank, and in his personal habits, generally resembled Field Marshal Montgomery.

I once remarked to him: 'You must belong to the Holy Army of Martyrs.'

'I am not a martyr,' crisply replied Dr Rossi. 'I enjoy it.'

But his greatest moments came when he rose before a hundred people at the provincial meetings to plead on behalf of his long-suffering district. I don't know why it is that unfortunate circumstances give rise to amusement: who can resist a smile at the name of Hogglestock (which Trollope obviously, if unconsciously, intended to provoke) and its perpetual curate, of whom Dr Rossi was the happier equivalent? But there is no doubt but when Dr Rossi delivered his pleas in his passionate Latin voice, the name of 'Gokwe' never failed to be drowned in waves of vulgar laughter.

Then Dr Rossi returned to Argentina for a year on a sabbatical of some kind. When he came back, something drastic had happened to Gokwe. His prayers had been more than answered: 'development' had taken place. There were no less than two banks, a garage, and a supermarket in the main square (which had never been called that before). So far from the nights being candlelit and silent, they positively throbbed with electric light, as did the air from half a dozen discos. Dr Rossi must have thought he had returned to Sodom and Gomorrah rolled into one. A profound convulsion was felt by his friends to take place in his soul. This was not what he had come to Africa for. Soon after his return, he put in for and obtained a lateral transfer to Nkayi, in the wilds of Matabeleland.

Meanwhile, the new game of Marxism-Leninism spread its merry circle. Africans are not children, but they do retain the happy gift of *reductio ad absurdum,* which the Irish and Italians used to have, until they got so sad that even their trains ran on time. This being Africa, there was going to be no nonsense about all animals being equal. It is true that the jolly fashion, 'comrade', flourished like flying ants after rain - rather sadly displacing (for a time, anyway) the graceful old forms of *baba* - father, or sir; *amai* - mother, or madam; *sekuru* - grandfather, or venerable sir, etc; whose family origins imbued them with a respect devoid of all servility. And, as often as not, the insultingly familiar edge was taken off the term by its transformation into *macomrade,* which roughly translates as 'comrade sir', as happened in Poland with *pan towarzysz* - lord comrade (trust the Poles not to spare the glory!). But people like our friends, the administrator and the mayor, acquired the curious title, 'chef', from somewhere, apparently ignorant of its origins in the kitchen.

(Incidentally, 'comrade' took a temporary dip in Shabani, when some wicked European spread the rumour that it was Russian for 'Kaffir'.)

Then somebody got the Maoist idea that it would be a good thing for white-collar workers to do a spot of manual work.

This did not go down very well with the people concerned. 'White collar' in Africa means just that, and on his first day, your African clerk turns up in white collar and tie and long trousers. Let the *Murungu* (white man) dress as if he were out shooting in the bundu: in town, the educated African dressed for town; and in these garments, he does not anticipate any task which requires him to shed them. His parents did not save their hard-earned dollars to send their little boy to school for any pick and shovel nonsense. (Strangely enough, the women were not included in this barbaric plan, although they do most of the manual work in Africa - perhaps for that reason; or the experimenters were rightly afraid of the Women's League.)

Nevertheless, in the first (and last) experiment, volunteers were called for. Volunteering in Africa tends to take a military form - the three 'U's', well-known to British soldiers - and the administrator's people (as he was running the show) outnumbered the others. The administrator, himself, incidentally, confined his participation to turning up in his Land Rover and instructing Mr Sango, of the Public Works Department, who was directing the actual work, to 'carry on', in an officer-like manner (the administrator, I mean; not Mr Sango). There were only two volunteers from the medical department: myself, probably looking for material for letters home (or 'England', as I should say, as Terry was now encouraging me to call Zimbabwe 'home'); and Phineas, the mortuary attendant - an unpopular job, usually held by foreigners such as Malawians or Mozambicans (like him), who felt insecure about their position in the country. Needless, to say, we got nobody from the private sector.

In short, we were supposed to dig a ditch to carry a water-pipe to a school, and again needless to say, I was the only white man in the line. It was Saturday morning. We were working beside the Selukwe road, and from time to time, Europeans, on their way to fishing, would pass in their vehicles, and they must have wondered what the government doctor was doing, swinging a pick in a gang of blacks, with another black man standing over him - a position that used to be filled by 'Dutchmen' - and what the doctor had done to get there. As they preserved a discreet silence on the subject, I do not know, although I told the story with great glee in the club afterwards.

Work started as usual at 8am, and by nine o' clock, the workers were feeling hungry. None of them except myself had had breakfast, rather expecting the government to provide. The voluntary principle is not a part of African culture: helping your neighbour build his house, yes; but as an abstract concept, no. Mr Sango looked unhappy. As the only one with any access to food, I volunteered to go back to the hospital for bread, which I duly did, although Rhoda, the cook, parted with it very unhappily, not surprisingly - she had to account for it. And to round off the morning's activities (which ended at twelve midday, sharp), Mr Sango, the good fellow, gave them all *doro* (or maize beer) at a local tavern.

All in all, the experiment was voted not a good thing. I don't know what was said in the councils of the local soviet, but it was never repeated.

Alas, an idealistic effort of my own also fell flat. There used to be a saying (no doubt, still is), WAWA - West Africa wins again - which could be extended to the whole continent, as I have more than once shown in these pages.

The rural hospital at Lundi, seven miles outside town, seemed to be outliving its purpose. It started life as the original African hospital, but when the new black wards were built at the main hospital, some time in the fifties, it fell into a sort of sleepy desuetude. Twenty miles out in the country, it would have been another thing. In short, more than half the beds were empty.

It was an irrational tradition, which I unthinkingly continued, for the doctor to visit the place once a week; when apart from my usual activities, I would deposit a certain quantity of reading matter, including the *Spectator* and the *Sunday Telegraph,* which were sent out to me. If this sounds like caviare to the general, I should explain that any African peasant who can read will read anything like a hungry man: I have even seen them studying the chairman's annual report of Barclay's Unit Trusts, I'd thought I'd thrown away. At Umvuma, when I got rid of some old books (mostly dictionaries), the nurses formed a rugby maul round them: at Shabani, I donated them to the African library. And any music too was welcome. When I replaced my LPs (which I usually did on UK leave, few being obtainable in Rhodesia or Zimbabwe), I would give them to Anderson to play on his old record player. I used to wish Smithy would pass his *kaya* with a United Nations delegation, while Anderson was listening to a Mozart piano concerto, and be able to talk about the most cultured as well as the happiest Africans - and make me minister of health, maybe; or, more acceptably, double my pension from high-power to low-power microscopic size. (Though that is not fair to Smithy: it was Mugabe who shrunk the dollars.) But all this is not the idealism I am referring to.

In the town of Shabani, as in all African towns, were a number of homeless beggars, who hung around the bus terminus, living on, and in, God knows what - certainly under the sun and the rain and the cold of winter. From time to time, one of these ragged, half-starved creatures would be admitted to the hospital, suffering from Tb, pellagra, and what-not, and sometimes all together. After they were bathed, clothed, and cured, arose the problem of what to do with them. If, or when, they drifted back to the bus terminus, sure enough they would reappear in the hospital in six months' time, if only in the mortuary. I decided to give these people a permanent sanctuary at Lundi hospital, and even bragged about my plan at the provincial meeting, and invited other districts to send their huddled masses there too.

Alas, in case after case, I was to discover, like Dr Patel at Samreboi, it had all been a disastrous failure. After a week or two, the beneficiaries disappeared. Three square meals a day, a clean warm bed, decent clothing, to say nothing of the *Spectator* and the *Sunday Telegraph,* were not enough to compensate these town mice for the bright lights of the bus terminus. The country life was JUST TOO QUIET.

Then word came that the provincial governor was coming to town, and would meet the local worthies and loyal citizens. The venue was to be the assembly hall of the largest mine township. For fairly obvious reasons, I did not anticipate a plumed hat and tea on the lawn: less obvious to the reader will be the fact that the governor, as well as representing the head of state, was a cardinal party gauleiter. And, for good reasons, I was the only white to turn up - I was by now the only one left in the town in government service, or, at any rate, head of department. Jock, needless to say, felt no obligation in the matter. (In any case, his department was still officially Belingwe.) Nor was any obligation felt by any of the private sector. Nor should they. You can't mix loyalty with politics and expect it to stay in place.

What occurred was more like the Munich *Bierkeller* than anything on a lawn. The hall was lined by the party *Jugend,* and the loyal citizens stood in patient rows, with myself as prominent in the front one as the proverbial sore thumb. We faced the stage, on which was a table, the usual supply of water, and a row of chairs, none of which was intended for the likes of me.

After the usual hour's wait, beyond the laughingly appointed time, the governor entered, followed by his entourage, including our friends, the administrator and the mayor (who had not yet received their marching orders): all the by now familiar local slave-figures, who seemed to have been painted black in Moscow; the totalitarian look or smell being as typical as the more wholesome Church of England one referred to some time before. The governor shook his fist in the black power salute, and shouted: *'Pamberi ne Zanu!'* (Forward Zanu - the Party), and the loyal (or prudent) citizens shook theirs and replied : *'Pamberi!'* - all except the doctor, that is, who began to look like a sorer thumb.

The governor spoke, 'rousing the meeting to enthusiasm' (or a good imitation of it), with lots more *'Pamberis'* and as many *'Pasi ne dissidents!'* (Down with dissidents, which referred to Mr Nkomo and his friends, their leader not then having kissed and made up with the leader of Zanu), to which the loyal citizens echoed: *'Pasi ne!'* I continued to stick out as before.

Before long, the governor (who would have needed to be pretty short-sighted not to) had noticed me. He came down from the stage, especially for my benefit (which did not flatter me a bit), and started dancing up and down in front of me, and shouting *'Pamberi!'* at me, which moved me no more than the echoing *'Pamberis'* around me. I stood with my hands crossed over my flies and stared through his boiling eyes, thinking, not so much of England, as of my late father, a man of independent spirit, and what he would have thought and done.

The ancestral spirit came to my aid - with a bit of my native cheek thrown in. I calmly looked at my watch and informed the man next to me - a reasonable chap, with whom I had had some conversation before, and whose *'Pamberis'* were not so enthusiastic as to prevent him from hearing me - that I had that old excuse, a critical case at the hospital. I then walked away, without saying 'bye-bye' to the governor. The party youths at the door looked very black, in more ways than one, but let me through, tamely enough.

Afterwards, my boldness surprised me and made me a little anxious. I was now a married man, with a family to raise in this land. At the next medical workshop, I inquired of a black friend in the PMO's office: 'What sort of person is the provincial governor?'

'He's a nigger. Why do you ask?'

I explained about the bad impression I must (as I meant to) have given at the meeting.

'Don't worry. You are a doctor. He used to be a garden boy. If you shouted at him, he would call you "sir".'

Ah well, the poor man is dead now, anyway.

2 - Family Life

Our first child, Michael, was born in Bulawayo. His mother was what is known as an elderly primigravida - having her first baby over the age of thirty - and there was no specialist gynaecologist in Shabani.

To begin with, he was rather lean: his mother's family carried the greyhound genes. But soon, on his mother's milk, though never even plump, he grew to a cuddly little creature, we called 'Baby Bear', always with a merry smile, and into everything, like any other healthy baby in the world.

Then Michael started keeping us awake - not through crying, but when he was able to climb out of his cot. Then he would come scrambling on to our bed, where we were sitting up, I reading Trollope to Terry: a habit we kept up for best part of a year, until it fell away, as such things do. 'Baby Bear' with his merry grin would want to join in. 'He *is* just like a baby bear,' said Terry. But soon we were calling him 'Night-life', which sounded like an African name. 'Sentencing Night-life Manyonda to six months' imprisonment, the magistrate said, "This kind of thing has got to stop",' as the newspapers used to say. But stopping it was another story.

Michael was born in March. In September, we took a holiday at Kariba. We were in an open boat, game-viewing. We drew up on a bank, where there was a pride of lion at their kill, a buffalo, no more than fifty yards away. Michael decided to start crying, a thing he rarely did, having no idea of the lions, of course. The guide asked Terry politely if she could keep that baby quiet: he could see the chief lion was thrashing his tail, and looking restless. He had already explained that the animal could be on us in two seconds. Terry felt wretched, and tried, not very successfully, to keep Michael quiet with her finger in his mouth. All were very relieved when we pushed off.

Every Saturday night, we had supper out, mostly at the hotel, even before Michael could walk, and he would crawl to neighbouring tables, being a friendly, outgoing little chap; so his mother, who was very much mindful of other people's comfort, hardly got her meal for getting up to fetch him back. Then he discovered the piano, which he was able to play and hold on to by a simultaneous process, with the delighted waiters, in their fezzes, holding their napkins, standing watching him, and applauding when he finished and crawled back to us.

Sometimes we varied it with supper at the mine club. One night there, Michael crawled about outside and found an old Coke bottle, which he picked up and gave a good licking. On Monday morning, his first birthday, he developed vomiting and diarrhoea. Oral rehydration therapy was new then, and I had had much success with it. That is what we gave Michael: simple sugar and salt mixture.

By the Wednesday, he was very ill indeed. He had grown peaky and listless, all his ebullience gone. A heart-broken Terry told me he was bringing back all the solution she gave him. I found her sitting silent downstairs. Michael was asleep in his bedroom. I said: 'You don't mind him *shupering*[1] when he is like this.' I could not keep the sob out of my voice. I knew then what it was to be a parent.

By Friday, it was the same. We became alarmed. I told Terry to take him to the private doctor at the mine.

And when he got into the doctor's office, Michael sprang to life, and started playing with the doctor's books. He had been absorbing as much of the solution as he brought back, and, with his mother's devoted nursing, it saved his life.

Michael was fifteen months old, when Mary was born, at Shabanie Mine Hospital. (Yes, the name was different from the town.) Michael's nose was not exactly out of joint, but he didn't show much enthusiasm for this event. He was silent as I drove him home, until he saw a cow, and said 'cow'. He liked cows.

He stayed with some Dutch friends, while Terry was lying in. I went round to be with him in the evenings.

Mary started life looking like me: after two years, she began to look like her mother. In her earlier stage, although she looked so like me that Terry said you could put her down anywhere in the district and she would be returned to the hospital, she had brown hair and

---

[1] Causing trouble. WD.

was very pretty, as she continued to be at all stages. Michael by now was a little blond angel.

I discovered a curious thing at the time. I could eat off their plates: I mean those of my wife and children, but off no one else's. This is the curious miracle of 'one flesh'. It persists to this day, and will remain, as far as my wife and I are concerned; but one day our children will outgrow it. For this cause shall a man leave his father and mother, etc. But this runs on too far ahead.

Michael liked to eat his evening meal, sitting on the concrete outside the veranda: a bowl of mealie porridge. Sometimes, before my own meal, I would join him, sitting on the step. One day, he put down his bowl and came running towards me, his loving little arms outstretched, and they and his face covered with porridge. Involuntarily, I shrank back. He tripped over my foot, went flying, banged his head and cried bitterly, his dirty little face crinkled up. I never felt so mean in my life. I picked him up and hugged him, porridge and all.

At bedtime, Michael liked to race round the front garden in his bare feet and little dressing-gown, just after dark. One night, as he was doing this, a police Land Rover pulled up in the road outside. A policeman got out and held up a six-foot cobra, they had just run over. 'This snake just came out of your garden, doctor.' That was the end of Michael's evening romps.

As Michael became more active, we had a four-foot wire fence put up, round the front garden, with a gate. One lunchtime, I happened to open the front door. A skinny little black brat in his rags was on the lawn, about to snatch Michael's football. The poor kid had never possessed such a thing in his life: a bundle of rags would be the best football he ever got. No doubt he came in by the gate: he was about ten years old. He didn't leave that way. Without touching the football, he took off and leapt the four-foot fence like an impala.

Once, we let the nurses' children in to play football with Michael. Alas, they were too old for him, and Michael never got near the ball. He ran after them in tears and was lucky not to get trampled. We found younger friends for him after that.

Anderson was now getting old and unsuitable for children. I pensioned him off, and we engaged a nanny, Norah, a rather sad girl. She had reason to be, as she could not have children, despite the best efforts of the provincial gynaecologist, when he visited the hospital. By now, all the specialists were making district visits every month, and greatly we appreciated them.

But Norah had some little nieces and nephews, who used to stay with her in the *kaya*, and these would play with our children, especially on the pedal-car we bought for Michael's birthday, and the trolley, Terry's father made for the children.

And there were many white and Indian and other black children for them to play with. These came to their birthday parties, for which Terry organised a regular treat. She hired a donkey-cart and its owner, and the high spot of the party was a drive up and down the hospital road for the children, accompanied by their mothers on foot. This started with Michael's second birthday, and the poor fellow was sick after the drive. His third birthday was his first of unalloyed enjoyment.

And not for nearly two years did he see rain in his life. Two, or even three years followed each other without rain. People starved in spite of the hand-outs of grain and the work programme they were given to pretend to earn them. One poor fellow collapsed and died on the work programme: 'probably through starvation,' as the PMO said. The usually dry country was now arid, and the fierce sun, unsoftened by the seasonal rains, beat down with hammer blows, as I wrote to people in England, after Hopkins, under which earth 'winced and sang'. One had to go to work, but Sundays found us pent up in the house by the terrific fire outside, as we might have been by the snows of Canada. Not till four o' clock in the afternoon did we take a turn up the hospital road and out the top gate, Terry pushing the shaded push-chair with Mary in it, Michael tripping along beside us under his little bush hat - round the back roads of the seedy little town, with their untidy gardens and security fences, with barking dogs exploding behind every one - round to the Selukwe road to the bottom gate and home again. And I wondered how long an English girl would last in a place like this - like the Scottish girls at Umvuma - and was glad, not for the first time, I had married a native, who didn't know any better.

Every other Sunday, when I was not on duty, we would go to the Anglican church, where I played the harmonium. Little white kids would run up and down the aisles, try to join me at my work, even climb on the altar; while black children, in bow-ties and best frocks, sat in good little rows, looking on at this behaviour with round eyes of astonishment. At the end of the service, I would allow Michael to have a go on the harmonium, when he would render his own composition, of the atonal school, which I called *Foggy Night on the River.*

Both children were now at the piano, especially Mary, who would sit for hours extemporising what sounded like Bartók. She had a prejudice against the black keys, so I suppose she was reproducing the pentatonic scale, the master was so devoted to.

Michael could certainly recognise a tune from at least eighteen months. He heard Rubinstein on a record playing the *Polonaise Militaire,* and said, 'Daddy!', which was very flattering. Once, when I was playing a record of the Dysart Pipe Band, he turned up the sound, before I could stop him, and fairly blasted himself off his feet. He sat down and cried, and I hoped it hadn't put him off Scotland for ever, if only for the sake of the Caledonian branch of the family.

Having children, of course, we had pets. We started with cats. First a kitten called Tabby, a girl; then a few months later, Tiger: same mother, next litter. Tabby did not seem to recognise her brother; spat at him, cuffed him, and generally tried to persuade him he was not welcome; until Tiger grew big enough to hit back: one day when Tabby forced him into a corner and he stood up on his hind legs and lashed out like Mohammed Ali. After that Tabby left him alone.

These cats did not last long; seemed half wild, and ran off, or else got killed by the dogs the medical assistants kept at their quarters.

These dogs also got the rabbits that succeeded the cats: a present from the vicar. They came with a special underground bunker, a sort of iron affair with a single entrance. One night there was a dreadful canine uproar, and next day we discovered that the rabbits had been dug up and presumably eaten.

All these disappearances we explained to the children as voluntary departures to cat land or rabbit land.

And as I said, I had a whole new large family to call my own. In pride of place was the patriarch, Terry's father, who invited me to call him 'Bill', as a concession to my age, as I was the oldest of his sons-in-law, who called him 'Dad'. He was a tall rangy man, then about sixty-five, who looked like what Australians used to look like, before they got so comfortable. In fact, he looked and spoke so like Ian Smith (except for his dark hair) that when Smithy appeared on telly one night (this being, of course, after independence), complaining about something, Michael said, 'Granddad!'

Bill had had the proverbial American career: cowpuncher, inn-keeper, veterinary hand, small farmer - never making any money for all his toil - and now was security officer on a pig farm, near Salisbury, where he lived in an old Rhodesian-type farmhouse: two *rondavels* connected by a middle section - the sort of place Terry was brought up in and ran about in her bare feet (as I discovered when she kicked me in bed, with a kick, as I told her, like a horse). Bill had a natural refinement: a dirty joke was abhorrent to him. He was a great reader and letter-writer in a fine copperplate hand, a great consulter of dictionaries. He had an encyclopaedic knowledge of the country: its history, its 'trades, their tackle and trim', everything that stirred or grew in the bush. He spoke Shona fluently, and when he came fishing with us, he would sit down with some passing African and chat with him for hours, having the man's life story out of him in the course of an afternoon, with a sociability and command of the language for which I could only envy him both. His attitude to the Africans was respectful but distant. Like D H Lawrence (whose stories he enjoyed when he found them on my shelves), he would have no 'mixing and mingling', and miscegenation was not in his book. He stretched himself when one daughter married a 'Dutchman', and one granddaughter later an 'Italian', but that was his limit.

314

Bill was born in the country, as was his wife, Betty. She was of Irish stock, and Bill blamed anything that went wrong in the family on those genes. (Incidently, his own parents came from the west of England, and he claimed descent from the Saxon kings of Essex.) Betty was an Irish pixie, 'all sense and spectacles', as I first saw her, sitting up in bed, reading Hansard (Zimbabwe), of all bedtime reading. She had worked as hard as her husband, not only at keeping the family going, but at such things as book-keeping, being an expert on income tax. Sadly, she died before Mary was born, though she lived to hold Michael in her arms.

Most of Bill's relations were in Salisbury, Betty's in Bulawayo: these being the older generation.

When we visited Granddad, taking the week-end off, we sent a message by 'Granddad's spider'. There were always one or two of these creatures - wall spiders - on the walls of the house. We told the spider to run up to Salisbury to tell him we were coming, and sure enough, the children would see the creature there before us. And what a long hot drag it would be in the car, with the two discontented little ones, unless they were mercifully asleep, with a welcome break at the hotel in Enkeldoorn on the way; and the same ordeal coming back. I would fall asleep at the wheel and Terry would take over. Thank God it was past the days when we had to carry guns and take the chance of an ambush, with or without a convoy. But that was before our married days, I am glad to say.

At least the days on the farm were a welcome break, and the children could see the pigs and run away from the geese, and 'drive' the tractor, as well as slip into Salisbury to the amusement park.

Brother-in-law Boyce (the 'Dutchman') and his wife, Terry's sister, 'Dozie', had a *real* farm - all 15,000 acres of it, a ranch near Gatooma. ('Dozie' was, of course, a pet name: most of Terry's family had pet names like the Victorians.) Their homestead could have been called 'Groot Schuur', like Rhodes's, it was so large, and looked more like a 'big barn' than the original. It was a simple house with an asbestos roof and mosquito-screened veranda, and measured 100 feet by 60. But inside was spacious luxury. First, the veranda itself, as wide as an English lane, where tea was served, extra beds put out, and, at the back, pumpkins and butternuts laid out to ripen, the deep freeze kept, and all manner of junk. Part of this was closed off as a garage. And on the veranda the children could play football and hockey, or just cycle back and forth. Within, were large rooms and many bedrooms, where one could retire and read in the heat of the afternoon. Around the house was a large garden, within the security fence, with magnificent trees in the front, surrounded by lawn. At the back, sheds for tractors and *bakkies* (pick-ups). Beyond the fence were the 'lands': the cultivated fields, planted with maize, sorghum, sunflower, cotton; and stretching beyond all, the Bushveld.

At four, when the main heat was off, we would take a stroll, beyond the gate, either to the left, among the lands; or to the right, where the dusty road soon entered the virgin bush, with the telephone line running above. Sometimes one saw game - a duiker or kudu; and once I saw a gymnogene, a weird-looking hawk, with a yellow face and feet. Then, when the children were tired, we would turn back for sundowners on the lawn.

Boyce was a hearty extrovert: you could hear him bawling Afrikaans or English down the telephone, half-way round the house, as if he didn't believe in the efficacy of the instrument; and a generous host, as was Dozie, a tall handsome woman with the cool of a duchess. And Boyce used to bawl at the workers, but I think they loved them both, if only from something that happened in the war.

The present building was not their first house. The first was burnt down. Boyce was away with the TA. Dozie looked after the farm, but left every afternoon to sleep in town. One day, she drove out, past the workers' compound, as usual, unaware that the guerrillas were hidden there. They could have shot her easily, and I believe it was significant that they did not. I do not wish to be invidious - some good people got shot - but it was widely believed that the popularity (or otherwise) of the *baas* and his family (at least, in some cases) had something to do with it. When Dozie had gone, they broke into the house, drank all the liquor, and had a regular party, before burning the place down. What the Koks missed most was three generations of hunting trophies.

They had three children - some of our children's many cousins - two tall sports-mad lads, and a daughter, I thought looked like Princess Di.

Terry's oldest sister, Rosemary lived with her husband, 'Muk', in Bulawayo. Rosemary was a slim, energetic woman, rather like her mother, who kept a spotless house and was never idle, always making things. She was devoted to her beautiful garden.

Muk was a colonel in the infantry, and, ironically, had fought for both Smith and later Mugabe, in the insurrection of 1981, when the Matabele swept down from the north, like a wolf on the fold, but found, not a fold, but Smith's old regiments, black and white (Muk's was a black regiment), who stopped them and saved Mugabe's throne at Entumbane, near Bulawayo.

Muk was another tall Rhodesian. Bill used to say the sun made the stock spring up: he regarded the inhabitants of our islands (including myself) as a race of dwarfs. Muk had a peculiar sense of humour, and described the Ashwin brides as 'the four ugly sisters'. The Micklesfields provided two more tall handsome cousins, a boy and a girl. Hugh was a geologist. Debbie was the one who dared to marry an 'Italian', though, like the 'Dutch' Boyce, he was as Rhodesian as Bill.

Muk died of cancer in 1986, before he was fifty.

And in Malawi, was another sister, 'Bobby', and her family, with whom we spent one happy holiday in that beautiful country. Bobby was most like Terry. And, needless to say, more tall, good-looking cousins, three boys and a girl. They moved about a lot, as husband Lionel was in the tobacco business: a charming man, the only one in the family, to Bill's eye, as 'short' as me, although he was born in Africa (Malawi), until we were joined by the 'Italian' Andy.

This was the immediate family: the 'extended family' would fill a book themselves, and as Bill has undertaken the writing of it, I will leave the task to him.

In 1984 my redoubtable Scottish aunt, Ina, came to visit us. We had invited a number of people whose hospitality overseas we had

317

wished to return, but at 70, Aunt Ina was the only one with the spirit to take us up. Admittedly, she was a seasoned traveller, having done a number of far-flung journeys on behalf of her church.

I picked her up at Harare airport, having left Terry and the children behind at Shabani. They would join us later on the tour of the country we had planned. I took her first to Bill's pig farm. He had certainly made an effort in converting one of the rough rooms into a passable lady's bedroom; but on the first night we had a problem.

Aunt Ina knocked on my door. 'Warren, there's an enormous spider in my room.'

I went to inspect. Sure enough, there was a wall spider, about as big as a man's hand.

'That's all right. It's just a wall spider.' They are, of course, quite harmless.

'I don't want to know what kind it is. I just want it out of my room.'

I fetched a yard brush. Bill came to help me. Of course, the things run like greyhounds, and this one did, all over the place, and ended up behind the dressing table.

So we had to move the dressing table, and continue the hunt in the dimly lit room. I took a swipe or two at the poor thing. We lost track of it. At any rate we didn't have a body to show. We told Aunt Ina it must have run out of the room. I don't think she was convinced, which wasn't surprising, because neither were we. She told me later, she switched off her light and made up her mind not to think about it or anything else that might be in the room, and slept soundly.

Aunt Ina had been given a message to deliver to Dr George (whose surname shall remain buried in shame) by his brother Walter in Edinburgh. I got him on the telephone and handed him over to Aunt Ina. She hadn't *asked* to meet him; thought we might get a cup of tea, but didn't expect him to shoot the messenger. 'So nice to hear from you,' replied George. 'Have a nice holiday. Goodbye!' Thanks very much! My words: Aunt Ina's thoughts.

We took a plane and saw the Victoria Falls. I took photographs with her camera. Then I tried to unload it, and ruined the film. We appealed to a young man who looked promising. A lucky choice; he was a professional. He showed me how to load and unload the camera (which Aunt Ina herself wasn't sure of), and I returned to the Falls alone to repeat all the pictures. 'And don't stand too close to the edge, Warren Durrant! I was very worried about you yesterday. I've got to get you back to your wife!'

We stayed at Wankie Game Park. One evening at supper, Aunt Ina felt chilly. It was July, winter. She walked back to our block to fetch a stole. After supper we walked back together, and saw the trees broken by a herd of elephants. Aunt Ina had missed them by about five minutes. Not a nice party to bump into!

We returned to Harare, picked up the car, and travelled down to Boyce and Dozie's farm, where Terry and the children met us.

Then on to Bulawayo, where Aunt Ina felt really cold for the only time. She met Rosemary and Muk there. Then to Shabani and home. Aunt Ina saw the hospital, and came with me to a clinic out in the bare winter bundu.

Then to Fort Victoria with Terry and the children. Michael had pointed out *mombes* (cows) to Aunt Ina and explained what they were. Aunt Ina spotted one. *'Mombe,'* she said. 'Cow,' Michael corrected her solemnly.

On to the Eastern Highlands - 'Scotland in the tropics': Melsetter, where Aunt Ina's room opened on the magnificent panorama of the Chimanimani Mountains, a picture window indeed. Then the Vumba, where she got nipped by a dog, fortunately vaccinated, otherwise we would have to think about rabies. Finally, Inyanga, the most like Scotland of all.

We dropped in at Gareth's place on the way back to Harare. He had made a pile of sandwiches, being forewarned.

And so to Bill's, spiders resolutely ignored. Last stop before the plane home. While we were alone, Aunt Ina said, 'That was the best day's work ye did in your life, Warren Durrant, when ye married Terry!' And I agreed. She also said, 'Now you've got children of your own, you will appreciate better how people feel about them.' 'Too true!' I replied.

Little boys and girls differentiate early, for all the opinions and practices of modern educationists. Mary certainly loved dolls as much as Michael loved his pedal-car, etc. And Mary developed an early interest in weddings. Whenever we saw one from the car, black or white, we had to stop until Mary had indentified the bride, like the queen bee. And before long, we got invited to some.

There were family weddings, but the one I remember most was that of an African colleague: or rather, it was his wedding breakfast. The poor man had got married some years earlier, and had children as old as ours, but had spent that time saving up for this obligatory event, which in the case of such a 'big man' as a doctor, included his whole clan, let alone his extended family. There were no less than a thousand guests, whom we joined in the meat and *sadza* (maize porridge), not being among the inner party. The latter ate rather more delicately in a separate room, into which Mary strayed to catch a glimpse of the bride, and was gently led out of. Then a disco started, which made such a tremendous noise, Terry and I could not bear it. We left early, after I had left the customary donation with one of the ushers. The formal ceremony, where the bride and groom sit like Egyptian gods, while the money is collected and the donors' names and contributions called out, came later.

After we left, Mary was disappointed. She was looking forward to a dance, seeming impervious to the dreadful noise. To compensate her, we stopped at a garage and let her slip out to buy sweets. She came running back in the path of an oncoming car. I shouted to her to stop. Thank God, it was a cold day and the window was closed or she might have heard me. Of course, one of us should have gone with her: parents should be everywhere, but aren't. I felt miserable with guilt and said so. So did Terry, no doubt, as she tried to comfort me. Parenthood!

Another delight of Mary's was hotels - posh ones. If there was anything she enjoyed more than a posh hotel, it was a posher one. The plush surroundings, the attention of the waiters (and what a fuss African waiters make of children!), made her shine like a little star and enter the place with the glow of a little princess. Auntie Rosemary won a week-end at the Bulawayo Southern Sun, which was a very posh hotel. This was a busman's holiday for her, on her own doorstep, and joyless enough without her husband, so she gave the tickets to us. It was a welcome break for us, perhaps not very thrilling for Michael, but was one of the high spots of Mary's little life.

Quite a different affair was what we called the 'Spooky Hotel' (which shall remain otherwise nameless). Our usual hotel in Salisbury was full, and they directed us to this place. We were booked in by a surly clerk, smoking at a rough desk. We took two rooms, divided between boys and girls. Michael succeeded in locking us out of his and my room, so we took the lift to the ground floor in search of the surly clerk. We discovered that the ground floor had no exit: just a corridor ending in a blank wall. For some reason, I tried one of the bedroom doors. It opened, and there was the surly clerk, like the Cheshire cat, without his grin, smoking at his desk.

We secured another key, and got into the room again. I switched on the light. The bulb exploded and sent the lamp shade flying across the room like a frisby. After that, there was no way Michael was going to sleep there. He could have been no more than seven. He shared his sister's bed and left the haunted room to me.

Besides these week-end breaks, we had our main holidays: best of all, a week or two in the national parks. Here, for about ten pound a night, one had a two-bedroomed lodge fit for a prince, with everything supplied, including servant, except food and drink. We went often to the mountains, where we made picnics, such as by the Inyangombe river pool, which I told the children was a natural pool, and Mary ever after called the 'national pool'. Here, Terry and the children splashed in the shallow water, while the river curved dark and deep beyond. We rowed on the dam lakes, and I tried to catch trout. At least, I could get the giant horse-whip into the air to the extent of twenty yards out, if I never caught anything. Michael would assist me, first waiting at the foot of the grass jetty, until I had cast the line, then galloping up to wind it in, then back and forth again. This was game enough, quite apart from the question of fish, and I tired before he did. Needless to say, there was football and cricket, in which Mary joined, and such activities as made me advise people to have their children before the age of thirty.

At Udu, at sunset, we heard the baboons barking on the *kopje*, beyond the lake, among the rocks above the flat-topped camel thorns

- *wha-hoo! wha-hoo!* - and the children barked back and made them bark again:

> *- concourse wild*
> *Of jocund din.*

Terry used to fear that children missed out in Africa: I was not so sure.

At McIlwaine, we had a lodge, high among the rocks and trees, above the lake, where the dassies, the children loved, would creep as close as their curiosity and their fear balanced out. No such fear restrained the cheeky vervet monkeys, who would get into the house and pinch things, if you weren't careful. There, we went game-viewing in the afternoon - not the best time - and saw buck, wildebeest and zebra in the long grass; hippo in the marshes, and hippo droppings like footballs on the roads; a giraffe or a herd of impala in the woods. Then back for a swim in the pool, before I got the *braai* (barbecue) going in the evening.

And evenings were best always. I smoked my pipe and drank a whisky, while the meat roasted, and the deep peace of the African night grew around me. At Kariba, I saw a bat hawk, with its strange scimitar wings, dipping and turning, snapping up as many as twenty bats before sunset. At another place, I saw the pennant-winged nightjars, fluttering their streamers from their wing tips, and in the night heard the cry of the common nightjar: *Good-Lord-deliver-us!* And everywhere, the shrill scream of the bush baby.

At home I would read to the children in the evenings. (We had television, but it was poor - black and white, and the programmes very limited.) They sat on either arm of my chair. First favourites were the Noddy books - in the original 'golliwog' edition, which had passed unnoticed in Zimbabwe, until the new PC edition arrived, which seemed to mean 'parochial consumption', as far as anyone in Zimbabwe could understand the strange Anglo-Saxon objection to golliwogs, which was seen as the poor old British lion losing his wits at last as well as his claws. The children spotted right away that Sid Golly's garage had been taken over by somebody called Bobby Bear,

I think. Useless to explain: I had to pass it off as a purely commercial transaction.

Other favourites were the Ladybird books, especially *The Town Mouse and the Country Mouse,* which was read many times, when Daddy had to finish, singing the carols to which Country Mouse returns in the church. Then I found a Victorian edition of the story, in an old book in the hospital library, which might have been written by Lord Macaulay for his unfortunate children (or nephews/nieces, perhaps?): 'The plain fare of his Rustic Cousin soon palled on the cultivated palate of the Town Mouse -.' The children didn't recognise it as the same story.

When Jock retired in 1985, we moved to the top house, which was more spacious and secluded, among the trees and three acres of rather wild garden. This was much better for a family than the rather pokey bottom house, which, for all its two storeys, had rather small rooms. We felt altogether more relaxed, especially Terry, who had to spend more time in the place than I did.

But it was not altogether secluded; or rather, its very seclusion seemed to attract the lunatics we treated at the hospital, among everything else. Perhaps the troubled minds of these poor creatures found some peace in this quiet spot. One day, as Terry was writing a letter in the dining room, she became aware of a presence behind her. Looking round, she saw a man dressed in hospital pyjamas, staring into space. She said, 'Good afternoon', walked calmly to the telephone in the bedroom, and called for the male nurses, who came and led the man quietly away.

Another time, after we had gone to bed, we heard a noise in the garden. 'Be careful, Warren,' said Terry, as she followed me to the back door. Outside, we saw a schoolgirl in her school uniform, calmly removing our washing from the line. She was a schizophrenic, poor thing; must have lately arrived, and not even changed into hospital nightdress. She wagged a reproving finger at us and said: 'You must not leave your washing out after dark!' A telephone call to the hospital saw the washing restored and the girl sent to bed.

We were having Sunday lunch, when a girl of sixteen burst through the front door and ran screaming through the dining room into the kitchen, where she hid under the sink. She was pursued by two young men, who took no more notice of us than she did. We thought this must be another mental case, but were rather disturbed when the young men tried to drag her out from under the sink, where she was clinging to the drainpipe, especially when they began beating her with the garden hose, combining insult (to us) with injury (to her). Finally, they got her away by dragging her out by the legs and the hair, leaving a considerable quantity of the latter on the floor.

Norah, who had come from her *kaya* to see what was happening, informed us that the girl was a perfectly normal schoolgirl, who had got a bad report and managed to lose it on her way home. The men were her brothers, who were paying her school fees and felt themselves aggrieved in the matter. She had no connection with the hospital, and must have run round half the town, like an antelope with the wild-dogs after her, before she sought refuge in our house. I thought I should have stopped the business, got rid of the two men, kept the girl in the house, and called the police. Thinking she was a lunatic had made me slow on the uptake, and I felt ashamed of myself. But such intervention would merely have postponed the thrashing I have no doubt she received when they got her home.

Another Sunday morning, just before lunch, I was taking a stroll with Michael, who was then about four. We took our usual route - through the top gate, round the back roads, to the front gate, and up the internal hospital road again. We were just opposite female ward, and I was looking forward to my pipe and sherry, when a ward-maid came out and called, 'Doctor, they want you in the ward!'

There was nothing to do with Michael, so, per force, we went together. Usually I could leave him in the duty room. There was nobody there to look after him, but I told him to wait there, all the same. In one of the first bays I found a woman in status epilepticus. All the staff on duty, including the ward maid, were gathered round the bed, when I saw, in the ring of bodies, the small pale face of Michael, under his little bush hat, just appearing over the edge of the bed, studying the scene with intense interest.

I gave instructions and left them to get on with it, retracing my steps homewards.Then I discovered that Michael, like Another before him, was not with me on the road; was, in fact, intent upon his father's business. A male nurse conducted him to the door, with the gentleness only an African can show towards children, a consideration Michael did not return, as he struggled to get back to the interesting scenes within. Finally, they shut the door on him, and when I called him, he exhibited the face of tearful rage of Noddy, as illustrated in his books, in that character's moments of frustration.

An old man in hospital pyjamas, sitting on a seat nearby, propitiated Michael with a piece of sugar cane. This was the first time he had tasted it, and the new experience provided a sufficient distraction. He followed me up the gravel path to the house, quietly chewing.

And when we got home, we ran into another problem, when Mary wanted to try the new goodie. After a good deal of protest from both parties, I cut it in half, and peace was restored.

3 – Zvishavane

About three years after independence, the name changes began. It consisted mostly of the Shonas claiming back the names which had been seized, not only by the pioneers, but by the Matabeles, who dominated the country before them. So Gwelo (Matabele) became Gweru; Marandellas, Marondera, etc. Shabani became Zvishavane. Names in Matabeleland stayed the same, except for some they took back from the whites, such as Esigodini for Essexvale. And the British Salisbury became Harare, which means 'none shall sleep', formerly for the roaring of the lions.

I never got used to the new name of our town, which sounded more like some place in Russia than Africa. After warning people in England that the Russians had not (entirely) taken over, I wrote, in the manner of Constance Garnett: 'On the family estate, near Zvishavane, Ivan Ivanovitch cast aside his fifth empty vodka bottle that day and exclaimed: "I am bored!" A loud bang from the next room announced that his sister, Sophia Ivanovna, had just shot herself. As Peter Simple would say: now write on...'

In 1984, we got two new doctors. Jock was still with us, so for one marvellous year, until he retired, we had four doctors on the station, and proportionately lighter work and more time off. The new doctors were Charles, a Zimbabwean, and Stephan, from Germany. Stephan did a three months' 'acclimatisation course' at Harare teaching hospital, where, among other things, they taught him to do caesarean sections, without which a doctor in the districts would be a burden to his colleagues. Charles had had the usual intern training of the country, so was fully equipped for district work.

Both were keen and made first-class district doctors. Charles (as I, eventually) was later forced out of the service by economic necessity (a subject I will return to later); Stephan by the termination of his two-year contract. Stephan is now in occupational medicine in Germany, but must regard his African days as the high spot of his medical life.

The only other German family in town was the Feldwebels. Brünnhilde was now a sister at the mine hospital: not for her the new order in the government service. I have said she was a German of the old school. She had married a German husband from South West Africa, raised three fine children, and had not been back to Germany for thirty years. She and I had many a merry evening singing the jolly old *Wandervogel* songs, which she had learnt in the Hitler Youth, and I, believe it or not, at the same time, at my Liverpool elementary school: nobody could accuse Mr Baldwin of not trying! Brünnhilde did not blame the British for attacking their German cousins: she probably saw the beauty of a good scrap as clearly as Clausewitz, but did not agree it justified any cause. To the point, she could not see why we did it on behalf of the Poles, whom she described, in her charming way, as the 'Kaffirs of Europe'.

So Brünnhilde, in the course of duty, and the spirit of friendship, paid a visit to the Moenichs. Stephan had his wife with him and a little daughter. Stephan was a tall man: his wife was a tall woman, and both she and Brünnhilde, for all their Nordic blood, were as dusky as Hindus.

Brünnhilde got a surprise. Another generation had grown up in Germany while her back was turned, and the Moenichs belonged to it. She reported to us, not exactly in horror so much as astonishment, that she had found the Moenichs taking morning coffee with the African 'garden boy', as, of course, she continued to call him. 'They are the most extraordinary people!' she declared. 'Nobody in Germany is like that!'

Brigitte Moenich had a different version of the event. 'This weird woman marched in, with the strangest ideas about Africans and everything else. I couldn't believe my ears. Nobody in Germany is like that nowadays!'

As the witnesses with the more up-to-date experience, we were inclined to give the verdict to the Moenichs.

The new families became good friends. Charles was a small man, a Tswana, as was his dainty wife, Nomsa. And all the children became friends and attended not only the Christmas party at the mine club, but the Sunshine Nursery School.

At the mine there was also a swimming pool, which afforded a study in racial habits. As at Samreboi, the African children swam in shoals, completely without parental supervision: no African adults appeared at all, in or out of the water. The Europeans came in family groups, as did the Coloureds. So did the Indians, but whereas the men and children swam in smart bathing suits, their women plunged into the water in their saris, and were taken home dripping wet in big cars. The Moenichs found the changing rooms dirty (I thought they were usual British standard), and got changed in the open air, to the astonishment of all other groups.

When I came to Shabani, I was approached by the medical school to take students. After independence, as well as local students on attachment, we had students from overseas, doing their electives. All were supposed to follow the doctor everywhere in his work, and observe, without engaging in any work themselves, or being made use of.

I remember all of them. Most of them were excellent, some otherwise. A pair of the otherwises was a strange American couple: two men who had served with the Selous Scouts, and were now reading medicine at the University of Zimbabwe - which says something for Mugabe's policy of 'reconciliation'.

They were like something from a fable: the fox and the wolf. They were older than the usual run of students. Moreover, they took notes, especially on our travels to the rural clinics, something other students did not do, nor were specially required to.

I soon became disabused with this apparent enthusiasm, when they informed me shamelessly that they were preparing to tour the districts themselves, during their vacations, selling patent medicines. After a week (they were down for two), they informed me they had seen enough of district practice (or, as they put it, 'one district hospital is like another': whatever they meant by that), and took themselves off, one of them owing me ten dollars I never saw again.

These were the only ones I had to make a bad report on, though I had to threaten another. This was a black lad who stayed at my house (as all did before I was married and had children, when they stayed at the guest house - the house I had stayed in when I first arrived). I knocked up young Barnabas one night to come and watch a caesar, when he informed me that he was only interested in the workings of a district hospital by day - he was going in for public health, anyway. The threat of a bad report got him out of his pit.

Otherwise, as I say, they were all good. Henry and Mike. Henry became a keen district surgeon: Mike gave his name to one of the wards. One night, we admitted a kid with kwashiorkor. After going through my usual routine, I asked for suggestions. Mike said, what about some heat. It was a winter's night. We moved the kid into a side ward and installed an electric heater, which thereafter became used specially for such cases, and was christened, the Mike Madzima Ward. Butch (white), who was an expert on English football and Middle East politics, as well as his own profession - interesting possibilities! Clips, who went in the air force: David, who became a pathologist. Two black girls from Bulawayo, one with an accent (Bulawayo Convent) like the Queen of England. From overseas, a German girl; Sam and Caspar (white and black together); Debbie and Pat, all from England. Hope I haven't forgotten any.

Pat had a special experience. She was sitting beside me in outpatients, when a thin anaemic-looking woman came in. She had a baby on her back, another at her side, and another one *in*side. When I had got through the medical business, knowing that Pat was rather into women's lib, I decided to lead the patient verbally through her typical day. The entire interview went through an interpreter for Pat's sake, as well as mine (although I could have managed the medical part myself).

I looked at her card. (The patients kept their own records, usually in plastic folders, as that way less got lost than when they used to be kept at the hospital.) I saw that she came from the next district, Chivi, which was even poorer than Zvishavane; so poor, in fact, that you could not see a blade of grass at times for fifty miles, and where there was only one doctor, at a mission hospital, further for this woman than ours.

'What time do you get up in the morning?'
'At the washing of the elephants.' (Daybreak.)
'What do you do then?'
'Sweep the house.'

'And then?'
'Light the fire.'
'And then?'
'Cook breakfast.'
'And then?'
'Go to the fields.'
'What do you do in the fields?'
'Hoeing, picking the mealies.'
'What do you have for lunch?'
'Nothing.'
'When do you finish in the fields?'
She extended her arm to indicate an angle of the sun.
'Then what?'
'Fetch water.'
'And then?'
'Gather firewood.'
'And then?'
'Pound the mealies.' She worked an invisible pestle.
'And then?'
'Light the fire.'
'And then?'
'Cook the *sadza.*' (Porridge.)
'And then?'
'Wash the pots.'
'And then?'
'Go to bed.'
'And what does your husband do all day?'
'Drinks beer and talks with his friends.'

Half-way through this catechism, Pat had been bobbing on the edge of her chair. At the last dreadful revelation, she exploded:

'It's about time these Zimbabwean women got their act together!'

Finally, I got a new type of student. The new policy was to take primary health care to the grass roots - to the villages themselves and the commercial farms. The ministry began to train three new cadres: village health workers, traditional birth attendants, and farm health workers. These people continued with their usual lives, being simply country folk with a little more education than their neighbours, who volunteered and were chosen by village councils. The traditional birth attendants (TBAs) were village wise women or female *n'angas* who had been delivering babies anyway. They all received short courses at the provincial hospital: the health workers in health education, which was the main purpose intended for them in the villages - they would educate the people about health, including nutrition, and teach them to make pit latrines and protected wells: the same on the commercial farms, where necessary. They carried some drugs, including chloroquine for treating malaria. They informed the people about the health programmes (maternity/child health clinics), and encouraged them to use them. The TBAs were given training in deliveries, and provided with fresh razor blades and tapes for dealing with the baby's cord (to eliminate the dirty practices which caused so much baby tetanus), and to recognise and refer complicated cases. They would keep in touch by attending the antenatal clinics at the rural health centres. All received a small monthly stipend, which fell short of a living wage and was not intended to be. As I said, they were simply villagers with training, intended to be educators.

All these people I encouraged to attend at my clinic visits - not that they would ever deal with more serious cases themselves, as the nurses did, but to inspire them in their work and extend their medical knowledge; and they were enthusiastic attenders. But when a lady had to undress, especially if she was known to them, they would all scuttle out of the room with anxious African modesty.

One day, on the golf course, Percy said: 'What about doing some prostates together?' I demurred. Prostatectomy is not an easy business, and is never an emergency. But I decided to have a look at it.

We did the old Freyer's operation. Percy tried to teach me the superior and more difficult Millin's, but I could never match his skill: my Millin's was no better than my Freyer's, so I stuck to the simpler operation.

But once you start something in Africa, you don't lack customers. Old gentlemen who had suffered in silence for years came forward in regular numbers. The reasons are complex. First, the doctor must get a reputation, then the thing must be near home. The people did not like being transferred (as had happened with such cases previously) to another part of the country, where they would fall into the hands of doctors and nurses of other tribes, who might do God knows what to them. Moreoever, if you died in such remote places, your family had to pay a lot of money to get your body back for decent burial in the land of your fathers.

Another consideration in favour of my 'doing it yourself' was due to the national shortage of urologists. Urology is a superspecialty, and if specialists are thin on the ground in Africa, superspecialists are almost invisible: less than half-a-dozen urologists in the whole country. So if I referred a prostate patient to the urologist in Bulawayo he would be sent home with a catheter to wait as long as a year or more for operation, and though most of them seemed to survive this otherwise unavoidable expedient the inevitable infection did not do them much good.

Then Percy said, what about thyroids? Endemic goitre is common on the high plateau of Central Africa, where, as in all high country, the soil is deficient in iodine. I had now got a contract for Percy at the government hospital, and although he only operated in the worst cases, he was soon doing one a week. But I never dared follow him in this tricky operation, and when he left, the cases themselves fell off to their previous number.

The better answer here was preventive, through iodised salt; but although available, it was four times the price of plain salt.

One afternoon, at the end of a five-hour session in the operating theatre, I began to feel ill. On my way out, they called me to see a case on the wards. I had to lean on the end of the bed, I felt so faint. When I got home, I felt so tired I thought I must be getting too old for surgery - which has been proved to be as heavy on the heart as manual labour, and not so healthy.

I had supper, and was thinking of an early bed, when I was called to the hospital again: a road traffic accident. Fortunately, the patient did not need more than observation, as I had hardly been able to drag myself to the ward, and on getting home, was only able to stagger into bed. Terry became concerned.

At eleven o' clock, they rang me for a caesar. I was only able to pick up the telephone: impossible to stand up.

It was Friday night. By a piece of administrative ineptitude, abysmal even for me, even though it was that golden age when we had four doctors on the station, I had let the other three leave for the week-end. Terry got on the line to the mine doctor, who was also alone.

He came and saw and diagnosed - at any rate, guessed - gave me a cocktail injection of all the things he had in his bag, and then the good fellow did my caesar for me into the bargain. Before dawn, Terry had to call him again for an appendix (not me). And he never even put in a bill for his fees.

Next day I felt slightly better, but towards evening, I developed awful stomach pains - no diarrhoea or vomiting - and felt feverish. Terry had started a four-hourly temperature chart, at the suggestion of my colleague, the night before. A dreadful sleepless night was succeeded by a stormy day. I found at last that Doloxene could control the pain, but I still felt feverish.

Then I had a good look at the temperature chart. I saw something that every doctor or nurse in Africa would (and all European ones should) recognise: a rising pattern like a step-ladder or staircase. This meant only one thing: I knew I had typhoid fever.

How I got it, I do not know. It was the typhoid season: there were at least a dozen cases on the wards. Maybe I hadn't washed my hands often enough; a piece of unwashed fruit from the market. My colleague from the mine agreed and started me on chloramphenicol.

Fortunately, Stephan had only taken one night - on Saturday he was back in time for a busy week-end.

On Monday, the delayed diarrhoea started. I feared for my family, and they put me in the mine hospital for a day or two, until it went off. But I still did not feel well.

It was three weeks before I had the strength to take a turn up the hospital road, and that did for me for another two weeks. My temperature rose every evening for most of five weeks.

I was well enough to read. I studied every morning: I studied whenever I could in Africa - more than I ever did, before or since, after leaving the medical school. I had to. And in the afternoon read

The Raj Quartet - all through it. When I was weary of reading, I picked up Poucher's photos of the Lake District, and re-lived old days on the hills.

And after five weeks, as I said, I was fit for work. It is good for us doctors to sample the diseases we deal in: it shows us the patients' point of view. And I was writing to people in England: 'It is at times like this that one appreciates the 'modern age' (pace Evelyn Waugh). Fifty years ago you might have got this letter from my widow.'

Until he retired, Jock and I would share a Sunday lunchtime drink on the veranda of the Nilton, or on cold, grey winter days, in the lounge. On the latter occasions, Jock, who hated the cold, would declare: 'This weather reminds me of Manchester.' (Where he had been an assistant medical officer of health). 'The most Gawd-forsaken place on earth! I'd sooner sweep the streets of Bulawayo.'

People would approach our table. One was Mr Gonzo, a watch-mender, who had a little desk on the pavement in the main street. He looked like Karl Marx, painted black. It was fatal to offer him a drink. He would take a seat and call the waiter himself, who knew his order (at any rate, for treats). An imported Scotch would arrive. Zimbabwe produced its own whisky, which I had described to curious connoisseurs in England in Thurberish terms as 'a rough colonial blend, but you have to admire its muscle'. It was good enough for me, at any rate, and as much as I could afford: imported being about four times as much. More than once, I instructed the waiter, 'Mr Gonzo takes Gold Blend when he drinks with me.'

Mr Gonzo (whose name means 'mouse' or 'rat', according to taste) would look pained and exclaim: 'But you are my doctor! Aren't you thinking of my stomach?'

I introduced him to Jock as a 'watch-doctor', a description which Mr Gonzo always reinforced: 'A watch-doctor, not a witch-doctor.'

He demonstrated his political incorrectness when I called him a bloated capitalist. 'I am a poor man. I am telling you the truth. I would not lie to you. I would lie to my wife; but you are a man. That is another thing.'

Once, when Jock had gone to the toilet, a woman with a baby on her back, who had been modestly sipping a Coke by herself at a nearby table, slipped over to me.

'You remember me? You save my baby.'

I expressed pleasure at this news.

'You cut me, and save my baby.'

A caesar. She unfolded the little fellow, and presented him for my inspection. Just before Jock returned, she added:

'You lack to fack me?'

I explained that that was not our usual fee. With a sly look at Jock, she gathered up her child and slipped back to her place.

'What was all that about?'

Another day, a black man sat at a nearby table by himself, looking about him in a rather agitated way. Presently, he approached us.

'Please can you tell me the way to Belingwe?'

'Sit down,' invited Jock. 'I can tell you all about Belingwe.'

He ordered the man a drink, and did so. The man had something else on his mind.

'I have just come from Ghana,' he said, rather breathlessly. 'I had to put down at Lagos airport, and you'll never guess what happened to me there. I asked to go to the transit lounge. I told them I was on my way to Zimbabwe. And do you know, they sent me to the arrivals lounge, and when I tried to get back, they said I didn't have a stamp in my passport. I told them I wanted the transit lounge: I was going to Zimbabwe, but they wouldn't believe me. They threatened me with the police. In the end, I had to pay fifty pound to get back into the transit lounge.'

I glanced at Jock, who knew the story of Terry's and my adventure. 'You were lucky it wasn't Christmas,' I said to the man, and told him my tale.

I had only one difference with Jock, and that was happily resolved. I report it to show the flip side of his admirably independent spirit.

As I have said, we took week-ends in turn, which included a Saturday morning ward round, when we saw all the patients, including the other doctor's. (This was before the arrival of Stephan and Charles, though we continued the practice with them.) I suspected meningitis in a baby Jock had admitted the day before. Meningitis is difficult to detect in babies, and the signs would not have been so pronounced at that time. I performed a lumbar puncture and got cloudy fluid. A British student, Sam, was with me at the time. I ordered treatment. The practised nurses were better at getting a drip into the tiny veins of a baby than I was.

On Monday, out of interest, I looked at the baby again, to discover to my horror that Jock had discontinued treament. I accosted him in the corridor.

'I didn't think that baby had typhoid,' said Jock The baby was on chloramphenicol, used in both diseases.

'Typhoid!' I exclaimed. 'Didn't you read my notes?' (Evidently not.) 'Jock, that baby has meningitis.'

'O, I didn't think so.'

'You should have seen it on Saturday. Anyway, I did a lumbar puncture and got cloudy fluid.'

'Was it really cloudy, or just misty?'

'Jock, normal spinal fluid looks like tap water.'

'O, I don't know. Sometimes it can look a bit misty.'

'Ask Sam. He was with me.'

'I'm not going to ask a medical student,' replied Jock, indignantly.

'Anyway, the lab reported pus cells and haemophilus bacteria.'

'O, I wouldn't go by the lab report.' (Which was produced by mere assistants.)

This was terrible. Egoism is an occupational disease in country doctors in Africa, almost a necessary evil: but this was sheer pig-headedness.

'Look, Jock,' I challenged him. 'If I am wrong, it does not matter. If you are wrong, the kid will die.'

This seemed to get through to him. He gave me an indulgent smile - the cheeky blighter!

'All right, Warren,' he condescended. 'I'll do it for you.'

He resumed treatment. I had the cheek myself to make sure, and the baby made a good recovery.

The best side of Jock (in which he was backed up by Joyce) was his almost embarrassing charity to lame ducks. He had two children of his own, but found time to adopt at least two others: an African girl who became a matron in UK; another, a Coloured girl, he 'found on a rubbish dump' in Bulawayo. 'Where's your mother?' 'She doesn't want me.' Jock took her to her home and found it was true. 'You can have her!'

In the time I knew him, he gave house-room to a demobbed young white soldier, who seemed a bit lost in his mind, with nowhere to go, before he settled him somewhere; and likewise a schizophrenic white girl, who became quite cheeky because Jock wouldn't play the piano to her - a thing, as I have said, he never did for anyone, as a rule. 'You're supposed to be entertaining me!' He managed to dispose of her after a week or two.

All in all, there's not much more you can do for your fellow creatures than share your home with them.

His individualism remained unimpaired as long as I knew him. One day, he discovered one of his patients - a young girl with typhoid - had been discharged by her mother. 'Why did you let her?' protested Jock to the ward sister, in his petulant falsetto. It was not unheard of for patients to do this (or parents), if they did not get better in five minutes, to go to the witch-doctor.

Here was a clear case for an appeal to the magistrate, under the Child Protection Act. Magistrates and their acts were not Jock's style: Jock's style was the citizen's arrest.

He got into his Audi and patrolled the town like a police car, until he found the runaway pair in the main street. He got out and ordered them into the back of the car, to the amusement of the afternoon drinkers on the veranda of the Nilton.

And his gallantry. Another time, Terry and I were sitting on the balcony of the bottom house, when we saw a girl running up to the hospital, screaming and beating herself with her hands. I suspected another lunatic. I soon got a call to the hospital - to the private wards (which were still in existence), to see Dr Scott. I found Jock sitting up in bed, stripped to the waist, covered in bee-stings, which the nurses were brushing off. I ordered Phenergan and pethidine.

337

Jock had been driving up to the hospital, when he saw the girl in a cloud of bees. African bees are the fiercest and most dangerous on earth. He jumped out and told the girl to get into the car. She did, and so did the bees, and soon Jock was in a worse case than the girl. How and when he got to the hospital, I do not know, but the girl, when I found her, was more comfortable than he was. He had shut the bees in the car, and the police waited till evening (when bees are calmer), before releasing them and recovering the vehicle.

In 1985, when he was seventy, Jock retired from government service and went (if not to sweep the streets) to live with Joyce in Bulawayo. He continued to do locums, including three months at St Paul's mission in Matabeleland, which was now haunted by disaffected bandits, who no more frightened Jock than they had in their previous metamorphosis as 'freedom fighters'. Then came news that he had died suddenly in his own home. He was seventy-three.

For years after he left, children on the borders of his old district would hurl the cry, 'Scott!' after me in my Land Rover. People change slowly in Africa. I expect the cry of 'Durrant!' was long being hurled after my successors.

Terry carried a small pistol in her handbag, during the war years. In 1980, she handed this weapon over to the police, not bothering to sell it, being more averse to such toys than even I was; and got an official receipt for it. (I gave my cowboy set away to a man who, with his wife, had shown me more hospitality in my selfish bachelor years than I had ever returned. What did I give his wife? Good question!)

Then, in 1985, Terry got a chilling notice through the post: 'Our records show that you have a pistol, licence number 123, expired 1981.' Obviously, the official record of the receipt had been lost. But that was not their fault! The mandatory penalty for possessing an unlicensed weapon was five years in jail. And this was a country where, even if a good lawyer got you off, you could be re-arrested on the stroke of a minister's pen as you left the law court.

Terry never threw anything away. (I don't think even I would have thrown that away.) We got our files out on the bed and had an anxious fifteen minutes before we found the receipt. In that time, we felt what English people have not felt for centuries, the deadliest fear I know - the fear of the State.

Yet another of our duties was covering the prison. We would be called there to examine the new intakes. I had a system of getting through them very quickly, without missing anything important. We also dealt with sick prisoners, either in outpatients or admitting them to the hospital. They were always accompanied by a guard, handcuffed to him in outpatients, handcuffed to the bed in hospital, while the guard sat beside it. There were also one or two women prisoners in a separate part of the prison.

Under the new order it was considered incorrect to allow the prisoners out to work on the roads, etc. This piece of socialist philosophy was not appreciated by the prisoners, and the prohibition was soon abandoned.

Capital and corporal punishment existed: the latter was abolished after independence, but while it was the government's intention to abandon the former, it was retained owing to the disturbed conditions which developed through the differences between the two main parties, which, as ever in Africa, were essentially tribal.

Another curiosity of the country was the abolition, some twenty years before independence, of trial by jury. I am ignorant of the reasons for this, but I can imagine that if you assembled twelve good Africans and true, they would be arguing from now until Christmas over a simple parking offence, especially when they were getting paid for it, and there was no planting or harvesting to be done. For a time, both systems ran concurrently, and you had a choice. It used to be said, if you were guilty, opt for trial by jury: if you were not guilty, for God's sake, opt for the alternative - trial by judge, sitting with two assessors.

After I had examined the new intake, the superintendent would give me a cup of tea. One of them told me a tale of Africa.

During the Congo troubles of 1964, many Rhodesian and South African youngsters took off to grab a piece of the action and the money. One such was the super, who left home at the age of sixteen, telling his mother that he was 'going south' to look for work. Instead, he went north, where he lied also to Mike Hoare about his age.

At length, he found himself in the dreaded Manyema of the Eastern Congo. 'One day, we ran into an ambush. When we got out of it, one of our chaps had a gunshot wound of his leg. His leg was completely shattered. We knew he was going to die of gangrene, unless we did something. There was no way he was going to see a doctor: they had all cleared off, if they hadn't been murdered by the *Simbas*. We didn't even have a medic with us.

'Anyway, we stopped in a clearing in the forest, and put him on the ground. One guy made a kind of knife out of a bully beef tin. We got a tourniquet on his leg, and we all held the guy down, while the other guy tried to saw his leg off with the knife. Fortunately, the poor bugger was semi-conscious by then. Anyway, we couldn't manage it, so we just *bopered* his leg with our field dressings and put him back on the lorry. He died soon after that.

'But what I most remembered about it was, while we were trying to cut the guy's leg off, a jet airliner went overhead. It must have taken about ten minutes to cross the sky. I remember thinking to myself: there's those people up there, reading their *Newsweeks* and eating their plastic lunches - they're in the twentieth century, while us, down here, are in the bloody Dark Ages!'

And the mortuary was always with us. The work here had certain spin-offs. I was able to study surgical anatomy, as I dissected - that is, anatomy in regard to operations. This I had always done: my first ectopic and my first ruptured spleen I had seen at post mortem in West Africa, and the anatomical knowledge I had gained enabled me to save lives later.

And one day, I detected a murder.

It was common enough to perform a post mortem on an alleged murder victim, determine cause of death, etc, but this was an unsuspected murder.

The police brought in the body of a man, found hanging from a tree in the communal lands (as the tribal trust lands were now called). The request form for post mortem said: 'Foul play not suspected.'

'Yes, doc,' said the policeman. 'We think he hanged himself.'

A wise doctor never accepts an assumption of that sort without question, and I had grown that wise long ago. I did a meticulous examination. There was a rope mark on the neck, proving that the subject was hanged alive: there was no question of a previous murder being made to look like suicide. Then, after the mortuary assistant had opened the body, I began my work. I found the expected congestion of the lungs and heart. I suppose I found Tardieu's spots (tiny haemorrhages) on the lungs, with the eye of faith: in an African, one obviously does not find them on the face.

Then, when we drew the scalp forward, there, over the left forehead, on the skull and under the scalp, was a small bruise. There was no fracture of the skull or evidence of damage to the brain.

On the way out of the mortuary, I met Jock, who was still with us, and asked him, pointedly, 'How do you get a knock on the head, when you hang yourself?' He made some joking remark about hitting it on a bough. His joke was more serious than he knew. I later saw a case where an old woman hanged herself in her hut and banged her head in the process, producing a similar bleed. Good job a clever lawyer could not then have got that story out of me!

It did not come to that. I voiced my doubts to the magistrate. He informed the police and they re-opened the investigation. The murderers were so surprised, they confessed. They must have thought the *chiremba* (myself) had been throwing the bones. They had knocked their victim unconscious with a knobkerrie, before hanging him alive to make it look like suicide. Final verdict - murder by hanging.

The significant detail, Watson!

Africans do commit suicide, though rather less commonly than Europeans. I wish I had made a study of their motives. Only two I remember from that point of view: a man who cut his throat after a business failure; and saddest of all, a lad of sixteen who hanged himself because his parents could no longer meet his school fees.

The most horrible occasion was the massacre of six party workers by bandits. These people were unpopular. Apart from selling party cards, as in Zambia, they would round people up to attend party rallies or political lectures. Complaints from schoolchildren, dragged away from their homework, appeared in the letters column of the newspapers. The bandits (who were the fringe of the opposition party) would take advantage of such discontents.

But the corpses were pathetic, each killed with an axe blow in the back of the head: the youngest being a boy of fourteen. (A party of white missionaries was axed later in Matabeleland: the disaffection in that case being a land dispute with the locals.)

The policeman told me the details. Under the guns of the bandits, the oldest man was made to axe each of his companions in turn, before being axed himself by the bandits.

Such actions seem incredible to the white man. The fellow had the axe in his hands; why didn't he have a go at his tormentors? He must have known he was going to die: he had nothing to lose. Quite simply, in a state of terror, people (especially simple people) act like zombies.

The Africans were full of contradictions. No people more biddable; none more obstinate when they decided to be. None was more devoted than the African woman. We had one on the ward, blinded in one eye by her husband. I wanted to send her to the eye specialist, afraid of sympathetic disease, when the good eye can go blind as well. She signed herself out: there was no one to cook for her husband. And none more vindictive when she felt herself betrayed, as we learned another day in the mortuary.

A village Lothario returned to his marital hut one night, stinking from his lover's bed, and fell into a drunken sleep in his own. His wife (a sleeping African, normally barely rousable) awoke; or maybe was even waiting up for him. She had had enough, as we saw from the thousand cuts he died from - or rather, dozen axe-chops; the last, the unkindest of all, which destroyed the offending organs. 'She meant to do it, doc!' commented the black policeman.

Young children were admitted to children's ward, where we had cots only. When they were too big for cots (say four or five), they went to female ward, and older children went on male or female wards. The younger children were admitted with their mothers, who slept on mats on the floor beside the cots, and in the beds with their children on female ward - another practice Europe has learnt from Africa, which has long since displaced the cruel practice of admitting young children without their mothers, which existed when I was a houseman. Mothers in hospital contributed in the matters of feeding, etc. As for the other children at home, they were looked after by grandmother, as are all African children between the ages of weaning (two) and schooling (six); when *Ambuya* teaches them their manners and the traditions of the tribe.

European visitors would appear in the African wards sometimes - police, mostly; sometimes a farmer bringing in a worker, or taking one home; someone visiting a favourite nanny, cook, or gardener.

One day, a friend came in and saw a little boy with a fractured femur, in gallows traction, which means swinging both legs from a beam. The children tolerate this literal suspended animation with great cheerfulness; after the first few days, when the fracture has become painless, twisting around and twining the cords and getting into all sorts of positions, like acrobats.

'What's the matter with that kid, Warren?' asked Fanie.

I could not resist the temptation.

'He's been a very naughty boy.'

I have mentioned mental cases. It used to be said, even by African psychiatrists, who should have known better, that lunacy, idiocy and genius were all rare in the African race. This seems to be a sort of wishful thinking, induced by their considerable bias towards conventionality: it is true that eccentricity, or even distinction, is viewed by them with suspicion. A man who has become very rich might be suspected of using witchcraft.

As to mental disease and mental deficiency (and, no doubt, genius), I should say they were as common among Africans as they are with us. We rarely saw depression, and never used antidepressant drugs [1] (which are among the commonest prescribed in Europe): but I

---

[1] A personal statement, and evidently inaccurate. I see from later statistics that the newly appointed community psychiatric nurse was treating 188 new cases of depression in 1987, in a population of 100,000 (and would be in my time) - still vastly lower than in Europe. WD.

suspect such cases may have gone to the witch-doctor, their condition attributed to witchcraft.

One lad of sixteen, admitted for something else, was found to be depressed. As with the suicide reported earlier, his parents were unable to continue his school fees. Education can be a slow process in Africa (as mentioned in Part I). Interruptions occur, owing to shortage of funds, mostly, and to requirements arising in the homes of the poor. So sixteen is a more tender age than it might be in Britain: two years or more short of 'O' levels in many cases.

I did not offer this lad antidepressants. I tried to offer him comfort. Prospects were better for further education since independence (so I hoped more than I believed): he should read anything he could lay his hands on - books, newspapers - advice hardly necessary, as said, to any African who can read. But I was sorry for the lad. What can be sadder than the unsatisfied hunger for education? Think of Jude the Obscure!

Teachers going to Africa will rarely have unruly pupils to contend with, any more than doctors will find litigious patients, in a continent where health and education are regarded as privileges, not rights. There are some sad exceptions to this rule: the demo at our hospital, a local school burnt down. But these are uncommon and usually due to failures of communication and other misunderstandings.

Schizophrenics we did see, probably because they caused the most social disruption, and the witch-doctor was less successful with them. And I am sorry to say our methods of dealing with them were necessarily crude. When they came in raving, we quite frankly chained them to the bed, until the massive doses of Largactil took effect. Then, after a day or two, they graduated to shackles and shuffled about the premises, while the nurses tried to keep an eye on them. They were nursed in the general wards, and, unless so restrained, with the limited staff available, could easily have wandered off into the bush, and the next we saw of them might be when the police brought in a box of bones, described on the form as 'found in the veld'.

When the lunatics were tranquil, we let their relatives take them home, where an African village was more adapted to 'community care' than a British inner city. Thereafter, they would be taken to their local clinic for monthly injections. Alas, some of them came into the bus terminus category, and gave the same recurrent problems.

Some of the schizophrenics were highly intelligent and well-educated. It almost seemed as if the culture clash in their brains had been too much for them. One in particular was called the *fundi* (student, or expert), who always had a book in his hand. One day, he challenged me on the ward.

'What's a beldam?'

I hesitated.

'Come on!' he bullied. 'It's your language.' The neighbouring beds sat up and took notice.

'It's an old woman,' I ventured.

'It means a *wicked* old woman;' coming down on me with the severity of a schoolmaster. Big grins all round.

When I consulted Collin's dictionary, I found we were both right.

The reader may ask about snake-bites, and I suppose a little lecture is in order. They rarely give much trouble in Africa, or at any rate, cause death.

They divide into two main kinds: adders, whose venom attacks blood and tissue, causing swelling and internal bleeding; and cobras and mambas, whose venom attacks the nervous system, causing paralysis. Serious, or systemic, effects (as opposed to local effects) rarely occurred; so our policy was to set up a drip, in case the antivenom (which has its own allergic dangers) was required, give a shot of penicillin (for infection and to reassure the patient), and observe. Six hours would decide the matter.

For there are two kinds of bite: the 'business bite', intended to kill prey, when the snake actually injects the poison; and the defensive bite, intended to deter a larger animal (such as man), when the poison is not injected, but the victim receives accidentally what the snake has on its fangs. This was the usual case with humans, and naturally, less dangerous.

The antivenom was kept in the fridge, and I had to remember to renew it yearly, even though it was used but once while I was in Zvishavane - by my colleagues from the mine on a white man whose whole leg turned black from an adder bite (internal bleeding), and who was very ill indeed. His haemoglobin fell to five grammes (one third normal), and he was in shock. They transfused him and gave him 50ml of antivenom - half our stock. He made a good recovery, and he was lucky.

If that cobra had bitten Michael, I would have been faced with more than one doctor's dilemma. First, whether to treat one of my own family, which is always inadvisable, as one's judgement is swayed by personal emotion; call in a colleague, with whom I might have disagreed; or take him to Bulawayo, a three-hour journey. And if I *had* treated him, whether to give him the antivenom right away, with its own risks, or wait for signs of paralysis. In a child, all the dangers are greater.

The cobras also spat - a syringeful (10ml) of venom into the eyes, which means a timely and copious wash-out. I only had to do this once - on a dog, when a woman brought in her little terrier with his eyes screwed up. This was before independence, after which we were forbidden to treat animals (see the chapter on Zambia); when I would have taken him to my garden and put him under the tap.

I had treated other animals - one or two dogs, stitched up under ketamine (hope vets approve) - but gave it up even before independence, as the African nurses were not happy about it. For one thing, they were afraid of getting bitten, or said they were. I think it offended their dignity, really: a feeling one must always respect.

As at Umvuma, at Zvishavane I had at least one distinguished patient: the sister of my neighbour, the former prime minister, Garfield Todd. True to the liberal principles of the family, she was content to be admitted to the common ward of the government hospital, but I got her into a side ward, if only because she was so ill.

There was some difficulty about the diagnosis; while I was thinking about it the lady died.

Sir Garfield (as he now was) proved as perfect a gentleman as Dr Mazarodze. His sister would probably have died anyway, and it might have been difficult to carry an action against me - which would not have stopped many people from trying, if rather fewer in Zimbabwe than elsewhere.

'I am not very proud of this case,' I confessed to Sir Garfield, in my office.

'Don't worry, Dr Durrant,' he said. 'Edie had had many operations before and would not have consented to another. Nor would we have wished it. She came to this country forty years ago from New Zealand for her health. She has had forty happy years here and she was only too grateful for that - and so are we.'

Terry's father was also an admirer of Mr Todd, as he was in his day; at any rate, as a performer. As to his politics, I am not sure. Bill's politics, I should guess, consisted of an enlightened fatalism. He recalled how an Irish candidate of Todd's party tried to make headway against a Rhodesian audience. 'You can't frighten me,' he boasted. 'I've fought elections in Ireland.' Before long, he was forced to change his mind and give up in disgust. 'You said you'd fought elections in Ireland,' they jeered. 'Yes,' he retorted. 'But in Ireland, I was talking to gentlemen.'

Garfield, who was supporting his candidate, then stepped forward, took his jacket off and threw it over a chair. He was a big man, as well as a distinguished-looking one. He rolled his sleeves up, and pitched into them. 'Now!' he retaliated. 'We've heard what you've got to say - now you're going to hear what I'VE got to say!'

As Terry's father commented, his candidate didn't win, but Garfield shut them up.

I could hardly connect this with the Christian gentleman who sat in my office; but, of course, he wasn't the first of his kind to put down the mob.

Behind the hospital was a *kopje*, Zvishavane Peak, the highest hill in the neighbourhood. Before the troubles, the white nurses would hold *braais* (barbecues) on the top. Later, it was considered dangerous: the guerrillas could be ensconced there (or at any rate, *mujibas*), watching the town. After independence, I often climbed it. About 500 feet high from its base, it gave wide views over the green sea of the veld. One could see the slag heaps of the next asbestos-mining town, Mashava, forty miles away, the road running north to Selukwe, and the toy town, sprawling widely and untidily below.

On certain nights, when I was called to the hospital, this hill took on a strange appearance, which was not shared by the other hills around the town. It was unique, like a magic mountain. It had to be a clear night under the stars. With cloud or with moon the effect was not seen. On the right nights the hill glowed white, less like a hill in tropical Africa than a hill in England at night, under the snow of winter. Terry's nephew, Hugh, the geologist, saw it; had never seen anything like it, and thought it must be a high load of quartz in the soil. I think it meant something to the Africans, as Inyangani did, and so many hills and rivers in the country. I regret that I never asked them. Perhaps they would not have told me. It loomed, on its special nights, a disturbing and ghostly apparition.

Then came sad news from Umvuma (now called Mvuma). The owner of the Falcon Hotel, John Holland, was killed in a car crash. The place was bought by a Canadian, who appointed the head waiter, Nelson, an excellent man, as manager. Nelson had a brother, who became head waiter. The brother was not an excellent man. The new owner conspired with the bad brother (who may have been called Satan, or Poison - both popular names for boys in a mythology which carries different values from ours, in which the Devil may, indeed, be accorded the status of a gentleman) - conspired with Satan to burn the place down and collect the insurance money.

Unfortunately for his scheme, he did his conspiring over the telephone, and he had insufficient knowledge of the operation of small town telephone exchanges in Africa.

During the often empty and tedious hours of her duty, Mrs Van Oysterbar would vary the reading of her novel with listening in on private conversations on the line, and in one of these, she overheard the final exchange of the plotters. She telephoned the police, who arrived to find Satan setting fire to a quantity of petrol in the lounge. I don't know how they got the fire out: I never heard of a fire engine in Mvuma. But the place was badly damaged.

The bad brother was arrested. The Canadian fled the country. Nelson got a job at the Enkeldoorn Hotel. The mine bought the building and turned it into a hostel for their male staff. The jolly days of the Falcon were over.

348

One day, Percy and his wife, Marguerita, added to the gaiety of nations, or, at any rate, Zvishavane, by laying on an expensive entertainment in the main street.

Percy had bought a new car - a Mercedes with automatic gears - and Marguerita went shopping in it. She parked it outside Toni's cafe, in the way permitted by the broad streets of Central Africa, that is, tangentially, with its boot pointing into the street. When she attempted to drive away, she did something to the unfamiliar gears, and shot the car backwards across the street. A Mercedes, of course, is built like a Tiger tank. Marguerita killed three ordinary cars, before ram-raiding the Parthenon cafe, on the other side of the street; admittedly, boot first, but ram-raiding was in its infancy then anyway, and this was Marguerita's first attempt. (Now, I understand, this mode has been widely adopted, so it seems Marguerita was ahead of her time, after all.) In the startled bowels of the Parthenon, she fiddled with the gears again and took off on a second voyage of destruction, killing three more cars and ram-raiding Toni's in turn, this time in the conventional way.

By now, the main street looked like the battlefield of Kursk, with wrecked cars all over the place, some on their backs, wiggling their legs in the air, like immobilised beetles. In the whole affair, nobody was hurt, or, at any rate, the only one to appear at the hospital was a badly shaken Marguerita, with a scratch on her cheek.

But then it turned out that Percy, in his leisurely old-fashioned way, had not got round to insuring the vehicle. Percy was not a poor man and his wife was said to be a South African millionairess. All the same, it was voted a most munificent spectacle.

One morning, a little girl was brought in, bitten by a hippopotamus, on her way to school. She had a big hole in her left upper abdomen. When we gently turned her over, there was another big hole in the back of her chest, on the same side, in which the collapsed lung was plainly visible, ineffectually trembling. She lay panting and grey on the bed in deep shock.

We resuscitated with fluids and blood, gave antibiotics, and when she was fit for surgery, got her to theatre. We started anaesthesia with a tube down the windpipe. When I was scrubbed up, I was able to make a closer inspection.

There was little damage to internal organs: some bruising of the lung, an abrasion of the stomach, and a six-inch tear in the diaphragm. The hippo had, in fact, performed what is called a thoracolaparotomy, an incision designed to open abdomen and chest at the same time. There was really little left for me to do but close up, like a registrar after a somewhat perfunctory chief.

Under the intubation anaesthetic, the lung had begun to re-expand, and the little girl was looking a better colour. First, I trimmed the tear in the diaphragm and stitched it up. Then I trimmed the chest wound, washed out the chest with saline, and closed it over a water-sealed drain (already described). As I put in the last stitch, a triumphant burst of bubbles came through the water and announced the full re-expansion of the lung. I trimmed the abdominal wound, over-sewed the abrasion of the stomach, and washed out the abdomen, before closing it also.

Next day, the little girl was sitting up in bed quite happily, but on the third day, she developed respiratory distress. I thought of respiratory distress syndrome (something first diagnosed after bomb explosions in Belfast), and thought the lung must have suffered more punishment than appeared. I ordered a chest X-ray, which showed the lung fields perfectly clear, but the heart displaced a whole width to the right - away from the wound.

I could not fully understand this picture. (In respiratory distress syndrome, one expects to see the lung solid with fluid.) But I decided to transfer her to Bulawayo, in case she needed mechanical respiration.

After a few days, she came back, perfectly well. She had required nothing more than oxygen, and the head of the intensive care unit explained in his letter that although this was indeed a case of RDS, the lung fields might well appear clear in the early stage.

Soon after that, I went away on my annual holiday with my wife and children, to the deep peace of the bush, where the cry of the fish eagle by day and the bush baby by night take the place of the ringing of the telephone.

When we returned, after two weeks, we found Charles had discharged our little patient, perfectly fit, and we never saw her again.

Then a sadder case. There are two important pitfalls in diagnosis. One is jumping to conclusions; another is taking the wrong turning. There are others, but these two are perhaps the commonest. In the second, you can go so far down the wrong road before you realise it.

I first saw him on my morning ward round, a little fellow of about ten, sitting up in bed with a cheerful grin on his face. It was about the beginning of the rainy season. He had been coughing for two days and had a temperature of 40^0. There were no signs in the chest.

I started him on penicillin. Next day, his temperature was normal, but he was still coughing. There were still no signs in the chest, and he still had his cheerful grin.

Next day, all was as before, but his temperature had risen again. I ordered an X-ray.

I did not see this till the fourth day, when there was no change, except that his temperature was normal. The X-ray showed central areas of consolidation on both sides. I suspected virus pneumonia, and changed the antibiotic to chloramphenicol.

After another forty-eight hours, things were the same: the cough, the temperature up and down, no chest signs, and still the cheerful grin.

I thought of Tb and started investigations. Of course, these took another three days, and the results were negative. I decided I was getting nowhere, and transferred the child to Bulawayo. He was there four days before he died.

Which means they did not make the diagnosis when he came through the door.

Medical or nursing readers may have made it already. All the clues have been given: Central Africa, the rainy season, an intermittent fever.

Of course it was malaria!

Several textbooks describe a pulmonary form of malaria. I searched the notes and made the miserable discovery that in all the investigations I had not ordered a blood smear. At any time, a couple of chloroquine tablets could have saved him.

Malaria is one of those so-called 'protean' diseases, which can take disguised forms, presenting pitfalls to the unwary. A well-recognised such presentation is vomiting and diarrhoea. Another, which I have never seen described anywhere, is catatonia.

I wish I had made a closer study of the several cases I saw, which might have added my name to a new eponymous syndrome.

Catatonia is usually a form of schizophrenia. In the malarial form, I have observed several of the classical features. Stupor, when the patient lies on his back and stares at the ceiling. Waxy flexibility, in which, with the patient lying on his back, the limbs may be manipulated into various positions, remaining there for minutes, at least. Another is statuism - such as the famous 'tea-pot position'. On one occasion, I had two girls on the same ward standing to attention at the foot of their beds like soldiers for hours together. The condition is differentiated from true schizophrenia by the absence of previous history and by a response to antimalarial treatment - and often (but not always) by a positive blood smear. The temperature is not always raised, and may be depressed. It is, I suppose, a form of cerebral malaria, and therefore a dangerous stage of the disease.

Professor Levy of Harare believed, like Potter of Oxford, that head injuries should be managed 'by the first one competent to do so', for reasons already indicated, which apply even more in Africa than in Britain. To this purpose Professor Levy (who was a neurosurgeon himself, one of only two in the country) gave a one-day crash course in Harare for district doctors, which I attended. His lectures included the three main conditions of depressed fractures, epidural haemorrhage and subdural haemorrhage. Depressed fractures, whether closed or compound, are not matters of urgency, and can be safely transferred elsewhere. But they are the commonest of the major head injuries, and for this reason are the more likely to amount to a burden on the limited specialist centres, and, conversely, will the more rapidly accustom the general doctor to opening the head and reducing his natural fear of handling the naked brain.

The most significant new thing I learned was the technique of turning a bone flap for epidural haemorrhage: previously, most of us had relied on the crude method of enlarging a burr-hole.

The wisdom of the professor's policy and his technique was to be borne out at my hospital two weeks later.

About two o' clock in the afternoon, an African clergyman of seventy was brought into the ward, having been involved in a road accident. He had a head injury but nothing else. On admission, he was confused (Harare scale, IV). I ordered the usual management, including skull X-rays. Within an hour of admission, he was down to grade I (no response to painful stimuli), with stertorous breathing and a fixed dilated pupil on the left side. His skull X-rays showed multiple fractures on the left side: his skull there looked like a jig-saw puzzle. Obviously, he was not going anywhere: we would be lucky to get him to theatre alive.

We intubated. I drilled a temporal burr-hole and came upon a blood clot. I then proceeded to drill four further holes around the first, as instructed by the professor, which I joined with a wire saw, and was soon able to turn a flap of skin and broken bone, as big as my hand, in the already fragmented skull. Beneath was a clot as big as my two fists, occupying a quarter of the cranial space, and dangerously compressing the brain. Clearly, the man had only minutes to live. With the new approach, the clot was easily evacuated.

I slipped a stitch around the bleeding artery, and proceeded to hitch up the dura, which covers the brain like a plastic bag. This was like trying to lift up a heavy fallen tent. I stitched it to the galea (underscalp), as best I could, to reduce the dead space and discourage secondary bleeding - more new stuff to me, I had learnt at the course. Then I got the jig-saw pieces of the skull together (some of which had come loose and I had washed with saline), before closing the scalp.

(Anything wrong with that lot is down to me, not the professor!)

In this operation I was assisted by Stephan, who next time round would be doing it himself, with little supervision from me. Indeed, I should hope head injuries are part of the house officer's curriculum at Harare now.

After we got the old man back to the ward, he lay unconscious for about five days. He was a Matabele, and his family wanted to take him to Bulawayo. I was not averse to this. They had a capacious car and our patient was becoming a feeding problem.

When we got in touch with the Central Hospital, some days later, we learned that he had been discharged fit.

Two months later, I was doing afternoon outpatients, when in walked our patient, as bright as a button. He was back in the pulpit, he told us. I called Stephan to join in the celebration.

I met the professor a year later at a surgical conference. He told me his one-day course had rather misfired. Since then, he was getting more transferred cases of head injury, if anything, than before. He thought perhaps all he had done with his lectures was to frighten people. When I told him about our case, he felt it had been worth it, after all.

By 1985, reports showed that malaria, resistant to the drug, chloroquine, was appearing in many countries neighbouring Zimbabwe. Chloroquine had, of course, been (still is) the chief drug used, not only to treat, but to prevent the disease. First, the countries of the east coast, then Zambia, were affected. I knew it was only a matter of time before this problem reached Zimbabwe.

At first, Fansidar was the drug recommended to treat these resistant cases, but soon the merits of the old drug, quinine, became recognised as appropriate too.

I decided to be prepared, and discussed the matter with the pharmacist.

'We should lay in stocks of Fansidar and quinine.'

Fansidar, he went along with; but 'quinine!' he questioned with astonishment and ill-disguised contempt, perhaps thinking the old doc was getting past it. 'That went out with Livingstone.'

'Well, it's coming back in again.'

He grabbed at his Martindale, after the manner of his kind.

'You needn't look at that,' I forestalled him. 'I'll show you the latest editions of *Medicine Digest.*'

He found the Fansidar without difficulty. Quinine was another matter: there was none in any of the principal medical stores of the country, government or private. I kept him at it, unbelieving as he was. Eventually, he ran some to earth on the back of a shelf in Gweru.

That year I took a holiday with my family in Malawi, with Terry's sister, Bobby and family. Malawi rivals West Africa as the white man's grave for malaria, and the resistant strains were reported there. At that time, the WHO recommended chloroquine prophylaxis in such areas, and to use Fansidar in cases of a break-through: not as stupid as it may sound, as there are three grades of resistance, and chloroquine exerts some delaying action against the first two. Nevertheless, it was a policy soon modified.

Ten days after we returned, Terry and I woke up feeling very ill. Terry had felt low the night before. Now she was shaking the bed with rigors, and I was burning up.

We telephoned the hospital for a nurse to take blood smears, and sure enough, they were positive. Stephan came to the house and gave us Fansidar. He gave it also to the children as a precaution; though, thank God, they were not affected. Everywhere in Malawi we had used mosquito nets. Only on the last night, in Bobby's house in urban Lilongwe, Terry and I dispensed with them; though, as parents caring more for our children than ourselves, we used them on their beds.

We telephoned the Dutch friends who had looked after Michael before. They now lived in Bulawayo, but kindly came and took the children away with them. Terry and I were quite incapable of looking after ourselves, let alone the children. Norah did everything for us.

Fansidar did nothing for us. It may be slow to act, or we may have got a bug resistant to that also. (Nowadays it is no longer used as a first-line drug, but as a back-up.) After forty-eight hours, Terry and I were still rolling on our bed of fire, like the souls of the damned. I suppose we got some sleep in the troughs of the fever. But by then, we were begging Stephan to give us quinine, which he did, and within hours, we were better.

Be prepared! When I got in the stock of quinine, little did I suppose my wife and I would be the first people to need it in Zvishavane.

A few months later, the first home-bred cases appeared. The PMO rang me up. 'I believe you have quinine in your hospital?'

There was corn in Egypt. Now we were able to help them.

One day, we got a big case of books from America - a gift to Africa. The Yanks don't do things by halves. Such books! They made the usual British thing look like the old war economy standard: the binding, the paper, the printing. There must have been well over a thousand dollars worth. All were about a year old, which I suppose made them dead ducks on the American market, but the shipment alone must have cost them. But the Americans' ideas about African country hospitals were as big as their hearts, as we discovered when we looked at the titles: *Magnetic Resonance Imaging of Brain Tumors, The Chemical Pathology of the Endocrine Disorders.* Just the kind of bread-and-butter stuff you need in a bush hospital! We selected a book of surgery - entirely theoretical: the actual business of operating would no doubt be set out in lavishly illustrated atlases in America; and a book on pharmacology: ninety per cent of the drugs were unobtainable in Zimbabwe, but it was nice reading about them - and sent the rest back to Head Office, which later admitted the arrangement had been disappointing.

Beside this, about every quarter we got catalogues from the same large-minded source - six copies of each; addressed to the 'Head of Surgery, Zvishavane Hospital', 'Head of Paediatric', etc, innocently unaware that these titles belonged to the same person. I did pass the 'Head of Pathology's' copy to the lab assistant, telling him not to get any big ideas. And the 'Head of Anesthesiology's' copy raised a few laughs in the theatre, where we saw an anaesthetic machine illustrated, that delivered half-a-dozen gases we had never heard of and none that we had, monitored all vital signs and measured blood gases; and, I told them, played *Ishe Komberera Afrika* at the end of the operation.

Then one night, a bus went over a bridge and into a river: a burst tyre, an accident becoming commoner as the country got poorer and imports fell. Not much water in the river, but a big enough fall to kill ten on the spot and produce fifty casualties, twenty of them serious.

Most of these were compound fractures: the sort of thing we could have dealt with in twos or threes; but twenty would have taken us a week, without going to bed - quite impossible. It was a good exercise in triage.

I called out all doctors and staff. We moved patients from the beds in the first bays, and went to work on the serious cases as they came in, with drips, dressings, antibiotics, and morphine. We secured an open lorry from the district administrator, and loaded most of the bad cases into the back, with blankets, as it was a cold night. We put some more in the ambulance, and sent all to Bulawayo, after warning them to stand by. The ambulance turned back, after one old man, who had lost the top of his head, died on the way, and whose body would have had to be expensively recovered by his relatives; before setting out again. That left five dislocations of hips and shoulders, we doctors dealt with between us, and many more cuts and bruises, the nurses dealt with. All done between 10pm and three the next morning. Not bad for a small hospital!

More other cases return to mind than the unrecorded cases of Sherlock Holmes - 'for which the world is not yet prepared'.

A man bitten on the hand by a puff adder. His arm crackled with gas gangrene to the shoulder. A surgeon had told me you could deal with these cases by debriding and packing, like gunshot wounds. I laid open the black flesh to its full extent and did my best, but the man died within two hours of the operation. I should have taken the arm off at the shoulder right away, but he was probably too far gone with toxaemia anyway.

A little boy with a fractured elbow - the commonest fracture we saw in little boys. But this had a tiny break in the skin - technically compound. Another surgeon told me you could safely suture such tiny cuts. Two days later, this arm was also crackling. This time, I took it off at the shoulder, without hesitation. Nor did I close the wound, but packed it open. After three days on penicillin, I inspected it. The black flesh was spreading. I debrided further (reluctantly removing the head of the humerus, which is usually left to preserve the contour of the shoulder), and re-packed. In another three days, the wound was clean. I closed it and the lad lived. Never again did I fail to do a full operation on a fracture with the smallest break in the skin.

A little boy with an abscess of the scalp. When I opened it, a litre of pus came out. I put my hand into the child's head, and felt - nothing! In alarm, I placed a drain, and sent the lad to Bulawayo. He returned in a few days, after no further surgical intervention, his brain re-expanded and the wound healing. Epidural abscess, caused by osteomyelitis of the skull, caused by head injury. He recovered on antibiotics.

A young woman with pelvic sepsis and peritonitis. We had more and more of these, which I treated by removing the tubal abscesses and washing out. It dawned on me that this was the onset of the Aids epidemic. But when I opened this abdomen, the pelvis was solid - 'frozen pelvis', the sort of thing caused in Europe by cancer (in my student days, at that). I suspected Tb, made a biopsy, closed the abdomen, and started Tb treatment. The biopsy was positive. The young woman was cured[1] but would never bear another child.

A young soldier from Mozambique, with a fractured femur. I inserted a Küntscher nail: an easy operation, which took me twenty minutes. But after three days, this one was pouring pus: something that had never happened to me before. I suspected Aids, and the test report came back positive. Meanwhile, I removed the nail, and the fracture healed on traction.

(Like all surgeons, I got dozens of needle-sticks, many surely from Aids patients. I just carried on: I didn't even think of squeezing my finger. A surgical needle is less dangerous than a hollow needle. When I got back to UK, I tested negative.)

A young man was brought in, unconscious. I tested his urine, which was loaded with sugar and ketone. I diagnosed diabetic coma, but two things were wrong. His pupils were constricted, and he was sweating: the opposite of diabetic coma. As I did not understand these signs, I ordered diabetic treatment. The lad died within the hour. Never ignore the anomalous sign. The anomalous sign is the significant sign: one ignores it at one's peril - and the patient's.

---

[1]Unless it *was* Aids-related (not tested). WD.

Soon after, came a carbon copy of this case. I was about to repeat my folly. Fortunately for the patient, I was due to depart for the annual bush doctors' refresher course at Bulawayo. (This was while Jock was still at Belingwe.) I was reluctant to leave the patient with the nurses, so ordered him to Bulawayo, where the correct diagnosis was made, and the case successfully treated. Organophosphorus poisoning from insecticides.

I had more cases which I successfully managed myself. But no one had then reported the ketone in the urine.[1] I wrote a letter to the *Central African Journal of Medicine,* and got an inquiry from as far away as East Germany about it. In the ensuing correspondence, someone added a 'Van der Merwe' touch (as the racialist black humour of South Africa is known) by suggesting that farmers use posts, instead of Africans, when marking out crops for aerial spraying.

A young girl, with all the signs of perforated typhoid ulcer. By now, I was having good results with these cases. I opened up her abdomen, and found the bowels all stuck together - plastic peritonitis. I explored and got a gallon of pus from the left side. Next thing, I found my exploring hand high up in her chest - empyema. Same thing on the other side. Good wash-outs throughout and bilateral chest drains secured a cure.

An ectopic pregnancy. The old books used to say, never forget to look at the other tube. I always looked, and this time, found a bilateral case, and had to resect both tubes. No more children, but a life saved, which could have been carelessly lost.

Not only black Africans are tough (if that is the word in this case). A white corporal dislocated his elbow, carried on - God knows how - to the end of his tour of duty in the bush, and came in after three weeks. After an enormous struggle, we reduced it, but the poor fellow would have trouble for life.

A black man, blown up by a land mine. His arm was jellified, and his urine loaded with protein. I took the arm off at the shoulder, but

---

[1] I later heard that these cases had lain semi-conscious in huts for some days and had evidently developed acidosis. WD.

he died, probably of shock. Should have sent him to Bulawayo, but he may have died on the way.

Then, at last, a case of locked twins: the thing I had expected at my first caesar. But a case with a difference. I did a vaginal examination, and could not believe my hand. I found the legs of a breech with a head between them. How had the baby done this circus trick? I did a caesar and got two live babies, the head of the second between the legs of the first, or vice versa: take your pick!

A girl with two upper front teeth knocked out by her boy friend. I cleaned them with saline and replaced them. She looked like Dracula. Wrong way round! I changed them, and after a week, she was her pretty self again. And achieved, in my ignorance, without splinting!

A young white cop, who drank a bottle of ouzo, straight off, in the police club, for a bet, and immediately collapsed. This was before independence, and he was admitted to the white ward, where the sister passed a stomach tube, and the place stank of aniseed. We dripped him, and when he came round, wondering where he was, he was greeted with the same riotous laugh such cases always received on white or black wards.

The old man with fifty per cent burns. He was a proud old Matabele, and when he forgot his manners he would complain, 'I've lived so long among the Shona dogs *(Maswina)* I've become a Shona dog myself' - to the huge delight of the (mostly Shona) nurses. As a lad he had met the great 'Rodzi'. 'And did you once see Shelley plain?' asked the nurses, or rather, 'What did you say to Rodzi, sekuru?' 'I said, "Good morning!"' 'And what did he say to you?' 'He said nothing.' Shame on Rhodes! Perhaps he was lost in his great thoughts, or already dying. It doesn't sound quite like him. Not many people can save a fifty per cent burn, and we did not save the old man.

Few of these cases would be seen in Europe, or, at any rate, in those circumstances.

And at week-ends, I would get out into the bundu - to begin with, leaving the family behind, as the children were not yet up to fishing, and ended up boiling in the car with their tormented mother. This situation would improve as they got older and we could all get out together, usually with Granddad, when he came to live in the old folks' cottages in Gweru; the children busily working with toy fishing tackle at imaginary fish (not much more imaginary than my own, most times).

So, in the early (post-bachelor) days of our marriage, it was more usually with companions such as Koos; and, no doubt, I was a selfish pig, as many 'post-bachelors' are.

For in my bachelor days, even during the war, I had gone fishing with Koos, he with his FN propped against a rock, and me with my cowboy set. Koos said (echoing D H Lawrence) that life was better on the *qui vive,* or the *pas op,* as Koos would have said. But one day, we were so little on the *qui vive,* engrossed in a conversation about Mahler, that we left our artillery draped over the chairs of the Portuguese cafe, frequented by Africans, some of them 'freedom fighters', no doubt, or in touch with them; before we remembered in the street and rushed back for it while it was still there.

One afternoon, Koos and I were fishing at a dam, when we heard screams from the *kopje* behind. Almost immediately, I guessed what they meant. We dropped our rods and scrambled up the steep stony hill, among the thorn trees, the sun baking the earth and our sweating, panting bodies. We wandered here, we wandered there, and still the rhythmic screams continued - *scream! scream! scream!* After a full ten minutes, they died down and we came upon the scene of the drama - a sight men have spent a lifetime in the bush and never seen - a python killing a buck. It had a baby duiker in its coils. The mother stood by, poised on her little toes.

When we appeared, the mother darted away, the python uncoiled itself and slid into the trees, all twelve feet of it, to return later to its meal. For by then, the little body was dead.

Then came some unpleasant business with the sisters. I have already explained how they were the 'officers' of the nursing service. The older ones had worked harmoniously with both doctors and nurses along the traditional lines of African district practice, but after independence, a new breed began to appear, who seemed to have derived ideas from the West End of London. They started to object to assuming certain duties, notably declaring persons dead on the wards and especially 'dead on arrival', something the older staff had done on the principle already described - the senior person on duty. These bright new things started calling doctors to do it, night and day, as if they were working in Guy's Hospital, or somewhere.

(The famous case of a lady 'resurrecting' in Gweru mortuary, the first of its kind in the country's history, did not help matters, needless to say.)

Of course, there was nothing more exasperating to a doctor who had been slogging in the hospital or banging round the landscape in a Land Rover all day, and got up to do a caesar at two in the morning, than to be dragged out of bed at 4am to declare someone dead before removal to the mortuary.

I put my foot down and issued a memorandum to the effect that this nonsense had to stop; that all should remember they were working in a district hospital and to observe the principle of delegation, without which our work would be impossible. And I sent a copy to the PMO.

The sisters retaliated by sending a copy of this directive up their ladder to their leaders, with a covering letter of protest. Some battle took place amongst the gods, which was never resolved, as far as I know, though occasional rumbles and flashes came down to us, notably a remark from some high lady about 'standards in Western countries', which I had already suspected had inspired the new attitudes.

I could have retorted to the Olympians that doctors could play at that game. What general practitioners in 'Western countries' did caesarean sections, and a lot of other things besides; and what would happen to the mothers and babies and most other people, to say nothing of the system, if *we* went by 'Western' rules? But the Olympians never asked for my opinion, so I never expressed it. On the ground, we were left in our bitter quarrel.

It reached its worst point when a dead body was brought in one night by the police, and the sister called Charles to 'certify' it. Charles refused, and the next thing, the police were banging on Charles's door, threatening and frightening the life out of the poor little chap, which they did with the more gusto as he belonged to the wrong tribe. Charles was dragged out of his bed to do his 'duty', and even taken to the police station afterwards to 'explain himself', and knocked about into the bargain.

This brought a sharp protest from the PMO, and the police chief was moved, but the hospital battle smouldered on, and was still burning when I finally left.

I wondered why I got so worked up about this matter. The fact itself was annoying enough, as I have explained, but there was something more. Some new spirit: the spirit of formalism of the modern world, displacing the generous spirit of the old world, especially the old Africa.

Then the PMO came up with a scheme for training expatriate doctors at the provincial hospital (something which was the rule when I first came to the country), and wanted me to move to Gweru to take charge of it, in a lateral transfer to a specially created new post of medical training officer. I may say now that the system of training them at the main teaching hospital, which was even then in existence, was far superior: they could learn more there in their three-month crash course, properly organised, than they could in twelve months in the rather haphazard circumstances of the provincial hospital. I rather think the PMO thought I had done long enough in the districts and might appreciate a move.

It brought, at least, benefits, for many incidental reasons, which were rather sad reasons. In the old days, men (and women - though the women were more usually unmarried and in missions) spent their whole careers in the districts, with all the advantages that experience and local knowledge give. Now things had changed.

In the first place was the matter of schools. District doctors could never afford private schools, but in the old days, every small town had good primary schools for white and black; and at the age of thirteen, the children could be sent to a state boarding school in the provincial town. The fatal flaw was a hopeless disparity on the black side. The black schools which existed were good enough to produce the country's new leaders, but there was not one tenth enough of them, to say the least.

So, with independence, came a vast break-neck expansion of non-racial education, and the quality of the system was inevitably swamped. Many of the teachers did not have 'O' levels. It was not quite the twelve-graduate situation of the Congo, but it was something like.

Which meant that government doctors, black and white, wanted to send their children to private schools.

When we moved to Gweru, we could send our children to a private non-boarding primary school and just afford it: the prospect of secondary education, as it loomed ahead, was something else, boarding or not boarding; and eventually, like everyone else, I had to review my position in the service altogether. As an African consultant, who was himself quitting the service, said: 'Unless you want your kids to go to Shumba Secondary School, Dr Durrant, you'd better get out and go into private practice;' as he was doing. The sad thing was, he went to Shumba Secondary School himself in its better days.

There was no private primary school in Zvishavane, and all middle-class people had lost faith in the government establishment. A desperate attempt was made to re-classify the schools into 'A' and 'B'; 'A' being the old European schools, 'B' the old black ones. As the 'A' schools were in the posher areas, now multiracial, it was hoped, though never confessed, that class distinction might save the situation left by the abandoned racial distinction of the past; but few (white or black) acquired much faith in this expedient.

Moreover, the government salary was not keeping pace with inflation and the rising cost of living. Sadly, when we left Zvishavane, we had to pay off our servants, knowing they had little chance of finding other employment.

The day came to say good-bye to Zvishavane. A tea party was given to us by the staff one morning, at which we attended as a family. We received the customary big clock - in the shape of Zimbabwe, which still hangs on the wall of our guest room. I solved the now doubly wretched business of making a speech by reviewing the progress we had made together in the ten years I had been with them: the immunisation programme, the sanitary programme, the Tb programme, etc, etc; how all our clinics had telephones, how 85 per cent of all deliveries took place in medical facilities, how our perinatal mortality rate was already below the government's target figure for the year 2000; and so on and so on. The atmosphere became strangely charged around me; tears began to gather in dark eyes; Terry too was looking dewy. My voice faltered, and I rapidly made an end.

O, my brave brown (and white) companions! as Sassoon says. These too were my fellow soldiers, and their names form a roll of honour. The matrons: Brewster, Johnson, Ashwin (later Durrant!), Jones, Mhlanga; the sisters: Masina, Mushaya, Sibanda, Banda, Mandebvu, Moyo, Mataka, Mutema, Munyoro, Kimpton, Grobelaar, Ziemkendorf, Wild, Drayton, Fourie; the medical assistants: Muguti, Chaumba, Mutamba, Marashe, Mutema, Dzauma, Mutonhodza; the ladies: Mrs Rioga, Muguti, Chikara; Chigumbo (health inspector); the clerks: Reynolds, Mantiziva, Jackie, the Sitholes, John and Peter, Rioga; Sam and Chikara (ambulance); the general hands: Molly, Rebecca, Eveline, Phineas (mortuary); Roda (cook); all those out in the clinics, and those on other stations, too numerous to mention: I shall always remember them, even those whose names I have forgot - may they forgive an old man's memory!

4 - Full Circle

At Gweru, I bought a house, nothing being obtainable to rent from the government: at 58, the first house I had owned in my life. And a very beautiful house it was, in a half-acre plot. I just about managed to keep the lawn under control myself with an electric mower, while Terry managed the rest, including a kitchen garden. We had trouble with bees in the house, which Terry managed to keep out by sealing one of the ventilators and smoking them out of the chimney - they fell into the sitting room in a huge dead ball. I was grateful for marrying a practical country girl - Harold Skimpole Durrant being a mere child in such matters.

I walked daily to the hospital, which was just down the road, but took the car for more rapid progress to emergencies which arose in the night. For I was a kind of all-round registrar, especially on the surgical side, and gave such training as was needed to expatriates and young local interns. My teaching methods in surgery were simple. First, I did the operation (say a hernia) with the pupil assisting. Then the pupil did the same operation on another case, with me assisting. After that, for that particular operation, he was on his own, unless he specially requested my help. A course which will no doubt make European surgeons shudder, but, as I do not need to say again, this was Africa.

They kept me at it to the day I retired, and my last night saw me piloting a young African doctor through a burst appendix with peritonitis - a successful and happy termination to the operation and my government career. But this is leaping ahead.

Came news that we were to receive two doctors from Poland: husband and wife, a surgeon and a gynaecologist, to boot. Poland was still (1986) a communist colony of the Russian Empire, and I feared the arrival of some sort of communist missionaries, and said so in my letters to England.

Within days of the arrival of the Stiritupskis, I was writing in a very different strain. 'If Jaruzelski thought he was sending us communist missionaries, all I can say is he boobed resoundingly.'

So far from preaching communism, so far from preserving a discreet or cautious silence on the subject, the Stiritupskis practically denounced it from the roof-tops. I lived in daily fear of their arrest.

Zimbabwean comrades, who incautiously approached them in a comradely spirit, got a big shock.

'Vot you are tinking is Rassia?' snarled Adam, a small, dark, fiery man, who looked like a scale model of Lech Walesa, even to the big moustache, which I learned was an anti-communist badge in Poland. 'Vorkers' paradise? Vot a joke! I tell you vot is Rassia, my friend. Rassia is Tird Vorld cantry viz atom bombs!'

'As for Rassians!' spat Elizabeth, a small fiery blonde. 'I tell you, Polish people vud razer hev zee Nazis!'

'Communism!' sneered Adam. 'Communism is dead in Polan'. Dead? It voz never born. I tell you, Polish people are 99 per cent Catolic. On'y communists are traitor shits!'

All this was very upsetting to the faithful of Zimbabwe, who looked for bread to what they thought was the source of the true bread, and got stones thrown at them.

Adam soon cottoned on to the local 'comrade' fashion, then still in full bloom. He sat in outpatients.

'Come in, comrade. Good morning, comrade. Sit down, comrade. Vot can I do for you, comrade? Get zis medicine, comrade. Call zee next comrade, pleess, Comrade Moyo!'

All this was rather lost on his unsophisticated victims, and even the nurses; but it was clear Adam was enjoying himself.

When their pay cheques failed to arrive after two months, Adam was on the line to Head Office in no uncertain tone. Finally, he shouted : 'From now on, I am on strike!', banged down the receiver, and walked straight home. By next day, his sense of duty to his colleagues (to say nothing of his patients) brought him back to work: the half-day strike was over. It caused a lot of fluttering in the dove-cotes of Head Office, who had never had this kind of thing before. (They were to get it later from their own people, as the service deteriorated.)

Then he asked me if he could use my private telephone for a certain purpose, which he more or less let us in on. While Terry was in the house, he would slip out of the hospital to our place to ring the

Canadian High Commission in a neighbouring country. It became plain that they had come to Zimbabwe as the first step in a plan of escape from their own country. Usually after these calls, he would leave with a sad face. Then one morning, he put down the receiver, ran into the kitchen and gave a startled but sympathetic Terry a big hug and a kiss. They had been accepted for Canada. Before long, they invited us alone to a small party, left their jobs without a word, and boarded the next flight to London.

Even before we left Zvishavane, Gareth decided to go back to Wales. He came out for an annual holiday for some years afterwards, when we would meet him and go away with him for a holiday ourselves, usually to the Eastern Highlands.

One day, in the British High Commission, the children saw Uncle Gareth's picture on the wall: not exactly a police notice, but looking remarkably like a wanted South American bandit, with his strong, swarthy features and heavy moustache. It was, of course, his new passport photo, awaiting attention, and our first intimation that the eagle had landed.

Once I took him to see the Mutarazi Falls: at 2500 feet, the highest in Africa. Even Terry had not seen them. On our previous visit, she had stayed with the children, as the thought of them scampering up and down that terrible drop was too much for our parental nerves. The scene is reached, walking down a valley in the Highlands, where one sees the strange tree ferns, like giant hairy phalluses. Then one comes to the V-shaped cliff. The narrow stream falls over the right arm of the V, in two thousand odd-foot steps, and can be viewed clearly from the left arm. Before one and far below is spread the vast panorama of the Honde Valley, fair as the Elysian fields.

On the viewing side there is a promontory, not at all unnerving, even to me who have no head for heights; but there is no doubt that only a little push is required to send someone over it, and they wouldn't touch anything for a long time. Gareth said he would like to shove his second wife off it, and we named the spot, 'Mrs Baker's Leap'.

Alas, in the government service, we got poorer and poorer. I had already cut Anderson's pension from fifty dollars a month to twenty. Now I decided I would have to stop it altogether. I did not want to give the old chap the shock of finding this out from the bank, when he went to collect it, so I went round to his house in one of the Gweru townships. I need not have worried about Anderson's welfare.

Malawians are no slackers. They were brought up by Dr Livingstone and his friends, under their policy of 'Christianity and Commerce', which is why so many of them have Scottish names, and although their mountain country is as poor as the Scottish Highlands, they have an equal reputation for industry and frugality. I discovered that Anderson (Thatcher style) had long since bought his house in the township; he and his wife were feeding themselves amply from the garden (like me, he had taken the wise course of marrying a strong and much younger woman); and, moreover, the couple were living in one room of the house and letting out the others to some lady lodgers, whose source of income had better not be further elucidated, except to say that it was secure.

In fact, I suspect that my pension simply covered Anderson's supply of liquor and tobacco: a double vice to which that admirable nation is over-addicted, and which has given them one of the highest rates of cancer of the gullet in the world; so perhaps I was doing him a service by cutting it off, though I rather doubt it.

All in all, Anderson was by no means discomposed by my news; even, if anything, extended sympathy to me and my family in our poverty.

And at Gweru, Michael showed organising abilities in creating the Gweru East Sports Club, comprising, like most such bodies in the country at that time, European and Indian members, for historical reasons, too complex to go into here. They shared their venue with Chaplin Secondary School (where Terry had boarded), until the governors of that institution, in rather cavalier fashion, enclosed it with a wall, and Michael's club came to an end.

They played cricket and soccer in season: on Saturday or Sunday afternoons; and I was dragged out of my armchair to supervise and instruct. Talk about the leadership activities of the blind! One bowler had an incurable problem: young Kalpesh, whom I rather unkindly described as bowling 'like an Indian student throwing a brick at a policeman'. And when it came to soccer, Africa burst in with the children of the school caretakers, who had never had more than a bundle of rags to play with before, and (temporarily) took the ball off the more privileged children, like a pack of wild dogs, sending them home in tears.

At least, Michael gained some local fame by his activities, and I was hailed by black children, on my way home, as 'Macklesfather'.

Finally, at the age of sixty, I decided to take early retirement from government service, and took a three-quarter share in a small private practice with an Indian, who went to live in South Africa as a sleeping partner.

The surgery was a simple lock-up, open eight to five, no night or week-end duty, and no house visits, except to a handful of my partner's friends. So, under the sign of Balti and Durrant, I set up in my own business for the first time in my life, in a street of other Indian stores, below Main Street.

What frightened me most was keeping the accounts. The other staff consisted of a clerk, Robert, and a nurse, Annie, with a stand-in nurse, Nyasha. But Indians are not in the habit of delegating finances, so I faithfully took on the books in my partner's tradition.

It was something I learnt faster then surgery, and its terrors were equally less. Soon, I was writing to an old banking friend in England (who was also musical): 'Our accounts would seem like a five-finger exercise to the symphonies of accountancy you must have conducted in your time.'

Dr Balti's wife had been used to sitting in the surgery, ostensibly knitting, while keeping an eye on the clerk and the nurse, who might otherwise have been subject to obscure temptations while her husband was in the examination cubicles, or otherwise off his guard. She suggested that Terry might like to do the same: Terry didn't.

Dr Balti instructed me not to let other Indian doctors into the surgery (they seemed to trust one another about as much as - I'd better not say). He gave me his address in South Africa with similar reservations; both including 'specially Dr Vindaloo'.

Indeed, I seemed to be fending off half the Indian secret service. Mrs Tandoori, up the street, was not only a patient but a frequent inquirer. Dr Balti had advertised his house for sale at what seemed to Mrs Tandoori a suspiciously low price. Even Dr Vindaloo broke in one day, but got nothing out of me.

And no love was lost between them and the Africans. The drains frequently got blocked, which Annie blamed on the 'horrible food' the Indian tenants above us were cooking. An African colleague in the next street cheered me with the assurance: 'Balti's a crook, and Vindaloo's another.' And, of course, Mrs Balti had warned me from her side - 'You can't trust them!'

The practice specialised in sexually transmitted diseases (STD), and again I was getting experience far beyond anything Europe could provide. I was seeing 300 fresh cases a month, which is more than most general hospitals in England; and nearly ten times the number of diseases, for in Africa, there are about twenty varieties to choose from. Species multiply in the tropics: eg, Roberts' *Birds of South Africa* lists fifteen species of eagle, on a rather different subject.

And more and more, I was seeing Aids. The first Aids case I saw was in Zvishavane, and went unrecognised by me until it was pointed out by the provincial physician, on his monthly visit: a young girl with extended shingles. Then, as I said, I recognised it in the terrible cases of pelvic sepsis we saw and operated on in females. In my new clinic, I saw it besides in cases of florid penile ulceration, which were stubborn to treat. Then the black spots of Kaposi's sarcoma, and the 'wasting disease'.

At first, I would test them, but the results took three weeks - a long trial even for the stoical African. The news was invariably bad: the signs were obvious enough before the test. The patients took the news silently: one schoolboy only shrugged his shoulders and said: 'Then I needn't bother about my 'A' levels.' I would always try to comfort them, telling them they had many years to live, and medical science was advancing so rapidly, a cure might be discovered in time for them. But I had little faith in my own words. Finally, I gave up testing them, or even voicing my clinical suspicions. They would do nothing about it, anyway. *Carpe diem* - the motto of Africa!

For the battle was already lost; or rather, it would be won through the brutal solution described by one local African specialist: 'We will outbreed it.' The PMO put it rather more scientifically, when he said, the disease would burn itself out with the vulnerable group: but that included most of the youth and wage-earners of the country. What would be left after such a loss?

A country like Zimbabwe was specially vulnerable, as the specialist said, because it had a highly mobile population. Most urban Africans (20 per cent of the population) retained a *pied à terre* in their ancestral lands, and moved between town and country. The enormous crowds at the bus terminus on public holidays were evidence of this. In more prosperous days, men would keep two wives: one at home (which was always the land), and a *mpoti* wife in town (for the 'pot' and bed). But now this luxury was beyond most of them, and it was the day of the harlot.

I went to work on a bicycle, leaving the car with Terry, who had to shop and ferry children to and from school. On my two-mile ride, to and fro, I would pass the beerhall, buzzing like a hive, especially in the evening, with music and prostitution. It was the market-place for the product, and my principal source of business.

The first World Aids Day was marked in Gweru in 1988 by a meeting of all interested parties in the Catholic hall. I was not on the committee, but sat in the audience. The proceedings were opened by a clinic sister, who announced happily: 'We are gathered here today to salute the great killer disease, Aids.'

She was followed by the PMO, a nice little Indian doctor, whom everybody loved but nobody could understand, because he spoke like a ham actor imitating Peter Sellers doing an Indian doctor. He sat down in a mystified silence, which remembered its manners just in time to produce an uncertain clap.

Next came the medical officer of health, I think, who spoke about condoms and 'safe sex'. He was followed by the Anglican bishop's wife: a large lady, as formidable in spirit as in body.

It is no part of African etiquette to cause embarrassment; but, I suppose, planning and coordination are weaker points with them than, say, the Germans. Therefore, I conclude that the bishop's lady had no prior knowledge of the contents of the MOH's speech: because her speech was a forthright denunciation of condoms and what she witheringly called 'safe sex'; but it was too late even for African powers of improvisation (which are considerable), and if the lady was going to say anything, it was no use giving an uncertain sound. She ended with a rousing appeal to 'Christian standards and the traditions of our ancestors'. By the time she had finished, the MOH looked like the little boy who had to stand in the corner.

And finally, and unhappiest of all, came the provincial physician, Dr Badza. Dr Badza gave a lucid and comprehensive survey of the disease, and should have left it at that. Unfortunately, being an African, he was a philosopher, and could not resist an incautious excursion into the tricky field of professional ethics. Under no circumstances, insisted Dr Badza, should any doctor or medical personnel betray the confidence of a patient, especially in the most delicate case of this disease.

He sat down amid polite applause. Then an old male nurse rose to his feet. The almost palpable scepticism of Africa (than which there is no scepticism denser) rose in his person. It was immediately palpable to Dr Badza, who knew the signs only too well: you could almost see the defensive hackles rising round his ears. First, the old man looked at the floor, like a practised barrister; then he looked up at Dr Badza, with an indulgent smile on his face, and asked: 'Doctor, are you telling us that if your daughter was going with a chap, and you knew that chap had Aids, you would not tell her?'

The old man sat down. Dr Badza rose to his feet, as bravely as he could. I must say, he stuck to his guns, even if he was destined to fall with them. 'No!' he protested. 'I would *not!* I *could* not under the ethics of my profession!' His voice cracked and became squeaky, as he tried to keep it up, but was soon drowned out by the tide of unbelieving laughter.

As to condoms, I discovered that private GPs were allocated a monthly ration of 500 to be given away freely. So, once a month, faithfully I would get on my bicycle with a rucksack and pedal up to the provincial medical store. My first appearance was greeted with surprise. It was plain I was the only GP in the town who was applying for his ration. I later learned I was the only one notifying cases of Aids. Far be it from me to play the good little boy at the expense of my colleagues: I expect they had given up the battle as already lost, which it probably was.

It was said that the African men had a prejudice against condoms. All I can say is, my 500 were gone long before the month was out, and I am sure I could have given away many more.

I offer this contribution to the subject for what it is worth.

The new surgery was busy at the beginning and end of each month, when people had money. In the middle weeks it was slack, and I would spend hours reading. From some puritanical habit, I would read only medical books in working hours: study. And indeed, one always had to in Africa, quite apart from the vocational pleasure I have described. I got through books on tropical medicine (again), on STD (of necessity), and pharmacology. But now and again, for a break, I would stand at the door and observe the street scene, of which my interpreters were Robert and Annie, and sometimes Nyasha.

Late one afternoon there was a power failure. There was thunder about and the sky was overcast. The Indian supermarket opposite was reduced to a dark cave. They started unceremoniously bundling the customers out on to the pavement. Robert explained they were afraid of shoplifters. The owner evidently did not wish his store to become an *Aladdin's* cave to his customers.

Sometimes, there was a hue and cry after a *tsotsi* (thief). It sounded like a pack of dogs. If you shouted 'stop thief!' in that country, people didn't just stare at you as if you had gone mad. Once I saw a single policeman following up, like a huntsman with the Quorn; and the thief would be lucky if the policeman dug him out.

This was called 'instant justice' and could also be visited on a motorist who knocked someone down. He was wise to drive on to the nearest police station and report the accident, where his failure to stop would be understood. Otherwise, he too could get a mauling.

This kind of thing was commoner at first in other parts of Africa than in Zimbabwe, but they all learn.

One day, a plain-clothes policeman tried to arrest a smuggled watch seller. This time the crowd was not on the side of the law. The policeman drew a revolver and fired a shot in the air, which made no impression at all. Finally, he hailed down a passing taxi and bundled his captive into it.

Another day, a rabid dog ran into our yard. The veterinary people came, calmly got a string round its neck and led it away.

I suppose Dickens's London must have had scenes like these.

And now I was earning twice my government salary for half the work. Working from nine to five (or rather, from eight to six) for the first time in my life, such are the hours most doctors work, seemed to me like part-time. So we were able to employ servants again: Norah, and a new gardener, John.

Norah occupied the *kaya*. One day she had an adventure. She was eating lunch outside her house, when a baboon appeared. We described it in a little rhyme:

Little Miss Norah
Sat on the floora,
Eating her bread and jam.
Along came a baboon
And sat on her spoon,
And Norah said, 'Frightened I am!'

The baboon got up without argument and climbed over the garden wall.

Other animal stories followed. Michael had another adventure with a snake. Terry would take the children to the swimming pool after school. One day a black mamba streaked towards them - or rather towards Michael. He was six or seven at the time and, unlike his previous encounter, remembers it clearly. He was in that most dangerous position - between the snake and its hole. Terry shouted, 'Run, Michael, run!' Michael was confused for a moment. He remembered my caution: if he stood up a black mamba in the bush, to freeze. Fortunately, on the present occasion, he followed his mother's advice.

A family were picnicking near a river, when a lioness appeared and picked up a young child in its mouth in a maternal sort of way. In an even more maternal sort of way, the mother jumped on the lioness's back and twisted its ears, until it released her child. The child needed nineteen stitches at the hospital.

A man got mauled by a leopard. This was while I was still at the hospital. The leopard either bit or clawed a hole in his head. I raised a flap of scalp and washed out a perforation of the skull beneath, before excising the scalp wound and closing the scalp.

At the risk of spoiling these stories, I have to confess that all these creatures, except the resident mamba, escaped from a local zoo, and the incidents could have happened in England (except for more awareness of 'health and safety').

Besides which, never having learned, we had more animals of our own. Again starting with cats: first a little girl, called Chocky after her colour. She did not last long, getting run over. I found Michael, then about four, weeping silently on his bed. Both our children had soft hearts. I suppose having pets develops their emotions: a rueful consolation, perhaps, as far as parents are concerned.

Then, as a consolation, Blackie, a boy. Alas, he was sleeping under the car one day when Terry took off. No, he wasn't run over. He climbed into the works and dropped off when Terry slowed near the school. She saw him go, and he didn't come back, not surprisingly, perhaps. At least the chidren did not cry; they felt they could leave him at school.

Then, at last, a dog: a Jack Russell, called Whisky. He grew up into a lively little fellow. He would race round and round the house when the mood took him, though he had plenty of walks, even though it was difficult to let him loose in town, except in the school grounds. Alas, he, too was run over.

Then another cat, boy, called Smokey: grey coat. But we did not feed him correctly - lean mince only, so he got rickets and couldn't climb trees or jump over walls. He survived to find a home with Dozie and Boyce when we came to leave the country (as will be told); and was followed by two beautiful fox terriers, Snoopy and Socksy. They too found a good home with an African lady who was obviously fond of dogs.

One day, after two years in the practice, I decided quite suddenly to leave Africa and take my family to England. The reasons were plain and mostly concerned our children.

We could see their way clear to the age of eighteen. We were not leaving for educational purposes, as people in England later thought. We had them in good private schools, which we would be lucky to match in the English state system; but after that, the future was problematical.

If everything in Zimbabwe were perfect, we would still have been members of a dwindling minority group. (At university, our children would have been in a mere handful of their own kind.) Minority groups have made great contributions to the world: the Jews are the outstanding example. But nobody knows better than the Jews the disabilities of minority groups.

Everything in Zimbabwe was not perfect. There was a million unemployed in a population of ten million. The economy was declining. The menace of Aids was already bigger than a man's hand, with its incalculable threat to the national life.

I sat on it for two days, although I was inwardly certain, before telling my wife, who readily agreed.

And Terry was going to feel the worst of it. The children would be easiest: they would adapt readily. I had done my work in Africa: my main concern now was to support my family. But Terry was leaving her native land, her family, and worst of all, her old father, with little prospect of seeing him again this side the grave.

We thought about the servants we were discharging, with no prospect of re-employment. I thought of lump sums, pensions - both would quickly wither in the rising inflation. Then Terry came up with a stroke of genius: we would buy them knitting machines. An African with a knitting machine is in business for life. We got one for Norah, and another for Beauty, John's wife (which eventually, John, too, learned to use). Years later, we got letters telling us they were still in business.

377

We were not going to come away rich. We sold everything. Through official and approved private channels, after eighteen years in the country, I realised £10,000, and received a civil service pension of £100 a month. I had enough savings in England to cover a modest house.

'Look thy last on all things lovely!' Africa would always have a place in our hearts - the 'great spaces washed with sun'. We took a last holiday: a few days at Hwange game park, where we heard the lions in the night; a lodge by the Zambezi - the wide Zambezi, the rolling river.

I wrote to England: 'I brought nothing into this continent (except, in Wildean fashion, my genius), and it is certain I shall carry nothing out of it - except a loving wife and children, incomparable professional experience, and a life of adventure.

THE END
October, 1995.